MARCH

When is a March not a March? Answer: When it's a Wildcat. The car in the left foreground is one of the first of 20 March 86As supplied in 1986 for Pat Patrick's American Racing Series, an attempt at a more advanced stepping-stone towards the Indy Car World Series than had been provided by the Formula Atlantic or Super Vee single-seaters. Thought up by Robin Herd, seen here standing behind the car's left rear suspension, the cars were powered by a 3.5-litre Buick V6 engine and were intended to perform the role handled in Europe by Formula 3000 with the likes of the 86B, seen on its wheels in the right foreground.

MARCH

The Rise and Fall of a Motor Racing Legend

Mike Lawrence

Foreword by Robin Herd, CBE

Motor Racing Publications Ltd

This revised and expanded edition published in 2001
by Motor Racing Publications Ltd
PO Box 108, Orpington, BR6 9TJ

© Mike Lawrence 1989 and 2001

This book is copyrighted under the Berne Convention. All rights reserved. Apart from any fair dealing for the purpose of private study, research, criticism or reviews, as permitted under the Copyright Act 1956, no part of this publication may be reproduced, stored in a retrieval system, or transmitted in any form or by any means, electronic, electrical, chemical, mechanical, optical, photocopying, recording or otherwise without prior written permission. All enquiries should be addressed to the publishers.

British Library Cataloguing in Publication Data

Lawrence, Mike, 1942-
March: the rise and fall of a motor racing legend
1. March Engineering (Firm) – History 2. Automobile racing – Great Britain
I. Title
338.7'228'0941

ISBN 1899870547

Printed in England by
The Amadeus Press, Cleckheaton, West Yorkshire
Bound by MPG Books Ltd, Bodmin, Cornwall

CONTENTS

(**Nigel Snowdon**)

Foreword

I have enjoyed working with Mike Lawrence on this book because it has revived a lot of memories and I enjoy Mike's company. He is not only one of the very few motor racing writers who writes well, he is also very perceptive about people and the sport itself. Sometimes he's been too perceptive for my own comfort; I don't think I would include this book as part of a CV.

Somehow I always felt that I'd be with March for twenty years and this is more or less what happened. I remained as an adviser in the wings should I be called on, as Max Mosley was for me after he left March to pursue a new career which led to his becoming President of the FIA. I have worked on other projects, including Formula One, and in areas completely outside of motor sport. My years with March, however, provided me with many of the greatest moments of my life.

This is an unusual work on motor racing because most books tend to be little more than a catalogue of results and technical facts which eulogise the subject. This one is unusual in that it deals with people as well as facts, and the bad side as well as the good; it is a portrait showing warts and all. The result is the true story of what went on, one of the few true stories ever written about motor racing, and it is a unique insight into the business of the sport.

Robin Herd, CBE

Introduction

Most of this book was first published in 1989 under the title *Four Guys and a Telephone* because that was how March began, with Max Mosley, Alan Rees, Graham Coaker and Robin Herd – and a single asset. In fact, the asset was not so much a telephone as a shared vision. Many people scoffed at their dream, but at the first Grand Prix of 1970 Marches took the first two places on the grid, with identical times.

The original book covered, almost to the week, the first twenty years of March, during which time it built very nearly 1,500 racing cars, from Formula One right down to Formula Ford. If you own the company which makes the world's third best television set there will be meat on your table and your children will never want for shoes. But when it comes to production racing cars, nobody will buy the third best, which is why few are constructors for very long or make many cars.

As a writer, I could not have had greater luck with my timing in 1989. Having worked on the book for 18 months, within weeks of delivering the manuscript, March came within an ace of folding, but was saved with perhaps only days to spare. There was a massive crisis and huge drama going on behind the scenes. It was a real cliffhanger, worthy of a soap opera, but March survived and made sure I had the story.

Better than that, I had the whole story. I wrote it and March paid to have it combed by a lawyer specialising in libel. I doubt if any author of a motor racing book has ever had such access to the nitty-gritty.

That was typical of the co-operation I received throughout. My study was piled high with documents from the team's archives, people told me things as they were and as they had been. Some stories I left out as a matter of good taste. Such a one was the story of a driver who was entertaining a young lady in his hotel room. The night was hot and his window was open – it was one of those which pivots from both sides. A member of the March team had the room below and his window was open. The two windows formed a periscope and, soon, most of the March team were admiring their driver's progress. They gave him high marks.

Inevitably, there were stories I heard only later. In 1970 Jackie Stewart knew that though the March 701 was quick from the box, there was no development in it. Ken Tyrrell therefore began to build his own car. At the Canadian Grand Prix, Jackie had a March and the Tyrrell 001 at his disposal.

Robin Herd and Jackie played a round of golf in Canada and Robin dropped a challenge: if he won the game, Jackie would race the March. After 15 holes, practice for the Grand Prix began and Robin was a stroke up. He suggested that Jackie should concede. "No way," said Jackie, "nobody has ever had a greater incentive to win a round of golf."

They played to the end and Jackie won. They then drove to the circuit where Jackie climbed into the Tyrrell and put it on pole.

Before I wrote the first word Robin Herd had said, "March is not about cars, it's about people, and for Heaven's sake let's tell the true story – you'll find that most of the best stories are told against us." Then, to make sure I was not short of stories told against March, he provided me with plenty, and the worse the light in which one cast March, and himself, the more he enjoyed telling it. The racing car maker who has not made mistakes has yet to appear, it is only the insecure ones who do not admit them.

Robin told me only one story which he said was 'off the record', and I would not have used it anyway. He also made one statement off the record, and that was his high opinion of a young designer in the March organisation. The reason for it being off the record was that he did not want other teams to come poaching. Max Mosley asked me to delete just one word from the manuscript.

Not only had there been drama as the manuscript was finalised, there had also been a change of leadership and, as luck would have it, I was in Robin Herd's house when he handed over the reins to Dave Reeves, who had been with March from the beginning. Dave had started as a fabricator and, twenty years on, he was Managing Director. That is a story which typifies the spirit that pervaded March from its inception.

The fact that this new edition, brought up to date, is titled *The Rise and Fall of a Motor Racing Legend* tells its own story. The sad thing is that the fall came about through a set of circumstances completely beyond the control of the men who made up March. They were not responsible for a downturn in the world economy and the subsequent collapse of the exotic sports car market. That is what happened, however, and a year-by-year contract with Porsche was not renewed. That punched a large hole in March's plans. It's hard for a small company to argue with world economic recession.

In his foreword, Robin Herd emphasises that the story of March is really a story about people. From 1986, however, they were not just men trying to win motor races and sell racing cars. They had done that so successfully that March became the first motor racing constructor in history to be launched as a public company. The advice was sound from an accountant's view, but it brought in corporate politics, and motor racing is quite difficult enough without adding corporate politics.

Motor racing is a job for enthusiasts, not bean-counters, and enthusiasm is the key to the March story. It was enthusiasm which set it up and enthusiasm which sustained it many a time when any normal business would have gone under beneath a shower of writs and debts.

Every one of the nearly 1,500 cars March has made is surrounded by stories of success, failure, frustration, humour, despair and triumph, so there are thousands of untold stories, and all I can hope is that this gives a flavour of what March was, what it did and what sort of people made the original dream into a reality.

Those people were, are, all racers. Racers nail their colours to the mast, they win, they lose, they get damaged in the process, but the essential thing is that they put themselves on the line. It's not an activity so much as an attitude. The racer's mentality is important to the story and it has never been expressed better than by Dennis Conner, the yachtsman, who has said, "The America's Cup is a game of life. Sailing is just how you keep the score."

The men who worked impossible hours to set up March and to sustain it through its many crises could have earned as much money servicing BMWs, and had a far easier life, but they were drawn to March because it was in racing, and every single one of the twenty or so men in the initial workforce went on to make his name in racing, as a mechanic, a team manager, a businessman. This story is about the guys at the factory as much as about the cars on the track, for the two are interdependent. One senior March man pointed out to me that even the factory cleaners had to work twice as quickly and twice as well than they would in a conventional factory.

For me the book began as just another job, but you would have to be a stone to have been around the guys at March and not to have caught their spirit.

I'd like to dedicate this new edition to everyone who made March, and to all racers.

Mike Lawrence
Chichester
April 2001

1 Silly Season

Hardly has one motor racing season begun than plans are laid for the next. Each season begins with questions and the opening races provide most of the answers: that new car which looked good in the workshop may not look so clever on the track in Brazil; Harry Hotshoe, a newcomer to Formula One, may have been overjoyed to have signed with a third-rate team, but soon feels he deserves better; Fred Fixit, team manager, dreams of the package no sponsor could refuse, while Danny Doodle, a number two designer, feels it's time his genius got the recognition it deserves. Since each one is a competitive individual, it's not long before Hotshoe is talking to Fixit who has been talking to Alan Ace, Len Latebraker and Paulo Puntero, who may not be wonderful but who does have a sponsor, Gasper Tobacco. Meanwhile Fixit has his eye on Doodle as a potential star designer and is talking to Melmoth Motors, who might supply him with engines, *if* he has the right package.

Alan Ace is interested in joining Fixit, *if* Melmoth is involved, but doesn't want Hotshoe in the team because he might show him up. Latebraker is a protégé of Melmoth but is under contract to Fuggifume Cigarettes, so they have to be approached as well. Gasper likes a package which involves Puntero, Ace and Melmoth, but has reservations about Doodle, for he has yet to prove himself as a number one designer, and so it goes on. Since everyone is at it, most of the time, the sport is a hot-bed of gossip and speculation, the press calls it the 'Silly Season', but really it's a courting ritual.

In theory a pack of cards is shuffled at random and Fixit *might* find himself holding four aces but, in practice, most of the court cards remain in the hands of those who already have them. Every so often, however, Formula One enters a state of flux, sometimes it's when new regulations come into force, sometimes it's when an innovation changes the parameters, such as when Lotus discovered ground effect or when teams switched to turbo engines. At such times the aces are up for grabs.

In 1969 there were new factors in the game, and two of the most significant were the Cosworth DFV engine and the arrival of direct sponsorship. Lotus had had exclusive use of the Cosworth DFV for 1967, but then it was available to anyone and during 1968 it powered the winner of every single Grand Prix. You could buy the best engine in the world for £7500 and Hewland could sell you a gearbox to go with it for a few hundred pounds, and this meant that more people could move into Formula One.

Sponsorship was new and it took time to get used to; for years European racing had been supported by the affiliated trade, particularly oil companies, but to tell Joe Public about this support they had then to pay for advertising. They were, therefore, *patrons* rather than sponsors, while in America you had Jimmy Bryan, say, winning races in the 'Dean Van Lines Special' and you had to be a close follower of the sport to know who built the car and engine, but everyone knew who put up the money, good ole D.V. Lines.

When the 3-litre F1 arrived, costs rose sharply and the traditional trade patrons blanched – there seemed no sense in writing ever bigger cheques so teams could go racing and then having to write even bigger cheques to tell the world you'd written the first ones. Realizing that times had changed, the sport's governing body, the FIA, allowed sponsorship and, as usual, Lotus was the first off the mark and while racing in New Zealand Jim Clark's Lotus changed from British green to the livery of a cigarette packet.

Some muttered about the end of civilization as we know it and it was certainly the end of one aspect of racing as we'd known it, green cars no longer fought red, blue, and silver cars, teams no longer represented countries but companies and the cars became mobile bill-boards. While there was tut-tutting among some, others saw that here lay the future – one could go racing and someone else would pick up the tab. Thus when the courting ritual started in 1969, there were these two other cards, jokers, in the pack.

In retrospect, F1 was entering the 'Cosworth' or 'British Kit Car' era, but nobody knew that at the time and there seemed any number of superior engines just over the horizon. There were rumours of an Alfa Romeo flat-12 (it appeared in 1976) and the Italian maker Tecno was predicted to be close to a deal to use it. Porsche was said to be poised to re-enter F1 with another flat-12. Matra was known to be developing a V12 engine and Ferrari was reported to have a 'broad arrow' V18 on the stocks but would field a flat-16 as an interim measure, but neither unit was ready before new rules limited engines to twelve cylinders.

The point is that it looked as if the days of Cosworth superiority were numbered, and one respected commentator was already calling it 'long in the tooth', then into the nervous welter of the rumour and gossip came the idea of four wheel drive. It had been tried by a number of makers over the years, but for various reasons had either not worked or had not been allowed to develop. Having made an engine whose power was stretching tyres and chassis to their limit, Keith Duckworth had come to the conclusion that a four-wheel-drive car was the F1 car of the future.

Keith dreamed of building a team around Jim Clark and, despite his legendary relationship with Colin Chapman, Clark was keen on the idea because Cosworth was the cream of motor racing engineering. Keith persuaded McLaren's designer, Robin Herd, to join him in 1968 to design a 4WD car. He also promoted the concept to anyone who would listen and the theory was given weight by the performance of 4WD cars in American racing. Let Ferrari and others build their exotic engines, 4WD could keep the Cosworth user competitive.

Poor Jimmy was killed in April 1968 and that knocked the stuffing out of Keith's dream, the car was no longer top priority and so did not approach completion until the beginning of the following season. Meanwhile, four-wheel drive became a buzz word in the courting ritual, another joker in the pack, anyone with an inside track on it was a man to court and Herd had overtures from every established team except Ferrari, plus others who were trying to establish themselves.

The progress of Robert John 'Robin' Herd had been remarkable; apart from possessing the charm and good looks of a schoolboy's hero (he probably has a decaying portrait in his attic) he was an all-round sportsman and academically brilliant. At the age of eighteen he had the choice of joining Worcester County Cricket Club or taking up an open scholarship to St Peter's Hall, Oxford. He chose the latter and even then he had a choice, "At school I was always better at Latin and Greek than science and you will find a few drivers who will agree with that." Apart from representing his college at eleven different sports, he took a double first in Physics and Engineering, and his exam marks for Engineering were the second highest in Oxford's history. The world beckoned and he chose National Gas Turbines, part of the Aircraft Research Establishment at Farnborough, where he worked on Concorde, published a number of scientific papers, and was appointed a Senior Scientific Officer at the unprecedented age of twenty-four.

He was presented with a career which had shown it could recognize and reward his talent, so promotion and responsibility were assured, there would be the respect of his fellow scientists with, at the end, an index-linked pension and, perhaps, a knighthood. There was, too, the chance to be a pioneer in technology, but for the young Robin Herd there was another factor to consider, he had been bitten by the racing bug. He was, and is, a racer, which is to say he thrives in crises and feeds on risk.

In the aircraft industry, the days had long gone when you might say that Sir Sydney Camm had designed the Hurricane or R.J. Mitchell had designed the Spitfire, a project like Concorde was a team effort between nations and any individual's contribution was only a tiny part. A racer is not content to put his initials on a blueprint which is passed to a section head for approval and, if passed, goes on to a committee and from there might become an anonymous part of a group effort. For a restless, innovative, engineer, motor racing offered the ideal outlet, but how to get in it was another matter.

In 1965 Howden Ganley was working as a mechanic at McLaren and trying to carve a career as a driver and he was friendly with Alan Rees, who had told him about this friend of his who was very clever and wanted to design racing cars. "By a coincidence, next day Bruce came into the workshop and said, 'I reckon it's about time we had a designer,' so I said, 'Alan Rees has got a mate who's very clever,' and Bruce told me to make contact.' " After a long session with Bruce, Robin resigned his safe career to become Chief Designer of McLaren, aged only 26. There his Formula One and Can-Am cars launched McLaren as a power in the sport and it was a short step to Cosworth and the car of the future.

In the 1969 courting ritual, the two drivers most desired were Jackie Stewart and Jochen Rindt. Stewart had narrowly missed the Championship the previous year, but was on his way to his first title in 1969. By contrast Rindt had yet to win a Grand Prix, although he was well nigh unbeatable in Formula Two at a time when all the aces took part; in most people's eyes he was the quickest driver in the world even though he had yet to open his score. Denis Jenkinson, *Motor Sport*'s Grand Prix correspondent, was in no doubt that the fault lay with Rindt himself and was so sure he never would win a Grand Prix that he promised to shave off his beard, his trademark, should he ever do so. As the 1969 season progressed, Jenks' beard looked safe as Rindt, who often started from pole, either retired or else was beaten by Stewart, who, while not quite so quick over the odd lap, had the knack of maintaining his pace over the distance of a race – Rindt drove on his nerve ends, Stewart applied formidable intelligence. Jochen himself was not the sort of man to harbour self-doubt and he had no difficulty in identifying his problem, he had never been with the right team at the right time. He was ripe for courting.

His F2 cars were entered by Roy Winkelmann Racing, which was the Lotus works team in all but name, and the team manager was Alan Rees. Rees had been one of the Winkelmann Racing team drivers, and a brave and quick one at that, until he retired at the end of 1968. Like all drivers he was ambitious, and while F2 was an ideal school for him to learn his new trade, he was not going to be content with it for very long for he was, is, a racer. As a close friend of Jochen, who used to stay with him in his flat in Maidenhead, Alan knew what was going through his mind, and it so happened that Alan had been at Monmouth School with Robin and the two of them used to sit at the back of Divinity lessons talking about such non-biblical topics as how they were going to become World Champion. Robin recalls, "There was the time when we were reading a passage from the Bible around the class and when it came to my turn, I lost concentration and read the next paragraph of the article I'd been reading in *Motor Sport*. I got thrashed for that." They had maintained their friendship and continued to hold the sort of conversations they'd had when they were supposed to be taking an interest in St Paul's Third Missionary Journey, except this time the subject was how they could build a Championship winner.

In 1967 there had been the possibility of a Herd-designed Winkelmann F1 car and the idea had support from Firestone and BP, but had been aborted when BP, in common with other oil companies, stopped picking up the tab for motor racing, but the seed of the idea of a new team had been sown and outside sponsorship seemed to make it a viable proposition once again. Meanwhile Rindt wanted to build a team which existed to service him alone. He admired Robin's work, was more than comfortable with Alan as a team manager, and had enough clout to raise the money. It began to look as if when the cards were shuffled, there'd be a new player at the table, one with a couple of aces in his pocket.

That was one strand in the courtship ritual, another came at the 1969 Racing Car show in January, when Alan went with another close friend of his, Graham Coaker. Graham had had a varied career which included accountancy and the Royal Engineers and was then general manager of a company, Faith Bumpers, within the Serck Group (the wife of a friend once thought he was up to no good when she saw Faith Bumpers' telephone number on his desk pad), but at weekends he raced a Brabham F3 car in British events. When he and Alan looked over the exhibits they were not entirely impressed and thought there was room for another maker of production cars, if they had the right designer. Alan was soon speaking to Robin and the idea of CRH Engineering (Coaker, Rees, Herd) was formed, with a view to making customer cars. So Graham (the production man) was talking to Alan (team manager), Alan was talking to Robin (designer), and Robin was considering his options and talking to everyone and F1 was soon included in CRH's plans.

Meanwhile another man entered the equation, Max Mosley. Max was a passing acquaintance of Robin's from their days at Oxford, where both had read Physics, but they had had little contact, in fact Robin had regarded Max as a bit flash, but then Robin was the scholarship boy from the Border Counties while Max was the cosmopolitan aristo who was up at a more glamorous college, was Secretary of the Oxford Union, and was one of the personalities of his year. Fluent, witty and multi-lingual, Max then read for the Bar and gained a high reputation in Patent and Trademark law. With his star in the ascendant and with good money coming in, he was at last able to realize an ambition and go motor racing. While he was still at Oxford, his wife had been given tickets to Silverstone, and since it was close and he was curious, they went, and that day Max discovered the passion of his life.

Two successful seasons in Clubman's racing led him to try Formula Two and to give himself a yardstick he had had his first car, a Brabham, prepared by Frank Williams to the same specification as the Brabham driven by Piers Courage. "I was at Frank's lock-up one evening when in walked Robin, who was moonlighting from McLaren by modifying the rear suspension on Piers' Tasman car." In the world of motor racing Robin was now the glamorous one, the brilliant designer, while Max was the tyro; one thing weighed against another, they talked, clicked, went back to Max's flat for dinner and the foundations of a lasting friendship were laid. During the evening they also decided that motor racing could bear another manufacturer, so that meeting laid one of the cornerstones of March.

Just as Alan Rees had discussed with Robin the idea of building cars so Max was soon discussing F1 with him, but the two strands were separate. In the autumn of 1968 Frank Williams had asked Max to accompany him on a visit to the States on the grounds that he had a degree in physics and the gift of the gab, because he was going to speak to Reynolds Aluminium about sponsorship. Frank was another who had been talking to Robin and was working at his dream package of top designer and big money sponsor, but it would be ten more years before he achieved it.

In a letter to Reynolds dated 6.11.68 Max summarized the discussions they'd had in the States. There would not only be an all-aluminium racing car but an all-aluminium

Alan Rees was a leading driver in F2 and here he leads his Winkelmann Racing team-mate, Jochen Rindt (both in Brabham BT18s) at the Crystal Palace on Whit Monday, 1966. Rees finished third on aggregate of two heats with Rindt fourth.

road car which would employ *modified versions of constructional techniques which are at present being developed in aluminium monocoque racing cars*. The idea was to create *a really startling illustration of the advantages of aluminium in road cars, and back it with a world-wide reputation gained on the racing circuits . . . we shall probably succeed in convincing the industry despite its undoubted inertia*.

The letter is a wonderful example of hype, but as Max says, "I knew nothing about racing car design and was given a grilling by a stress engineer, but fortunately he turned out to be concerned with oil pipelines in Alaska, so we managed to confuse each other and he made a favourable report. Unfortunately, Frank had had the bright idea of bringing along a driver and chose Bruce McLaren, who was winning everything in Can-Am. Alongside Bruce, Frank and I were nothing, so he walked away with the money."

Unsuccessful though it was, the trip planted in Max's mind the idea of creating a team with Robin and the letter to Reynolds also contains the first instance of what would become a recurring theme in the March story, the idea of tying in with a big firm to form a long-term relationship in which the racing team acted as a consultancy. Over the years the thinking behind a lot of March decisions, good and bad, can be traced back to Max's trip to the States.

Max drove in F2 for a season and half before he found he'd reached his limit and wasn't going to be World Champion after all, but thanks to his contact with Reynolds, he had grasped the implications of sponsorship, something some F1 teams had yet to do and, of course, he'd raced against Alan in F2 and knew Graham Coaker. In early 1969, then, among Robin's many options were CRH, a project with Max (we'll call it M-H), and the Rindt connection, and while Robin knew all that was going on not everyone else in the equation did.

Still, the courting ritual was bringing together a designer, a team manager, a production engineer and a new type on the racing scene, the commercial manager. With his legal training, fluency in languages, and his understanding of the potential of sponsorship, Max was the ideal fourth element and he began to devote his spare time to putting together the right package. Max's idea was for Robin to design both a four-wheel-drive car and a conventional one for Jochen, but since it was a new team, dealing with a new breed of patron, they had to have more than ideas and bright-eyed enthusiasm.

There was, however, a solution to the problem: the Cosworth F1 car. At that time the car had yet to race, in fact it never would race, but initial testing had been promising. Since Duckworth's interest in it had waned with Clark's death, Robin felt sure he could take over the project, and in early 1969 a document of intent was drawn up.

ARRANGEMENTS WITH J.R.

Requirements

1. The top priority is to get into F1 next year. The money which is made is not important, but it is vital to have the best equipment and the best driver. Failure to get into F1 would be a major set-back. We would lose on prestige and the team might be dispersed.

Jochen Rindt, a driver every team would liked to have signed.

2. We want a set-up which enables us to get hold of the Cosworth Car and all the sponsorship and prestige that goes with it.
3. We need Rindt, if we can get hold of him.
4. We must be in a position to design and build our own F1 car as soon as we have the means to do so.
5. We must be in a position to seek sponsorship for our own F1 car both financially and prestigewise.
6. Our own car and its sponsorship must be independent of Rindt and any tie-up with him separately negotiable on each occasion.
7. RH and MM must be earning while our own F1 set-up is arranged. This might take some time.
These arrangements can be satisfied if a sensible arrangement is made with Rindt. The main features of such an arrangement are:
a) No formal service contracts. The best way of avoiding these is to ask for shares in R's set-up, e.g. 45, 45, 10. Otherwise he may think we are using him to build our business. Ecclestone to get no share but commission on money he introduces.
b) Realistic salaries, i.e. 15 for RH, 5 for MM. Then a large sum (up to 70) for Rindt before profits are calculated.
c) Freedom for MM and RH to travel at company's expense in search of further sponsorship.
d) RH to be Chief Development Engineer, MM to be team or general manager. Both therefore free to run own company. On no account RH to be taken on as designer. If the design question is raised, RH to say this is a difficult area which he would like to separate from racing and look after himself, but he would always bring his designs to R's company because he has a share in the same.

At the same time we pursue the rest of our plans by setting up a company with RH, MM, and AR as equal shareholders. The company would do the new car and eventually sell same to Jochen. In this event it could be explained to Rindt that although he was not getting the benefit of any materials contracts, the whole energy of our set-up was being devoted to give his show the best run in F1 with an exclusive design. At this point Alan, if he wished would move in as team manager.

Rindt could go on having the exclusive use of our F1 cars as long as he wished. But as the cars became better known and more successful, the purchase price would rise. But so too would the profits of Rindt's company.

As this arrangement is only a different way of getting into F1 it would seem right that the dividend (but not salary) earned from RH and MM from the Rindt company should be paid to the RH, MM, AR company. The profits of this company, consisting of these monies plus profits from the building and sale of the new car, would be dealt with as originally planned.

The reference to Bernie Ecclestone is because he was Jochen's manager, but at the time this document was written there was no thought of anything beyond F1 in this strand of the ritual which omits any reference to CRH or Graham Coaker, and while Alan Rees is mentioned, the first time he saw the proposal was in 1989. This was the M-H strand; Alan and Graham were still talking about CRH unaware that RH was talking to MM and JR and while they were including AR (not GC) in their thinking they hadn't got round to telling him.

Robin was attracted by all his friends' proposals, but was not limited by them since almost everyone was after him, but there seemed no point in selling his talent for a salary when it was possible to exploit it for a percentage, and the more he turned over his options, the more it made sense for him to go freelance and, further, to merge Herd-Mosley with CRH because by doing that the four most important elements would be covered. Formula One would be the flagship and a range of customer cars would generate money, just like Brabham and McLaren were doing. There was, too, the North American Can-Am series, which offered fabulous purses, most of which went into the pockets of the works McLaren drivers in cars which Robin had designed. As a result McLaren was selling cars at a hefty profit and that money was going into Bruce's pocket when it might be going into Robin's.

Moreover there was (is) a motor racing industry in England unlike any in the world, if you wanted spaceframes, Arch Motors would make them, Specialised Mouldings could take care of the bodywork, Hewland would supply transmissions and so on. Provided you had a design all you needed was a credit line and a workshop to assemble the components, so the initial financial commitment was small and the potential profits were large. There was another attractive aspect to the idea of making production cars; according to the rules of the courting ritual if Jochen was talking to Robin and Max, then he was also talking to others, and setting up a company, with friends, meant that Robin was not dependent on Jochen. It was unstated at the time but one then had a greater awareness of a driver's mortality.

2 The Longest March Begins with a Single Step

By the end of April the components of what was to become March existed, but had not been assembled or even introduced to each other, and negotiations between Mosley and Rindt continued on the one hand while, on the other, was CRH. After he had visited Graham's house and ran a measure over his Brabham, Robin drew a simple spaceframe Formula Three car which used some Brabham and Lotus parts. It was not so much a serious design, more an intent, a first small step; it would have been a surprise had it been a great design, for Robin had stepped straight into F1 with no experience of the junior formulae.

The car had to have a name and since the USA was exciting everyone with its lunar flights, the drawings were labelled 'Apollo'. Robin says today, "It was typical to choose a name like that, we were young, we were confident, we were brash, we were heading for the moon ourselves. What we could never understand, considering we were so bloody marvellous, was that nobody liked us." It was the Sixties when youth could do anything and there was more than a hint of the partners seeing themselves as the motor racing Beatles, but later when Max went to register the company he found the world and his dog had beaten him to it, everything was being named 'Apollo'.

By the end of April 1969, the position was that Graham, Alan and Robin had laid the foundation of CRH with the design of an F3 car and had been to see John Frayling with a view to him building the body. Max was still racing and acting as an emissary in his spare time and various drivers were being approached with what was still a fairly vague notion of building an F1 car for 1970.

With the first car under way, CRH entered the ritual and, apart from Rindt, the first driver to be wooed was Chris Amon. Chris was thought to be as gifted as any driver around, but his bad luck was proverbial. He seemed never to be in the right team at the right time, he would lead races but some fault would deny him his win. In 1969 he was with Ferrari, which was in one of its troughs and from which it would not emerge until Fiat bought into it later that year Amon was not a happy man and he was receptive when Robin suggested that there might be a new team looking for a number one driver.

Chris says, "I knew Robin from my McLaren days and I had a very high regard for his ability. We had dinner during the Spanish GP meeting in mid-April and he said he was talking to Rindt, but if that fell through was I interested? As presented to me the idea was one driver, two race cars and a development car, a tight dedicated package, and that was the basis on which we negotiated. I found it very attractive because of my experience at Ferrari, where they'd been trying to run on all fronts, F1, F2, sports cars and getting lost in the middle. At the time I felt we had a sensible understanding, we'd touched, and all the problems which arose between myself and March later were because they changed the package. Anyway we left it in the air and got talking again in September."

A meeting was called at Robin's house in Towcester on 17 May, and Graham arrived having just raced at nearby Silverstone. There Graham and Alan were introduced to Max as a consultant to CRH, but they knew him from racing, so it was no problem, and someone to look after the legal and commercial side made perfect sense. Robin is a man who lays great store on personal relationships and loyalty so it was typical that he would include all his friends and merge the two strands. At the time it was an agreement of intent, nobody gave up his day job, but as a first step it was decided to start building the F3 car.

Max Mosley, barrister, Formula Two driver and member of the original March 'gang of four'. **(Nigel Snowdon)**

The following week Graham sold his Brabham because it was occupying valuable space in the garage adjoining his house, space which would be needed for the CRH/Apollo project. Thus the first March began to take shape in a quiet, leafy, suburb of Reading, the most unlikely place imaginable for the start of a new racing car company. Carol Coaker says, "The neighbours were thrilled by the idea and there would always be kids around during the day and various people dropping by in the evening. I had to stop giving dinner parties, but would pop into the garage and ask, 'How many for supper tonight?'" So around the table might be young Ronnie Peterson, or Rolf Stommelen, or anyone with an interest in what was going on.

Actually building the first car was Bill Stone, March's first employee. Bill is a Kiwi who had come to Europe to be World Champion, raced his car during the summer and in the winter earned money for his season by working for racing outfits building the following year's cars. That first car still exists and stamped on to the chassis frame is S1/69 (S for 'Stone'). One advantage for Bill was that he then had a McLaren M4A, which Robin had designed, so was able to get advice on setting it up straight from the horse's mouth.

Meanwhile Robin had enlisted the help of John Thompson, a fabricator whom he'd first met at McLaren and whom he'd taken with him to Cosworth because, as he says, "Good fabricators have a combination of creativity, initiative, and an artistic temperament," and he points to a number of fabricators who have gone on to the heights of motor sport. At the time drawings were rudimentary and Bruce McLaren designed the camera car for the film *Grand Prix* in a note book. "Front and rear suspension off the sports car, seven-litre engine, straighten that tube, beef up the back and whoosh, bonk, there we are." It worked too and McLaren built three 'Whoosh Bonk Specials' and made a lot of money from them. The point is John could work from almost nothing and make adjustments in the metal, which is why Robin, not the world's greatest draughtsman, had persuaded him to join him at Cosworth.

"What we were doing was all top secret," John says, "because we were still employed by Cosworth. I'd make bits and pieces in my spare time and go down to Graham's garage at the weekend to fit them, when Bill was racing, along with Pete Kerr, who was Winkelmann's chief mechanic when he was available. We were, in fact, making the car up before the design had been completed and I wasn't quite sure what was going on. I knew about Rees, but I didn't know about Mosley, in fact I didn't even meet him until I'd left Cosworth and we had set up in Bicester."

After the meeting at Robin's house, initial work went ahead on preparing to launch CRH Engineering and quotes were solicited for such as adhesive badges. Max flew to Geneva and explained to Rindt that the new plan was to create their own team, and build customer cars, but they would still like him to drive for them. This did not suit him at all, there was no sense in leaving Lotus for an outfit which was little more than an idea, but he knew about the F3 car and said contemptuously, "You vil never git togezzer your schoolboy dream, I will not drive a car built in Grem's sheck," so the project became known as 'Gremshek' and Dave Reeves, one of the first employees, now Managing Director, had his contract typed on Gremshek Engineering notepaper.

Like Amon, Rindt wanted a dedicated package, so he dismissed the idea of being a hired driver for an outfit which was now set on making customer cars. With his contacts he could set up his own team; he already had a first-class manager in Bernie Ecclestone ("He is a *real* businessman") so he needed only a designer, and the designer he wanted was Robin Herd. To get his own way he tried to split the partners. To Max he said, 'You come in with me, we don't need Alan and Graham, and to Alan he said, 'We don't need Max'. It was an anxious time for Max, Alan and Graham, for although they were friends, they had not worked together in business and knew that was another matter entirely. It's one thing to discuss a bright idea, it's quite another when your future depends on it and none was sure that one of the others would not break ranks.

Then Rindt, together with Ecclestone, began to pressure Robin and he was tempted. With Jochen he would be a designer, pure and simple, and not have to worry about niggling details like trying to run at a profit and keeping the customer satisfied. In the meantime Max maintained his contact with Rindt, trying to persuade him to drive for Gremshek, while at the same time he applied his formidable powers of persuasion on Robin.

One element which was no longer part of the equation was the Cosworth car, because it didn't work, and nor did any of the other 4WD cars made by other makers. From the idea, in 1967, to its completion two years later, aerofoils and wider tyres had solved the problem of an excess of power while creating problems for a 4WD car. It is ironic that the first designer to fit an aerofoil to an F1 car was Robin in a test with McLaren at Goodwood, but the idea was put on ice because McLaren was not in a position to exploit it and, by the time it was, others had also stumbled on the idea. Cornering speeds and forces had increased so much that when a 4WD car entered a corner the inside, unloaded, front wheel would spin and cause understeer, in short it did not like going round corners, which is a handicap in a racing car. There were two ways of overcoming it, either bias the power towards the rear, which negated the idea of 4WD, or use a limited slip differential which would cut out wheel-spin, but at the time no suitable differential was available (there is now) and Bruce McLaren, who also built a 4WD car, described driving one as 'Trying to sign your autograph with someone nudging your elbow.'

Thus Max's negotiations with Jochen centred on a conventional car (with the possibility of 4WD should the problems be ironed out) and the one ace in his hand was Robin, except that Jochen was confident that he would have that ace in his hand, so what had started as the courting of Rindt became the wooing of Herd. Years later Max remarked, "One of the statements which has made the most impression on me was by the economist J.K. Galbraith, who said that once power and wealth lay in land, then it was in the means of production, but now it is in talent." The problem Max faced was that power lay in Robin's talent and for all his persuasiveness, he argued from a position of weakness. There was nothing tangible apart from the embryo F3 car, and for all the enthusiasm there was no money. Of course, if Jochen joined the money would follow, but Rindt could not see how that was to his advantage, since he could pick and choose who he drove for and anyway he wanted his own team where he would call all the shots.

Robin thought this way and that, with all options having their attractions, and it was not until early August that he finally committed himself to Gremshek, which was registered as a company the following month. It's interesting that the only two directors of Gremshek Engineering were Graham and Robin, for it was to be the production side of the company, but it was soon swallowed up by March and nobody seems to know what happened to Gremshek Engineering.

Another meeting was called at Robin's house and this time the discussions were detailed, the four partners committed themselves to the project, worked out basics such as cash-flow, a factory, machinery and sponsorship and each agreed to put up £2,500 initial capital. The die was cast, they were resigned to not having Rindt but they would have two cars on the grid at the first F1 race of 1970, just seven months away.

Alan and Robin were helped out a few weeks later when Stewart clinched the World Championship, because at the beginning of the season Alan had found a bookie who was offering odds of two to one against Stewart, had invested £500 and had persuaded Robin to do the same. Eighteen years later Robin's £2,500 would translate into an eight-figure Stock Exchange value, which is a better return than your friendly neighbourhood building society offers.

To call the plan ambitious is to use a weak word, for all they had was intent, £10,000, and the car taking shape in Graham's garage, but they also had the confidence of youth, and ignorance of the difficulties they would face. To put £10,000 of 1969 into perspective was like setting up a modern factory and F1 team with £80,000 today. Pause for laughter. A name had to be chosen for the outfit, and they fell back on March, an acronym of their initials, Mosley, Alan Rees, Coaker and Herd; the alternative was 'Charm', which would have been asking for trouble, and Carol Coaker designed the logo, which served for twenty years.

Alan says, "It's important not to give the idea that what we were doing was foolish. It's true nobody else had ever before set up as we did, but in those days everything was so much more simple you didn't need so much time to design a new car and we didn't think we were taking that much of a flier, we had a fairly sensible plan. We'd taken account of the credit which suppliers would allow, the deposits on cars, and so on. The only problem was that we didn't attract the sponsorship we thought we'd get."

Alan's view is expressed with hindsight, but if we look at the perception in 1969 we can see the logic – all the elements for success were in place and star drivers were interested but then all good drivers wanted to be behind the wheel of a Herd car. The one uncertainty was sponsorship, but with the right package and with Max fronting the operation that appeared to be a formality.

Of his decision Robin says, "The deciding factor was Max, Max beat Bernie. I don't think now it was the right decision. Had I gone with Bernie and Jochen we'd have had only one car and we could have built a 711 instead of a 701, but Max did a very good talking job and I knew him well while Bernie was hardly known in racing. If today Bernie said, 'We're going to do a car for Senna, are you interested?' I think one might have a different view of things.

"March has been a marvellous experience, but it was probably the wrong decision. I've never fulfilled my potential as a designer because I ceased to design and became an engineer, in other words instead of creating cars I made them work properly. There are a number of drivers who will say that I was pretty good at that, so I think I fulfilled myself on that side, but from a design point of view I never really did that much at March after the 711. I regret that I didn't fulfil my potential as a designer, but if I had I could not have created March, the company, it was one thing or the other."

It was not only Robin who had a big decision to make; Max was one of the brightest barristers of his generation so he was putting a considerable career on the line. He says, "My father told me we would certainly go bankrupt, but it would be good experience for a later career." Graham, too, was giving up a secure job for an uncertain one, although he saw it as swopping 9 to 5 for an adventure, and only Alan was making a positive career move since March meant he was graduating from F2 to F1.

When they made their commitment the partners were resigned to not having Rindt on the strength, but Amon was interested, and there was this youngster, Ronnie Peterson, who was obviously very good. Alan, the racer, had been following Ronnie's career and was convinced he was a driver whom March could take under its wing and develop. He says that then it was much easier to spot future stars in the lower formulae, the progression up the ladder was simpler in the days when top F1 teams were run with fewer mechanics than a good F3 team employs today. "These days, the driver is still important, but natural ability and skill are not as important as then. The equation is more complicated now, and before I select a driver for Arrows, I have to get to know him very well, take him out to dinner and that sort of thing."

March needed a number two with potential, the next Stewart or Rindt, and Alan drew up a short-list of candidates: Tim Schenken, Howden Ganley, Emerson Fittipaldi, Reine Wisell and Ronnie Peterson. That much was simple, almost any fan could have done the same. To put them into an order of merit and to pin the future of a new team on the choice of just one of them was a different matter entirely. It was hard enough to decide who was the better Swede, Peterson or Wisell; Reine had the higher profile and was to be plucked from the crowd by Lotus, but at the top level was to prove inconsistent. As for Schenken and Ganley, both were to drive in F1 but with the wrong teams at the wrong time and neither fulfilled their potential.

When Ronnie won the F3 race at Monaco in May, Alan's mind was made up, not because he had won, he could have learned that from a magazine, but because of the way he won, something which only a driver could have detected. Alan spoke to him at Crystal Palace the following weekend just after Ronnie had ceded best, by a length, to Schenken, but he might have won had not his plans been foiled on the last corner when lapping a backmarker. Then Alan wore his Winkelmann hat and suggested an F2 drive later in the year, but Ronnie had to decline due to a commitment to Tecno, but when that fizzled out Alan repeated his offer.

Since Max had hung up his helmet, his Lotus 59 was gathering dust, and he did not need much persuading to lend it to Winkelmann so that Ronnie could drive in the Albi F2 race in September, and there he proved a revelation. During practice he hung on to Jackie Stewart on a soaking track, an impertinence which ended only when Stewart, rattled, made a political pit stop. Ronnie had problems in the race and finished fifth, but his performance in practice convinced Alan he had found the future star he was looking for, and after the race he and Ronnie sat down to some serious discussion which led to Ronnie committing himself to a three-year contract with March.

"With hindsight," says Alan, "I chose the wrong driver. I should have picked Emerson Fittipaldi. Ronnie was quicker, but Emerson was the more complete driver as proven by the fact that he won two World Championships and the 1989 Indianapolis 500." There are a million *what ifs* in motor racing and in 1970 most team managers were kicking themselves that they had not spotted the potential of either Peterson or Fittipaldi, but Alan's choice was to have a fundamental effect on March long after he himself had left the team. He actually made the right choice because Ronnie's personality was precisely suited to the mood of the young company in a way which Emerson's, perhaps, was not.

In the meantime Jochen continued his courting and might have gone to McLaren except that Bruce wouldn't include the lucrative Can-Am series in the deal, he was keeping that for Denny Hulme and himself. He came close to signing for Brabham, but in October he won his first Grand Prix, the American, and during it Graham Hill crashed and his injuries were such it was felt he would never race again. At that point Chapman needed Rindt and, more to the point, Ford wanted him in a Lotus and was prepared to stump up the cash, so Chapman offered him more money than Brabham and, moreover, promised to build his team around him, complete with a new car on the stocks. Thus Jochen got the deal he had been after and had not had to risk any of his own money to get it. Denis Jenkinson did shave off his beard and grew another one and racing historians still debate whether Jenks' new beard is original, a replica, or what.

Meanwhile the confidence of the partners brought in others and Ray Wardell became March employee number two. Alan brought in Pete Kerr and others from Winkelmann Racing and the mass defection tore the heart out of the team, which folded soon afterwards. Bicester, a sleepy market town near Oxford whose one claim to fame was that it had more pubs per head of population than any town in England, was chosen as the team's headquarters.

Pete Kerr (left) and Bill Stone (right). Stone was the first official March employee and Kerr, previously chief mechanic at Winkelmann Racing, was another involved from the earliest days.

Nobody has ever denied a connection between that statistic and the choice of location, but it was also close to where Robin lived, close to Oxford, a new industrial estate was being built on the outskirts and it was near to Silverstone, which was convenient for testing. March took over a 3000 sq ft unit and when the company moved in it consisted of Bill Stone and Ray Wardell, a Ford Transit van containing all its effects, tools and spares, and the 693 on a trailer. Bill had his old Thames van, which held all his worldly goods, and his McLaren. "They showed Ray and me where Bicester was on the map, gave us the keys, and we drove up in convoy."

While they set up the unit they lived in the Transit; they'd get up in the morning, cook breakfast on a camping stove and then get on with the job. They soon tired of this and moved their sleeping bags to the flat roof of one of the offices in the unit, sheer luxury. When Graham Coaker had served his notice, he took charge and really got the place humming.

After a while the partners took a deep breath and took over two other units, and John Thompson moved into one in order to set up the prototype workshop. "I used to go to Robin's house in the evenings after work and look at his drawings and then try to make something of them; it usually happened that the proper drawings were done after we'd made the bits. I started off in a bare workshop and had to bring in the equipment and so on. We were helped by suppliers who extended us credit because we had no money, everything was going forward on bluff."

Dave Reeves was another early recruit; he had been trying to make a go of race car preparation and had looked after Max's Clubman's car. "Business was slack when I was offered a 'key position' in an exciting new team. I soon discovered that the 'key position' was bashing out brackets alongside John Thompson." In those days the workshops were pretty bare and by the time the first F1 cars ran there was no machine shop and only one lathe, but then that was all that was needed. As word spread that on the new industrial estate, which was then open to the fields, there was an exciting new racing car outfit, it brought others knocking on the door. Some had never seen a racing car before, but if they were good, they stayed, if not they were shown the door, there was no time to train them.

Despite a slow puncture, Ronnie Peterson brought the March 693 home third on its début at Cadwell Park on 28th September, 1969. **(Nigel Snowdon)**

March had been an open secret in racing circles, but the first inkling the public had of its existence was on 28 September, a fortnight after Albi, when Ronnie raced the March 693 in the Lincolnshire International F3 Race at Cadwell Park. Although he suffered a puncture in his heat, and managed to come in fifth, and had clutch problems in the final, the result was:

1. Tim Schenken (Brabham)
2. Howden Ganley (Chevron)
3. Ronnie Peterson (March)
4. James Hunt (Brabham)
5. Reine Wisell (Chevron)

It was a thoroughly respectable début and showed that March could hold its own with the best. With its report of the race *Autosport* broke the news about March and the author had been well and truly knobbled by Robin and Max, for he tells how the first F1 car was *already under construction*, while in fact only preliminary sketches had been drawn. There was *a team of technicians with unrivalled motor racing experience and an efficiently integrated production procedure*. Formula Ford buyers were assured that their cars would have *suspension characteristics specifically demanded by the radial ply tyres demanded by the formula – which meant studying the tyre behaviour figures supplied by the tyre manufacturers and making extensive use of a computer at the design stage*. Wow, this was really motoring – the nearest most people had come to a computer was at the movies (*The Italian Job*, *2001*, etc), where they were shrouded in mystery. Robin was *thought by many to be the most brilliant racing car designer in the world*, and Max had apparently obtained *very considerable financial backing*, although he would have been sleeping easier had that been the case. An announcement of the drivers for the F1 team was expected *in a couple of weeks*.

Robin and Max are the two most persuasive characters you'll meet this side of a poker game on a Mississippi steam boat, put them in harness and you feel sorry for the hapless, eager hack whose pen raced across his pad in mounting excitement. What a story, what a scoop! Robin says, "I had actually written a computer program to calculate tyre behaviour, but its capacity was rather less than perhaps Max implied. It was not a deliberate lie, it was exaggeration which stemmed from enthusiasm, and while that may look like hype from the outside, we believed it, after all we were living on enthusiasm, we certainly didn't have much money."

That report was just the send-off March needed, though Robin and Max now have the grace to blush when reminded of it, but, in fact, what it predicted turned out not to have gone far enough. Most people found it hard enough to swallow as it was, but had it said that instead of building two F1 cars, and a spare for development, March would build ten Formula One cars in 1970, they would have rolled on the floor and clutched their sides. Yet that is what did happen. Not even the four partners would have believed it, or half of it in September 1969, but the courting ritual was still in progress and the next six weeks would see March go from a magazine article, which few believed, to a position which grabbed everyone's attention.

3 Lubricating the Deal

While the factory was being prepared, and Robin was designing the cars, Max was beating his drum. He had an acute sense for publicity and knew if he shouted 'We're the greatest' loud enough, someone would take notice. He didn't stint himself, and before long the racing world heard that March would not only run its own team but would sell F1 cars – March would listen to anyone who could talk while waving money.

Roll up, roll up, see the boy wonder design racing cars. You sir, you look the sturdy sort of lad who could be a Grand Prix star, put your money on the plate and enter the booth. You, the shaveling, just the sort to put fear into the feckless foreigner in F3, we'll take a cheque, kindly join the throng. Despite the evidence of your eyes, the emperor is fully clothed! You don't believe me, then pray be at Silverstone on 6 February when you will see things which will astound you.

Max was doing the trick of Wile E. Coyote in the 'Road Runner' cartoons. He could keep running over the edge of the cliff *provided he didn't look down*, and since he didn't look down, he kept running on thin air. There is a strong streak of conservatism in racing and this brash approach was not welcomed in all quarters, and some sat back and smiled and waited for March to fall flat on its face, although Colin Chapman, who recognized kindred spirits, was not one of them. The claims were too extravagant to be believed, nobody, not Lotus, not Ferrari, not Brabham, had made a début such as Max was predicting and before long some had decided that March stood for Much Advertised Racing Car Hoax.

After all, there was nothing more tangible than a rudimentary F3 car which had hardly rocked the world. In its second race, at Montlhéry, Ronnie had been blinded by the low sun, hit some straw bales and the car flipped and caught fire. His career might have ended there and then had not the marshals and Ray Wardell dragged him from the car and doused the fire. In its third race, at Brands Hatch, the substitute driver, James Hunt, could only bring it home tenth. It was hardly a dream beginning and Max said, "James drove it unspectacularly. We would have preferred him to have gone a lot quicker."

Following the announcement letters came in from hopefuls offering their services, among them one from a young scientist who was disenchanted with the *lack of pace and initiative displayed by large companies*. It was clear this man had the racer's attitude (also a BSc and a PhD). March was suited at the time, but the letter was kept and later Dr Harvey Postlethwaite was called from ICI, where he had been working on the *evaluation and application of the new generation of high-strength, high-modulus composite materials, especially carbon fibre-reinforced elements*. What's that? And what had it to do with price of fish or motor racing you may have asked in 1969, when carbon fibre was then something giving Rolls-Royce headaches with the RB211 jet engine.

Meanwhile the courting ritual was becoming serious as the F1 season drew to its close. Max had been against the signing of Amon on the grounds that his retainer would sap the company's resources, but he was overruled by the others, who felt that they needed a top-line driver to give them the results they needed and to test and develop the car. Once they were winning, everything else, the credibility, the sales, and the sponsorship, would follow. Alan says, "I wasn't aware of any problem with this point of view, it seemed the logical thing to do." Twenty years later people have different memories and about the only thing everyone there at the time can agree on was that there was argument, but only in the sense of debate, not in the sense of quarrel. That is why this account has sometimes apparently contradictory statements; the truth is to be found in the space between the contradictions, but the base line is that nobody could conceive of the way that March would snowball because it had never happened before.

So Max continued to woo, although it would not be long before this clash of philosophies came to the surface again. March did not have the cash to pay Amon's retainer in full and so Max proposed a deal whereby Chris would receive a modest sum, £10,000, two Can-Am cars and a share of the sponsorship Max was hoping to raise. Amon was interested, but was slow to commit himself since Ferrari had a new flat-12 engine ready to race. In testing it seemed very promising – until the fuel injection started to give endless problems and crankshafts constantly snapped.

"It was a difficult decision for me to make because Ferrari was an established team," Chris says, "and the new car was faster and had a lot of potential, but with all the unreliability I could see a repeat of '69. The idea of running with a Cosworth was very attractive because Stewart and Rindt had them and they were the two to beat." At that point he decided he could not waste another year, he needed a Cosworth and the dedicated package built around him, ("I knew they'd signed Ronnie, but I was under the impression that was only for Formula Two") was exactly what he needed. In September he had a meeting

Disenchanted with Ferrari, Chris Amon left Maranello in March 1970, only to have yet another disenchanting year with March. **(Nigel Snowdon)**

with Max, Robin and Alan in a hotel near Heathrow and they agreed terms verbally, based on the idea of Chris being the centre of the F1 effort. Says Chris, "Alan kept saying that although they were going to make customer cars, the F1 effort was going to be an entirely separate operation (*and so it was*), but it was blindingly obvious that it would lead to a dilution of effort (*and so it did*)."

Rolf Stommelen also figured in the ritual and at various times it was proposed that he would have a car bought with the assistance of Ford of Germany and run by his long-time sponsor Eifelland Caravans or that he be run by the works. Max drew up a full budget which included every detail (office expenses, National Insurance stamps, etc) and concluded that while a single car for a star driver on a £50,000 retainer would cost £156,890 for the year, Stommelen could be run without a retainer for £35,700, and that included a built-in profit margin. In the event, Stommelen's backers bought him a Brabham for F1 and a March for F2 but Max's estimates are revealing, especially since March was capitalized at only £10,000.

Meanwhile Ken Tyrrell and Jackie Stewart had just won the World Championship using a Matra chassis and a Cosworth DFV engine. When you have a winning combination most people are content to leave well alone, but Matra, part of the French aerospace industry, had developed its own V12 engine and was keen that Jackie should use it, and made it clear that it would not provide a chassis for a different engine. Matra was linked with the Simca group, which had just been taken over by Chrysler, and it was inconceivable that Chrysler would allow a chassis built by one of its associated companies to be powered by a Cosworth engine which had 'Ford' writ large on its cam-covers.

Stewart was not keen on an untried engine, and he had tested it in secret, but felt he had to have a Cosworth, yet despite his title his options were limited. He would not drive a Lotus because he felt that the cars were not built with proper regard to safety (his one drive in a Lotus had been in the 1964 Rand GP) and buying a car from Brabham or McLaren was out for both were contracted to Goodyear while Tyrrell was with Dunlop. Ken Tyrrell approached BRM with the idea of buying a chassis which would be fitted with a Cosworth, but was rejected on the grounds that it wouldn't do, Old Boy, to fit a British Racing Motors car with an American-financed engine even if it was designed by a Lancastrian and built in Northampton. If Jackie went to Ferrari it would mean cutting out Ken, who had given him his big break and had just helped him to the Championship, so his only realistic option was March.

Alan Rees could see this and he persuaded his partners that sooner or later Tyrrell would come knocking on their door. "I'd been in racing since 1958, much longer than the others. I'd always liked to work out questions in the sport and I could see there was nowhere else he could get a car from." This was beyond their wildest dreams, but Alan took them through the logic of Tyrrell's dilemma and they pencilled in Stewart as a March driver, while crossing their fingers.

Elsewhere Ferrari was playing out its part in the courting ritual and it had its eye on Jo 'Seppi' Siffert. Seppi, 'the last of the late brakers', had been in F1 for five years, driving for Rob Walker, who had been an entrant for nearly twenty years and whose partnership with Stirling Moss has passed into racing legend. His association with Siffert had been less spectacular, but had resulted in a win the 1968 British Grand Prix, the last World Championship race won by a privateer. Ferrari wanted Siffert not because he was an outstanding F1 driver, he wasn't, but because he was the best sports car driver of his time and Ferrari ran a team of sports cars. Further, Ferrari would give him two full racing programmes and something on which he had set his heart, the recognition of a works F1 drive.

One of Jo's outstanding qualities was his straightforwardness and he could not receive an approach without squaring things with his current teams. Porsche understood his dilemma but did not wish to lose him, especially to Ferrari, but there was a solution to the problem and that was that he stayed with Porsche, which would buy him a drive with an F1 team. An approach was made to Brabham, but neither Jack Brabham nor his partner, Ron Tauranac, was keen on the idea since Siffert was not a top-line driver. Jack was prepared to step down to make way for a star, but it would take more than just cash. Siffert's only option was March, but March had agreed terms with Amon and had a contract with Peterson, but despite this apparently insurmountable problem, Max listened.

Meanwhile, in America, Andy Granatelli had his eyes set on Europe. Andy had been a promising driver until he had crashed during the Indianapolis 500 and thereafter he set his heart on winning the race, if not as a driver, then as an entrant. Year after year he appeared at the circuit with teams of cars on which no expense was spared and year after year they disappointed. Then he entered a youngster

In 1970, Jo Siffert (seen here on the left of his Gulf-Porsche team-mate Brian Redman) was eased into the March Formula One team to prevent him from going to Ferrari. **(Nigel Snowdon)**

called Mario Andretti and the combination was not only successful in the American Championship but, at last, in 1969, Mario took a Granatelli car into the winner's circle at Indianapolis. Granatelli's life's ambition had been achieved, it had taken him twenty-three years, and Heaven alone knows how much money, but when he finally cracked it he wrote a book, *They Call Me Mr 500*. He was still only forty-six and that's young to have climbed your personal mountain, so he looked for other peaks.

Andretti, a naturalized American from the age of fifteen, had been born in Italy and had been hooked by the sport when he saw his hero, the tubby but sublime Alberto Ascari, drive a Lancia to victory in the 1954 Mille Miglia. While he developed in the tradition of oval racing, Mario did not have the insularity of most Americans, for his roots were in Italy. For both Granatelli and Andretti, F1 was a new challenge. Mario had already tried his hand at the game, and had been on the pace, so he was confident he could be the first American from the track and oval tradition to make his mark. Further, there was a commercial bonus; Granatelli marketed an oil additive and his cars had STP logos plastered all over them. Now that the FIA had waived its objections to sponsorship, F1 could be used to spearhead the marketing of STP in Europe.

While that idea was growing in Granatelli's mind, Max happened to meet Bill Dunne, STP's European representative and since Max was speaking to anyone who would listen he and Bill were soon engaged in conversation. Before long Max and Andy were talking not only about buying a March for Andretti but also about STP sponsoring a works team. Max was duly sent a copy of *They Call Me Mr 500* and he duly raved about it, and might even read it one day.

Within a few weeks of the partners committing themselves to the project it was starting to snowball beyond anyone's wildest dreams. When Max spoke, there were no ifs, buts or maybes, if someone wanted a car, the car was his and the growing number of men at Bicester would work until they dropped to make sure it happened.

As Alan had predicted, Tyrrell approached March to buy three cars.

Almost simultaneously, Siffert and Porsche also approached March and they too were made welcome. This upset Chris Amon, for he'd understood the team was going to be built around him and in his eyes it was lunacy to try to run a second car for an established driver, and events proved him right. He says, "Max explained that the money which Seppi would bring would be of benefit to me, it would help the development of my car. This was news to me, as I'd understood it the money was already tied up. I had no objection to Jo as a person, but he wasn't in the package I'd been sold, but by then I had no option, I had committed myself. First I was told about Siffert, then about Ronnie being in F1, whereas I thought he was to be only in F2, finally about Tyrrell, the bombshell."

Later he made the best of a *fait accompli* and said he was glad to be taking on the World Champion in equal cars, but what else could he say? By then he'd burnt his bridges with Ferrari and had nowhere else to go. "I never did accept the idea of Stewart running the same car, but by then I had no choice. The idea of running against him in the same sort of car had a certain appeal, but it was a long way from the small concentrated team I'd been sold on." Chris could argue but was stuck with his decision, and the first crack in the relationship appeared.

With Siffert in the number two seat, Ronnie was disappointed, but Alan, Max and Robin took him aside and promised that they would honour their contract. Contracts in motor racing have often, too often, been regarded as hopes rather than binding articles and Ronnie was later to say that he would have been left out in the cold by any other team. While Alan, Robin and Max were, are, the sort of men who would not want to break their word, their virtue was to reap its reward, for eventually Ronnie was to do more for March than March was to do for him. Max then began to approach private teams with the offer of the loan of a car and engine if they would run Ronnie in 1970.

Amon did not get the concentrated package he'd been promised, but in fairness to March everyone except perhaps Max thought of him as the centre of their effort, but they also thought they could juggle balls in the air while twirling a hoop. They couldn't and Chris has every right to be sore, but they did not see it as breaking their word, they saw themselves fulfilling their obligations to Amon and *at the same time* doing all these other wonderful things because they were young, it was the Sixties, they were the motor racing Beatles and could make their own rules. The decent, dedicated, core of the operation is shown by the commitment to Ronnie, nobody wanted to break his word, but here and there the word was stretched to the limits of its meaning not out of deceit but because of the sheer drive of the enthusiasm which was carrying them forward.

On 13 November *Autosport*, with obvious wonder, ran the story that Amon, Siffert, Stewart and a second Tyrrell driver would all be seen in Marches and Ronnie Peterson would not only be heading the March F2 effort but would also be seen in F1. The fact that Stewart was going to drive a March put everything in a different perspective, he was The Man and nobody questioned Ken Tyrrell's judgement so it was confirmation that March was not selling snake oil, for behind Tyrrell and Stewart were Ford and Cosworth and that was Muscle. Six F1 cars from an outfit which had been public for only six weeks was unbelievable, and on the same page *Autosport* ran a cartoon showing Tyrrell pushing Stewart towards the Gang of Four and saying, *Go on, Jackie, just go and ask the nice man if you can see your car.*

People could laugh at the cartoon, and scoff at the claims, but the signatures were on the contracts, so the laughter was nervous. Between them, the two March teams were playing with two aces and a fair spread of court cards, so the other players at the table were right to be nervous. Then *The Times* ran a piece on March and took the logical view that if March could make such ambitious predictions then there had to be a powerful backer committing at least a six-figure sum. That was a sensible assumption. Amon had believed it because his retainer would be over £70,000, not that he ever saw all of it, but because the four principals were were all known and respected. If anyone had said they were committing their futures on a capital of £10,000, he'd have been scoffed at, nobody would be that stupid. Max's only public comment was that the backing was 'adequate'.

There's all the difference in the world between an article by a reporter in a motor magazine, fleshing out his piece with extracts from a press release, and an article in *The Times* when it held an unparalleled position in journalism, so even the most sceptical among the racing fraternity took a sharp intake of breath and speculated on the 'Mystery Backer', and the motoring press took it up and suggested that £150,000 was the minimum needed to do all that Max had claimed and in fact they weren't far out, as March's accountants would discover in due course, the problem stemmed from the shortfall. As for the Mystery Backer, Ford was one nomination, so were Guinness and Huntley & Palmer biscuits, even the Ministry of Technology figured in the rumours (it was the Sixties and the Wilson government). Naturally Max did not go out of his way to deny the existence of a Mystery Backer and it became part of the mythology.

There was no Mystery Backer, but there nearly was one. In the course of his legal work, Max found himself operating the British end of an international case involving the trademark of the German chemicals company Bayer. Some Bayer directors were intrigued by the fact that the man who wore wig and gown during the week spent his weekends in overalls and helmet. One thing led to another and soon Bayer was talking about a long-term involvement with March, for it was developing a new type of plastic, and the reasoning went that this material could be used to make a racing car which would be the most spectacular way imaginable to launch the product. It would be a long-term project, but in the meantime Bayer money would launch March. It was the Reynolds package but with plastic instead of aluminium.

Meanwhile negotiations were going on behind the scenes with other potential sponsors and buyers and the press was full of possibilities. Rumour had it that a German team was going to buy one, an Italian team, and so on, the 1969 Silly Season was vintage. Robin says, "I remember the day we moved into the third unit and Max was late arriving. He breezed in and said, 'It's now ten Formula One cars we have to build, and we're running in three months' time.' I looked around the shop and it was literally bare walls and a telephone, and the phone wasn't even connected."

Another cartoon appeared in *Autosport* in December and this one depicted a racing car with an elephant's heart instead of an engine and the caption read: *Following the advent of March comes news of yet another Formula 1 challenger, the April. The company, formed last Tuesday by a group of Albanian businessmen over lunch at the L'Écu de France, is the brainchild of Count Haemoglobin, an Argentinian now residing in Capetown. The most interesting feature of the car is its means of propulsion: a twin overhead ventricular elephant heart with transistorized nervous system. The power is transmitted to the road through a fluid flywheel (working on a hydrocharged water-wheel principle) and then via a 5-speed Hewland gearbox. "The beauty of this type of unit is its torque and reliability," says its brilliant young designer Robert Beard. "I first got the idea while watching* Jungle Book *last Monday with my Aunt Doris." There are already plans for F2, F3, F4, FF, F5000, Can-Am, saloon and Indycars, which they hope to have ready for the Boxing Day Brands.*

The humour may be blunt, but the subtext is clear, March was creating enormous excitement, but nobody could quite believe it and what nobody knew was just how close it came to folding before it had begun. Max: "We were kept going by deposits and credit from suppliers who believed in us and besides in those days people were much freer with credit. I think people were less aware of the value of money, interest rates were lower, and people tended not to think as they do now in terms of one per cent per month. It got to the stage in late November when I calculated that we had just ten days before all our money ran out. Then during the next seven days Tyrrell paid deposits of £3,000 each on his three cars and we were through the wood. This was followed at the beginning of December by Porsche paying us a first instalment of £10,000 to run Siffert and at that point we had a reserve."

That much had been calculated from the start, but Max then made a shrewd move. "We needed to borrow money to buy engines and we went to our bank and arranged an overdraft which we promised to pay back in four to six weeks, and we did. That put us in good stead for the big crisis later on, for banks tend to be very impressed by people who borrow to a certain date and then repay on that date, because it doesn't often happen. So by the spring of 1970 we had considerable sums of money on deposit."

The bluff had worked, March was on its way.

4 Mad March Days

Not everyone in Bicester was delighted that March had moved in and some on the local council thundered about racing cars roaring through the main street on market day. When Jackie Stewart was due to visit the factory for a seat fitting, the mayor was invited to meet him and he turned up with his chain of office and the corporation. Jackie charmed them all and by such strokes were things smoothed over.

There was justification for the council's anxiety, since March had applied for planning permission to use the units as warehouses and then, to make 'sheet metal components'; there was no mention of motor racing, for few would have recognized it as a serious industry in 1969. It was a raffish, peripheral activity in which ordinary folk did not indulge, but Jackie was the acceptable face of it with his fashionable hair, fashionable wife, fashionable cap and shades – he was young, hip, and coining it, a totem of the time. March never has had proper planning permission, but Bicester has been kind to the company, which is now a major local employer, and since other outfits it has spawned sprouted all over the district, it's been a happy arrangement.

While the F1 cars were being built in one workshop, in another customer cars were taking shape, all based on the Gremshek 693, although they now were wholly March. The chassis itself was crude, nothing like as advanced as those made by the opposition, but then it had been done in a rush and, as one of the new designers, it was the first spaceframe Robin had drawn. There was not time to re-think for there was this pressing little matter of making more monocoque F1 cars than any team had ever made in one build season and the only time that record has since been beaten was in 1972, by March.

The season loomed, but everyone buckled down and got on with the job, regarding the clock on the wall as an enemy or, at best, an ornament. Talk to the people who were there at the time and they look back on the experience with wonder. It's like asking people what it was like to live through the London Blitz, it was tough at the time, but there was this wonderful feeling of pulling together. As

The March factory at Bicester photographed in January 1970. **(Nigel Snowdon)**

with the Blitz, you get the stories like the time Alan Rees' secretary came in to start work and found everyone hard at it. She asked whether they'd had breakfast. 'Breakfast?' came the reply, 'we haven't had last night's dinner yet.' If Alan had letters to dictate that morning, he had to wait, because she took the lads back to her house and rustled up bacon and eggs.

Bill Stone remembers, "Our first mechanic was a guy called Bill Wright, who worked in a garage in Bicester. He called on the day we moved in and kept coming back after he'd finished work. He'd done no motor racing at all, but we took him on and be turned out to be an excellent mechanic and is still in racing in America. We employed all sorts of odd people, some weeks anyone walking through the door was taken on and if he was no good we sacked him, we couldn't waste time teaching him. Whenever we were stuck for bits we used to make them because sometimes people wouldn't supply because we hadn't paid them. I don't know what kept us so inspired. I look back now and wonder how we worked so hard."

Robin says that it was a form of willing exploitation, the idea was so novel that it inspired people to push themselves to impossible limits, including the management team. Speaking at the beginning of 1989 he also said that a similar situation existed in the March Racing F1 effort, with an eager young team given their head at the top level and attacking the problem with enormous energy. "The problem will be how to sustain that energy when the novelty wears off."

By Christmas there were around two dozen employees and in their spare time they played as hard as they worked; their Saturday night parties became famous. Police, called by neighbours, would issue stern warnings about the noise and then, as soon as their shift was over, would turn up to join the party. There was, too, the mechanic who was getting married, so the lads took him out for a very wet lunch and the poor chap was legless when they got him back to the factory. That afternoon, as Robin and Max showed round some VIPs, they were unaware that the odd lump under a dust sheet in one of the building bays was a comatose bridegroom. He was a Glaswegian and his father had a fierce temper, so later that day the lads carried him home, dumped him on the doorstep, rang the bell, and ran away. He is now a respected figure in the industry, but in the early days his Glasgow accent was so thick that Bill Wright, himself a Scot, had to interpret for him, but his excellent work spoke in a different tongue.

Those early March men included names which would become familiar to racing buffs over the years. There was Bob Dance, who worked on Andretti's car, and who would become chief mechanic at Williams and Lotus, one of those rare mechanics who become legendary; Roger Silman, who started as a fabricator and later became a team manager with March, then with Toleman, and would go on to run the World Championship-winning Jaguars; Peter Briggs, who would become team manager of Surtees and is now a successful Honda dealer was there, so were Dave 'Beaky' Sims, John Gentry, Nigel Stroud, Keith Leyton, Jim Brady, now of Brady Fabrications, and John 'Ace' Woodington, while Bob Sparshott, who would run the March which won the first F3000 Championship, worked on Andretti's car.

To these names, and others, have to be added Dave Reeves, MD of March Engineering, Bill Stone, who now manufacturers kit cars in Bicester, Pete Kerr, chief mechanic at Arrows, John Thompson, who runs an internationally renowned fabrication business, and Ray Wardell, now an engineer in the States. With apologies to anyone left out, the March *Class of '70* hasn't half done well for itself, but then they are all the sort of men who'd want to get involved with something as exciting as March in its early days. The other thing is that the company gave them all their head and didn't pigeon-hole talent.

As the year turned and cars started to be delivered to customers, the cash flow became quite healthy – building racing cars was obviously a doddle. Max says, "In the early days we were awash with money, but it wasn't to last. In the January Walter Hayes of Ford asked to see us. He asked, 'How much is Ken Tyrrell paying for his cars?' 'Six thousand pounds.' 'Are you sure it's enough?' he asked, and we said, 'They're only costing us £3,000 each to make,' which is what we thought they were costing, and we were pleased at our mark-up. Walter said, 'I don't think that's enough, tell Ken they're nine thousand.'

"We didn't realize that Ford was paying for his cars and when we phoned Ken and told him we'd upped the price, he didn't turn a hair; we thought we'd get the froth job to end all froth jobs. When he did get upset was when he found out that the price of his spare car was £9,000 as well, because Ford was only paying for his race cars, and to this day he is still sore about that. Hayes had been shrewd enough to know we had been underpricing ourselves and it's a funny thing with some big firms like Ford that if they value a supplier they will often tell him to charge them more because they don't want him to go out of business. Later that year, the money we made by upping the price probably saved us from bankruptcy."

On 6 February, the press was invited to Silverstone for the March launch, but before that the Mosley publicity machine was already in motion as Dave Reeves recalls, "The BBC tv programme *Wheelbase* decided to do a film on Stewart's 701, but it wasn't quite ready. One expert, I think it was me, decided that on black and white television Amon's red car could pass for Jackie's blue one. The BBC crew turned up with two massive buses and ran six-inch-diameter cables everywhere, there was none of the modern video on the shoulder stuff. The buses arrived the night before and everything was set up for the shoot, but in the morning all hell broke loose. Colour television was just coming in, but, of course, none of us owned a colour set and we didn't realize the BBC shot everything in colour.

"We rushed the car to a local garage, cajoled the owner to spray it blue, then rushed it back before it was dry, but the hand prints plastered over it didn't show up on screen. If you saw the programme you might have noticed that some of March's staff seemed terribly camera shy and always seemed to have their backs to it – those were the guys who also worked for Cosworth."

Andrew Marriott, then with *Motoring News* had been signed as March's Press Officer and as the day of the launch

March 701 Formula One cars under construction at Bicester in January 1970. **(Nigel Snowdon)**

Robin Herd, Alan Rees, Graham Coaker and Max Mosley with two of the 701 Formula One cars outside the factory four days before the official launch. **(Eoin Young Archives)**

dawned he was going through all the agonies of an expectant father. "At the time there was a character on the scene we called The Lurker. He was one of those guys who manages to get in anywhere without a pass and if you picked up a magazine which had a photograph showing a driver celebrating a win, or a team lining up behind their car, there would be The Lurker, but only if it was a big deal, he didn't muscle in on anyone's picture. In order to accommodate the television companies, we'd arranged an early, secret, session at Stowe Corner, where they could film Stewart driving the car. It was really hush-hush because we didn't want to spoil the impact of the press presentation, but when I went down to Stowe, there was The Lurker smiling at the cameras. For me it was the accolade, I knew the day would be all right."

Not only the press arrived, everyone who was anyone in motor racing was there, the paddock was packed and there were even punters in the grandstands. There had been so much doubt about the project that everyone had turned up to see for themselves and among some there was the feeling that there would be no more than speeches and a half-finished car, but then came the announcements. The first was that STP Corporation would be sponsoring the works team and may we present Mr Andy Granatelli? Unveil the bright red STP March 701 which Chris Amon is to drive. Against all expectations there it stood, ready to run. In fact it had already run, nothing had been left to chance. Unveil Stewart's blue Team Tyrrell car and please welcome the World Champion also Johnny Servoz-Gavin, who is to have the second Tyrrell car. Sharp intake of breath all round.

Second announcement: Andy Granatelli has bought a car for Mario Andretti. Sorry it's not here, it's already on its way to South Africa for testing prior to the first race. With two cars in front of them, everyone had to believe that. Either announcement would have been the main story in any magazine, but here were two whammers one on top of the other. In the days before trans-atlantic flight became routine, someone like Granatelli was an exotic and the British press welcomed him with open arms completely unaware that American racing, for all its glitz, was light years behind.

There was, too, the novelty of sponsorship and few knew the base line in the auditor's books so it was thought that perhaps STP was investing more money than it was, and if people wanted to think that, it did them no harm.

Max was not finished, he had a third whammer up his sleeve. Another car would be entered for Ronnie Peterson, but the sponsor would have to remain secret for the time being (it surely did, there was no such animal). After the other announcements this had to be taken at face value, especially since Ronnie was there to have his first experience of driving an F1 car, so the Peterson deal passed into the headlines as fact.

The racing world had been dubious about the idea of four Marches running in F1, but now there were six. Moreover two were present and they fired up and ran, with Amon putting in some quick times which impressed some members of the press, who assumed it was turning a wheel for the first time. In fact Howden Ganley had been the first person to drive an F1 March and had put two days' testing in Amon's machine, so it was reasonably well sorted, but of course if people wanted to think it was running for the first time, nobody was going to tell them otherwise. Howden says, "I thought it was pretty brave of them since I wasn't an F1 driver, but I did a lot testing for them in the early days."

The two 701s drove round the circuit, with Stewart discovering aspects of his car he didn't quite like, and they were joined by Bill Stone and Mike Endean (who now runs Xtrac) in the latter's 708. In the meantime the first F2 car, destined for Eifelland and Rolf Stommelen, was sitting on its stand at the Stuttgart Racing Car Show.

Chris Amon recalls, "It was one of those bright but frosty days in February and everyone was wearing overcoats and scarves except Max, and this sums up March for me, he was there in a suit. I said, 'Aren't you cold, Max?'

The Tyrrell branch of the March launch at Silverstone on 6th February 1970. Ken Tyrrell sits on the left hand front wheel with his drivers, Jackie Stewart and Johnny Servoz-Gavin behind him, official Ford interest is shown by the presence of Walter Hayes seated on the right hand wheel and Keith Duckworth (to Stewart's right), while the presence of Robin Herd, Graham Coaker and Max Mosley shows the importance March placed on the deal.

'No, I'm fine. Of course the Nomex underwear helps but one has to make the right impression.'" Chris seems unsure whether it's a pro-Max or anti-Max, story but Max was right, it was Media Opportunity and March needed a business front as well as a display of racing expertise and in this he was ahead of the game.

"There was a quiet moment during the day," says Max, "when I stood in the paddock and looked about me with the whole of the racing establishment milling around and thought, 'From nothing to this in six months is really quite something.' I think it meant more to me because I'd been on the outside of motor racing. Only four years before I'd been on the other side of the fence looking at people like Clark, Hill and Chapman, yet here I was . . . I felt an enormous sense of achievement."

It was a dream launch, the most exciting in racing history, and the mass media was full of it, *they are the innovators, the brilliant young team having an all-out crack at Grand Prix racing, introducing a brand new name to an ultra-competitive field.* Even the normally staid *Illustrated London News* had March on its front cover. No new team has attracted as much attention and publicity as March; they were photographed and filmed from all angles and became the centre of attraction in the pits. Robin says, "One result of the publicity was that I was propositioned by four film stars – the trouble was that only three of them were women."

From some quarters came the sound of words being eaten and the only comfort for the consumers was that the cars had not yet raced. When it came to competing it might well be a different story, they hoped. Some people then began to rationalize their dislike of the newcomers by accusing them of having the audacity to build too many cars, it was allowing anyone who could pick up the tab to enter the hallowed halls of an exclusive club. *Brace yourself, Carruthers, for the sight of who's just walked through the door.*

March's first F1 car, the 701, was a conventional design. It was a near-miracle that it existed at all, to have had technical innovation on top would have been asking too much. Besides, the car was designed to be used by customers as well as the works and it was essential that it be easy to work on and set up. Since safety and reliability was of the essence, Robin had been conservative with the result that the finished car was overweight by nearly 70 kg. Ken Tyrrell was to criticize this, which was a little unfair since he had been one who had emphasized safety and reliability even at the cost of ultimate performance, but it was typical of the compromises Robin had accepted when he had opted to go with March. In essence he had chosen to service customers, whereas had he gone with Rindt he would have serviced a client.

The 701's monocoque was of 18-gauge LM72 aluminium strengthened by cast magnesium bulkheads and pairs of longitudinal tubes. Front suspension was by equal-length wishbones and outboard coil springs and the short uprights derived from the Cosworth 4WD car, and since they were contained within the diameter of the 13in front wheels, a good turning circle was achieved. At the rear the Cosworth DFV bolted directly on to the back of the tub and behind that was the usual off-the-shelf Hewland DG300 gearbox. Rear suspension was by reverse lower wishbones, twin radius arms, outboard coil spring and damper units and a top transverse link. Since broken drive-shafts were then the Achilles' heel of many GP cars, Robin went for simplicity and strength with BRD tubular shafts with Hookes joints at each end and Spicer-Glaenzer crosses. Rubber doughnut joints helped absorb transmission shocks and central spigots sliding in outer tubes, after Brabham practice, prevented them from becoming extra universal joints. 10½-inch ventilated disc

Chris Amon demonstrates the 701 at the launch at Silverstone on 6 February, 1970. On the same day Stommelen's Formula Two car was displayed at the Stuttgart Racing Car Show. **(Nigel Snowdon)**

Andy Granatelli, Mario Andretti and Vince Granatelli at the March launch. **(Nigel Snowdon)**

brakes with Girling-AP calipers were mounted outboard front and rear and their cooling was aided by the distinctive six-spoke Cosworth-style wheels, which became a March trademark for years to come.

"Keith Duckworth was the first person to take wheels seriously," says Robin, "he came up with a concept of wheel design and when I look at the wheels on some cars today I realize just how advanced he was. When I designed our own wheels I used his theory, but although there was a family resemblance ours was a different wheel, I hadn't taken the drawings or anything like that. At the time there was a bit of an edge between Keith and March because he had offered me a fabulous deal to stay with him which included a share in the company, but since I'd gone my own way he was the spurned lover, as it were. Now Keith was very proud of his wheels, and he'd every right to be, and a few months later he was showing the 4WD car to a visitor, who said brightly, 'I see it's got March wheels.' Keith reached 100,000 feet."

Most distinctively, the 701 featured aerofoil sections on each side of its glass-fibre body. Max says, "We needed additional tankage for some circuits so these auxiliary tanks were put on the sides of the car and Peter Wright, who designed the body, shaped them like that. We had to have a reason for their shape so I cobbled up a press release referring to 'low aspect ratio' wings (meaning they were short) which were designed to stabilize the car in turbulent conditions. It was all absolute rubbish, but we were living on hype."

That's what Max, as Bullmaster, believed, but Robin is quick to point out that those side tanks were very close indeed to the profile of the inner sidepod of a ground-effect car, but that comes as no surprise when one learns that the same Peter Wright created the first ground effect F1 car while working for Lotus. Robin says, "Every designer receives bright ideas from people. I had one once from someone who said that since our Indy cars went anti-clockwise on a banked oval, we should build cars with vertical wheels on the near side and horizontal wheels on the off side so they would simply run around the wall! Another crank suggested that if we enclosed the side aerofoils on the 701, and sealed the space on either side with sliding skirts, we would create massive downforce. It's just as well that I ignore people like that.

"In fact, Peter's pontoons did, quite deliberately, generate a degree of downforce, but it was wasted by the fact that the rest of the design was fairly messy with the springs in the airstream and so on."

Rolf Stommelen, Eifelland Caravans and Ford of Germany had negotiated for an F1 March but had eventually decided on a Brabham, but Eifelland bought a March F2 car for Stommelen and four F3 cars for other drivers. In the long-term the negotiations with Ford of Germany were to be significant, for Ford's competition manager was Jochen Neerpasch and, after that first contact, he and March were to remain friends and when he moved to BMW the long and fruitful March-BMW link was forged.

Malcolm Guthrie, a driver/patron, bought two F2 cars. *Tell you what, Malcolm, we like you and the way you operate, so we're prepared to trust you with the running of our team if you would like to buy, er hem, run it. There'll be full works backing and we'd like you to team up with Chris Amon.* Who could refuse an offer like that? For an amateur driver it was the Big Time on a plate.

Another caught up in the excitement of watching whizz kids make the impossible happen was Ted Simon, who wrote the first fly-on-the-wall look at F1, *The Chequered Year*. It describes March's first season from the best possible angle, the eye of a shrewd writer in a complex world new to him, and it is not only one of the best books ever written on the sport but its frankness, as it recorded the cock-ups and conflicts, influenced other writers and it was a landmark in motor racing journalism. If the present account differs in detail from Ted's it is because when he wrote it Max in particular didn't level with him in every detail, "I now wish I had because memory has lost so many details but, at the time, it seemed important to exclude him from some developments. We didn't grasp the fact that by the time the book came out it wouldn't matter."

Every motor racing fan, including the present writer, owes a debt of gratitude not only to Ted Simon but to Alan, Graham, Max and Robin for allowing him to push back the envelope of reportage. It's not a small point, it's an important part of the revolution March wrought.

The works F1 Marches were to run on Firestone tyres, while Team Tyrrell used Dunlops. Despite STP being on the cars (and there were soon STP stickers on all the milk floats operating from the dairy next door to the factory) most of the money came from Firestone, who contracted March to undertake 2500 miles of F1 and F2 tyre testing at a rate of $100 per mile for the first 500 miles, $50 per mile for the next 500 and $15 per mile for a remaining 500 miles plus 1000 miles of F2 testing, $84,000, or about £27,000, in all. STP's contribution was about £1000 per car per race, but that made the difference between March surviving and going under.

Robin recalls, "Just after the launch at Silverstone I went out to South Africa for tyre testing. We were out there with Amon and we didn't have a couple of parts for the car and so couldn't run. I telexed to Bicester that the failure of such and such a bit to arrive was screwing the issue. Back came the reply from Max: If I didn't get on and earn the tyre testing money, there wouldn't be any issue left to screw."

By then Robin was himself more aerodynamically efficient because he'd shed over twenty pounds in the previous three months. Nowadays he could make a mint with *The Bicester Diet* (design a range of racing cars in three months). He recalls, "There was also the matter of Jackie Stewart's seat. This was before moulded foam seats and we had the idea of taking him to Specialised Mouldings and having him sit in damp clay from which we would make the mould. He was absolutely delighted and came out with things like, 'These boys are really on the button, Ken, why didn't you think of that?' We preened ourselves, but Tyrrell's chief mechanic muttered, 'Two days. Jackie always needs two days before he's happy with his seat.'

"In those days a seat was a seat and we used the mould we'd made for Jackie for all our seats; everyone had a Jackie Stewart seat. We arrived at Kyalami for testing and while Chris went out and drove merrily around, Jackie did one slow lap and was back in the pits. 'Ken, this seat, I canna drive in this seat. There's no way any human being could drive in this seat.' By the end of the day he'd done a few laps, constantly complaining, while Chris had done 200 miles in a Stewart seat.

"Jackie was still unhappy and the Tyrrell mechanics had to make him a new seat overnight. Next day, 'Ken it's no better, it's still terrible.' Again he did only a few laps while Chris did his 200 miles. Eventually it was, 'Ken it's

Mike Endean's 708, the first customer car, at the March launch. (**LAT**)

impossible, I canna drive the car with this seat,' and he stormed out of the car with Ken doing a froth job. Jackie came up to Chris, 'Chris how's your seat?' 'Seat?' said Chris, 'Seat?' It was something which he didn't even think about. 'Oh, it's fine, Jackie.' Remember, it was a Stewart seat. 'Chris can I sit in your seat for a moment?' 'Sure,' said Chris, wondering what was going on. Jackie got into the car and was delighted, he'd never been so comfortable. 'Ken, why canna I have a seat like this?'"

When pre-race testing was over at Kyalami, the Grand Prix circus got down to the serious business of qualifying. Stewart's complaints had been in testing, when it came to qualifying, he was his professional, brilliant self and he went out and claimed pole. Then Amon showed he was right to think himself the equal of the World Champion and in an identical car he equalled Stewart's time. March looked good, no question. When you were young and brilliant, Formula One was easy peasy, there was this baby with endless candy who was eager to hand it over. Rindt, who had set the process in motion, could make only fourth on the grid, but that was with a three-year-old design, nobody thought what would happen when he got his hands on a new Lotus. What was important was that the weeks, the months, of talking, of dithering, of negotiating, of committing, of working, of worrying, were behind.

Max says, "The most amazing moment of all came just before the start at Kyalami. As the grid was forming, Robin and I walked from our pit which was at the bottom end of the lane up to the front of the grid, savouring the whole thing. Everything we'd set out to do, we'd done, and there were two of our cars sitting at the front with equal times, and you could feel the annoyance, hatred almost, of some of the Grand Prix establishment because we'd pulled it off. It was one of the most extraordinary moments of my life. For our part, we were pretty arrogant, as one tends to be when one's young. I've often talked over those times with Robin and we agree that the biggest mistake we made was being too pleased with ourselves. I suppose it was hubris."

5 March Hares

The records cannot lie, the March 701 won three of its first four races and started from pole position three times. The records say that no new team in the post-war history of F1, with the exception of Mercedes-Benz, has ever opened its account with such a string of success. It's the truth, although not quite the whole truth, but then few racing statistics are simple.

March's dream beginning didn't last for the rest of the afternoon at Kyalami. Stewart sailed off into the distance, while Amon had a tussle with Rindt which left his nose cone damaged and he had to call into the pits for another. After 15 laps, Chris was making ground on the leaders when the welded filler cap in the radiator header tank failed, the water escaped and the engine overheated. Then the same thing happened to Andretti – someone had goofed for no two F1 cars had ever retired with the same silly fault. Stewart led until his tyres went off and then first Jack Brabham and then Denny Hulme (McLaren) passed him, both on Goodyears. The term 'tyres went off' covers a multitude of reasons, few of them the fault of the tyres, in most cases the driver and/or the chassis are not in harmony with the rubber, but since Stewart was the most sympathetic of drivers, few doubted that the car was at fault.

Stewart and Tyrrell knew they had a problem with the rear end set-up and went away to try to rectify it. Jackie had already decided that the car was not what he wanted, he found it capricious, slow to react and unresponsive to adjustment. Ken was in the position that he had just won the World Championship yet was dependent on other makers, which made him extremely vulnerable, so had already decided to build his own car, and he achieved the rare trick of keeping it secret until he announced it. While Tyrrell had already decided to defect from the March camp, the partners could find plenty to be pleased about. Max took the view that the broken weld was a teething problem which would be rectified, and so it was. He could point out, too, that Amon had been catching the leaders at such a rate he could have won. Besides, pole position and third was still a remarkable debut and it didn't matter that it wasn't a works car. A March was a March and it proved his promise that every customer would have as good a car as the works.

While the partners were pleased, Chris Amon felt that his world had fallen apart. The race proved that he had been right all along, it was a mistake to try to run a works team with two top drivers and the season should have begun with all the effort centred on getting his car competitive and reliable. March was trying to do too much, it was spreading itself too thinly, and the result was inevitable failure. From the elation of equalling Stewart's pole time, he descended into despair and his relationship with the team would never be the same again.

Chris remains the most gifted driver never to win a Grand Prix. Some put it down to luck, others say it was because he was so disorganized, you could never rely on him to find his hotel so how could you expect him to choose a team? Some say that deep down he lacked confidence, his personal make-up did not back his gifts, and he needed everything done for him. If the car was right, he was right, but he couldn't draw on inner reserves to inspire a team and mould them to serve him as others have done. Whatever the reason the fact remains that Chris and/or his team could never mesh to produce the right results in a race, yet his sensitivity with machinery made him unsurpassed as a test driver. Perhaps this is the clue; most drivers go racing to stretch themselves, and it's a public expression; Amon raced to integrate himself and it was a private expression which found its purest form on the test track, where the only three factors were himself, the car and the road.

By contrast, Jo Siffert, an uncomplicated man whom everyone liked but few worshipped, has always been overlooked so far as March has been concerned. Articles about him, and his biography, treat the March period like a comma in his career and yet it was his first works F1 drive. Max: "Jo was a very nice straightforward person who was difficult to communicate with because he spoke four languages and none of them properly, one always had this feeling one didn't really know him." His mechanics, though, felt very close to him because he was a man with no side. Alan: "Jo did not get a fair deal from us, we did our best for him with the resources available but the main effort went into our number one driver, Amon, and what was left over wasn't enough."

Three weeks after the South African Grand Prix, Stewart and Amon were entered in the Race of Champions at Brands Hatch, where their cars were unstable and would not put their power down properly, and since they were using different tyres it was clearly a design fault. While Amon floundered in practice and the race, Stewart took a deep breath and set pole, something which Chris could never have done, for he lacked the reserves of belief to tip the balance. Chris says, "It was quite a good car on fast, smooth circuits and a real handful on bumpy ones. With hindsight I made the mistake of trying to dial it into the circuit when I should have simply gone out and driven it, because as it came out of the box it was as good as it was ever going to be, there was no development in it."

In the race itself Amon retired with engine problems while Jackie eventually inherited the lead when first Jack Oliver's BRM retired and then, three laps from the flag, Brabham coasted around with a dead engine. For March it was a success, a win in only its second race, and two successive pole positions, but a cool look at the performance showed all was not well and that it had been a demonstration of Stewart's talent and character, plus a lot of luck, and not something to get really excited about.

Back at the factory Robin was under siege as he tried to find ways to shed weight and solve the handling problem, while at the same time he tried to sort out the customer cars. All the junior Marches were based on the Gremshek 693 with glass-fibre bodies which looked like miniature versions of the F1 car, but it was soon apparent that they were too heavy and not slippery enough for FF1600 and F3, and the chassis was not stiff enough for F2. collected one of the Germans poked a piece of wire down a spark plug hole and smiled. He then took off the head and from each of the cylinders took a can of beer which he passed round to the lads. "We didn't believe you wouldn't take off the cylinder head to look at it." So runs one of many versions of the story, but Graham Coaker and his men were so busy building cars that the idea of industrial espionage didn't occur to them and besides they weren't that sort. Even although BMW was unimpressed by the chassis that story was told in Munich as well, where a tick was placed against March.

The F3 cars were never really in the hunt, although in a German national race at the Nürburgring in April, three of them occupied second, third and fourth behind a Lotus, but that was to remain the 703's finest hour. In Britain a privately financed works team was set up, co-ordinated by Andy Marriott, but it would not be until late May that they first appeared in a race. Andy recalls, "Our drivers were Tom Walkinshaw, Geoff Bremner and Ian Ashley and once we did get started we did a great deal of testing with Robin on behalf of Firestone, developing its new F3 tyres.

"It was a transitional period, the last year of the one litre screamers and the first year that F3 cars ran on slicks

Race début for the 702 was at Thruxton at the end of March 1970. Amon finished tenth in the final after a pit stop to have a loose nose-cone removed. (**Nigel Snowdon**)

In the F2 opener, at Thruxton, the best placed of the four Marches on the grid was Rolf Stommelen, who started from 12th place, while the best result was Amon in tenth. Chris decided to vote with his feet and vacated the seat and so allowed Ronnie Peterson a valuable learning year in F2. Stommelen gave up on his 702 within a month and Eifelland bought him a Brabham BT30, while BMW bought one to evaluate against its own works chassis, but after the test parked it in a corner. Once the build season drew to an end, however, the 702 received closer attention and became more competitive. Howden Ganley did most of the testing and he recalls he was running once or twice a week, so a serious effort was made on it.

BMW needed special fitting, for its car was the only one not to use a Cosworth FVA engine, so it sent over a dummy engine to be put into the frame. When the car was or used wings. It was not unusual to have 30, even 40, cars in a race and sometimes a handkerchief could cover the first ten on a slip-stream circuit, so even a sixth or seventh place could be quite good. We made a great deal of progress during the year and were not far off by the end, but we were a fraction too heavy and the car was too bulky, but what was learned was acted on. No other company was making cars for so many classes and Robin had a lot to learn about the junior classes, because he had started in Formula One." One area in which March had nothing to learn was braking, and the 703 led the field in that department, but the aerodynamics were not special and the cars soon sprouted bib spoilers. Still, it was good experience and the 1971 cars would benefit.

Dave Morgan in a customer car was to be most successful March driver with three seconds and three thirds late in the season, and these performances were more meritorious than their equivalents today, racing was closer and there were more future F1 stars in F3 than there has been for some years. There was, too, a sprinkling of other places in Britain and Germany, but the car was basically too much of a compromise to be successful.

As for the Formula Fords, their buyers enjoyed some small measure of success in minor races and in a European Championship race at Hockenheim, Ian Taylor won a slip-stream battle to record the first international win of a non-F1 March. Taylor, who was to become an F3 champion in a March, was the most successful user of a 708 and won half a dozen races, but most of them were in minor meetings.

One outstanding problem, the question of how Ronnie Peterson was to be run, was resolved over lunch with Colin Crabbe at the RAC Club on 5 April. Crabbe ran *Antique Automobiles*, one of the first firms to specialize in historic cars, and Colin has had a distinguished career as a driver in Historic racing. In 1969 *Antique Automobiles* had bought and run a McLaren M7B for Vic Elford which had performed creditably and won WC points, until he was involved in an accident not of his making and the car was written off. "I cannot forget the date," says Max, "because that morning I took my wife to hospital and then interrupted lunch to phone and learn of the birth of my eldest son. We'd put together a really good package, we would provide a car and engine on loan for the season to anyone who would run Ronnie, and we'd approached a number of people. It was a very good way of getting into F1 with a superb driver and works backing." Ronnie didn't receive a retainer, but he and Colin split the starting money, which was typically £750 per race.

When the Grand Prix circus arrived at Jarama, Madrid, for the first European race, March arrived with a revised rear suspension lay-out with the bottom wishbone replaced by parallel lower links and inboard rear brakes but like every other team was met by two problems, one potential, one actual. The potential problem was the new Lotus 72, which was one of Chapman's advances when he re-wrote the racing designer's manual. It didn't perform well in Spain and was put aside for a re-think, but within a short time was to make every other car on the grid obsolete. Meanwhile March had signed Geoff Ferris, who had worked on the car under Chapman and Maurice Phillippe and he was set to work on March's 1971 F1 car.

The actual problem was that there were 22 entries and only 16 starters and some people blamed March for building too many cars. The average two-car team needed the guarantee of starting money or else it was financial suicide to take cars to a circuit. The drivers took the racer's view that the 16 fastest should start, but that did not suit either the teams or the organizers, who wanted to guarantee all the stars and perhaps also include some local hero to bring in the punters. "FOCA has been credited with revolutionizing F1," says Max, one of its two mainstays, "but I maintain March brought it about. When the 3-litre formula began in 1966 for reasons of engine supply and cost, grids went down to 15 or 16 cars. We revived F1 and showed that anyone could do it, all you had to do was take a Cosworth engine and a Hewland gearbox and build a car around them."

In those pre-FOCA days, the organizers called the tune and the Spaniards decided to assure places to all former World Champions (Brabham, Hill, Hulme, Stewart and Surtees) and the number one drivers from teams not led by a Champion. Thus ten places were allocated and the remaining twelve entries were left to fight for the six vacant slots. Between practice sessions the team managers locked themselves into a caravan to discuss the situation with the inevitable result of so many competitive people arguing a point: deadlock.

Max could not take part in the discussion because he had laryngitis so he sat and listened to the circular debate conducted by the Grand Prix Constructors' and Entrants' Association. It was a salutary lesson in how business should not be discussed if that business would go anywhere except up its own backside and it planted in him the seed of Mosley, the FOCA man. "The GPCA invited me to a meeting in late 1969 at the Excelsior Hotel, where I was met with a degree of hostility, being the brash newcomer, but they felt they ought to have March on board and when they went along to meetings to discuss things such as prize money they felt they ought to take me along because I was a lawyer. Later we all went together to Brussels to meet the organizers, who were then much stronger because they were the national clubs who made up the FIA, and our side all went in a group because nobody trusted anyone else and all were afraid that someone would break ranks and make a private deal.

"When I saw the standard of negotiation I couldn't believe it. This went on for a year or so and then Ron Tauranac sold Brabham to Bernie Ecclestone. I'd known of Bernie because he'd been Rindt's manager, but to me he'd just been this rather shadowy figure on the edge of the scene. Within about 20 minutes of him turning up at the meeting, it was apparent that here was someone who knew how many beans made five and after about half an hour he moved around the table to sit next to me, and from then on he and I started operating as a team. Within a very short time, the two of us were doing everything for the GPCA, instead of everyone moving around in a block, and from that developed FOCA."

Outside the endless, futile, debate in the caravan Amon was presenting other problems as he became increasingly unhappy with everything he saw around him. He had two cars at his disposal, his regular race car and a development chassis which had lighter-gauge sheeting and components, but both had endless problems, brakes, gear selection, the best engine being in the wrong car and so on. Everything around him confirmed his view that March had bitten off more than it could chew and he'd found himself in the middle of Team Shambles. Normally a cheerful and outgoing man, when Chris was upset – which was not often – he was famous for his wobblies, which ranged from the white wobbly, when he would throw down his helmet and gloves and stomp off, through his rainbow wobbly, and up to the full-blown purple wobbly. The team had the benefit of the full repertoire and relations between them and their driver went even lower.

Max, who had not been keen on employing him in

the first place, was manoeuvring to get rid of him. Before Amon had even been signed, Max had drawn up a memo which spelt out the position: Amon would cost £75,000, Siffert, helped by Porsche money, £24,000, while Peterson, who would drive for no retainer, would cost £10,000. The estimated Peterson budget (including resale value) breaks down as:

1 chassis	£1500
1 engine	£4000
1 mechanic	£2000
rebuilds etc	£2500
total	£10,000

O happy, innocent, days!

"I had a fixed idea in my mind that we didn't need Amon. I thought if Stewart won everything in a March, that's fine, it's a March, regardless of who's running it but Alan wanted him at all costs and the works team was his thing. I thought we had to be making money or we would soon not be making cars, but Alan maintained that success would bring money in its wake and Robin was wavering between the two points of view. I tried at every opportunity to get rid of Chris, not because I didn't like him, I did and I do, but I thought he was wrong for us at the time. He was absorbing money, was bringing nothing, and was not a winner. Stewart would get the job done for us perfectly well while Siffert and Peterson made a respectable team and we would have made money running just them. Porsche was paying us £30,000 to run Jo and our Firestone contract was worth £27,000. I was trying very hard to get rid of Amon and Robin and I had a meeting with Granatelli, but for various reasons we finally stuck with him."

Both sides wanted the split yet neither knew what the other was thinking; moreover Matra wanted Amon and Chris was keen. Had that happened, March would have saved money and the whole history of the company, and of Amon, might have been different, but the matter was never aired. The one problem with Max's view, as Alan is quick to point out, is that just as Tyrrell was vulnerable by having to rely on customer cars so March would become vulnerable if it had to rely on Tyrrell, for while Siffert and Peterson made a respectable pairing, neither was likely to win races in 1970.

On the track, Robin's new rear suspension was working well, in fact it was working rather too well because extra grip generated extra stresses and during first practice a cross member at the back cracked on Stewart's car and then the same happened to Siffert and Amon. Modification was simple, the member was made of U-section alloy, so welding another strip to it made it into a box-section, but doing it meant that the works cars missed second practice. While Stewart claimed third place on the grid behind Brabham and Hulme, Amon had to be content with sixth, and his mood got darker. Andretti and Servoz-Gavin also qualified, but Siffert failed to make the grid although he had gone quicker than some seeded drivers.

Max then approached the organizers with the idea that the non-qualifiers should start the race but not receive any money. He had, he assured them, the full support of everyone else. More cars on the grid and costing not a single peseta was a great idea and the organizers asked for proof of the agreement. Max then wrote a petition in a note book and charged along the pit lane getting signatures. It was presented and Siffert, with the other non-qualifiers, took his place on the grid.

Fifteen minutes before the start the organizers changed their minds, again. The whole meeting had been marked by indecision, and there were acrimonious scenes as they enforced their curious decision. There was chaos on the grid, even brawls, but eventually just 16 cars started and when the race got under way Stewart charged into the lead and stayed there until the chequered flag, the lap charts say so. It wasn't quite as simple as that because early in the race Oliver's BRM and Ickx's Ferrari collided and burst into flames and while the conflagration was well off the track, foam and water from the fire fighting equipment seeped on to the tarmac and caught out Hulme and Brabham, who both spun. Brabham charged back into contention and was about to take the lead at two-thirds distance when his engine let go, so Stewart's win was as fortunate in Spain as it had been at Brands Hatch.

Details become forgotten over the years, only statistics are remembered, and they say that March won a World Championship race at only its second attempt and, to add to the jubilation, Andretti brought his car home third. True, he was a lap down and there were only five finishers, but the record books say that March finished first and third. Amon, however, had a miserable time starting with a clutch which wouldn't disengage, so he was last away, and then his engine wouldn't fire on all eight cylinders and trips to the pits did nothing to solve the problem. Eventually he called it a day, a very unhappy man, but Chris had reason to complain, his car *wasn't* being prepared properly; everyone was working as hard as they knew how, but there simply weren't the hours in the day to do the job with the resources available. On the other hand, some drivers would have seized the opportunity to stamp their personality on the team.

During the week after the Spanish GP, Chris was a

In the Spanish GP Jackie Stewart scored March's second F1 win, and first World Championship victory, in the 701's third race.

Servoz-Gavin with the second Tyrrell-entered March finished fifth in Spain, two laps in arrears. **(Nigel Snowdon)**

The front row of the grid at the 1970 International Trophy at Silverstone with, from camera, Amon (701) in pole position, Stewart (701), Hulme (McLaren) and Gethin (McLaren Formula 5000). Amon scored his first Formula One win. **(Nigel Snowdon)**

busy man because he was to drive a Ferrari sports car in the Monza 1000 Km on the Saturday, and his March in the International Trcphy at Silverstone on the Sunday. He practised at Monza on the Thursday then flew to Silverstone, where his March had new Firestones, which suited it perfectly, and while Stewart was delayed with problems Amon set fastest lap of the day. Then, while Chris was busily taking second place at Monza on the Saturday, Silverstone suffered a downpour so nobody could approach his time and he had pole.

The race was run in two heats and in heat one, which was dry, Chris drove off into the distance, with his car working in perfect harmony with its tyres, and the fact that he'd had so much to occupy him over the previous few days that he'd not had time to brood was probably equally as important. It rained by the time the second heat began and this time Jackie had the tyre advantage, since he started on wets while Amon fitted intermediates, but when the track began to dry Chris hauled him in and was content to sit on his tail until the end, knowing he was a long way ahead on aggregate.

So Chris took his first F1 win and beat Stewart in a similar car, which seemed to vindicate his talent. The problems of Spain were forgotten, and so too was the question of dumping him. It was not yet the end of April, yet March had won three out of the first four races and taken three pole positions; Stewart led the Drivers' Championship and March led the Constructors'; it seemed as though nothing could stop the outfit's progress, yet never again would it know such a pinnacle of success in Formula One.

6 Learning Curve

After the dramas and politics of the first few races, the rest of the 1970 season was straightforward, if any F1 season can be called that. March was on a high when it arrived at Monaco and Amon dominated most of first practice. Then, as it was drawing to an end, Stewart bolted on some new, softer, Dunlops and clipped 0.6s off Chris' time to claim pole. Chris, full of confidence from Silverstone, went out in the dying minutes of the session, but at Casino he was baulked by Rodriguez' BRM and by the time he got by he was so busy shaking his fist he missed his braking point and ended up by the side of the track with a bent car. He therefore started the race in the development car, which, for diplomatic reasons, was called his spare.

Since the second qualifying session was wet the first day's times decided the grid, so again Marches occupied the first two places with, as usual, Hulme and Brabham the main opposition. Monaco limited the number of starters, so Granatelli scratched his car because, after the Jarama fracas, he wanted nothing more to do with qualifying, although Andretti took the racer's view that he'd always had to earn his place on any grid.

Siffert started 11th, although the team's watches had him third quickest and they are supported by his performance in the race, and two places further down was Peterson in Colin Crabbe's car. Ronnie had an original spec 701, without the inboard brakes and revised rear suspension, and was running on Goodyears. With the works on Firestones, Tyrrell on Dunlops, Robin joked, "The tyre companies will soon be running out of excuses." March itself never ran out of excuses in the early days.

Ronnie was making his F1 debut with minimal testing since with only one chassis and one engine that was a luxury one dreamed about, but he posted a time equal to Graham Hill's Lotus and was quicker than Surtees' McLaren and both BRMs. He also equalled the time set by Johnny Servoz-Gavin in the second Tyrrell car, but Johnny crashed in practice and didn't make the start. During one practice session, which was wet, Ronnie arrived opposite the pits with the car sideways but under perfect control. Colin Chapman's eyes lit up and he turned to 'Beaky' Sims, "Who's he? I want him." It was the start of an eternal triangle between Chapman, March and Ronnie.

Stewart took the lead and pulled out half a second a lap on Amon, who had Brabham breathing down his neck until he slithered by just after quarter distance, but Chris was soon back with him scrapping for second. Then Stewart's spark box gave up the ghost and he lost two laps having it replaced, so Chris was now fighting for the lead. Then Rindt and Siffert, third and fourth after a lot of the field had retired, began a charge which took them closer to the leaders until Seppi's car developed a misfire. Amon was in with a chance, until he came up to lap Rodriguez, who, as usual, had no wish to be lapped, and by the time Chris got past, Brabham had a useful cushion. Whether or not Chris could have done something about that we will never know, for at three-quarters distance a bolt sheared in his rear suspension and his race was over. Peterson was driving a sensible first race, and Siffert was struggling to reach the finishing line with a fuel feed problem which caused his engine to misfire and he baulked Brabham, who lost six seconds as a result. This allowed Rindt, who was really motoring, to close up on Brabham, forcing him into an error on the last corner which cost him the race.

The only bright spot for March was Peterson's drive to seventh, but that was also last place and was to be his best result all year. Because of the constraints of his budget it could hardly be otherwise, but it allowed him a season of learning his craft without pressure. Stewart's failure had not been the fault of the car and, in a funny way, the failure of Amon's lightweight car was a vindication of Robin's policy of building rugged, reliable, cars. Siffert's fuel system failure, again, didn't reflect badly on the design, for it was another of those things which happen in racing, but Seppi's crew, who felt he might have won, grumbled that so much effort was being spent keeping Amon happy that their man was not receiving his fair share of attention.

Meanwhile both the works F2 cars had new chassis, for both had crashed at the Nürburgring and, in rebuilding the cars, there had been the shedding of some weight. Thus they appeared with lighter wheels, modifications to the suspension geometry, different spring rates, F1-style wings and a revised body. All this was an improvement, but the design was a lost cause even with Ronnie at the wheel, a man who drove his way through most problems.

Back at the factory, as Bill Stone recalls, "During 1970 we had an incredibly busy time until June trying to get all the cars out, and then everything went dead. There was nothing to do and we laid off some of the men." March was to employ some assemblers on a seasonal basis until 1976, but these were normally racing mechanics looking for winter work. "To give you some idea of how hard we worked, when I married Max's secretary I went to work on

A fine practice shot of Jackie Stewart who led at Monaco until he was forced to retire by engine problems. **(Nigel Snowdon)**

In mid-May the chassis of the first Can-Am car, the 707, was ready and Chris shook it down at Silverstone minus its body. The prospect of the two cars, which were part of his retainer, perked him up because it was the first step in establishing an Amon Racing Team, which might lead to independence and long-term security even after he'd hung up his helmet. In the event, an agreement was made that the works would retain the cars, and the books would be balanced to suit, because Chris was not getting on with the team and felt that if the crunch came the Can-Am cars could become a major bone of contention.

Overall the 707 bore the distinctive signature of Robin Herd with its cast magnesium bulkheads and 20 gauge sheet aluminium skin, but the detail design had been executed by ex-Lola man Martin Slater (a friend of Graham's) and John Clark, a freelance designer who was involved with most of the early Marches, while further refinements were made during its construction by John

The sole March finisher at Monaco was Ronnie Peterson, making his Formula One début with the Antique Automobiles-entered car, who took seventh place, two laps in arrears. Here he is seen in practice. **(Nigel Snowdon)**

Saturday morning, got married in the afternoon, we went on our honeymoon and I was back at work the following Tuesday.

"It was not difficult to work so hard because everyone was doing it and there was the feeling of all being in it together and trusting each other. Those of us on the shop floor had weekly meetings with Robin and he would produce his diary with all his points written down. He would then allocate these jobs and cross them out in his diary, confident they would be done. You just got on and did them, there was nobody constantly looking over your shoulder, and he didn't raise the point again unless something hadn't been done.

"With a bit more time on my hands I took a long look at the FF chassis, which I'd always thought was a crude affair, and then designed and made my own using March bits. It was a lot lighter, had round tubes instead of square ones, and I won three races in it. It was probably the best of all the March FFs, although *Autosport* took to calling it the 'Starch'."

Thompson, Roger Silman and Peter Turland. Many of its components were shared with the 701 so it had F1-style front suspension by coil springs and double wishbones, while at the rear was a single top link with parallel bottom links.

Bolted to the back of the monocoque, with extra tubular bracing, was a mighty 7.6-litre aluminium-block Chevrolet engine which gave 685 bhp feeding through a 4-speed Hewland LG 600 gearbox and 23-inch-wide Firestone tyres. There was nothing startling about the car, which continued the thinking Herd had pioneered at McLaren, although the aerodynamics were different to normal Can-Am practice in that, in place of the usual full-width nose, the front wings swept over the wheels and an F1-style nose-cone protruded proud. A side-effect of the massive rear tyres was that the beast was very wide indeed and the cockpit had enough room for a normal-sized passenger. Thus when Amon complained about some front end instability, Robin volunteered to sit beside him to experience it at first hand, and some of the mechanics

Views of the production shop and the prototype shop at the March factory at Bicester during 1970. Note above the 707 bonnet propped against the wall and the monocoque being worked on. (**Nigel Snowdon**)

muttered that he'd designed it that wide so he could hitch rides in it. Three 707s were built, two for Amon with the third going to Helmut Kelleners, who raced it in the Interserie Championship, the European equivalent of Can-Am, which was mainly centred on Germany.

A month passed between Monaco and the next Grand Prix at Spa, but when the circus reassembled in Belgium two of its regulars were missing, permanently. Bruce McLaren had been killed testing a Can-Am car at Goodwood and Johnny Servoz-Gavin had retired. He said he had lost confidence in himself, "Fear has won me over." It's not the only time a driver has retired for that reason, but few have had the guts to admit it.

Once again two Marches sat on the front row of the grid with Stewart on pole, Amon third, and Rindt's Lotus between them. Since Monaco March had made Chris a new monocoque, which shed about 60 lb, in the tub itself, in the tanks, in the radiators, in all manner of details. Further back, Peterson was in ninth place and his car had been updated to heavyweight works spec, while the only other March, Siffert's, was tenth. Ronnie very nearly didn't make the start because he was stuck in traffic and committed the cardinal sin of queue jumping on the road to the circuit. Unfortunately he also ran over the foot of the traffic cop who was trying to redirect the queue jumper, so he was hiked off to the hoosegow. Only at the last minute did the organizers manage to spring him.

In the race Chris went into the lead and while he soon had to give way to Stewart, he stuck on the blue car's tail, biding his time, then took the lead once more and began to look unassailable. Meanwhile Rodriguez' BRM was on a charge and moved up the field to take the lead and Amon hung on just behind the BRM, while Stewart's engine blew up. For lap after lap Chris was looking down Pedro's exhaust pipes, expecting the engine to give at any moment, for it normally did when pressured, because BRM cut too many corners when building its engines, but this one held together, and even though Chris set a new lap record of 152.08 mph in his pursuit, at the end he was 1.1 seconds behind.

He says, "I couldn't believe it, Pedro just towed past me, I'd never seen a BRM go so well; he'd not been special in practice, sixth on the grid and well off the pace. I tucked in behind and got a tow, but there was no way I could pass him on power. I'd not been taking the Masta kink flat, nearly, not quite, so on the last lap I held back and did it flat, and I wouldn't want to do it again. It worked because I got my nose in front, but on the run up to Stavelot he passed me again."

Chris had done everything which could have been expected from a driver, and in the normal course of events would have won, but Rodriguez had experienced one of those magical days which sometimes fall on a driver not quite of the first rank, a day when everything works in harmony and he lives as an ace. Moreover, Amon's luck, it was the first time a BRM had won a race in four years. Still, Chris's six points for second promoted March to the head of the Constructors' Championship, four points ahead of Brabham.

Siffert had finished seventh and Ronnie, after many

Jo Siffert in the Belgian Grand Prix in which he took seventh place, two laps in arrears, but not running because of loss of fuel pressure. **(Nigel Snowdon)**

problems, had limped over the line too far behind to be classified. As he clambered from his car he was greeted by Pierre Plod, who whisked him back to the calaboose. There he stayed for the next two days until freed on his promise he would return to face the full majesty of Belgian justice for trying to get to the circuit to race. In the event, the matter was smoothed over and the charges dropped, but to Ronnie fell the honour of being the first March driver to see the inside of a cell, though he would not be the last.

In the Dutch GP which followed a fortnight later, Stewart appeared with a new monocoque, for as well as secretly building his own car, Ken Tyrrell had instigated a weight-saving programme on Jackie's March and the new tub was skinned with 20-gauge aluminium instead of the usual 18-gauge. By then Tyrrell had chosen Servoz-Gavin's replacement and the seat went to another Frenchman, François Cevert, who was to entirely justify his elevation. The Dutch race was the turning point in the year. Having tried the Lotus 72 at Jarama, Rindt had reverted to a 49 while Lotus sorted out the teething troubles, but it reappeared in Holland and Jochen put it on pole with Stewart alongside and Amon fourth. The rest of the Marches, Cevert, Peterson and Siffert, were in a tight little group at the back of the field with Siffert the slowest despite receiving many of the weight-saving features of Amon's car. In the race itself, Rindt took the lead on lap three to win easily from Stewart. Amon's clutch failed on the line, he was out after two laps and, of the rest, Ronnie was the only March finisher, down in ninth place.

After the Spanish GP Rindt and Chapman had worked together to improve the Lotus 72 and the car was built around the driver's requirements in exactly the same way as Jochen had wanted to work with Robin. His second GP win of the season was joyless, however, because early in the race his close friend, Piers Courage, had crashed and had been burned to death. Piers had been very popular and

François Cevert joined the Tyrrell team at the Dutch race as replacement for Johnny Servoz-Gavin. **(Nigel Snowdon)**

that on top of the death of Bruce McLaren, another of the good guys, cast a pall over everything.

Shortly afterwards Helmut Kelleners débuted his 707 at the Nörisring and led both heats until retiring with gearbox problems, a considerable feat since works-assisted Porsche 917s were present and the car was far from right on its debut since it had troublesome brakes and imperfect weight distribution. Later Kelleners was to win the Interserie round at Croft (scotching the rumour that the car was so big it would have to negotiate the chicane by doing a three-point turn) and some national sports car races. He finished third in the Interserie Championship, but, given better reliability, might have won it, for the 707 was probably the class of the field and the lessons learned on his car were transferred to Amon's.

Rindt won again in the French GP at Clermont-Ferrand, and Amon came home a strong second, but the meeting had really been about the new-found speed of the Ferrari and Matra V12s, which had dominated both practice and the race until side-lined with mechanical problems. Robin, Max and Alan began a critical analysis of the situation and decided that since they were wonderful, and March was wonderful, then the drivers had to be at fault. A cooler view would have said that March had begun the season with a sound 1969 car, and now the 1970 cars were coming on stream the inevitable was happening. One result of this was that Lotus had taken the lead in the Constructors' Championship.

Dampers had always been a problem on the 701, because the car did not like bumps, and the team had reverted to Armstrong units by the French GP, then in testing at Goodwood prior to the British GP had discovered a great improvement in traction by changes to the rear roll centre and kits were made for all six cars which started at Brands Hatch. The great improvement at Goodwood did not translate to Brands where, as in the Race of Champions, the 701 proved a pig to drive. Stewart, who had taken pole in the earlier race, could do no better than equal that time, which meant that half a season's development had resulted in zero advance, at least at Brands Hatch. The catch was that the time which had won

Chris Amon with his works 701 in the French Grand Prix. He finished second. **(Nigel Snowdon)**

him pole in March was good for only eighth place on the grid in July, while Amon was in an even worse state, down in 17th place and slower than Andretti, Peterson and Cevert.

Andretti had returned to Europe with his March modified by Frank McNamara, who had built the car Mario had driven at Indianapolis. Granatelli had hoped that March would build him an Indycar on top of everything else, but that was pushing things too far, so he had turned to McNamara, whose junior formulae cars were going quite well in Europe but whose career as a constructor was to be interrupted by the sudden death of his wife and his own disappearance.

The race itself was exciting for the spectators. First Ickx led in his Ferrari until his transmission broke, then Rindt led until hauled in by Brabham, who had the race in the bag until, near the end of the last lap, his car ran out of fuel, and as he coasted to the line, Rindt passed him to take the flag. Then Rindt was disqualified because his rear wing was judged too high, so Brabham had won, but the disqualification was quashed after an appeal so Rindt had won again, his third race in a row. After all that excitement, Rindt had his hands on the Championship and March was looking desperate. A modified part on Andretti's rear suspension had broken and Stewart had a puncture, and when he called in at his pits, the car burst into flames because a clutch line had melted and the leaking liquid had ignited. Siffert had a standard March part break on his rear suspension, while Amon plugged home fifth, a lap down.

If that was a bad result, it was as nothing to the German GP at Hockenheim, where seven Marches entered, six qualified (Siffert was easily the quickest in fourth place, but that was almost certainly a timekeeper's mistake) and only Cevert finished, in seventh. To make things worse for Amon, who retired with a broken engine, Jacky Ickx brought home the Ferrari, which could have been his, a strong second to Rindt's Lotus. Chris says, "About the only amusing thing in an unamusing year came at Hockenheim. The only Cosworth car which could match the Ferraris was Rindt's Lotus, but I figured if I could organize the start right I could get a tow, and that worked out, but I had no hope of passing anyone. In the stadium section I really had to throw the car about, it wouldn't go round on rails, and it was case of throw it at the corner, use plenty of throttle and slide it through. After I retired Max came up and was livid. He said the way I was sliding the car might give people the impression it didn't handle very well!"

By the German GP most of the early season optimism had evaporated. Hard facts in terms of times and performances had concentrated the mind and Robin began to admit to mistakes he'd made on the 701. More fundamental than a designer's discontentment with this detail or that were that the compromises he'd had to make meant that it was a competent, user-friendly car which was quick straight out of the box but it was a shallow design which revealed all of its secrets at once and there were no reserves which might be teased out.

If Chris looked with envy at a re-vitalized Ferrari, so Robin looked at Rindt stringing together his fourth consecutive victory and thought of the chance he'd had to concentrate on one design for one driver and not, as then, having to worry about a whole range of customer cars, which were not adding lustre to the March name, while at the same time worrying about a new range of cars which might do the job the following year.

There was, too, the matter that all the swank of a few months before was rebounding and the people who had looked with annoyance as Max and Robin had swaggered up the grid at South Africa were laughing up their sleeves at 'Team Bullshit'. That was the least of their worries, though nobody knew it at the time because March managed to keep a united, ever-smiling front; there was an impending financial crisis. When the last car had left the factory a few weeks before, it had marked the last time that anyone arrived at March with a substantial cheque in hand and nothing was coming in apart from the F1 team's start and prize money. With only a few dozen cars on the circuits, the demand for spares was small and March's only solution was to draw in its belt a notch or two and some of the poor performances later in the year were the result.

On the same day as the German GP Xavier Perrot, March's Swiss agent, ran a standard (heavy) 702 in the German F2 Grand Prix at the Nürburgring, and won, and in second place was Hannelore Werner in another 702, which remains the highest place a woman has scored in an international F2 race, but one has to add that despite its title the race was, effectively, only a German national event called the 'F2 Grand Prix' to placate the organizers, who had lost the real Grand Prix to Hockenheim.

After Germany, the rest of the season became something to get through, hoping for the odd points result. Stewart and Amon were fourth and sixth on the grid in the Austrian GP, but Jackie retired early with a split fuel union, and though Chris ran as high as fifth in the race, his shock absorbers were rooted (penny pinching by the team) and he had to finally settle for eighth. "Max made a point of telling the press I'd given up half-way through, but my mechanics made a point of showing them a broken seal on the damper and the fluid seeping from it."

Ronnie missed the race because he had no engine, since Cosworth insisted on doing all the rebuilds itself, which was fair enough but for the fact that the works closed for a fortnight's holiday in August. For several seasons this led to a race across Europe by team truck drivers all intent on being first in the queue with their engines when Cosworth re-opened. With no spare unit, Ronnie was beached.

The addition to the regular March runners at Hockenheim had been the privateer Hubert Hahne, but when he failed to qualify for his home Grand Prix he uttered the German equivalent of *We wuz robbed*, his solicitor issued writs and when March headed home after the Austrian race, as soon as the transporter crossed the German frontier it was impounded by the police. Hahne claimed that he had been sold an uncompetitive car as was proven by the fact that he, a works BMW F2 driver, could not get it on to the grid.

Max went into overdrive, but it still took over a week for the team cars to be ransomed and then after thrashing

Hubert Hahne in practice for the 1970 German Grand Prix with his silver 701, financed by magazine magnate Axel Springer. When Hahne failed to qualify, it led to litigation with March. (**Nigel Snowdon**)

out a deal which would see Hahne take his 701 to Silverstone, where Ronnie would drive it, and if he failed to achieve an agreed lap time Hahne had won his case. Hahne was happy with the arrangement, for Peterson was a novice who could not possibly go as fast as he. Ronnie turned up, equalled the agreed time, and then lapped two seconds beneath it to do conspicuous service for his employers. There wasn't much Hahne could say about that so he returned to Germany and retired from racing.

The Italian GP brought Rindt's fatal accident in qualifying when one of the front brake drive shafts broke on his Lotus, causing him to turn into a barrier. Despite losing the second of his two closest friends within months, Stewart qualified fourth and, the master of slip-streaming came home second though unable to match the pace of Regazzoni's Ferrari. It was a fine drive by any standards, but following on Jochen's death the day before and a sleepless, troubled, night, it was a magnificent example of professionalism. It was he rather than March who took second.

By contrast Amon was in a black pit because his March was down on power; a week in the hands of the German authorities had not helped matters, and it showed at a power circuit like Monza. Chris was hauling a gutless car around and all he had to show for it was a place three from the back, and had not all the Lotuses been withdrawn after Jochen's death he would have been bumped off the grid, but, given the way he felt, he would not have been unduly worried. While Peterson and Siffert retired with blown engines (Cosworth was going through a sticky patch with its quality control) not even that relief was his. It was the professional in him who brought the car home seventh, and lapped.

Monza was to be Stewart's last race in a March. A few weeks earlier in a minor race at Oulton Park he had débuted the Tyrrell 001 and had dominated until side-lined with fuel feed problems. He had practised it at Monza, but still unsure about its reliability, had elected to drive his 701. Robin says that if Tyrrell had not built its own car March might have won the Constructors' Championship; it still had a chance after Monza, but that view overlooks the fact that since it had two or three times as many cars on the grid than any other constructor, it jolly well ought to have won. On the other hand if Tyrrell had not been diverting so much attention into his own car then Jackie's 701 might have enjoyed better reliability (he scored points in only four races, unusual for Tyrrell) and he might have won the Drivers' title.

Shortly after Monza Graham Coaker left March. He has hardly appeared in this story as a personality because setting up a factory to make cars is not as glamorous as running them – he stayed at home and did the chores while the rest of the boys were out playing. By the time of the Austrian GP, the financial crisis was becoming so bad that Max was ready to quit, unless he had control of the finances, and that ultimatum was to lead to Graham leaving.

Graham was older than the others and had a different style, professionalism against optimism as his widow, Carol, says. As the man in charge of production cars, he believed that side of the business was of paramount importance to the future of the company for, after all, it was subsidizing the F1 team, not the other way around. He'd built a factory out of nothing, an operation which had run on adrenalin, and knew that if it was going to continue to do the job properly there had to be capital investment, you couldn't rely on maintaining the buzz.

Graham's view put him against Max (Alan is quick to say that he never fell out with him), but his was a tenable position because the F1 team was sapping March's resources and there wasn't enough money to run it properly. The main motive of March was to be in F1 and customer cars had always been a way of ensuring that. Graham knew he was out-voted and took it in his stride, the parting was amicable and Alan, Robin and Max still speak warmly of the man who, in the long-term, did so much to secure the future of March, for, by all accounts, he was a thoroughly likeable and competent man who had brought tremendous energy to bear on the problem of setting up a new factory from scratch.

Most, not all, of Graham's shares were bought by Jonathan Guinness, a merchant banker and Max's half-brother, and when the company found that it could not pay his agreed leaving settlement he opted to take a 1971 F2 car instead. At about the same time John Thompson also left to set up his own fabrication business, which has since built Ferrari F1 monocoques and such prototypes as the

Swiss driver Xavier Perrot with his Squadra Tartaruga-entered March 702 scored a surprise win at the Nürburgring in the **Preis von Deutschland**, *run the same day as the German Grand Prix at Hockenheim.* (**Autosport**)

Ford RS 200 and recent Jaguar sports-racers, but which started off mainly as a March subcontractor.

After Monza Amon took his 707s to join Can-Am; he was supposed to have done the full series but both he and the works had been rather busy, so he arrived in time for the final three rounds. In his first race, at Donnybrooke, he ran as high as second until encountering fuel feed problems when one tank would not empty into the other, and finally finished fifth, but in the final two rounds he picked up a couple of fourths (it would have been third at Riverside but for a return of the fuel feed trouble) so it was not altogether a wasted trip and nor was it a poor showing since Can-Am was then at its height. To judge by Kelleners' performance in Interserie, had Chris done a full season he might have upset the McLaren steamroller.

In the last few European F2 Championship races, Ronnie got the improved 702 wound up and ended the season with a fifth, a fourth and a third. After the race at Rouen in June – *Robin: How did Ronnie get on? Roger Silman: Led all the way until he spun on the last lap, I don't know why. Robin: Probably surprise.* On that occasion Ronnie finished sixth and it was also the first time that two cars had gone to a circuit and both came home in one piece. His best finish of the year was third at Hockenheim in October, but he had started from pole, which showed the progress which had been made. By the end of 1970 the 702 had reached the position where it should have been at the start of the year, but since March was not letting the grass grow under its feet, it was a springboard for 1971.

Even though Rindt was dead, and there were still three Grands Prix to run, it was almost certain he would become racing's first posthumous World Champion and that took pressure off everyone, except possibly for Ronnie, because Chapman began to woo him, but his

In the Can-Am series Amon took two fourth places and a fifth with the 707. Here he is seen at Laguna Seca. (**Dave Friedman**)

The Formula 3 race at Oulton Park in August 1970. Cyd Williams (Brabham BT28) leads the March 703 of David Morgan and the rest of the pack. None of the leaders here finished in the first three and the race was won by Carlos Pace (Lotus 59A). In this race there were five drivers who later competed in Formula 1, plus Tom Walkinshaw (later head of TWR) and other drivers who were later very successful. **(Autosport)**

contract had been drawn up by Max and would have given Houdini a hard time. Graham's departure also took pressure off March, not because he was obstructive but because his going resolved the debate; the emphasis on F1 was agreed policy so everyone was united. Chris felt good because he had reached terms with Matra for the following year and, perhaps, because, now that Stewart had decided to race the Tyrrell, he was not being compared with him.

In the Canadian GP Stewart dominated until a front hub broke, but then he had a new development Cosworth, which was a great advance, and March didn't have the clout to tout for it. After Stewart retired, the Ferraris of Ickx and Regazzoni stormed away to a 1–2, but third, and winner of the Cosworth race, was Amon. Robin says now that the team was too young and inexperienced to get the best out of Chris, but towards the end of a season when there had been so much to learn, team and driver began to knit together. There was even talk of doing 1971 together, which was not so much courtship, more a mild flirtation, where each side flattered the other and felt better for it. Amon already knew he was going to Matra and March knew it could not afford to keep him and would promote Peterson to the number one seat, but it was good to end the relationship on a friendly note.

There was no such flirtation with Siffert, who was to end the season without scoring a single point, which was more of a vindication of Amon's view than it was a measure of Siffert's ability. Jo may not have been regarded as one of the tiny handful of aces, but he wasn't far off as he showed with BRM in 1971, when he scored a brilliant win in Austria and finished fourth in the World Championship (the highest non-Cosworth user) before dying in a minor race late in the year.

In the US GP at Watkins Glen there were six drivers who might have won *if only*, because it was one of those lotteries where all the leading contenders had troubles. Moral victor was Stewart, who led most of the way, but one of the remaining five who might have won was Amon, except that he had to stop to replace a front tyre. If that hadn't happened he would have been second on the last lap, when Rodriguez' BRM ran out of fuel, and that would have seen him win his first GP and the $50,000 prize, but Rodriguez could have said *if only* as well, and so could have Stewart, and Ickx, and so on. Apart from the effect it might have had on each driver, no team could have benefited more than March, both by taking its first WC win and by arriving at Barclays Bank, Cornmarket Street, Oxford, with a cheque for $22,500, the entrant's traditional share. As it happened it was Emerson Fittipaldi in a Lotus who took the flag and his win ensured that the Championships went where they deserved to go, to Jochen Rindt and Lotus.

Robin says, "One of the moments of the year for me was after the race when we were having dinner and Chapman came up; after Jochen's death there had been some doubt whether he would enter the race and he said, 'The only reason I came was to stop you bastards winning the Championship at your first attempt.'"

The final race of the year came on 25 October in Mexico, where Chris Amon qualified fifth and finished fourth behind two Ferraris and Hulme's McLaren. The conditions in which the race was run were farcical as the crowd spilled to the edge of the track, so the drivers raced through a wall of humanity on some parts of the circuit. It's a tribute to the drivers that nobody was killed and none was sorry to see Mexico dropped from the calendar.

Max says, "You had to psyche Chris and I only discovered how to do it at the very last race of the season. By the time we went to Mexico everyone had given up and I went there on my own and by then we knew that Chris was leaving and everything was arranged for the following season, so there was an end-of-term feeling. By that time I had learned what made Chris tick, you had to say something like, 'You've got no chance today, you're on Firestones and they're no good for this circuit. We're also about 30 bhp down, so just try to keep the car going and aim for a finish. Forget about winning because you've got no chance.' If you told him that, you would get an amazing performance, but if you said, 'You've got the best car, best engine, best tyres, best everything then he would go to pieces, because it was then all down to him. If you told him it was a lost cause before he started, then he couldn't be blamed for failure and he would pull out an incredible performance."

Chris's response is, "That's absolute rubbish, I don't recall that at all, but I do remember being told all year we'd got the best car, the best everything. If Max did say that, by that time I don't think I'd have been listening to him. I don't really think he was in a position to tell me about racing cars."

If March had been any other team, everyone would have applauded its first year in racing, for it finished third in the Constructors' Championship behind Lotus and Ferrari. When something is billed as a wonder car and it turns out to be ordinary there is a sense of let-down and, frankly, all the hype had got up people's noses, but its first year was nothing to be ashamed of. There were lots of other teams who could have wished to have done half so well, Brabham, McLaren, BRM and Matra among them, but none of them came under such close scrutiny, so their mistakes were less public.

Andy Granatelli was to say that March had achieved more in its first year than any other débutante team, including Mercedes-Benz, and the records show he was right. One lightly refers to the Can-Am car, which was a detail in the year, a car which was not quite good enough to win, yet one could draw up a long list of Can-Am cars which were much inferior to the 707 whose constructors were doing nothing else than trying to win in Can-Am. One thing that Granatelli did not say was that he became so exasperated with his 701 that at the end of the season it was dismantled and the monocoque was used as a flower box.

At the end of the season the accountants found that March had made a profit of £3000. No business can survive very long when it is making only three thousand pounds a year, but even that figure disguises the true position. Max says, "We started to run out of money in June and stayed in that position ever after. The fundamental problem was that building racing cars is a capital intensive business, you have to keep spares for customers in the stores, for example, but until they want them it's money lying on the shelves doing nothing. At the end of 1970 the total value of our assets was about £250,000 and we had our initial £10,000 plus £3000 profit in our first year. Take £13,000 from £250,000 and you're left with a deficit of £237,000, which was basically provided by our suppliers." It might also be added that a substantial amount of money was owed to Chris Amon, whose solicitor was urging him to issue a winding-up order. Eventually he got some of it, not all, but it took time and had he felt so inclined he could have ended March there and then.

"When it became clear that they were in difficulties, Robin and I borrowed £20,000 from relations and friends as convertible debentures. Later, after I'd left the company, the debentures reverted to shares, Robin was able to buy almost all of them and everybody who sold made a small profit. We never did make enough to get out of trouble, though, and a lot of the deals we made were to keep us going in the short-term, but were unprofitable in the long run."

Thus it was that March went from an all-star line-up to stitching together odd deals to support Ronnie, who, at the beginning of 1971, showed promise but who had yet to win an F2 race let alone a World Championship point. In effect, March's future rode on Alan Rees having made the right choice of junior driver.

7 Team Shoestring

STP was happy to continue with March since its products had taken off in Europe thanks to its exposure in racing, but although its logo was everywhere on the cars, it was only because there was no other sponsor,and it actually paid for only a fraction of the costs. Sponsorship was still new and Max is the first to admit that his efforts to raise it were amateurish compared to some of the operators who have appeared since, but for a while it looked as though he would land a lucrative deal with Firestone and Ford USA to run a Can-Am team, and that would have made all the difference, but then Ford abruptly pulled the plug on motor racing.

The brutal fact remains that when the partners set up March one of the founding ideas was that the F1 effort would be sustained on sponsorship, but Max had not attracted enough and that was really the root of the financial crisis because the production car side made money (it could hardly fail to) while the F1 team had absorbed it. Since sensible levels of sponsorship were not raised, Max was forced to make deals which were not in the company's long-term interest, but which did generate cash in the short term.

Thus he agreed to run the Spanish amateur, Alex Soler-Roig, in Formula One for £15,000. It was a ludicrous amount even then and, taking inflation into account, would not buy a season of F3 today, but March was desperate and the pile of pesetas Soler-Roig handed over in a hotel room kept it afloat for a few more weeks. In the long term March lost heavily on the deal and it became just one of many factors which was to plunge it into an even deeper crisis. Some money came in by selling the 701s; Jo Siffert bought one and so did Frank Williams and Tom Wheatcroft, while the group of stockbrokers who supported Mike Beuttler had a new 701 built up from spares. That kept things ticking over in the short term, but the racing car industry is seasonal, like ice cream, and serious money would not flow until the early part of 1971.

While Max was stitching together deals, Bill Stone took over Graham Coaker's job and Dave Reeves took Bill's. Meanwhile Robin was getting on with the job of designing both the new F1 car and, what in the long-term was to be more significant, a monocoque for F2 and F3. "It took us three or four goes to get it right; I did the detail mechanical design, Roger Silman and Dewar Thomas who made the prototypes put in a lot of their ideas as well, and John Thompson's operation actually built the production tubs. Apart from the fact that it worked, and was still winning races in 1977, it was very well production engineered and I think we can be pleased with it. When the car was finished, I was away at an F1 race, so Dewar simply took it up to Silverstone and did 60 laps in it, which is something one cannot imagine happening today."

Apart from a sharp new body and the monocoque itself, which had the engine as a semi-stressed member supported by detachable multi-tubular frames, the broad layout of the design was similar to the 1970 cars, although there were detail changes such as narrower wishbones and the use of foam-filled fuel cells, which were required by new regulations. In fact these bag tanks were to lead to March rediscovering the principle of the gas turbine. Bill Stone: "We used to get the bag tanks into the monocoque by using a vacuum cleaner to suck all the air out so we could squeeze them into their space. Once the season started we had to deal with the first car to be damaged and had to remove the tank. We drained the fuel and hooked the vacuum pipe on as usual. So far so good, but the fumes motoring through the vacuum cleaner caught fire in the electric motor and it took off like a jet engine and finally burned out in a smouldering heap in the corner."

Unlike the first customer cars, the 1971 range was ready at the beginning of November and to give it the best possible send-off Max invited a number of journalists to Silverstone to drive a 701. Since most hacks secretly believe they're undiscovered World Champions, it was an offer not to be refused and the result was yards of print as each one bored his readers by describing the experience of driving an F1 car slowly and repaid March with glowing adjectives. Max also invited an unusual number of drivers to test the cars, which were actually very good, so between the drivers' grapevine, the press reports and the fact that the cars were ready in plenty of time, a good story spread and orders came in, particularly for the F2 car, which ended up in some capable hands.

To live down the 702's reputation, Max put together a rentadrive package whereby drivers paid £8500 for the season and received a car and an engine for each race. 'A car and an engine' is used advisedly because, depending on circumstances, there was a lot of swapping around and sometimes the engines were pretty tired, but since the object of the exercise was to spread the good news about March rather than to make a quick buck, the team worked hard to give everyone as good a deal as possible.

In 1971 the 713M achieved substantial success in Formula Three. In the first heat here at the Crystal Palace in August Roger Williamson (Holbay 713M) leads James Hunt (works Holbay 713M) and Steve Thompson (Ensign). Hunt won the heat, but Williamson by this time with financial support from Tom Wheatcroft, won the 20-lap final. (**Nigel Snowdon**)

Mike Beuttler, Jean-Pierre Jarier and Jean-Pierre Jaussaud were among those who took advantage of the scheme, while others, such as James Hunt, negotiated one-off drives. By contrast, the F3 cars (which now had 1600cc engines but restricted by a 20mm throttle flange) tended to be bought by drivers whose names are now only vague memories, but there were two exceptions, Roger Williamson who bought a 713M on hire purchase with no hope of meeting the repayments unless he was successful, and James Hunt, who was in a works car.

Robin had done a belt and braces job, and apart from the monocoque model (the 713M) had made a spaceframe F3 car (713) which had the new body and a chassis similar to Bill Stone's 'Starch'. Oddly, all but two of the spaceframe cars went to Germany and it seems that Fritz Fastpunter was conservative in his choice of chassis. Another variation on the theme was a Formula B (Atlantic) version of the 712/3M, which was to establish March's first firm foothold in the States.

In late January, again ahead of schedule, the new F1 car was announced. Circumstances had dictated that the March 701 should be conservative, but its successor had to be altogether more advanced if March was to maintain its momentum. When it appeared, the 711 was the most distinctive F1 car of its time and the man responsible was Frank Costin.

Now Frank is the sort of man for whom his friends would walk over miles of broken bottles in their bare feet, for he is multi-faceted, brilliant and kind. He was the first man to apply serious aerodynamics to an F1 car (Vanwall in 1956) and the last that those who know and love him would choose as a business partner. That's not for the usual reason – he's the straightest man you'll ever meet – it's because he is such a devout worshipper at the shrine of engineering excellence you cannot ask compromises of him.

Robin says, "With the 711, we had significant help on aerodynamics, and hence the layout of the car, from Frank Costin, but Frank had a smart-arsed financial adviser who tried to out-flank Max. If he and I had been left alone we would have worked out, I really enjoyed working with him. Looking back, the car probably gained more by the packaging which was imposed on it by the body than by the aerodynamics themselves, although they weren't bad. Geoff Ferris, who had come to us from Lotus and later went on to Penske, also made a big input with me being in overall charge.

"We made an agreement with Frank for a fixed fee and a couple of weeks later there was a letter from his adviser saying he rejected what we had agreed, having agreed it, and he wanted the payment calculated on the differential in drag, so much money for so much notional gain in performance through the aerodynamics. It was cloud cuckoo land to try to do it like that." The bright idea never did make any money for Frank because he never got paid for his work. "I am sure he still feels pretty sore about that, but he was talked into it by his partner while we were prepared to pay him the fee he had asked."

Frank Costin (with a chuckle): "Robin's absolutely right, it was cloud cuckoo land, but the idea came from me. I put it to them that if they went to Cosworth and asked for an extra 20 bhp, they'd have been shown the door. I reckoned I could design a body which would be the equivalent of more than 20 bhp and took the view that you get what you pay for – you get a big advantage, you pay a lot, you get nothing, you pay nothing."

Robin continues, "We went to Kyalami and Ronnie

got stuck behind John Love in his 701 going down the straight and couldn't overtake him, which tended to make us think the 711 didn't have less drag. In fact, I think that the aerodynamics of the 701 weren't as bad as we thought at the time." It is, however, a fact that Ronnie's engine was down on power.

Unlike most other F1 cars of the time, the 711 had a fully-enclosed engine with air for the carburettors fed by a NACA duct in the driver's head-rest fairing. Frank now admits this was a mistake on his part because he had not seen through the loop-hole in the regs which would have allowed him to mount an air-box (counting as part of the engine) on top of the injection intakes, which became the demon tweak of 1971. One feature which marked out the 711 as a Costin design was the enclosed cockpit, a feature which can be traced from the Lotus Eleven, via the Vanwall, to the 1967 Protos F2 car, one of whose drivers had been Alan Rees. The most memorable feature of the body, however, remains the high-mounted 'Spitfire wing' front aerofoil, which being mounted in 'clean' air was extremely effective and could run almost horizontally to generate the required downforce with minimal drag. Some people doubted that the single mounting pylon for the wing was strong enough, so at Kyalami Robin and someone else stood on the wing and proved their point;after all it had to withstand several hundred pounds of wind-generated downforce, so it had to be able to bear the weight of two men.

Geoff Ferris is on record as saying that the problem with the overall concept was that it was designed primarily for low drag with downforce being an afterthought, something to be generated by the wings, whereas it might have been better to have gone for a wedge-shape to use the main body to generate downforce in harmony with the wings.

With so startling a body to divert the eye, it is not surprising that the car beneath the skin has received comparatively little attention, but it was perhaps Robin's finest design. It had been influenced by the Lotus 72, which is hardly surprising since Geoff had worked on that, but then so is every car on an F1 grid today. Where Robin and Geoff were clever was to learn from the Lotus and make a car which was simpler, friendlier and, in 1971, generally quicker.

Under the skin was an entirely new, stiffer, tub formed of 18- and 16-gauge NSA aluminium and it was a full monocoque, unlike the 701, which had a 'bath tub' monocoque. In front of the foremost bulkhead, made of 3/16in Dural plate, was a tubular subframe to carry the front suspension. The front coil spring and damper units were mounted inboard activated by rocker arms from the tubular unequal length double wishbone front suspension. The ventilated disc brakes were mounted inboard all round with BRD constant-velocity joints at both ends of the front drive-shafts. Apart from anything else, this cleaned up the airflow to the small side-radiators. Rear suspension was by outboard coil spring and dampers, lower wishbones, long top radius arms pivoting on the engine bulkhead and short transverse links.

Apart from Cosworth-engined cars for Peterson and Soler-Roig, the works had also reached agreement with Alfa Romeo to use its new flat-12 engine. Until it was ready Alfa Romeo supplied its four-valve-per-cylinder, 2993cc (86 x 64.4mm) V8 sports car unit. This was not too special even in sports car racing and was heavier than the Cosworth DFV while being neither as powerful nor as reliable. Andrea de Adamich had had one in his works McLaren in 1970, but he spent most of the first half of the season failing to qualify and March was not exactly squeezed in the crush to get the engine.

Max says, "The immediate attraction of the deal with Alfa Romeo was money; we got something like £20,000 plus free engines and rebuilds, and we did perhaps think that the engine might prove better than the Cosworth." That was not entirely wishful thinking because late in the 1970 season de Adamich had qualified quite well, around mid-field at some circuits, and had also finished races. While there was no point in most teams taking a chance on an unproven engine, March's position was somewhat different to most teams.

"I believe it actually did produce more power. It certainly revved 1000 rpm more than a Cosworth, but the power was only at the top end and there wasn't the same power useful curve. As it turned out, it never was any good and apart from its peaky power output, it was badly engineered with pumps and pipes all over the place and the engines would be different every time they arrived. At the time we did the deal, in the background was the possibility of the new flat-12 engine and one could see a wonderful relationship building up. It was obvious to me that our ideal course was to become tied in with a big motor manufacturer who would provide money, free engines and everything else, but it didn't quite work out." The flat-12 took much longer to develop than expected and it did not appear until 1973 (in an Alfa 33 TT 12 sports-racer) and it was not until 1976 that it finally ran in F1, in a Brabham, and then it was as poorly engineered as the the V8 had been.

"When I went to see Carlo Chiti, who was head of Autodelta, Alfa's racing division, we were sitting in his office drinking coffee when I noticed he was breaking up sugar lumps and throwing them under his desk. Then I saw a little wagging tail, and then another. Chiti was a very soft-hearted man and he used to take in stray dogs, of which there is no shortage in Milan, and they were looked after in the Autodelta factory. The trouble was that every ambitious young man who wanted the catch the boss's eye also started to take in dogs and they ended up with 70 or 80 strays in the place."

As part of the deal March had to take Andrea de Adamich and Giovanni Galli, who was always known as 'Nanni', the pseudonym he adopted when he started racing against his Mum's wishes. Then he goofed and started to win races, which is a dumb thing to do if you want to remain anonymous, but the nickname stuck. Neither man was an ace and they mostly took it in turns to drive the Alfa car, but since a deal had already been done with Soler-Roig, the team could hardly be said to be choosy. "De Adamich was a lawyer," Robin muses, "and the funny thing about lawyers is they all think they're

Andrea de Adamich who drove for March in 1971 as part of the deal with Autodelta.

engineers. I remember Andrea once saying to Max, 'If the World Championship was for talking, you and I would lap the field.'"

Seven 711s were made, the works used four, one was sold to Skip Barber in the States, who made use of the 3-litre racing engine equivalence in Formula A/5000 but without success, and Frank Williams bought both a 711 and the ex-works spare, 701/6. At the end of the season a seventh car was made up as a show car for Ronnie's native Sweden. Both Cosworth and Alfa Romeo engines drove through Hewland FG 400 gearboxes and, as an aside, Hewland has an interesting way of labelling its transmissions, HD stands for 'Heavy Duty', while the FG obviously gave its designer problems, for it stands for F***ing Gearbox.

Howden Ganley: "I was with BRM at the time and one day we were all testing at Silverstone. BRM went off at lunch time, Ronnie had to go back to Sweden and March asked me if I'd like to carry on testing the 711; things were a lot more relaxed then. As a result I had a direct comparison and it was a very nice to car to drive, better than the BRM – and there wasn't much wrong with the BRM, although like the 711 it was probably better suited to fast, smooth circuits." Once again we're in *can you imagine that happening today?* country, but just like the man in the shaver ad, Howden eventually bought one (711/6, Ronnie's car) for his collection of Historic F1 cars.

The 1971 F1 season kicked off with the non-Championship Argentine Grand Prix, run in two heats. March was too busy to go, but was represented by three private 701s, all of which finished in the top six. In truth there wasn't a quality field, but when the works Lotuses dropped out, Chris Amon inherited the lead in his Matra to score his second, and last, F1 victory and he was followed 22 seconds later by Henri Pescarolo's 701.

The serious start to the season was the South African GP at Kyalami, where March arrived with three 711s for Peterson, Soler-Roig and de Adamich, but there was to be no swagger along the pit lane this time. For once Frank Costin had boobed in his calculations, the NACA duct failed to deliver cold air (a layer of hot air was trapped over the engine) and the cars overheated. Both problems were solved only when the rear bodywork was removed. If there wasn't much to crow about at Kyalami in 1971 (the best performance was Peterson qualifying 13th and finishing tenth) at least the team was more relaxed. It was no longer the brash newcomer, Max was no longer having to beat a drum, everyone had discovered how difficult F1 was and had matured as a result. Further, since nobody expected anything from Soler-Roig or the Alfa car a lot of pressure came off; if either did well it would be a bonus, if they struggled it didn't reflect badly on March.

As for Peterson he was still unproven, but whereas so much effort had gone into trying to please Amon, and that had been one of the features of the year, Ronnie was simple and straightforward and commanded absolute devotion from everyone who worked with him. Robin says, "About the only thing you could say against him was he was a bit tight with his money, but show me a racing driver who isn't. Against that you could list nine hundred and ninety-nine good points."

Max says, "He was simply the best driver we ever had. When it came to engineering his car, what one mainly did was to build up an air of excitement around him, he would do the rest." That made all the difference, the fact that the 711 wasn't immediately competitive became a setback, not a disaster, because racing was fun again. At the Kyalami prize-giving, March got an award for something or other, slowest qualifier, first retirement, it could have been either. When the compère said, 'Robin Herd please accept this' someone called out, 'He's gone back' and someone else shouted, 'To the drawing board!'

Before the works F1 cars were in action again, the European F2 season began with a non-Championship race at Mallory Park. There Ronnie put his works car on pole and led until a ball-joint in his steering seized and deposited him into the bank. The race was won by Henri Pescarolo in a Frank Williams 712M and he and Ronnie shared fastest lap, but after that bright start, the three-car Williams team rarely figured in the results. The trouble, as usual with Frank those days, was lack of cash, which meant the engines did not often get rebuilt.

Ronnie's crash at Mallory Park led to incidents which highlight both the March rentadrive system and his character. Somehow a special Hart engine intended for a customer had been installed in Ronnie's car, but when Ronnie hit the banking, the car flipped and his foot remained firmly on the loud pedal for long enough for the engine to cry 'Enough!' and commit hara-kari. Max was left having to employ some nifty tongue work to placate the engine's owner.

When Ronnie crashed, the car's body shattered and some spectators, including a small boy, received minor cuts from the debris. When he heard of this, Ronnie's reaction was to autograph one of the front wings and send it to the boy. At the time he had just survived a huge accident and was in some pain from a bruised hand and nobody would have noticed had he not made the gesture, but touches like that make you understand why he was one of the few top-line drivers about whom nobody has ever uttered an unkind word.

A little later Robin decided to try a wide-track version of the 712, so the team went to Thruxton with Ronnie and took along one of the rentadrivers, Niki Lauda. Robin says, "We didn't rate Niki at first, he'd not done very well in F3, but when you talked to him you realized that he had a very good head on his shoulders and we took him testing to give him a bit of experience. Niki went out to set a base time, then Ronnie took over the same car and I drove Niki to the back of the circuit to watch him. Ronnie came round on the warm-up lap, sideways on with the car leaping into the air as it went over a bump. Niki took one step back and literally went pale. 'Robin,' he said,

The first Formula Two race of the European season was at Mallory Park where Ronnie Peterson (above) set pole position but crashed and the winner was Henri Pescarolo with a Frank Williams-entered 712M (below). (**Nigel Snowdon**)

'I could never, ever, drive a racing car like that.'

"He was still shaken when we drove back to the pits and I asked what time he thought Ronnie had done. He said, 'I did 1m 14.0s, he must have been two seconds a lap faster, 1m 12s.' In fact Ronnie's best lap was 1m 14.3s and I thought then maybe this guy is going to be good. He could never drive with the same panache as Ronnie, but achieved his results by the application of his intelligence, which is why it took him longer to make his mark and for us to take him seriously, but later in the year, at Rouen, he was quicker than Ronnie and had to be told in no uncertain terms that that was not part of the plan."

From being the joke of F2, March became the pace-setter and Ronnie the star, but in the first few races of the season a pattern established itself: he would lead or contend the lead, and would then retire with engine problems, although once he crashed after being blinded by dust thrown up by someone else's accident. One exception to this general rule was at Thruxton on Easter Monday, when, after a long duel, he took the lead with two laps to go and then was baulked by a back-marker and finished second, 0.6 second adrift. Since the winner was Graham Hill taking his first victory since his accident 18 months before, the emotional crowd had no sympathy at all for Peterson's bad luck.

At Silverstone on the same day Graham Coaker was driving the March 712 he had accepted in lieu of his leaving settlement. He had decided to run with minimum wing in first practice and then build up from there, but on his third lap he went over a bump, the air caught the underside of the wing, sent the car out of control and he wrapped it round a concrete marshal's post, badly breaking a leg. In essence it was a similar crash to the one which later would make Manfred Winklehock the star of one of the most lurid shunts ever recorded on film. Still, it seemed that it was a fairly routine accident, even if Graham would have to spend a couple of months in traction.

Frank Williams had ordered a 711 and, since Ronnie was free, he was entered to drive it in the Race of Champions, but, as practice got under way, the car was still being built. He was allowed to start but from the back of the grid with a ten second penalty and was making progress through the field when, on lap 14, one of the front inboard brake shafts sheered as he entered Clearways and the car snapped to the right, fortunately on to the grass infield. Since a similar failure had killed Jochen Rindt and since no fault in the material was found all the 711s were immediately converted to outboard front brakes.

When the cars arrived for the Spanish GP at Barcelona, March still had not solved its cooling problems, so the cars again ran without radiator cowls or engine covers. None of them could qualify in the top half of the field and all retired, so it was a race to forget, but their apparent slowness did have a reasonable explanation. March had upset things in 1970 by introducing as many as six extra cars into the field, but a year on there were even more and Cosworth was finding it difficult to supply and service all its customers. In the late season North American races, Stewart had received the first of the 11 series DFVs and these had been trickling into the system, but since March's number one driver was a novice, and its number two was a make-weight, it was not near the head of the queue for one.

The next time Ronnie was at the wheel of an F1

In the Race of Champions at Brands Hatch Ronnie Peterson drove this 711 for Frank Williams but crashed when one of the front inboard brake shafts broke. As a result all 711s were converted to outboard front brakes. **(Nigel Snowdon)**

March was at the International Trophy and there he had one of the Alfa Romeo engines. It was Galli's turn to drive, but he'd injured his hand and putting Ronnie in the car was a useful proving exercise. A loose plug lead quickly put paid to even the slender chance he had, but he was driving in his usual press-on manner when his throttle stuck wide open and he smashed into the bank at Becketts. One of the front wheels was torn off and it caught him on the side of the helmet, knocking him unconscious.

March's bank manager had been nervous about becoming involved with a racing team, so they attempted to reassure him, and when Robin saw Max in the pit lane he said, "You know we gave tickets to our bank manager? Well I am afraid he has seen our entire assets pass before his eyes on the end of a crane."

Ronnie was taken to the same ward in Northampton General as Graham Coaker, but there was no happy reunion for Graham was very ill indeed. At first it appeared that Graham had done nothing more than break a leg, but the stress of the crash had triggered perforation of his stomach, something which could have happened under many circumstances, and he was operated on but soon developed septicaemia and had to be transferred to an intensive care unit.

The metaphysical idea of a wheel of fortune might have been invented with motor racing in mind since March went to the Monaco GP as a joke team and came away heroes. Qualifying started badly with a deluge during which Soler-Roig lost a wheel because a part had been machined incorrectly, Galli's car was suffering from fuel starvation, and Skip Barber, who'd entered his 711 in three Grands Prix before taking it home to the States, had endless problems because his gearbox had been assembled wrongly.

Ronnie Peterson, the most loved driver in March's history. (**Nigel Snowdon**)

After running as a semi-privateer with March in 1970, Ronnie Peterson became March Formula One team leader in 1971. (**Nigel Snowdon**)

Ronnie's car had revised rear suspension with a new cross member, longer top links and repositioned springs. It was also fitted with front brake discs made of copper in conjunction with the Copper Development Association in America. This body existed to promote the use of the metal in industry and the theory was that copper brake discs would give a higher coefficient of friction for a given brake pedal pressure and would dissipate heat more readily. In testing at Silverstone the discs worked well, but there the long periods between braking allowed them to cool, but at Monaco, a circuit notorious for the strain it puts on brakes, they acted unpredictably during practice and were abandoned.

Ronnie was not his usual out-going self, the four crashes he'd had had got to him, not in the sense he had lost confidence in himself for he'd not been to blame in any of them, but people were muttering he was a crasher and on top of that there'd been all the engine failures, and now the blind alley of the copper brake discs. It seemed that nothing was gelling, but it also intensified his determination to be the element which made everything cohere and that was the springboard of what was to be his first clear demonstration of greatness.

Stewart led the race from start to finish, despite brake problems, but all eyes were on Peterson as he disputed fourth with Rodriguez, who was using every trick in the blocker's manual. Eventually the youngster forced Rodriguez into a mistake and then picked off Siffert and Ickx in a display which combined determination, bravery and precision, to finish 25 seconds behind Stewart. Had he not been side-tracked with his copper brake discs he might have qualified higher than eighth and there might have been a different result.

A year before the team would have been in *If only* mode, if only Rodriguez hadn't delayed their man he would have won, and they would have been right, but now they celebrated as though they had won. Alan's choice of Peterson had been vindicated, not that anyone in March had ever questioned it, but outside the whispers were going around. It also demonstrated that with an engine as good as the opposition, the 711 was as good as the opposition, and that was something on which to build the rest of the season.

The celebrations were not unrestrained because, as Robin says, "It was very poignant because on the day March turned the corner, when Ronnie came second at Monaco, Graham Coaker died. As so often happens in life our feelings were mixed. The blow of Graham's death was softened by Ronnie's success, something marvellous had just happened, but the news about Graham seemed to cut it from beneath our feet. I'm not sure which was the greater emotion."

8 March Makes its Bones

March was beginning to gain respect. It had been one thing to appear in a blaze of hype and a 'Mystery Backer' (some had assumed there was a pipe-line from STP through which money gushed), but when a team is struggling on all fronts and fights back, then racers begin to warm to it and start to accept it into the fraternity. It was obvious that the team was being run on a shoestring and, as always, the mechanics' grapevine knew the true position. "There was a simple formula for finding out which hotel we were staying at," says Robin, "you took a map and drew a circle around the circuit as far out as it was practical to be – the nearer you were the higher the prices, and you'd find us in the cheapest hotel on the edge of the circle."

Because the Belgian GP had been cancelled there was a four-week gap between the Monaco and the Dutch races and the Badischer MC organized the Jochen Rindt Memorial Race at Hockenheim. Before half-distance Ronnie was second and catching Jacky Ickx's Ferrari, but then his clutch failed, and although he dropped back he still kept his place. True it was a non-Championship event and over only three quarters GP distance, but most of the leading teams and drivers had been present and Ickx broke every available record at the circuit, so it was not a hollow achievement.

In practice at Hockenheim Ronnie had tried an Alfa engine, a move instigated by Max, for he could see March and Alfa Romeo heading towards a mutually beneficial future, with March perhaps becoming the F1 arm of Alfa Romeo, free from the worries of sponsorship and engine supply, or even as a specialist consultant improving Alfa's road cars. This was still in his mind when the team arrived at Zandvoort for the Dutch GP, where Ronnie had two cars, one with a Cosworth, one with an Alfa unit. All the team cars, plus Pescarolo's 711, were fitted with the revised 'Monaco' rear suspension and Soler-Roig had an anti-vibration tweak on his as well. Skip Barber was there with his car and finished in the only European WC event for which he qualified, then he went home and discovered that running an F1 car in FA/5000 was not such a good idea after all.

Ronnie set his qualifying time in his 711-Alfa in the first (dry) session and then switched to his Cosworth car for the second (wet) session, preferred it, and opted to race it. In appalling conditions he brought it home fourth ahead of four world champions, who had not coped as well as he with a deluge falling on an already slippery track. Ronnie had come of age as a driver and the following weekend won his first European Championship F2 race at Rouen, where Niki Lauda's pace, and fourth place, was the first public indication that he might be more than a rich no-hoper.

Elsewhere customer Marches were doing well and Roger Williamson's private 713M was sharing the honours with Dave Walker's works Lotus in British F3 racing. Williamson's grit as he prepared his car himself for the Monaco F3 race had impressed Tom Wheatcroft, who took him under his wing and so freed him from the tyranny of having to win the money to pay off his hire purchase payments. By contrast, the main works March F3 driver was proving fast but erratic and was earning an unenviable reputation for hot-headedness. He was someone who was obviously going nowhere fast, chap name of Hunt.

Alan Rees had increasingly become the odd man out of the March triumvirate, not as a result of disagreements but because Robin and Max had drawn closer and most teams operate with just two people. The one big disagreement, however, came at the French GP, where, with the courtship of Alfa Romeo in mind, Max insisted that Ronnie drive the Alfa-engined car. Alan strongly resisted, he'd been nurturing Ronnie and saw no reason to jeopardize the chance of a good result, possibly a win, to make a political point. Yes, he knew March was heading for a serious financial crisis because the build season was over and no more money was coming in, but the way out of it was to get results, everything else would follow on that, and using the Alfa Romeo engine was not the way to get results.

Max dug his heels in, and Robin supported him, the way forward was with Alfa Romeo, they had an acute engine shortage because they didn't have the money to have them rebuilt. Ronnie was furious. Like any driver he wasn't concerned with how cars got to the circuit; had that been his buzz he would have been an accountant, and he couldn't see why his chances of the World Championship, and he had a chance of the title, should be blown. Each argument had merit but in the end only point of view could prevail, Ronnie got into the 711-Alfa and, being Ronnie, gave it all he had and qualified 12th, easily the quickest of the four March 711s. In the race it was soon apparent that the Alfa engine had been a mistake, since it was down on power and blew up before half-distance. After that a truce was called and as Ronnie said to Alan, "It was a big bang, but a happy one." But the damage had been done, there

Ronnie Peterson's March 711 in the pits at the Dutch Grand Prix. After a deluge of rain in the closing stages of the race, Peterson finished fourth. (**Nigel Snowdon**)

American Skip Barber bought his 711 for Formula 5000 in the United States, but entered three European races. The only race at which he qualified was the Dutch race in which he finished 14th, ten laps in arrears. (**Nigel Snowdon**)

In the French Grand Prix on the high-speed Paul Ricard circuit Ronnie Peterson drove a 711 with Alfa Romeo engine which he blew up in some style. (**Nigel Snowdon**)

was a growing rift between Alan and the others.

It was not expressed in hostility but Robin and Max had drawn together and as Max said much later, "There were two different ways of approaching the same problem, but in the end you had to choose one way. Robin and I would sometimes have completely different solutions to the same problem, but there was never a single time when, after discussion, we did not end up in complete agreement and he's the only person I've ever dealt with of whom I can say that. One often ends up going along with someone else because it's expedient, and one still has reservations, but with Robin we might have started with different views but we'd always end up with the same one, sometimes my original view, sometimes his, but most of the time we independently arrived at the same solution."

Alex Soler-Roig, whose only finish of the season had been at Hockenheim, had become cheesed-off and left the team, but nobody thought they were seeing the departure of a potential star, and since Galli hadn't been getting a fair crack of the whip, they put him in Soler-Roig's car at the British GP. Apart from the three works cars, and the Williams car for Pescarolo, Mike Beuttler's backers had bought him the ex-works 711/2, but of the five, only Peterson qualified in the top half of the grid and, helped by retirements, he came home second behind Stewart's Tyrrell with Pescarolo fourth.

Although it was apparent that the company was heading into severe financial trouble, the elusive first works Grand Prix win looked as though it might come at any time. When the team arrived at the Nürburgring, all three works cars had strengthened rear uprights and Peterson's had cowls over its radiators and Bilstein gas-filled dampers, but even so he could make only seventh on the grid and that was 6.5 seconds off pole. In the race he ran as high as fourth and eventually finished fifth after a pit stop to remove the battered glass-fibre around one of his radiators, evidence of how hard he'd been trying.

In Germany Chapman was still trying to sign Peterson and he offered March £35,000 and Wilson Fittipaldi for Ronnie's contract. There was a small snag in that Wilson wasn't Chapman's to offer, but when Max discovered that Emerson Fittipaldi had yet to sign his contract with Lotus for 1972 he offered him a drive at March, but it was only a wind-up, they couldn't afford him.

So far as the works team was concerned, the Austrian GP was a race to forget, not even Ronnie could qualify in the top ten and he could finish no higher than eighth, although Pescarolo made it to sixth. The cars were suffering from an aerodynamic problem in that the nose was lifting, the centre of pressure came back and the car understeered, with the result that the tyres scrubbed. Robin says that the problem had him baffled for a while, it was the first time he had encountered it, and the following year solved the problem by making the car less pitch sensitive.

The race itself was notable for a pole to flag win by Jo Siffert's BRM, which was universally popular; the fact that, even without finishing, Stewart clinched the World Championship; and that a local hero had persuaded Levi Jeans to buy him a drive in a works March. Niki Lauda qualified second from last and retired just after half-distance with severe handling problems, but that did not deter him from his ambition to get into F1, and since nobody else took him seriously, he approached the only team which did. Robin has acquired a reputation as a talent spotter and Lauda is often cited as an example, but he says, "I didn't spot just one talent, I spotted thousands! I use the word 'talent' in its biblical sense, as coin of the realm."

Most people, if asked to give an assessment of March on 1 September 1970, would have returned a favourable report. It was promising in F1, at least when Ronnie was at the wheel, and looked likely to win a race before long, which is more than one could say for Surtees, McLaren or Brabham. Its F2 car was the cream of the field and by then not only had Ronnie won four races in the works Cosworth-engined car, but Dieter Quester's unique 712-BMW had also won. As for the 713M, Roger Williamson had shown that the only thing which stopped him winning every race was Dave Walker's works Lotus. All in all, things looked rosy; nobody else was competitive in all three main single seater formulae.

Behind the façade things were different, as Max explains, "Despite all our borrowing at the end of 1970, and the deals we did, and despite all the success we had, in 1971 we made a loss of £73,000, so we were actually bust. That loss of £73,000 sucked in our £20,000 loan, our £10,000 initial capital and the small profit we'd made in 1970, so we had an overdraft of £40,000. Although we struggled along, we were desperately short of money and during the whole time I was with March, we never did make enough to get out of trouble." The reason for the shortfall was that creditors from the previous year had to be paid, the initial capital plus earnings did not cover capital investment in the works, and the F1 team was draining resources because there was no big sponsor picking up the tab, STP's contribution would now have got it small stickers on the rear wing and not the main billing.

"Probably the most significant deal that we did was

with Lauda; he brought 2.5m Schillings (£43,000 – £35,000 for an F1 drive, £8,000 for F2) in September 1971, at the moment when the real crisis was coming, and that saw us over the winter. In today's money that is something like a quarter of a million pounds, a helluva lot of money for a 22-year-old to borrow from a bank, but we couldn't afford to be philosophical about that." It was an unprecedented move and race commentators and journalists took to calling him *The man who got the bank loan for £35,000 pounds*, and lesser mortals would gasp at his audacity.

"As soon as Niki signed a contract with us I phoned our bank manager and said we would have the money by the end of the month, and he desperately needed an excuse to keep us going. Then Niki rang up to say his bank had cancelled the loan. Grandfather Lauda, who had considerable influence in Austria, had found out about his plans, and since he disapproved of them, he had brought pressure to bear. Niki had gone to his grandfather and said, 'Look, I don't mind you not giving me any money for my racing, but don't interfere with my attempts to do it.' His grandfather had agreed not to and Niki then said he'd get another bank to back him, which I didn't really believe. I said, 'Get your father to guarantee the money and you can have the drive,' and Niki duly did."

Lauda Senior's guarantee was written on the same typewriter as Niki's covering letter, on the same sort of paper, and signed illegibly with the same pen. Niki's father also appears to have had an identical command of English to his son. The guarantee reads like the legendary school absence note: *Johnny could not go to school yesterday because he had a cold. Signed, My Dad.* Max says, "It's all we had to go on, so we took it. Anyway Niki found another bank to back him and the money arrived, much to the astonishment of our bank manager, who said 'It's like the TSB putting up the money, I can't believe it.' Had it not been for that I don't think we would have survived the winter."

When March arrived for the Italian GP, the public air of breezy confidence still prevailed and privately the team thought that this could be the race which might give Ronnie his first win, because the 711 went well on speed circuits and, because Monza is Monza, Autodelta had become personally involved.

After first practice the Alfa-engined cars were not doing very well and as Robin tells it, "Chiti said 'We have a special development engine, but leave it to us, it must be put in the car very carefully.' So the Alfa mechanics put in the engine very carefully and then de Adamich went out and broke the sound barrier, he improved his time no end. Before the end of the session, Chiti said, 'You must call him in. We must take the engine back to the factory to examine it.' So as practice ended the car and engine were disappearing out of the circuit, which meant of course it could not be examined. Andrea raced with his non-development engine, which was much slower. Heaven alone knows how big the development engine was, or what was in it." The official line was that it had a three bearing crankshaft in place of the usual five-bearing crank.

With a race average speed of over 150 mph, all the Marches, and many of the other cars, ran without aerofoils and no matter what anyone says about Frank Costin's body, it proved itself at Monza. In qualifying, none of the Marches were exceptional, although Ronnie took fifth on the grid, but when it came to racing in a slip-stream battle, they came into their own. Peterson was in the leading bunch most of the time, but, late in the race, Amon took the lead in his Matra and appeared to have it in the bag, but he had a two-layer visor, the idea being that as the top layer became dirty, you peeled it away and had a clear one underneath. Chris managed to peel away both layers and lost his lead because he had no protection for his eyes. It remains a unique reason for losing a race.

With Amon falling back, and many of the other aces out for various reasons, Ronnie found himself battling for the lead with other tyros such as Hailwood, Gethin, Ganley and Cevert. Lap after lap they swapped the lead and everything came down to the very last corner and the sprint to the finishing line. Ronnie led into the corner but Gethin scrambled inside him, smoke coming from his tyres. On any other lap it would have cost him time, but Gethin knew that his V12 engine gave him an initial advantage on acceleration in the sprint to the line a few hundred yards away.

Ronnie tucked into the BRM's airstream and pulled out to overtake a hundred yards from the finish, but Gethin crossed the line one-hundredth of a second, a few inches, ahead of the March with Cevert (Tyrrell) and Hailwood (Surtees) fractions behind. Ronnie, in fact, overtook the BRM a few yards beyond the line. It was the tightest finish ever recorded in F1 but Gethin won with his head; he even raised an arm in salute, so if there was any dispute the gesture might sway the result.

Frank Costin learned later that Ronnie's engine was not fresh from Cosworth (his brother Mike is the 'Cos' of Cosworth), but a well-worn development unit built by Race Engine Services which was at least 35 bhp down on a good DFV. March's enforced penny-pinching had cost them, and Ronnie, their maiden WC win; but for Frank the fact that so tired an engine had done so well demonstrated the effectiveness of his design and he asked March to do tests at Monza to verify his claims and settle up. Frank's calculations showed that he was due a bumper pay day, but since there was no money in the kitty, Max stalled and Robin denied there had been any improvement, pointing out that the 711 hadn't been able to pass John Love's 701 on the long straight at Kyalami, but he did not volunteer that then Ronnie's engine had been down on power. Frank couldn't afford legal action (March had a barrister in situ) so he dropped his claim and did not receive a penny for his work. Had he pressed his case, and won, it would have been the end of the company.

A week later Ronnie won the F2 race at Tülln-Langenlebarn and although nobody knew it at the time, for there were still two rounds to go, that clinched him the European F2 Championship. Then in the Canadian GP, which was drenched, he confirmed his stature by coming home second to Stewart. He had been the only driver to press the new World Champion and they had pulled out a huge amount on the rest of the field. Ronnie even led laps 17 to 31, but just after Stewart regained a slender lead an

Two views of a 712 Formula car at a March test session at Silverstone in August 1971. **(Nigel Snowdon)**

Henri Pescarolo with Frank Williams' 711, now with an airbox, in the Gold Cup race at Oulton Park in August 1971. Pescarolo won the first heat but retired in the second heat after a spin. **(Nigel Snowdon)**

errant back-marker swiped the March and knocked the front aerofoil askew. Despite that handicap Ronnie still managed to finish nearly a minute over the third placed man.

With that drive Ronnie became runner-up in the World Championship, and just in case anyone still had any doubts about the Swede's talent, he followed that with a storming charge to third in the US GP from 11th on the grid. Not only that but March finished third in the Constructors' Championship for the second year, beating the likes of Ferrari and Lotus, and that with only a single serious car, plus some help from Pescarolo, whereas in 1970 the grid had been showered with Marches.

In the junior formulae March rounded off the F2 Championship with wins by Peterson at Vallelunga in the Rome GP, and Beuttler, also at Vallelunga, a week later, in the Madunina GP. Ronnie also took two non-Championship races during the season and Pescarolo, Pace and Quester each took wins. What makes March's 1971 F2 season all the more creditable is that no fewer than 16 drivers went on to works F1 drives, nine would win Grands Prix and two, Lauda and Fittipaldi, would become World Champions.

Roger Williamson ended his F3 season winning one of the British Championships and finishing runner-up to Dave Walker's works Lotus in the other.

Helmut Kelleners bought the only sports car March made in 1971, a '717' which was an up-date of his own 707 fitted with an 8.3-litre Chevy engine with the weight distribution rearranged, but he had endless reliability problems, the modifications did not work as hoped, and his only points finish was a third at Helsinki behind series-winner Leo Kinnuen's Porsche 917 and Peter Gethin's McLaren. Before the end of the season he had switched to a Porsche 917.

That was the public face, the story in the record books; the reality was that the company was hobbled financially. Robin says, "There are two things you need in a racing team, a bloke to get the money and a bloke to make the car go quick – all successful teams have that combination. We had Max and Alan trying to sort out the business side and two people doing the same job doesn't work. Alan wanted to spend everything on F1, on the basis that the results would bring in the money, and he was right. Max was saying, that's all very well but we don't have the money to spend on F1, so we can't do it, which in the short term was absolutely right as well.

engine in France, but at the end of the season I was told I was no longer wanted and I had to accept it, but I would say I remain on good terms with both Robin and Max. I refute the suggestion that I wanted to spend money we didn't have. I've been in team management for twenty years with four different teams, Winklemann, March, Shadow and Arrows, and the only time I haven't had financial control was at March. You can make of that what you will." In effect CRH had disappeared and what remained was M-H.

A deal was thrashed out which would make a new team, Alan Rees Racing, a favoured customer of March with the cars supplied at special rates, profit sharing and so on, but for various reasons this never happened. Because Alan left after two years, his contribution to March has often been overlooked, but when the team started he was

Ronnie Peterson, seen here in practice, scored an easy win in the non-Championship Rothmans International Trophy Formula Two race at Brands Hatch on August Bank Holiday Monday, 1971. Peterson took six of March's ten Formula Two victories and easily won the European Formula Two Championship.

"We had had this divergence in basic philosophy and I had to go with one or the other for we were near bankruptcy, although I have to say that I now have much more sympathy for Alan's view. It was a difficult time for me because I had been at school with Alan, but by that time I had more in common with Max and he had access to money, which was the deciding factor. Had Alan and I gone off together I think we would have quickly gone broke. It was as civilized a split as you can have, but I hated it because he was a good friend."

Alan says, "There was no big row, the only open disagreement we ever had was over Ronnie using the Alfa

the only partner with significant experience of the sport. Apart from choosing Ronnie, he had also drawn on his expertise as a driver to make huge strides with the 702, and while nobody could have made it into a good car, his work prepared the way for the superb 712M. Alan had also set up the racing team from scratch, so his influence continued a long time after he had left. Whatever the rights and wrongs of the case, the unwieldy management structure with which the outfit had started had been whittled down to the ideal number of two bosses, just as Alan has operated since 1978 with Jack Oliver at Arrows.

9 Year of the Lemon

March entered its third year in the most precarious position it had ever been in, yet the production car side was booming. Twenty cars would be made for each of F2, F3 and Formula B, with a further four for the British Atlantic series. These were all developments of the 1971 cars with chisel noses and side radiators, but the spaceframe option for F3 was dropped. Six FF1600 cars went to America, but the Formula Fords had never been very successful and March had only made them because it had a spaceframe on the stocks and it was as easy to make an FF as not. They had never received any serious attention, nor did they make much money, and 1972 was the last year the model was listed.

John Cannon, a Canadian domiciled in London, ordered a car which was 722 to the rear bulkhead and then had F1 parts. It was fitted with an Oldsmobile V8 engine prepared by Race Engine Services to run in FA/5000. This caused a mild sensation when Cannon put it on pole in the opening European round of the F5000 Championship, but the engine was not quite up to the Chevrolets most runners used, and chassis development did not keep pace with its rivals, but it was still a regular top six finisher and came home a very close second in the Rothmans race at Silverstone but that was run in a monsoon and Cannon was a very able wet-weather driver. More than that, however, it was a significant car in that it pointed the way to the F2-based Formula One car which was to appear later in the season.

Formula One was still very important to March and the reasoning went that if it could make a technical breakthrough with its 1972 car then Ronnie could win the World Championship, and on the back of that success it

John Cannon with the March 72A at Silverstone where he finished second in the Rothmans Trophy in 1972. (**LAT**)

could dig itself out of the financial pit into which it had fallen for then a superb Cosworth car cost no more to build than a hopeless Cosworth car.

The March-Alfa Romeo relationship fizzled out at the end of 1971 but a by-product of it had been that Ronnie had driven one of the Alfa Romeo Tipo 33/3s with de Adamich in the Watkins Glen 6 hours, and won. Afterwards Robin had questioned him closely about the Alfa's gearbox because it was located between the engine and the rear axle line, not behind the axle line as was usual, and being told it was a good unit decided that this would be the key to the breakthrough.

While Robin worked on his main effort for 1972, March built the 721, a developed 711, and when it first appeared it still had the 'Spitfire' front wing, although the voluptuous rear bodywork was new. By its second race this had given way to a full-width chisel nose with most of the surface fixed, but with small trim tabs on the trailing edge. Apart from that (Stewart's Tyrrell with a full-width nose had been easily the quickest car through the Paul Ricard speed trap in 1971) the body of the 721 was recognizably the successor to the 711. Four 721s were made, two for the works drivers, Peterson and Lauda, one for Frank Williams, who retained Henri Pescarolo, while the fourth went to Eifelland Wöhnwagenbau, for Rolf Stommelen.

This last car, which was entered as the Eifelland 21, was a standard 721 with a body designed by Luigi Colani, a freelance designer whose main claim to fame was furniture but when you saw the body he drew you wondered how comfortable his chairs were. Colani's design was messy compared to the standard car and its two most notable features were the single mirror mounted on a high stalk in front of the driver and the air duct to the engine in front of the cockpit. The periscope mirror was a styling gimmick and the forward air duct did not work because, by the time the air had passed around the cockpit sides, it had slowed and was barely able to raise the effort to drop into the carburettors. One other Eifelland innovation was 'the world's first progressive titanium springs', but these showed no improvement either and over the year the car gradually eased more and more towards works specification.

The opening races of the year produced the sort of results which you might expect from an up-rated year-old design. Ronnie, ill during the Argentine GP, managed to finish sixth, though lapped, with Pescarolo eighth and Lauda 11th and last, two laps down. Niki in fact did not pass a single healthy car since he had qualified last as well. Ronnie followed this with second in the non-Championship Brazilian GP, and that without a clutch for the entire race, and then took a decent fifth in South Africa after running as high as third until his rear wing worked loose. A look down the Kyalami qualifying times, however, shows that while Ronnie was ninth fastest the other four Marches were 21st, 22nd, 24th, and 25th of the 26 starters. Whatever results March was getting were due to Peterson and it began to look that Lauda was just another rich no-hoper after all.

Still the team could afford to be fairly relaxed about it, Ronnie had opened his points score, some teams would have been delighted with a fifth and a sixth, and the technical breakthrough was nearing completion. The March 721X had, as its main theme, a low polar movement of inertia, something which Porsche had been using successfully, which led to the gearbox (Alfa Romeo internals in a March casing) being placed in front of the rear axle-line, and not behind it as was usual. Theoretically this should have reduced the 'dumb-bell effect' and the layout should have increased cornering speed in the hands of a driver such as Ronnie Peterson. From the start it was known that it would be a nervous car, but Ronnie's amazing reflexes, it was reasoned, should overcome this as in some modern jet fighters, which are built unstable, the advantage being in the quickness of response. Thus the 721X had the same basic lay-out as the 721 (née 711) except that the monocoque was slightly more square, and new double wishbone and rocker arm rear suspension was used with high-mounted coil springs angled at 30 degrees from the horizontal.

Ronnie was enthusiastic about the car in testing, but he was never one to be able to analyse a car. He had one for the Race of Champions, where a loose wheel delayed him for a long time, but his relatively poor grid position told its own story, though nobody wanted to hear it. He then took a 721 to the non-Championship Brazilian GP, where he came home a splendid second despite losing his clutch and driving the last few laps with a slow puncture.

A surprise came at the Good Friday meeting at Oulton Park, which hosted a round of the John Player Championship, a British national F2 series. There Niki took the lead on the first lap and held it, driving impeccably in atrocious conditions to score only the second race win of his career. It has to be said that there were only 14 entries, most of them were privateers and the man on pole, David Purley, had his throttle cable snap a few yards after the start but it was a win none the less and since Niki had finished second in the opening round, at Mallory Park, he led the Championship.

In the European F2 Championship opener at Thruxton, Peterson led home Cevert and Lauda to record a March 1–2–3. It seemed as though F2 was going to be March's happy hunting ground once more, but things did not quite turn out like that. The basic problem was that the '72 cars had been subtly changed, there was new bodywork (and a slightly more shallow front to the tub to accommodate it), a wider front track, and side radiators, but the changes did not work as harmoniously as they should have done. As a parallel, imagine Rita Hayworth with the eyes made slightly smaller and moved together, the nose a touch larger, the lips thinner and the cheek bones smoothed down, just a fraction. The result is not a sex goddess but the girl next door. Since the F1 team was soon in deep trouble the junior formulae cars did not receive as much attention as they needed and they slipped behind the opposition.

The situation was further worsened by the fact that Ronnie had a works drive in Ferrari sports cars, so his commitments did allow him to appear often in F2, while the driver who might have upheld March honour, Niki Lauda, was plagued all season by more than his fair share of

Wilson Fittipaldi with his Team Bardahl Brabham leads Niki Lauda with a works 722 in the Formula Two race at Mallory Park in March 1972. (Nigel Snowdon)

Ronnie Peterson with the 722 which he set fastest lap at Mallory Park in 1972, the first round in European Formula Two Championship. (Nigel Snowdon)

Niki Lauda on his way to a win in the wet with the 722 Formula Two car at Oulton Park on Good Friday 1972. **(Nigel Snowdon)**

problems from Race Engine Services engines. In fairness they were not the only ones since 1972 saw maximum capacity in F2 rise from 1600cc to 2 litres and the Ford BDA engine, which was standard equipment, was unhappy when stretched. Those drivers who had either an 1850cc Brian Hart unit or one of the four 1927cc Cosworth BDFs (which were allocated to the four leading teams) had an unusual advantage and it was not often that Niki was one of them since he mostly drove with a Race Engine Services unit which was stretched beyond its limit.

March did not shine in F3 for, apart from the works team of James Hunt and Bernard McInerney, none of its cars was driven by a rising star and in fact most went to Germany to run in a national championship which did not have the status of the British or French series. Roger Williamson started the season with a March but soon switched to a GRD, a very good car built by a new outfit set up by a breakaway group from Lotus, and that combined with another good car from another newcomer, Ensign, left thin pickings for everyone else.

After a disastrous showing in the Monaco F3 race there was a dust-up in the works team. This had been farmed out to a private outfit, but the March works had had so much on its plate that it had not been giving the F3 project much attention and Hunt found his car had not been prepared for the race. He then accepted a drive in another team's March and one thing led to another. Hunt and McInerney left and were replaced by Jochen Mass and Russell Wood, neither of whom achieved much. Mass left before the end of the season and his place was taken by Jean-Pierre Jarier, who didn't have anyone shouting 'Hold the front page!' either.

March was trying to juggle too many balls in the air at once and some fell. The one bright spot was Formula Atlantic, where the British Championship became a hard-fought affair between the American Bill Gubelmann and home-grown Cyd Williams, who dominated in their Marches.

All this was something which would become apparent over the season, but when March arrived with two 721Xs at Jarama it faced a crisis – the car was no good. The team was elated when Ronnie matched Stewart's Tyrrell in pre-race testing, but Jackie was experimenting with different suspension settings, treating a test as a test and not going for a time. When it came to qualifying, the picture was different. Ronnie put his 721X ninth on the grid, the same slot he had taken in South Africa, so an optimist would say that the new car was starting where the 721 left off and would only get better, but that was due to Ronnie ignoring the problems. As for Lauda he was, by more than two seconds, the slowest man in the field and you do not listen to the opinion of the last man on the grid.

Robin says, "When it came to the 721X, Ronnie and I had the same attitude, we wouldn't let facts interfere with our belief that it was a winner. Niki got into the car at

An almost legendary relationship, Ronnie Peterson, here at the wheel of the 721X, and Robin Herd. **(Nigel Snowdon)**

This photograph, taken after the finish of the Race of Champions, shows the lines of the 721X. Peterson finished 12th after a pit stop. Fittipaldi, who won the race, acknowledges the applause of the rather thin crowd as he sweeps by. **(Nigel Snowdon)**

Jarama, did two laps and came in and said 'No way, your car's no good,' but our attitude was that it was the driver who was at fault. Part of the problem was on the human level, Ronnie had an amazing ability to create devotion, he was a wonderful human being. By contrast it was difficult to believe that Niki was a racing driver, he wasn't like anyone else on the scene, he was this funny little guy with an odd nose and buck teeth.

"With his clinical mind, however, he could see what was going on, he had mortgaged his livelihood, his life really, and he must have despaired. He was dead right. He was right to despair and he was right about the car, which was a complete and utter cock-up from beginning to end, and ultimately it was my fault. Apart from that, there were several contributory factors, one of which was Alfa Romeo. Alfa supplied us with a full set of ratios, but only the one set, so after Ronnie had made his choice our job was to persuade Niki that his optimum ratios were what we had left over; this was advanced race engineering at its very best. Apart from that, the 'box had a dreadful gearchange and a terrible differential.

"Our fundamental problem, though, was weight distribution. One of my basic rules was do tyre testing with the tyre company, which was Goodyear in 1972; that way they produce tyres to suit your car, because if you make a car which runs outside the parameters of the tyre, it simply won't work and we were using a standard Goodyear product. The most important thing you can do in racing car design is to keep the tyres happy and that is what we failed to do with the 721X. We changed the weight distribution so much that it grossly overloaded the front tyres, so it produced ridiculous understeer going into corners and then the diff would lock up and eventually, and I stress 'eventually', it produced ridiculous oversteer very suddenly, but it was a splendid way to learn how to drive a racing car."

Howden Ganley, himself a successful designer, says, "Robin does have a tendency to do himself down, I thought it was a clever idea." In fact, so did most other designers and and in 1989 several cars appeared with the same style of gearbox, among them the March CG891. Had March had more clout and Goodyear been willing, it could have been made to work provided tyres were tailor-made for it. Max says, "We made the basic mistake of going for a complicated solution when, given the state of our finances, we should have gone for a simple one." At Jarama, there appeared a simple solution and it was also a March.

Mike Beuttler's backers, a consortium of stockbrokers (Ralph Clarke, later Chairman of March, Alistair Guthrie, Malcolm's brother, Jack Durlacher and David Mordaunt), had ordered an F1 car and, seeing a possible escape route from the 721X, Robin had one made along the lines of John Cannon's F5000 car, on a sale or return basis. Bob Sparshott did most of the work on the car, which had a 722 tub with extra tanks, F1 rear suspension and a Cosworth DFV and which was dubbed the 721G, the G for *Guinness Book of Records*, because the whole project, beginning to end, took only nine days. That must be a record for any F1 car, let alone one which led races and scored World Championship points.

It was not race-worthy on its début in the Spanish GP, but in the next race, Monaco, Beuttler managed to qualify ahead of both Pace (711) and Stommelen (721) and finish a creditable 13th in appalling conditions. Beuttler was no ace and he was driving under the constraints of a privateer on a low budget, so he could not afford to take chances, but the performance raised a few eyebrows.

At Monaco Peterson had a ZF differential instead of the usual Weismann, but even in conditions which emphasized the driver he could manage no better than 11th and four laps down on Beltoise's BRM. "Among the many criticisms Niki has made of us," says Robin, "is one which says I was trying to con him when I started pouring STP into the 721X's differential at Monaco. He was most upset when he saw it being done, but in fact it was a desperate attempt to try to free it by using a lighter oil."

In the next race, the International Gold Cup at Oulton Park, Ronnie had a car with 721 rear suspension and Hewland FG400 gearbox internals in place of the Alfa Romeo bits, but that made little difference and he crashed anyway. After one last outing with the 721X, in the Belgian GP, where Ronnie finished ninth and Niki qualified, and finished, well behind Beuttler, March decided to cut its losses. The 721X was dumped and the works made up two 721Gs and from then until March pulled out of F1 at the end of 1977 its F1 cars would be in essence the same as its F2 cars.

They began as a desperate move, but served March well; it's hard to imagine the company being able to stay competitive and even to win Grands Prix had it gone the conventional way, one only has to look at the number of teams with much more money which didn't do as well. The 722 was not embarrassed by having a Cosworth DFV attached to a tub designed for a smaller engine, in fact the V8 configuration made for a much stiffer installation and the relative slimness of the cars gave them a distinct advantage in a straight line.

The works first fielded 721Gs in the French GP where Ronnie qualified ninth, ran as high as third before a roll bar broke, and finished fifth. It was not a world-shaking result but an improvement, but the damage to the confidence of the works drivers had already been done and the effect on Niki was clear, 23rd on a grid of 24 with only Beuttler slower. He has recorded how at one time he came close to committing suicide, he'd mortgaged himself up the hilt and was clearly not going to make it in motor racing.

A longer-term problem was the damage the 721X did to Ronnie's confidence in Robin as a designer. At the start of 1970 Robin had said that Ronnie would be World Champion in three years and to the last man everyone at March believed it, but so far 'the most brilliant designer in the world' had not delivered the goods. On a personal level Ronnie was happy at March, but he was also ripe for courting and at the French GP, Colin Chapman did just

Peterson with the 721X in practice for Monaco in 1972. **(Nigel Snowdon)**

In the rain-soaked Monaco race, Peterson, seen here leading Stewart round Station Hairpin, finished a poor 11th. **(Nigel Snowdon)**

Mike Beuttler with the Formula Two-based 721G with which he finished 13th at Monaco in 1972. **(Nigel Snowdon)**

that, and he made an oral agreement which soon became a signed option to drive for Lotus. As the year progressed, it looked the best move possible for him as Lotus and Emerson Fittipaldi won five Grands Prix and both World Championships.

Robin and Max were shattered; the future of March in F1 depended on Ronnie, and Max started to mutter about legal proceedings against Chapman, but the approach had been made properly and when Ronnie's contract expired at the end of the year he would be a free agent. In fact Ronnie had received offers from every team except Matra at the end of 1971 and while many drivers would have simply torn up their contracts and gone for the bigger pay day, Ronnie was an honourable man. Max anyway was probably more furious because he'd been outflanked by Chapman, but then so had most people in motor racing at one time or another.

Anyway, everyone outside of March could see it happening, Ronnie was far too good to stay tied to a team going nowhere, and while it was true that March had bent over backwards to nurture him and advance his career, it was also true that he had more than repaid them in terms of results. When one driver is typically ten places ahead of his team-mates on the grid, then that driver is doing more for the team than the team is doing for him. It's ironic that after Ronnie decided to leave, he found himself among the leaders again and had March started the year with the 721G development might have made it into a winner by mid-season. At Brands Hatch he was in fourth place with two laps to go when fuel feed problems made him spin into a couple of parked cars. He spun again in the German GP, but gathered it together and came home a splendid third behind the two works Ferraris.

At the Nürburgring Peterson qualified fourth while Lauda in a similar car was 24th, over 20 seconds slower. Had anyone predicted that within 18 months Niki would be leading the Ferrari team and on his way to becoming a triple World Champion he would have been avoided in case his condition was contagious. In fact at the 'Ring he was outclassed as usual by Carlos Pace running in Frank Williams's old 711, who had been putting the car in the middle of the grid much to the embarrassment of team leader Henri Pescarolo, who had a 721.

Both the Austrian and Italian GPs are best forgotten, for March's engines weren't good enough to be competitive on such power circuits, and Ronnie anyway had a miserable time at Monza because by then he'd signed his Lotus contract and Max gave him a hard time, with the result he was unsettled and kept spinning in practice. The trouble was that everyone was so devoted to Ronnie that they took to heart what anyone else would see as a good career move. It wasn't so much anger as hurt and Ronnie himself hated leaving, but knew that he must.

Absent from the last races was Rolf Stommelen because Eifelland had been taken over and motor racing did not figure in the plans of the new owners.

Since it was imperative that March rebuilt its engines for the long trip away to North America, Ronnie was back on form in the Canadian GP, where he qualified third behind the McLarens of Revson and Hulme and at the start he shot off into the lead. The circuit was very dusty, so behind him quite a number of people started to have problems as dirt got into their throttle slides, but Jackie Stewart was not among them and he got by on the fourth lap. Ronnie then settled down to a lonely drive in second place until three-quarters distance, when he encountered a bunch of backmarkers intent on their own race. After five laps of being baulked he tried to force his way through, connected a front wheel against one of Graham Hill's rears and snapped a steering rod. He rushed into the pit lane, overshot his pit, and was disqualified when he was pushed back the wrong way.

Niki Lauda at the wheel of the 722 at the Crystal Palace on 29 May, 1972. (Nigel Snowdon)

Rolf Stommelen and the bizarrely styled Eifelland in the 1972 French Grand Prix. (**Nigel Snowdon**)

In those final races it was almost as though Ronnie was trying a bit too hard to leave March with a win as a goodbye present because in the US GP he crashed in practice and damaged his monocoque. It was a desperate situation, but a couple of mechanics drove into the nearby town, stole someone's wrought iron gate and cut it up to make new bulkheads. With a Jerry-rigged car Ronnie started from 26th on the grid, stormed through the field to finish fourth.

By contrast Lauda started from 25th place with a perfectly good car and finished 19th and last, ten laps adrift. It's true he had fuel injection problems, but there was no way he could have responded in the same way as Ronnie. Robin says, "We destroyed Niki eventually. I remember speaking to Jackie Stewart and asking him what he thought of Lauda and he was very critical of his driving, but now I think he was just out-psyched, he had lost his confidence. We all know he eventually overcame it, but it was only recently that I understood what he must have been going through, because since taking up rally driving I had a period of experiencing the same thing myself. I'd recommend rallying to every engineer because then you begin to understand what drivers go through and I maintain you can get more performance from a driver than you can from a car.

"There's one other thing about Niki which we should put right. At the end of 1972 we wanted him as a full works driver without him paying and then STP pulled out. He went off to buy himself a drive with BRM, although eventually BRM waived his fee and made him a full works driver, but the point is that he believed he was putting himself even further into debt. We didn't want to lose him, but we had no sponsorship. Then Max persuaded STP to reconsider and we ran with some STP money in 1973 – as I remember it was £15,000. Niki never would believe that Max had not deliberately engineered his departure from the team and still holds it against him, but Max was entirely innocent.

"Niki's complaints and criticisms of us are fundamentally justified, they're a little simplistic, but only just. We did some terrible things to him, but none with malice aforethought. We grew to like the guy and although you wouldn't believe it from his books, he's got a terrific sense of humour."

While Niki's performances were embarrassing in F1, a week after the US GP he won the John Player F2 Championship. This was a national affair which consisted of the three British rounds of the European Championship plus two races at Oulton Park, the second one to carry double points. Niki had won the first Oulton Park race, then had a difficult season in the European series when time and again he was robbed of good finishes due to the

Peterson with the 721G in the Austrian Grand Prix, one of two races in which the team's prospects were ruined by poor engines. (**Nigel Snowdon**)

epidemic of engine problems. At Oulton Park his engine stayed in one piece and he came home a good second to Peterson, who, despite the fact that he contested only two of the five rounds, finished runner up in the series. In third place at Oulton Park was James Hunt in a 712 which the works had loaned him for a few races late in the season. That result together with a fifth at Albi and a fourth at Hockenheim did a great deal to revive Hunt's career and the following year to see him in F1 with Lord Hesketh's March.

Back at the shop, Bill Wright was a first-class motorcycle trials rider who used to delight his colleagues by riding up and around the low brick wall outside the factory. Dave Reeves remembers, "Bill Wright was teaching Bill Stone how to ride a trials bike and they used a very large mound of soil nearby as a practice ground – they'd ride up and down this mountain. One morning unbeknown to us the contractors had taken away the back half of the mountain. Dead on half twelve Bill Wright started his bike and with poise and expertise rode up the side of the mountain. Suddenly there was an unexpected silence and then that sickening crump we all knew so well. There was a cloud of dust and from behind the mountain emerged this bedraggled figure pushing the remains of his bike. It was like something out of a film and I don't think anyone who saw it has laughed so much before or since."

Bill Stone had his trials bike in the workshop when a party of students from the Oxford Polytechnic MC arrived on a works visit and when one of them saw it he showed interest because he'd built a motor cycle for record breaking and further, he had ambitions to get into car racing. Bill had retired when he realized he was the granddaddy of Formula Ford but since the student was keen, and they got on, he went with him to choose a second-hand FF car and then they became partners in a fabrication business which started to make racing cars designed by the student, whose name was Adrian Reynard.

Ronnie had one other commitment to the team, the John Player Challenge Trophy Race at Brands Hatch, and there he nearly did leave March with a win. The race had a wet start, but the outlook was changeable. Ronnie gambled on wets, took the lead and pulled out a big lead until about one-third distance, when the track began to dry and he had to pit for new tyres. Still, he'd made a point by leading Emerson Fittipaldi, the new World Champion and his future team-mate.

The highest March finisher in the race was John Watson, who had been making a name for himself in F2. When Eifelland pulled out of racing its 721 was bought by Paul Michaels, a car dealer and enthusiast who runs Hexagon of Highgate, and he entered Wattie in a Formule Libre race at Phoenix Park, Dublin. John won the race and he says, "I may be the only driver who has good things to say about the 721. When Hexagon took delivery, it was in a pretty tired condition and there wasn't time to prepare it properly, but we got a good result. By the time I drove it at Brands Hatch, the mechanics had done an extremely good job on it. Quite apart from the fact it had conventional 721 bodywork, which made no difference, it felt like a proper car. It was as they say, user-friendly, not the most competitive car in the field, but relatively easy to drive. Since I was making my F1 début and the conditions were difficult, with a light mist and a wet/dry race, it was the ideal car for me in the circumstances – and we got a good result." Wattie brought it home sixth, and highest March finisher, in a fairly strong field. More than that, his performance was noted widely and favourably and it launched him into a distinguished F1 career.

After Brands Hatch Ronnie left March without breaking his F1 duck and while he was about to enter the most successful phase of his career, he left with mixed feelings. Apart from the fact that March had given him the chance to shine, and being a thoroughly decent man, he understood terms like 'gratitude' and 'loyalty' (some drivers have to look them up in a dictionary); he'd also been close to so many there and, despite the ups and downs he'd had, was never again to be so happy with a team. After he left, it became an article of faith at March that one day they'd build a good enough car, and be in a strong enough position, to woo him back.

In the meantime if March was to stay in F1 it needed a top-line driver, someone whose name might attract more sponsorship, and Max began to court a driver of enormous talent whose team had decided to call it a day. Please welcome the return of Chris Amon. After the dramas of 1970, Chris and Max had buried the hatchet and had become quite good friends. Chris needed a berth, Max was persuasive, and declarations of intent were made on both sides. There was no money in the kitty (March made a profit of just £3000 in 1972) and Chris would not receive a retainer but Max would do his best to raise sponsorship, which would be shared. Originally Howden Ganley was pencilled in for the number two seat, but March couldn't afford that so he was erased and as part of the deal Chris sold his engine-building facility at Reading, which had been a fairly disastrous operation, and that then became March Engines.

Everything looked rosy until Chris wrote Max a letter in which he expressed the hope that Max was doing everything he could to find sponsorship because he, Chris, was mindful of life's little luxuries such as food. Max took this entirely the wrong way and thought Chris was looking for a way out and would happily skip to another team if the money didn't arrive. Chris denies this, but it was a classic case of miscommunication. "I was surprised to hear on the radio I'd been dropped. Later Max more or less admitted he'd made a mistake, but I can't for the life of me think why he did." Amon eventually found a seat with the disastrous Tecno project, which effectively ended his career, while March faced 1973 with neither a star driver nor a new car. As things turned out, it was a blessing in disguise.

10 Bavarian Honeymoon

In the three years since March had appeared there had been some fundamental shifts in motor racing and by 1973 conditions had so changed that no new outfit could hope to enter and cover Formula One down to Formula Ford. The health of motor racing is always an accurate indicator of the economy and in those pre-Oil Crisis days, the sport was expanding at a rapid rate with new categories and more championships and as this happened each class became more specialized and professional. In 1972 there had been six non-Championship F1 races plus the Rothmans 50,000, a Formule Libre extravaganza with a big enough purse to attract works F1 cars; in 1973 there were only two non-Championship races and both were combined F1/F5000 events.

The same process was taking place in F2. There had been seven non-Championship races in 1972 but in 1973 there were none and it was felt that the 17 races there were three too many. In fact at the beginning of the year no fewer than 22 races were scheduled and the plot was one took part in 12 'base' races and then could score points in four others of one's choice provided they were in different countries, but in the end five of those races were cancelled. Apart from the odd appearance by an F1 driver, F2 had ceased to be a pay day for stars, new demands on their time had made it impossible, thus it became a separate, specialized, field and by the end of 1973 the day of the privateer with a car and some volunteer helpers was over.

As competition intensified in each category, so manufacturers found it hard to maintain competitiveness on all fronts. Lotus, for years the most prolific production racing car maker, pulled out in 1972 to concentrate on F1. Brabham, a leading maker for ten years, did the same at the end of 1973 and the few customer cars it made in its last year suffered from lack of development as the company concentrated most of its attention on F1. The same happened to Ensign, which had made excellent F3 cars before it turned to F1 when the customer cars suffered and trickled away to nothing.

This shift was to be responsible for March's revival for, with only £15,000 from STP, its 1973 F1 programme was a very low-key affair and instead of the F1 team taking the lion's share of attention, the customer cars received it, and benefited. In 1972 March made 11 Formula One cars in three distinct types, which must be a record, in 1973 no F1 cars were made, but existing 721Gs were modified. In place of the 60 inch front and rear track, which was the same as the 721 and 721X, the 1973 version had 56 inch front track, 58 inch rear track and the wheelbase extended by three inches to 97 inches although the most obvious difference was that all 1973 Marches reverted to front-mounted radiators.

For the opening WC rounds in the Argentine, Brazil and South Africa one works 721G, for Jean-Pierre Jarier, and Mike Beuttler's car were the sole March representatives, for Frank Williams had his own Iso Marlboro cars. Neither March driver distinguished himself, but then nor did the team for Jarier suffered from gearbox problems in all three races.

The choice of 'Jumper' (Michael Herd, aged two, couldn't quite say 'Jean-Pierre') was a surprise to most people, for he was almost unknown. He'd had a rentadrive F2 March in 1971, and took a couple of thirds, and then he had returned to F3 for a season, but had not quite had team managers tripping over each other to get his name on the dotted line. Robin says, "We obviously needed a good driver and Jarier had impressed me in an F3 race at Clermont-Ferrand, where he was driving a second hand March which was under-prepared and under-financed, but my goodness, the aggression he showed. He was the most aggressive driver we ever used and I simply cannot understand some of the problems he had in the latter part of his F1 career."

While the F1 team was the shadow of its former self the production car side was healthy and March was about to have its most successful season, partly because of the shifts motor racing was undergoing, partly because the cars were good, and partly because of a special deal. In the spring of 1972 Jochen Neerpasch, then with Ford of Germany, had phoned to say that he wanted to run Jochen Mass in the non-Championship Nürburgring F2 race and could March provide a car with a Ford engine? The snag was that they would probably lose on the deal, and money was tight, but in the back of Max's mind was, as ever, the tie-up with a major manufacturer.

Max says, "Against any commercial sense we ran Mass, he won, and Neerpasch was delighted. It did him an enormous amount of good in Germany, and as the direct result of that he asked us to meet him at Monaco because he was moving to BMW and it was there we did the deal for the forthcoming BMW F2 engine. Jochen offered us an exclusivity with free engines for our works cars, but we had to order and buy 50 engines. We couldn't possibly afford them, but we reasoned they would probably be good and we could probably sell them. Knowing how these things operate, we figured it was highly unlikely that all 50 would arrive on the same day, but they would trickle through, so that gave us a potential get-out, where are those engines you promised us? When it became known that BMW was going to build an F2 engine everybody was after them, but by that time we had a contract signed and sealed."

At about the same time, March became interested in the idea of setting up a BMW dealership and offering a range of March-modified cars, a British version of Alpina. Max had meetings and dinners with representatives of those who then held the British BMW concession, agreement was reached, the site was chosen, and key personnel were ready to spring into action, but it all petered out because there was not enough money to set up the agency.

On the racing front, to spread the BMW engines around a sports racer was made for the popular European 2-litre Sports Car Championship. The 73S, which was basically a two-seater version of the F2/3 cars, showed promise in the winter Southern African Springbok Series, and Jody Scheckter led races with it, but its aerodynamics were not up to scratch and it did not receive the development it needed since it was wasn't a top priority so after the first couple of European rounds its drivers became spectators to the main contest fought out between Lola, Chevron and Abarth. Still, on the strength of Scheckter's performances the cars sold well and mopped up the surplus BMW engines but Jody came close to not having a car to spread the word.

As a mark of friendship between nations, the mechanics at BMW had put a mild girlie magazine in the packing case along with the engine for the benefit of the workers who had to slot it into the prototype 73S. When the South African customs officials prised open the crate they immediately impounded the engine because it was instrumental in importing pornography into a pure, Christian, country. It took all of Max's skilled tonguework to release the obscene, vile, decadent, engine so it could race and play its part in furthering Jody's career.

After a promising start, the 73S was to prove a disappointment on the track, but of greater long-term significance was that Tom Hanawa's Le Mans Company imported seven of them into Japan along with a 732 with which Motahuru Kursawa won the Japanese F2 Championship. Japanese racing was still fairly primitive, but it was growing and through Hanawa March established a toehold in what would develop into one of its most important markets.

By contrast to sports car racing, Formula Two was an entirely different story. The 732 reverted to the same dimensions and lay-out as the 712, Hunt's late season performances had done the company a favour as well as the driver, so the front track was narrowed and the side radiators thrown away. Robin then turned most of his attention to the aerodynamics of the car and the result was a subtle improvement which worked on almost any circuit. The distinguishing feature of the 732 was a full-width nose cone which covered most of the height of the front wheels; there were no separate, adjustable, front wings, though often a splitter was fitted at the bottom of the nose cone. As on the 1972 Surtees and Lotus F2 cars, the nose cone nearly touched the deck to eliminate lift from air passing beneath the car.

In the opening F2 round at Mallory Park Jarier, March and BMW won easily from the reigning F2 Champions, Hailwood, Surtees and Ford. Jean-Pierre Beltoise had an outing in a works car there, but the engine blew up on the second lap and a con-rod went through the window of the time keeper's box just to confirm his retirement. Later in the race Colin Vandervell's BMW engine went the same way and exploded with such force that flying shrapnel removed the air box from Jarier's car, which was just behind. The early BMW engines had a design weakness in the con-rods and there were at first just four examples of a revised version, and all four were in Jarier's engine. Apart from that and a batch of faulty valve

Toine Hezemans with his March 73S-BMW competing in the round of the European 2-litre Sports Car Championship at Paul Ricard where he retired because of overheating. The 73S proved unsuccessful in 1973, mainly because it was heavier and did not handle as well as the Lola T292 opposition. **(LAT)**

March started the 1973 Formula Two year with a brilliant win by Jarier with the 732-BMW at Mallory Park, the opening round of the Championship. (**Nigel Snowdon**)

necessary and this handed the race to Reine Wisell, who gave GRD its only F2 win.

Come the next race at Pau, problems in practice saw him start from the back of the grid and Max Mosley threatened him with the sack if he tried to take the lead on the first lap. In the event he behaved himself, finished second to Cevert's Elf and took maximum points as the leading non-graded driver.

From then on the ambition of every driver was to beat Jarier, and the driver who seemed most likely to do so was Roger Williamson, who abandoned his GRD for a March in June and led his heat in his first race with it at Rouen before sidelined with a misfire. He then won at Monza and would have taken Misano as well but for an electrical failure in one of the heats. Since Jarier had been absent from both Monza and Misano, a confrontation between the two drivers was eagerly awaited but, tragically, it was never to take place.

March completely dominated the year, taking 11 of the 17 races, with Jarier accounting for seven of them, and yet so far as marques were concerned it was one of the most varied years in the history of the formula with cars from Lotus (a works team which fielded 'Texaco Stars' for Peterson and Fittipaldi, who were severely handicapped by their Lotus engines), Brabham, Motul (run by Ron Dennis and Neil Trundel's 'Rondel' outfit), Elf, GRD, Surtees, Pygmée (run by Mike Earle and former driver Rod Banting, who formed BERT – Banting Earle Racing Team), Royale and the one-off 'Scott' designed by Patrick Head for Richard Scott, which later formed the basis of the successful Delta FF2000 cars.

In the 1973 Spanish Grand Prix Henri Pescarolo deputized for Jarier (driving elsewhere in Formula Two) and after qualifying near the back of the grid finished eighth. (**Nigel Snowdon**)

springs later in the year, the BMW engine showed impressive reliability as well as superior torque.

To prove Mallory was no fluke, Jarier followed it with a win at Hockenheim, a very different sort of circuit, but then he threw away the next two races, largely because of his aggression, for he wanted to lead at the first corner and once in the lead to win by the largest possible margin. At Thruxton he was involved in a start-line mêlée and the race might have gone to Mike Beuttler's 732, but he collided with Gerry Birrell's Chevron two laps from the end and the race went to Pescarolo's Motul M1. Jarier then threw away a win at the Nürburgring when he spun after hitting a puddle because he was pressing on harder than

Since March had an exclusive deal with BMW, something which did not stop some from buying a March and putting the unit in another chassis, some muttered that the performance was all due to the engine but if had been as simple as that, the March 73S-BMWs would have dominated 2-litre sports car racing. The fact is that the BMW unit had only a slight edge on the Cosworth/Ford-based unit which most people used, but F2 became March's main concern and, indeed, part of the contract with BMW was that Robin should make it so. Thus while Max looked after F1 Robin had come up with a car which was by no means new but which had had attention lavished upon it, with the result that it was a harmonious package.

If March had been reliant on BMW for its success in F2, what could explain its performance in Formula Three and Formula Atlantic? In 1972 there had been mass defections to GRD, and its 372 had been a fine car, but GRD was content to rest on its laurels, and although it sold a lot of cars at the beginning of the season, by the middle of the year you were spoiled for choice if you wanted a second-hand example, since most of the serious runners had switched to March.

Jarier was busy throwing away the F2 race at the Nürburgring on 29 April, so Henri Pescarolo drove the works F1 car in the Spanish GP. New regulations demanded deformable side structures and both Beuttler's and the works car had them, together with a narrower track and a 732-style body with a front radiator. Both qualified near the back of the grid and though they finished both were out of the points and lapped, Pescarolo twice. Jarier was back in the works car for the Belgian GP at Zolder, but both he and Beuttler were way down the grid and they were among the ten drivers who had accidents on the treacherous surface of the track, which had broken up and was being repaired within minutes of the start.

March's F1 season looked as though it would be an embarrassment, but at the next race, Monaco, things suddenly looked brighter. James Hunt had a patron, Lord Alexander Hesketh, and they had planned a season in F2. Then Hesketh hired a Surtees TS9B for Hunt in the Race of Champions and James brought it home third, inches behind Denny Hulme's McLaren. That settled the matter, F2 was forgotten and Hesketh bought 721G/3 and at the same time lured the designer, Harvey Postlethwaite, away from March to develop it.

Also making his début at Monaco was David Purley with a March rentadrive. David, who was long on bravery but short on natural talent and mechanical empathy, had flirted with F2 the previous year and was leading both British Atlantic Championships with his 722. Purley was a great character with a whole body of mythology surrounding him, like the time at Pau when he couldn't sleep because his hotel room overlooked one of the bends on the track and some local boy racers were screeching their cars around. Some Castrol spread on the corner resulted in the sound of tinkling glass and bent Renault and then the air was undisturbed for the rest of the night.

Four Marches started at Monaco and although you had to look in the lower part of the grid to find them, at least it was progress where none had been expected. More was to come when Hunt proved the sensation of the race by running as high as sixth until, five laps from the end, his engine blew. It was the first sign that Britain had a new star.

After Monaco March Car Hire had a busy time and Reine Wisell, who had lost his drive at Lotus to Ronnie, booked the car for his home Grand Prix, the first time Sweden had hosted a WC round. It was slightly ironic that he had to do that to try to re-launch his career, since he had been generally thought to be the best Swede in 1969, but coming up against Emerson Fittipaldi in the same team had destroyed his confidence, for Fittipaldi could always find the odd extra tenth. Reine qualified quite respectably and was easily the quickest March, but his front suspension broke on the warm-up lap. Hunt was absent, Jarier retired with a broken throttle cable, but Beuttler did a good job to finish eighth.

At the French GP Jarier qualified seventh, but retired with a broken drive-shaft; Wisell hired another drive, but had a fuel leak and overheating problems, while

***Jean-Pierre Jarier with the '731' in the Belgian Grand Prix at Zolder. He crashed on lap 61 when holding sixth place.* (Nigel Snowdon)**

Hunt cheered up everyone by coming home sixth, splitting the two Ferraris. March also felt it had part of the main celebration because Ronnie finally scored his first GP win after a season which had seen him the quickest man in the field, but also the unluckiest. It was typical of Ronnie that he spent most of his time celebrating his win in the March pits among his friends.

The 1973 British GP will always be remembered for Jody Scheckter's spectacular crash on the second lap which wiped out a third of the field, among them Roger Williamson in the works car. Williamson's mentor, Tom Wheatcroft, had done a deal to run him for the rest of the season and Jarier had stepped down to concentrate on the F2 Championship, since by that time he had won four of the nine rounds and it was better to be winning in F2 than struggling in F1.

Thanks to Postlethwaite's patient development work, Lord Hesketh's car now had the edge on the other Marches and Hunt was able to exploit it to the full. After the re-start he worked his car up to third place behind Revson's McLaren and Peterson's Lotus, a remarkable feat in only his third GP, and while he eventually had to bow to Denny Hulme's greater experience, his eventual fourth plus fastest lap was success beyond anyone's wildest dreams. One other driver to make his mark at Silverstone was Niki Lauda, who, driving with determination with which few would have credited him a few months before, had his BRM in second place for a few laps. He had been making progress all year, but Silverstone was the turning point and from then on he was to turn in a string of performances which led to Ferrari in 1974.

For those who collect obscure facts, the Dutch GP saw four Marches start and all were driven by Englishmen, a unique occurrence, but only Hunt was to finish, in a superb third place behind the Tyrrells of Stewart and Cevert. So much for the statistics. What the race will always be remembered for is that one of Roger Williamson's front tyres threw its tread and his March ploughed into a barrier, which bent back. Roger's car slid along it, ripped away one of the side fuel tanks and when the car came to a halt it was upside down and alight.

The marshals appeared not to know what to do, a fire tender parked a few yards up the track on the other side would not come to the rescue because the race had not been stopped and spectators who wanted to help were restrained. Purley was just behind and he stopped and tried to deal with the fire, which was then a minor one. In desperation he tried to lift the car to free his friend while marshals looked on, some holding fire extinguishers. Then the fire which could have been easily dealt with, flared up and poor Roger was asphyxiated by the fumes. A driver of immense promise was lost through bungling incompetence.

Film of the accident and Purley's rescue bid made television and press headlines all over the world and he was later awarded the George Medal. In the same Honours List Mike Hailwood also received a GM because at Kyalami he had saved Regazzoni when both their cars had been involved in a multiple pile-up, Clay had been knocked unconscious and his BRM had caught fire. The difference was that the mass media did not have film of Hailwood's heroism, so made less of it, for there were no images with which to titillate the punters at home.

Purley was always to say that he had done what

For the Dutch Grand Prix Tom Wheatcroft rented the works '731' drive for Roger Williamson. Here Williamson is seen shortly before his fatal crash. **(Nigel Snowdon)**

David Purley with his rentadrive '731' in the 1973 Dutch Grand Prix at Zandvoort. He pulled out of the race in a vain attempt to rescue his friend Roger Williamson from his burning car, for which he was awarded the George Medal. **(Nigel Snowdon)**

James Hunt, seen here at Mallory Park in March, was one of the sensations of the 1973 season at the wheel of a car entered by Lord Hesketh and developed and modified by Harvey Postlethwaite. **(Nigel Snowdon)**

anyone would have done for a friend, and the incident adversely affected his career. From then on he was David Purley the Hero, not David Purley the Driver, and while he felt honoured by the GM, as an ex-Para officer who had been in the thick of things in a guerilla war in Aden, he knew something about heroism. David was a hero, but his bravery was to be shown much later when he sustained massive injuries in a racing accident and underwent years of agony so that he could walk properly again. When he could do so he got back into a racing car, proved that he had lost neither his nerve nor his speed, and then walked away from the sport on his own terms, without a stick or a limp.

After the Dutch tragedy only Beuttler and Purley ran Marches in the German GP where David was last in practice by over 25 seconds, but the rest of the GP circus knew what a personal mountain he was climbing after being so intimately involved with the death of a friend and they gave him moral support, for by strict reckoning he should have been excluded under the 110 per cent rule. In the race he played himself in and and regained his pace so finishing 15th and second last was a great personal triumph even although it's buried in the basement of motor racing statistics.

By the Austrian GP Hunt's car had received considerable modification, but even so he was only marginally quicker than Jarier and Beuttler, who lined up just behind him on the grid, in mid-field, but none finished. Beuttler qualified remarkably well (12th) in the Italian GP, but retired, while Purley, who qualified last, came home ninth.

By that time Jarier had been confirmed as the European F2 Champion, having won seven rounds, and he

At Zandvoort the ever-improving James Hunt, seen here leading Gijs van Lennep's Iso Marlboro, took a strong third place with the Hesketh-entered '731'. (**Nigel Snowdon**)

took to wearing a T-shirt saying *Superfrog*. Jarier kept a Simca Étoile at the factory for use when he was in England and he couldn't understand why it progressively grew more breathless over the year until eventually it was hard-pressed to go at all but then he didn't know about the attention it had been receiving from March's dedicated employees.

"At the time," Dave Reeves recalls, "Murdock Road petered out into a field just past the March factory and at the end of the road the contractors had left a pile of soil as a sort of barrier. The game was to take the Simca up to the junction with Launton Road, then drive back past the factory accelerating all the way and see who could brake the latest on the loose earth in front of the mound. One bloke, Keith Leyton I think, left his braking too late, hit the mound and disappeared over the top. To everyone's amazement he and the car survived, so now the game was to see how far we could jump into the field. Needless to say, the car didn't survive."

The lunch-time kart racing around the workshops, however, came to an end when someone nearly decapitated himself going under a work bench. It is probably better to say nothing of the discovery that magnesium swarf burns brilliantly (there are still rings in the roads around the factory where dustbins melted the tarmac) and if you set fire to a skip full of magnesium it buckles the skip so it won't fit the lorry, and as for the acetelyne bombs . . . The spirit of the early days was still alive. "We got up to tricks I wouldn't allow today," says Dave, JD turned MD, and when he was appointed as Managing Director in mid-1988 it was not only because he is a superb crisis manager and production engineer but he was the man to put the heart back into March Engineering.

Vittorio Brambilla had been going well all season in his March-BMW and he finished his year with a couple of wins, which added to two seconds and a number of other place finishes gave him second in the Championship. Moreover, by winning at Albi he became the first man to out-drive Jarier all season. Brambilla had clearly matured as a driver, for in his early days he was prone to red mists in front of his eyes and his driving style was, well, controversial. Add to that the build of a wrestler and it's not surprising that he was nicknamed the 'Monza Gorilla'. In his F3 days he once had a problem with his car when testing at Monza and his brother Ernesto went out to help him. The problem fixed, Vittorio offered to give his brother a lift back to the pits and then the red mist came, he forgot about his passenger and put his foot down in his usual way. Ernesto was found, hurt and not amused. face down at Parabolica.

Much later, when the press began to call Andrea de Cesaris the 'Monza Gorilla', Vittorio was most indignant and declared, "*I* am the only true Monza Gorilla." The man had a sense of humour and, despite his reputation, Robin says he was one of the four best test drivers he has ever worked with. The others are Lauda, Giacomelli and, in Robin's view the very best, Brian Henton.

Another March driver to pick up an F2 win was

Jacques Coulon, a French university lecturer, who had a special Firestone compound for the penultimate round at Vallelunga and then came a strong second to Jarier in the last round at Estoril. Coulon looked set for better things, but his career later faded. Still, wins by privateers such as Williamson, Coulon and Brambilla proved the claim that everyone received the same equipment. It was true in 1973, but was not to be so in the coming years.

In the other categories, nobody who bought a March sports or FA/5000 car was in danger of developing a drink problem through a surfeit of victory champagne but in Formula Three March cleaned up everywhere and not only took all three British Championships, but the Italian and Swedish series as well. The one non-March driver who did conspicuously well was Alan Jones in a GRD, who finished only two points behind Tony Brise in the John Player (British and European) Championship, but like so many others Brise had begun the year with a GRD and then switched.

In Formula Atlantic in Britain, once Purley was diverted by F1, Colin Vandervell's March won one of the championships from John Nicholson in his one-off Lyncar, and Nicholson won the other from Vandervell.

When the teams headed to North America for the final rounds, the World Championship had already been decided in favour of Jackie Stewart. None of the Marches (Jarier, Beuttler and Hunt) distinguished themselves in the Canadian GP so it was all the more surprising to see Hunt qualify fourth for the US GP at Watkins Glen. He liked the circuit and his car was working perfectly. The meeting itself was overshadowed by the death during practice of François Cevert and the withdrawal of Team Tyrrell.

Ronnie Peterson started from pole in his Lotus, as usual, but in his wheel-tracks was Hunt and they stayed locked together for the entire race. In the whole of motor racing history there has rarely been such a close race-long duel for the lead on a medium-fast circuit, slipstream battles are another thing entirely. They were never more than a second apart, James running with less wing being faster on the straight, while Ronnie had the advantage in the corners. At the flag Hunt was just two-thirds of a second down.

Hunt's brilliant second showed that in the right hands a March could be as quick as anything on the grid. That was the difficult point, had March ended the year with a string of no-hope performances it would have been easy to bow out of F1 to concentrate on consolidating the success gained in other formulae, but Hunt had shown that March was still agonizingly close to the works' first GP win and it was impossible to turn one's back on that. The trouble was that the Hesketh car was in the right hands not only in the sense that Hunt was driving but it was backed by a proper budget and a full-time engineer. Harvey Postlethwaite was in the position which Robin could have been in had he gone with Rindt instead of throwing in his lot with March.

11 Formula Two Steamroller

In 1974 March made 30 F2 cars and dominated the category with no excuses, for the BMW engine was available to all. The Brian Hart version of the Ford BDA engine was probably its equal, but few were prepared to take the chance and the German engine became standard kit by the end of the season. The category itself became even more closely defined as a separate entity, the number of rounds in the Championship was pared from 17 to ten, the appearance of a graded driver became a rarity, costs rose (the BMW engine needed a £1000 rebuild after every race) and the formula was centred on the Continent. In 1972 there had been five F2 races in Britain, three of them rounds for the European Championship, but in 1974 there were none.

It also became noticeable that some European countries, especially France and Germany, were investing in their rising talent in a way Britain was not. Thus the works March team ran Patrick Depailler sponsored by Elf Petroleum, which had initiated a scholarship scheme for French drivers and backed the French Alpine team, which entered its cars as 'Elfs', a policy that would lead to a preponderance of French drivers in F1. March's other works driver was Hans-Joachim Stuck, son of the great pre-war Auto Union driver, who came to both the F1 and F2 teams as BMW's protégé with sponsorship from Jägermeister, a German hangover treatment. Along with the driver, BMW also provided March with engines prepared under Paul Rosche which had an edge over the opposition.

The 1974 customer cars were all further revisions of the 1973 cars but the works F2 team soon arrived with 741 style bodywork, which had a full-width nose cone and side radiators, something which did not please the customers who felt, not unreasonably, they should have the same mods. So far as the F1 cars were concerned, there was a new monocoque built on the same principles as the earlier cars, although the 741's rear wing was mounted further back and its overall dimensions were slightly altered.

While the F2 side was strong, in F1 March was down to the two works cars after the first couple of races. Lord Hesketh had been so pleased with his racing that he had asked Postlethwaite to design a new car and had also commissioned a new V12 engine, although he pulled the plug on it before it was completed. Hunt's days in a March were numbered.

The 1973 US GP had been Beuttler's last F1 race before his backers hit trouble; it was a time of economic instability when property prices rose sharply and secondary banks got into difficulties. He had driven under the constraints of a privateer, where it's better to settle for 11th than try for tenth and risk damaging the car, but he and his team had enjoyed themselves, and he'd always been dependable. To judge by some of the fire he'd shown in his F3 and F2 drives had he been in a properly funded team which could have stood the odd ding or blown engine he might have made a useful F1 driver. We shall never know, for he turned his back on motor racing and died in San Francisco early in 1989.

On 13 January the grid for the Argentine GP saw Hunt in fifth place in his modified 721G and, near the back of the field, Howden Ganley and Hans Stuck in their 741s. The difference between them, six rows of the grid and 2.5 seconds, was not all down to Postlethwaite's superiority to March, for Hunt was very special in his early years. Ganley had been taken on without a retainer or even the guarantee of lasting the season because sponsorship was still problematical and if someone came along with a bag of gold it would be bye-bye Howden.

Hunt made a superb start in the race, avoided a first lap mêlée which slowed some of the leaders, and actually led for several hundred yards until he arrived at a corner and found he had no clutch. He careered on to the grass and retired a few laps later with overheating precipitated by his excursion. Howden managed to get up to sixth until the last lap: "I was suffering from severe wind buffeting which made overtaking difficult because I was being shaken about so much I couldn't see, so I might have even gone higher. We'd had problems in qualifying with the fuel breather, the car was actually finished in the paddock, so we ran five gallons light, and on the last lap I discovered we'd taken a little too much out. A point for sixth place would have been very useful."

Stuck started the race from 23rd on the grid and had not made much of a mark by the time he retired with transmission problems, yet mention his name at March and eyes light up. Robin says, "Hans was like having a giant, good-natured puppy in the team. I remember once at Enna, it was a Saint's day or something, and he had a room with a balcony overlooking the main square. He'd been quickest in the morning warm-up and went back to have a shower. As he came out of the shower he heard this procession, people were carrying a chair with the

Madonna, that sort of thing, and remember this is Sicily so it's a big deal. Hans immediately flings open the door to the balcony and, stark naked, starts yodelling. Hans is a big man in every way and at the sight of this huge naked yodelling Viking they dropped the Madonna and everything dissolved into confusion. I had to go and bail him out so he could start the race.

"Another incident, also at Enna. The main street there is very steep and they sell a lot of water melons by the side of the road. At the top of the hill was a woman with a big pyramid of melons. Trust Hans, he walks up to the pyramid and takes the bottom one, whereupon fifty or sixty melons go bounding down the hill crashing into cars, shop fronts and people, there were scooters swerving to avoid them, the lot. I had to bail him out on that occasion too. his biggest problem was that he was so tall and heavy that it was hard to fit him into a car, but he was a marvellous driver, with terrific car control. When it comes to car control, he and Ronnie were in a class by themselves."

No March driver, not even Hunt, acquitted himself particularly well in the Brazilian GP, but the works cars were still doing, in effect, pre-season mileage and they suffered wires falling off and air in the fuel. Howden says, "The 741 was a very nice little car straight out of the box once the buffeting had been cured and about the only serious thing wrong with it was its DG gearbox, but soon afterwards March changed to Hewland FGAs.

"I had a lot of time for March. I'd heard all kinds of horror stories about the way they treated drivers, but they were 100 per cent straight down the line with me and one thing I don't think anyone's ever given Robin proper credit for is his knowledge of aerodynamics. When he was at National Gas Turbines he did work on the ducting of Concorde and then when he was at McLaren he was the first person to run a wing on a Formula One car in a test at Goodwood. I've always felt he knows things about air that nobody else in motor racing does."

The Hesketh team stayed on a few days at Rio to test its new car, the Hesketh 308, before joining some of the rest of the circus for a non-Championship race at Brasilia (where Howden finished fourth), which was to be the last time Hunt raced a March. From there on he drove the Hesketh 308, which broadly followed March thinking, but it was far from being a March clone, perhaps Son of March describes it best.

While the Hesketh proved an immediate advance, the 741 did not receive the development which might have seen it move up the grid. With March being tugged between F1, on a bargain basement budget, and consolidating its position in the junior formulae, something had to give and the emphasis shifted on to the latter, but it was a case of emphasis rather than priority because that first works F1 win was still possible.

The unstated policy paid off at the first European F2 round at Montjuich Park, Barcelona, which was dominated by the works Marches, who swapped the lead several times until Stuck got the better of his team-mate when they encountered a back marker; a 1–2 was a good way to start the season.

By the time the South African GP came at the end of March, the question of the second F1 seat had been settled. Howden Ganley had been offered a lot of money to drive for the Japanese Maki F1 team, which seemed better than hanging on at March and waiting to see if anyone came along with the gelt to kick him out. He calls it jumping ship but given the dire state of Maki it was like stowing away on the *Titanic*. Vittorio Brambilla on the other hand had persuaded his F2 sponsor, Beta Tools, to promote him. Stuck, growing in confidence with every race, qualified seventh and finished fifth at Kyalami, while Brambilla had a quiet debut, qualifying 19th and plugging home to finish tenth.

Vittorio did not keep such a low profile at the Spanish GP and during practice demonstrated that when chicken wire catch fencing is hit at 160 mph it can stop a March 741. While this was an advance in the knowledge of Man it kept Vittorio out of a wet/dry race, where Hans came fourth despite a puncture. True, he was two laps down but it was his second points finish on the trot.

The turning point for Hans came at Monaco when he attempted to pass Hunt on the third lap. They collided and Stuck's car was launched into the air and into a spectacular crash from which he was fortunate to escape unhurt. At least he escaped without physical injury; what it did to his edge is another matter, he was never quite the same driver afterwards.

The F1 season which had started so promisingly then slumped and March would only score one other WC point in the season, when Brambilla inherited sixth place in the Austrian GP. Only once after Monaco did either driver manage to qualify in the top ten (Stuck, British GP, 9th) and most of the time they were were languishing near the back of the grid, sometimes not even qualifying. The final score, incidentally, was Brambilla 3, Stuck 2 – this refers to the number of tubs each destroyed in the season.

Elsewhere, by contrast, March was often the main name in the results sheets. Stuck had followed his win in Barcelona with another on home territory at Hockenheim, where he sliced 1.5 seconds from the lap record. That was before his Monaco shunt, and thereafter Patrick Depailler usually had the edge, although it was mid-season before Hans lost his points lead and he had an outside chance of the title up to the last round. Stuck's late-season performances were extremely erratic, however, for sometimes he was off the pace, and even when he re-mounted the victory podium, at Enna, it was after spinning three times.

The works Marches usually had things their own way except at the Salzburgring, where Jacques Laffite won in his 742-BMW, which had been rebodied by Tico Martini, and the second of the three races at Hockenheim. There Jean-Pierre Jabouille's Alpine-BMW won in the absence of Depailler (who was driving a Tyrrell to second place in the Swedish GP) in a race which was shortened by rain. Apart from the fact that it was the only time in 1974 that a March did not win a Championship race, it was the only time that one of Josef Schnitzer's BMW engines or a car using Firestone tyres won, and the Alpine (aka Elf) was the last spaceframe single-seater to win in a major category.

Early in the year the 731 showed considerable promise and Stuck finished fourth in the Spanish race at Jarama. (**Nigel Snowdon**)

In practice for the Spanish race Brambilla, seen here, crashed heavily, but although he was uninjured, the car was a non-starter. (**Nigel Snowdon**)

The other result which was not quite according to pattern was the Swedish round at Karlskoga, where March persuaded Ronnie Peterson to put on a show before his home crowd. It was a good thing to do, but there was also the little matter of the Lotus 76 being hopeless, a Colin Chapman own-goal, and Ronnie was not happy at Lotus. On the other hand there was this friendly team, which was dominating the junior single-seater formulae and needed only a star to make it a winner at the top level . . . Ronnie duly went out and won while Patrick Depailler came second, which won him maximum points as the first non-graded driver.

One person who was not so happy with March was Bob Harper, a Hong Kong millionaire who bought a pair of cars for David Purley and Dieter Quester in a team managed by Mike Earle. Now Mike's experience of running Marches started with Purley in 1972 and, with only a couple of breaks, extended to the end of 1988. Nobody has more experience of the customer cars and while he has remained a March enthusiast, he does not wear rose-tinted spectacles.

"Bob Harper was a great character who had made his millions by the time he was 42 and then thought it would be fun to run his own team in Europe. He came over and ordered two cars and, give March its due, they were delivered in just ten days. We weren't expecting that and it meant they arrived on the Thursday before the first round at Barcelona on the Sunday. Bob was all for trying to make the race, and to give you some idea what sort of man he was, and how very, very, wealthy, he was all for chartering a Hercules and air-freighting the cars, team and transporter out to Spain.

"I persuaded him that it wasn't such a good idea and we arrived at Hockenheim with our new cars only to find that the works Marches had new bodywork with F1 style nose cones and side radiators and they ran away and hid. After the second race Bob wanted to know when we were going to get the new tweaks and we were told that the works was still evaluating them.

"March totally lost their way in 1974 so far as customers were concerned. You'd phone the works and give your name and be met with something like, 'Ah yes,

Jackie Stewart with the Tyrrell-entered 701 in the 1970 Dutch Grand Prix. For Tyrrell the 701 was a stop-gap, but the cars performed well in the early part of the year. At Zandvoort Stewart finished second behind Rindt's improved Lotus 72. (Nigel Snowdon)

Jo Siffert in the German Grand Prix with his works 701. Siffert had a thoroughly miserable season with the March team and in this race he was classified eighth, although not running at the finish. (Nigel Snowdon)

Chris Amon with the 701 in the 1970 French Grand Prix at Clermont-Ferrand. In one of his best performances of the year he finished second behind Rindt's Lotus 72. (Nigel Snowdon)

Jo Siffert, whose works drive with March in 1970 was financed by Porsche. (Nigel Snowdon)

Ronnie Peterson, leader of the March team in 1971–72 and the friend of everyone at March. (Nigel Snowdon)

Frank Williams was a consistent private entrant of early March Formula One cars. Here his 711 is driven by Henri Pescarolo in the 1971 German Grand Prix but the Frenchman retired because of suspension problems. (Nigel Snowdon)

Ronnie Peterson and the works 712 March in the non-Championship Formula Two race at Brands Hatch in August 1971. (Nigel Snowdon)

Ronnie Peterson with the works 722 Formula Two car at Mallory Park in March 1972 where he set a new Formula Two lap record. (Nigel Snowdon)

Niki Lauda with a works 721G at Clermont-Ferrand in 1972. He retired early in the race because of drive-shaft trouble. (Nigel Snowdon)

Jean-Pierre Jarier with the March 732-BMW on his way to the first win of many in 1973 in the Formula Two race at Mallory Park in March. (Nigel Snowdon)

One of the sensations of 1973 was James Hunt with the Hesketh-entered and progressively modified 731 Formula One car. Here on his début at Monaco, he ran as high as sixth but was finally classified ninth, although not running at the finish. (Nigel Snowdon)

Roger Williamson in practice for the 1973 Dutch Grand Prix in which he so sadly lost his life. (Nigel Snowdon)

Leading member of an unsuccessful team: Hans Stuck with the March 741 in the 1974 British Grand Prix at Brands Hatch. (Nigel Snowdon)

Roger Penske's March 751 with Mark Donohue at the 1975 British Grand Prix at Silverstone. Entered as a Penske, the March was driven into fifth place by Donohue in the race, stopped short because of bad weather. (Nigel Snowdon)

Alan Jones on his way to a win at Brands Hatch, with the fast but unreliable 75A Formula One-based Formula 5000 car entered by RAM Racing. (Nigel Snowdon)

Vittorio Brambilla with the 751 in the last Grand Prix of 1975, the United States race at Watkins Glen in which he finished seventh. (Nigel Snowdon)

Alex Ribeiro with the Formula Two 762-BMW on his way to second place at Thruxton in April 1976. (Nigel Snowdon)

A major success at Monaco overshadowed the team's poor performance in the Grand Prix. Tom Pryce, later Shadow Formula One team member, won the Formula Three race with his March 743-Holbay. **(Nigel Snowdon)**

you're customer No. 36, I see you've bought three cars from us, but you've been complaining.' If you phoned up Chevron you'd usually be put straight through to Derek Bennett, who would say in his broad Lancashire accent, 'You want to buy a car, lad? Come up Saturday and we'll make you a pot of tea while we knit one up for you.' They were lovely, lovely, people to deal with.

"Bob Harper, being the sort of man he was, threw away his Marches and bought Chevrons. March's priorities were different at the time and they probably made more money from the sponsorship for their works F2 cars than they did from selling cars. It became important for them that the works team won and this attitude, which was to beat the customers, was a recipe for discontent." There were times in the year when the Harper Chevrons looked as though they might steal March's thunder, especially when Tom Pryce joined the team for the odd race, but they were running on Firestones, which were not up to Goodyear.

In the Monaco Grand Prix Vittorio Brambilla with his Beta Tools-sponsored 741 leads the Tyrrell of Depailler during practice. Brambilla was eliminated in a first lap multi-car accident. **(Nigel Snowdon)**

Stuck could have clinched the F2 Championship in the final round at Vallelunga if he won and Depailler finished out of the points but while the Frenchman won pole and both heats, Stuck was poor in practice and did well to fight his way up to second place on the aggregate of two heats. That crash at Monaco perhaps cost him not only the Championship but robbed motor racing of a first-class F1 talent, although Hans became a supreme sports car driver.

In the other classes, Jean Ragnotti began the 2-litre Sports Car Championship with a good second place in his works-assisted 74S-BMW, which was a subtly improved 73S, but 1974 was the year of the Alpine-Renaults and so complete was their dominance that they killed what had been a thriving and popular category. Ragnotti, like many other BMW users, soon found that the cost of using the engine made his eyes water and switched to a Cosworth FVA, which blunted his edge but by the end of the year the 74S was a well-handling car, probably the best in the field, although it was still hampered by less than optimum aerodynamics.

John Nicholson's one-off Lyncar, designed by ex-March man Martin Slater, continued its winning ways in British Formula Atlantic, but a strong runner-up in the premier series was the March of Jim Crawford, who belied his comparative inexperience in a year when most of the best young drivers, including Tony Brise and Alan Jones, chose Atlantic over Formula Three. In the latter class, however, Brian Henton's works March had a field day and he was to win no fewer than 17 races in one of the most successful F3 seasons ever.

'Superhen' was a colourful character, a man who started life in a council house with his widowed mother, who wheeled and dealed to find the money with which to go racing, and who, on advice from a journalist, had celebrated his win in the British Formula Vee Championship, a minor class if there ever was one, by announcing he was going to be World Champion. The idea was that shouting from the rooftops had done Muhammed Ali no harm, but, as Max had discovered, adopting so brash a way of drawing attention to oneself gets inches in the press but since motor racing is a conservative little world, in the long term it does more harm than good. He also gained a reputation for being arrogant and temperamental, which he happily admits he was in his early days, but the reputation stuck to him long after he'd matured and become one of the most pleasant characters in the sport and, in the late Seventies, the only British driver to have a fan club.

In 1974 he had the works March F3 drive (the 743 was virtually the same as the 733) and won race after race, but late in the season he and the team were faced with an extraordinary situation and March became perhaps the only team in history to use an illegal engine and then draw the attention of the scrutineers to the fact.

That year saw new engine regulations with capacity increased from 1600cc to 2 litres while retaining a 21.5mm air restrictor. The team had previously used Novamotor engines, but switched to what we will call the *Bentford* version of the engine. This proved not to live up to the claims made for it at the beginning of the year and was coming under pressure from the Novamotor-Toyota unit which, though heavier, had better torque and a longer active life.

Despite the engines, Henton managed to dominate the season because, he says, March had got its act together at the start of the year, but when the Toyota engines came on song Max Mosley was extremely miffed at *Bentford* and started to bang the table and demanded to know where were the fantastic engines promised before pre-season. Late in the year *Bentford* delivered a new engine for Brian at Oulton Park and it came with the warning that it had a new camshaft which revolutionized the engine.

Brian went out in the first practice season and found

In the Formula Two race at Montjuich Park in April the works 742s took the first two places. This is the winner, Hans Stuck, who slipped ahead of team-mate Patrick Depailler when they were lapping a back marker. **(LAT)**

Fourth place at Montjuich Park was taken by Gabriel Serblin with a standard 742 on his Formula Two début. (LAT)

he was pulling 7000 rpm, 1000 rpm more than he'd seen before and since the engine was fitted with an air restrictor, this could not be possible with a legal engine. He did a couple of laps and then parked the car, "Summit's up here," he said, "I've not been out of fourth gear and I'm two seconds under the lap record."

The team looked over the engine but could find nothing wrong, it passed the vacuum test on the air restrictor, there was nothing visibly untoward, but they had their suspicions. They faced a problem, a Championship was in their grasp, they had no spare unit, they felt they had to trust a firm with a reputation like *Bentford*'s, so Brian had to use the motor. "I made a good start in the race, but the track was greasy. I spun at the first corner and the entire field went by. I reckon I re-started 15 seconds after the last car went by and it was a short race, but with that engine I simply sliced through the field and won by a ridiculous margin."

At the end of the race, *Bentford* took the engine back but March was furious that a scam might have cost Henton his title and, worse, might have blackened its name. Like everyone else March has stretched the rules to their limits,

The European 2-litre Sports Car Championship was Alpine-dominated, but Jean Ragnotti took second place with his 74S-BMW in the first round at the Paul Ricard circuit. (LAT)

and has hyped its products, but that's motor racing, blatant cheating is another matter entirely and no constructor can afford to be caught doing it.

Most blatant cheating in motor racing has involved individuals or works teams who are not selling their product, and most of the instances of running oversized engines in F1, for example, have been desperate moves to either attract a sponsor or to keep one happy. It is impossible to tell the difference between a 3-litre Cosworth DFV and a 3.3-litre DFL but, since most engine builders are straight, an F1 team which wants to do that needs another angle, such as a close friend running a larger engine in a hill climb car, the team to be also running a sports car using the bigger engine, or else the team to own the engine builder. These suggestions are for amusement only, a bane on he who thinks that any of these ploys have ever been used, but if a customer car maker cheats it's a quick way of committing commercial suicide.

At the next meeting, Brands Hatch, Max Mosley insisted that the suspect engine be put into the second car, which was run for the Brazilian José Chateaubriand. Putting the suspect engine in Chateaubriand's car was a wise precaution, for if it was as bent as they suspected, it would do less harm to the team's Championship chances. They still could not find anything wrong until a mechanic put his hand over the air restrictor when the engine was running; it should have choked but it kept on running, so it was clearly getting air from another source.

Max, who was there to supervise *Bentford*'s exposure, instructed the chief mechanic, Mike Rowe, to alert the scrutineers; he could hardly protest his own team, but he wanted the exposure to be as public as possible. The scrutineers turned up, the engine was run, a mechanic put his hand over the air restrictor and the engine continued to rev merrily. The scrutineers took the point and sealed the engine in the usual way, but that presented no problems to *Bentford*, who were able to reverse the ingenious way they had devised to circumvent the air restrictor.

When an engine is started, if it backfires it can blow out the diaphragm which controls the fuel mixture, so *Bentford* had put a valve in the oil gallery so that when the oil pressure was low it was open and thus allowed the pressure of a backfire to escape and not blow out the diaphragm. When oil pressure went up the valve closed and sealed the oil gallery. Thus much was perfectly legal, but what *Bentford* had done was to reverse the oil gallery so it was closed when oil pressure was low, which meant it could be presented to scrutineering and pass the vacuum suction test on the air restrictor because, when the engine wasn't running, there was zero oil pressure and hence the valve stayed closed. When the engine was running the valve opened and allowed extra air into the carburettors, which gave a hefty boost in power.

By the time the engine was examined, the oil gallery had been reversed and the RAC upheld *Bentford*'s appeal even though it had been demonstrated at Brands Hatch that the engine would run with the air restrictor blocked off. March's response was to switch to Novamotor's engines, and, as it happens, Brian did not need assistance, since apart from his one, unwelcome, dodgy win he took 16 other victories and both the British Championships.

It had been a mixed year, the F1 team was a make-weight struggling along on an inadequate budget, yet in the junior formulae March was supreme. It was the old problem of F1 versus production cars and this time the answer seemed clear cut since there was no sponsor on the horizon for the following year, for the Oil Crisis had seen cut-backs on all sides, so Robin and Max announced their retirement from Formula One.

Behind the decision was more than just a missing sponsor; the Oil Crisis was threatening the production car side because sponsors were cutting back all over and a large number of races were cancelled. By the end of 1974 March was profitable and almost self-sufficient on the production side and had it not been so the position would have been easier; if you're an assembly shop employing race mechanics in the winter build season you simply don't hire as many extra hands and you don't order so many bodies or whatever from a sub-contractor and, besides, poor showings in F1 weren't doing the company's image much good and the production side was anyway subsidizing the F1 team.

Meanwhile Max was able to announce that March cars and spares would be cheaper for 1975, partly because of the withdrawal from F1, partly because March was almost self-sufficient on production. Not many people saw much reduction, but it was a breezy thing to say in the November of a year of economic crisis when people were thinking what to buy for the following year. Further, March offered customers an insurance package through John Heynes, a Lloyds underwriter – you pranged your car, you took it back to the factory and two days later you collected it and didn't have to take a bag of gold with you. It was the standing joke that John was the major sponsor of the works cars (there was a record number of shunts in 1974), but apart from his business involvement he also helped out a number of drivers, including Nigel Mansell.

March had had a radical re-think vis-à-vis the customer and there would be no repeat of the sort of treatment to which Bob Harper had taken exception. The withdrawal from F1 also induced customer confidence and, hand on heart, everything said at the time was true at the time, but Robin and Max being the sort of people they are, if the door leading to F1 opened only a couple of inches, they'd be through it like a shot. Both had too much pride not to do so. Until the works had won a Grand Prix March was still somehow a failure, and it probably went back to that lingering saunter up the pit lane at Kyalami at the first race, when they'd been so pleased with themselves. There was still an account to settle, with themselves.

12 Ins and Outs

March's retirement was shorter than one of Frank Sinatra's, but it concentrated the minds of some who held purse strings, and a few weeks later Robin and Max were able to say they had changed their minds and would be entering a single car for Vittorio Brambilla. This late decision meant that, unlike its usual practice, March began the year with new customer cars and its old 741s.

Early in the year the magazine *Motor* published an interesting road test since it had been able to attach its 'fifth wheel' performance recorder to the back of a 741 (a Mosley stunt) and for the first time was able to put F1 performance into perspective. It recorded a 0–60 mph time of three seconds dead and 0–100 mph in 6.3 seconds. In 1974 even a Ferrari Daytona could go 0–60 mph in only 5.3 seconds so the armchair racer was duly impressed.

Overall, the F1/2 cars looked much the same as they had in 1974, although the front bodywork was no longer flat from the nose cone to the cockpit but raked sharply up towards the driver, but the chief difference was a wider monocoque. New rules called for crushable side structures for F2 and it was decided to incorporate these into the tub rather than hanging them on the outside, but despite other detail changes such as redesigned bulkheads the structure was essentially the same as the 1971 cars, while F3 and Atlantic models retained the original-style narrow monocoque.

With the wider (and stiffer) tub went a narrower track, longer wheelbase and a slightly different weight bias. The result was a car which was an improvement over the '74 models in F1 form but not quite as good in Formula Two. March's priorities, however, were shown by the fact that the customer cars were built first and the 751 did not appear until the South African GP.

In the meantime there was the feeding of the involvement in Japan. Through his Le Mans Company, Tom Hanawa invited Peter Gethin and Brian Henton to run in F2 Marches at Fuji. Brian says, "March made the nicest F2 cars you could buy and the 742 was an absolute classic. I'd done most of the testing on the 752 and knew it was a dog by comparison, and at Fuji there would be a 752 and a 742, but Peter had the choice since he was the star who'd won a Grand Prix and I was just the coming man. On the trip out to Japan Peter casually asked me about the new car, 'Oh it's wonderful, it's the business, the best car March has ever made, a real step forward, blah, blah, blah.' We arrived at Fuji and Peter said, 'I'm sorry, Brian, but I have the choice and I've decided to use the 752.'

"I swallowed my bitter disappointment, took the 742 with good grace, and was over a second a lap faster. I won the race easily and was headlines in Japan. I had the whole thing, 'Future World Champion,' you name it, but I was no better a driver than Geth, it was simply that the 742 worked and the 752 didn't."

Vittorio Brambilla alone began the F1 season with a strong 12th place on the grid in the Argentine and it was not lost on the men at March that he shared the sixth row with Ronnie Peterson, who was easily the quickest of the two Lotus drivers. Lotus had reverted to running 72s before the end of the '74 season and it had been a lost cause then, but in 1975 it was an embarrassment mainly because it couldn't make the new generation of Goodyears work, while they suited the Marches perfectly. As Lotus slid down the grid, Ronnie's F1 career went with it and rumours were rife that he was about to switch to Shadow, where Alan Rees was team manager. Robin and Max looked on enviously as Shadow courted him, but there was nothing they could do, they had neither the car nor the money to offer as a dowry. In the end Ronnie stayed with Lotus, but the scenario would be played out again the following year.

Brambilla, who, at 37, was the oldest man on the grid, scored an unexciting ninth place in the Argentine and retired in Brazil. When he arrived in South Africa he had both his new 751 and a new team-mate, Lella Lombardi, the first woman to appear in a WC event since 1958. She had surprised many when she came fifth in the '74 European F5000 series and she became the protégé of Count Googhie Zanon, an Italian aristocrat who had quietly assisted a number of drivers, and he had arranged for her to join March.

At Kyalami Brambilla put his new car in seventh slot on the grid, the best March qualifying position since South Africa the previous year, but he lost his oil cooler in the race and retired. Lombardi qualified last, slower even than some local drivers in their second-hand cars, and the back of the grid was to be where she would to be found throughout the season. Max says, "I don't take the view that a woman will never win a GP, but Lella just did not have what it takes." As we will see there were some mitigating circumstances.

Lombardi had a couple of lacklustre outings in the Race of Champions and the International Trophy but when the European GP season got under way Brambilla soon demonstrated that both he and the new March were better than anyone had guessed as he put it in fifth place on the grid in Spain behind the Ferraris of Lauda and Regazzoni, Hunt's Hesketh and Andretti's Parnelli and he was to prove time and again that season that it was no flash in the pan.

The Spanish GP very nearly did not take place, for the organizers at Barcelona had prepared a circuit which was lethal and the armco barriers were in a disgraceful state, with missing bolts and washers, loose posts etc. It was indefensible and the members of the Grand Prix Drivers' Association flatly refused to drive. Consternation! Soon everyone was at each other's throats, drivers, the organizing club, team owners and officials from the FIA. The central issue was beyond debate, the circuit was downright dangerous, but it sparked off a row which had been brewing for some time.

Formula One had become more professional since the advent of sponsors, more money was involved and the circus itself was more conscious of the need to put on a show. The sport's governing body, a cosy little club, had failed to keep touch with the times, the Grand Prix Drivers' Association had become more powerful, while team owners who now had considerable investments, and sponsors, to keep happy, had organized themselves into the F1 Constructors' Association. While the constructors' association was very powerful behind the scenes (it had already established the principle of selling organizers a complete field for an agreed fee) it was still slightly less influential than the GPDA. In other words all of the constituent elements of Formula One were out of step with each other and, if you like, the employers were facing a vocal employees' union. Just as the Spanish GP of 1970 had seen Max appalled at the amateur way in which business was conducted, so the Spanish GP of 1975 was the turning point which was to see the Mosley and Ecclestone partnership begin its long and painful passage to bring stability to the sport.

Eventually the race got under way but at the first corner Andretti was nudged from behind, ran into Lauda and started a chain reaction which eliminated the Ferrari and Depailler's Tyrrell, then Arturo Merzario and Wilson Fittipaldi both retired in protest at the race being held. Sheckter's engine blew up and the oil it left on the circuit did for others. Then a wing strut failed on Stommelen's Lola as he breasted the brow of a hill and that threw his car into a barrier and flying wreckage killed three officials and a photographer.

The race was stopped and since it was at one-third distance, half points were awarded. Thus Jochen Mass (McLaren) scored his only GP win, while Brambilla and Lombardi, who had kept out of harm's way, came home fifth and sixth and Lella became the first woman to score in the World Championship, admittedly only half a point, but it is still the only top six finish by a woman.

At the next race, Monaco, she found her true level and did not qualify, while Vittorio again started fifth on the grid and was up to third on the first lap when Tom Pryce and he touched and his steering was bent, causing his retirement a few laps later. His progress continued in Belgium, where he qualified third and led briefly, but to do so he was harder on his brakes than they liked and they gave up the ghost. For economy's sake March had F2-spec brakes, which were adequate in most conditions, but which couldn't cope with really hard work.

But Brambilla had led the race and March was suddenly a force in F1 again, but good as he was, and he was digging a big hole into which to bury his reputation as a rock ape, Robin and Max knew that if Ronnie had been in their car they would have already have gained that elusive first works win. Then in Sweden Vittorio took pole, the first time a March had headed a grid since 1970. Nobody could believe their eyes when the computer print-out

Vittorio Brambilla in practice for the 1975 Spanish Grand Prix at Montjuich Park. In a troubled race, stopped short after Stommelen's crash, Brambilla finished fifth, with Lombardi in sixth place. **(Nigel Snowdon)**

***Vittorio Brambilla and Lella Lombardi discuss their March problems at the Belgian Grand Prix at Zolder.* (Nigel Snowdon)**

showed he had lapped in 1m 24.63s when no-one else had even looked like breaking the 1m 25s barrier and some blamed the Texaco 'hospitality unit's generator for upsetting the computer. Next day, on a much slower track, Brambilla did just a few laps and was again much quicker than anyone else and, for good measure, he gave Lombardi's car a whirl. Then he and Robin stood conspicuously at a hairpin goading the other drivers as they tried to approach his time. Nobody could understand it yet none was convinced by the bland assertion, "We were lucky enough to get nine of the ten variables right."

Everyone had a theory about the car's new found speed; they could point to the narrow track and relative stiffness of the springing (some muttered that the 751 was a glorified kart) and to the fact March was using wider rimmed rear wheels. Any team could have done the same, but since none did it appears that engineers were not convinced. All in all it has remained a mystery.

Robin, however, can solve the puzzle, "The organizers were timing the cars with a light beam, and when one saw this, it occurred to one that if one could station one's pits by the start line it opened up all kinds of possibilities for lateral thought. I was given the very important job of holding out the pit board and the trick was to swing the board in front of the timing beam when one of our cars was about fifty yards away! That's how March achieved one of its greatest moments of glory."

No matter how he got on to pole, Vittorio actually led for the first few laps and seemed in command of the situation, but then he had to pit to replace an overheated front tyre and later went out with a broken drive-shaft.

While March was making enormous progress in F1, legitimately and otherwise, in F2 it had an upset awaiting it. The works fielded Michel Leclère and Patrick Tambay and were supported by the sheer weight of numbers from customers, for 25 cars had been built, although some went to Japan. Nobody would have bet serious money against another Bicester steamroller, for March had not been headed in the F2 Championship since late 1972 and, further, two of its main competitors were out, Surtees to concentrate on F1, while GRD had folded, and there was only token representation from Alpine and Chevron. Everything looked set for another season of March glory, but things didn't work out like that.

Brian Henton had already discovered that the 752 lacked the subtle harmony of the 742, but he had seen the best of it, for when it came to the European season, things had changed for the worse. Goodyear was the only F2 tyre supplier in 1975 and at the start of the season decided to supply only 25-inch diameter rears, whereas all March's winter testing had been on 23-inch diameter rubber. Further, most of the testing had been done with a Ford BDA engine, for it was cheaper to run but it was 45 lb lighter than the BMW unit, and since the new wide monocoque cars had their weight biased more towards the centre of the car, and the tub was heavier to start with, this all combined to produce a car with unsatisfactory weight distribution and rear suspension geometry which produced both understeer and oversteer on tight circuits, something which Tambay and Leclère were unable to dial out.

Later it was also discovered that the engine installation itself was not rigid enough, which did not affect the F1 cars for their V8 Cosworths provided inherent rigidity, something which was lacking on a semi-stressed straight-four BMW unit. Then the Paul Rosche engines were initially fitted with tappet shims which were too soft and this led to a spate of valve spring breakages.

All this might have been weathered except that as well as backing the works March team Elf Petroleum had also shrewdly invested in Jacques Laffite and Tico Martini. During the winter Martini, with considerable input from Laffite, built his first F2 car, there was just the one, but it was made without compromises. Throughout March's history it has had to consider two things: the selling price and the customer. Price becomes less important if a car is winning, but if, say, needle roller bearings in the front hubs would be an improvement, any production car maker has to consider that they need to be taken out after practice, cleaned and then repacked, and that might be beyond a customer running with one mechanic.

One car made without compromise was enough as Laffite won five out of the first six races and wrapped up the Championship by mid-season. Later in the year he was to suffer engine failures, for Josef Schnitzer had committed himself to more work than he could handle, but when the Martini failed, quite often the two Alpines of Larrousse and Jabouille, and only two were made that year, were on hand to cause further aggravation to the March contingent. March still ended the year with five Championship wins, and second and third in the series, but since it dominated the field by weight of numbers, and the works team did have favourable treatment from BMW on engines, it was not a cue for dancing in the streets of Bicester.

1975 was the year that March got its sports car right and the 75S had new bodywork which had been developed

At Thruxton in March 1975 Ronnie Peterson drove a brand new 752 entered by Ron Dennis's Project 3. After spinning, he climbed back through the field, but was eliminated in a seven-car accident. (**Nigel Snowdon**)

Brian Henton was one of four drivers with a works March 752 at Thruxton. Henton finished second in the first heat, but started the second heat with odd-width rear wheels and after a pit stop he dropped to the tail of the field. (**Nigel Snowdon**)

Brian Henton was a driver for whom Robin Herd had very high regard. (**Nigel Snowdon**)

in the MIRA wind tunnel, but it came too late, since Alpine-Renault had destroyed the European 2-litre Sports Car Championship by its dominance, so the cars had to run in a junior class in the World Championship of Makes, which not many people took seriously. Just how good a car the 75S was can be gauged by the fact that versions were still winning races in Japan eight years later and, incredibly, scored points in the Group C Championship in 1982 and 1983, which must be a record for any post-war sports-racer.

In the main British F3 Championship all was well, however, as Gunnar Nilsson and Alex Ribeiro did most of the winning in their works 753s, which kept the narrow 713-style tub, beefed up at the back with a cast rear beam instead of a fabricated one. Robin says, "It was a very tight finish to the season and while Gunnar came to the last race with a handy lead, in theory Alex could still take the title if he won and Gunnar did not finish. Everything depended on the last lap of the last race at Silverstone and as they disappeared out of sight we knew only one of them was going to come round and I guessed it would be Gunnar. He was a lovely guy, but he was a manipulator, a lovable manipulator, and sure enough he had Alex off into a bank."

Nilsson and Ribeiro finished first and second in the BP series with Danny Sullivan third in his Modus with equal points to Alex. Late in the season Gunnar managed to get a drive in a Formula Atlantic Chevron and promptly won five races on the trot so was reckoned to be the coming man in racing. Both he and Alex were pencilled in for the '76 March F2 team, but, a straw in the wind, in fifth place in the BP F3 series was Larry Perkins in a new make, a Ralt.

One thing which was odd given March's domination

At Thruxton Patrick Tambay drove an Elf-sponsored works March and finished second overall to Arnoux (Martini), the dominant combination in 1975. (**Nigel Snowdon**)

The Formula Three race at Thruxton in March 1975 was won by Gunnar Nilsson with the works March 753 and Nilsson went on to win that year's BP Super Visco British Formula Three Championship. (**Nigel Snowdon**)

of Formula Atlantic the previous two years was the reluctance of drivers to buy the 75B; only three did so in Britain and none figured strongly. It was perhaps one of those cases, which happens more often than most people believe, when a rumour goes the rounds that such and such is the car to have. In any case Formula Atlantic was riven by politics and although it limped on for a few more years in Britain, in 1975 it more or less self-destructed.

Another anomaly, given the poor results March had previously achieved in F5000, was the sight of a one-off car winning races. John Macdonald's RAM Racing had begun the season with a Chevron and a number of drivers, none of whom delivered results. Then it bought a March 75A (a 751 by any other name) powered by a 3.4-litre Cosworth-Ford GAA V6 engine and took on Alan Jones. In his début race, at Thruxton, Jones led until encountering problems which saw him finish third. Then he won at Brands Hatch and Silverstone and really put the cat among the pigeons. In the final races of the year Jones and the March were the class of the field, while the engine ran properly, but too

Swedish driver Nilsson, later a member of the Lotus Formula One team, after his win at Thruxton. (**Nigel Snowdon**)

often it did not and Jones eventually finished seventh in a championship dominated by Lola.

One would have thought that this would have led to a spate of orders for the car, but in 1976 only two were built. The economic upheaval which followed the 1974 Oil Crisis and the huge increase in the price of crude imposed by OPEC was having its effect. F5000 began to die on its feet, for few could afford to run in so expensive a junior formula and all around motor racing was having to tighten its belt. One result of this was that there were fewer British drivers coming up through the ranks, they were already a rarity in F2 and it's significant that the top six finishers in the British F3 Championship were a Swede, two Brazilians, an American, an Australian and a Belgian.

The key to this shift was the economic upheaval which followed the 1974 Oil Crisis. No sport is more sensitive to outside influences than motor racing, soccer, rugby and cricket all continued after a fashion during WW2, for example, but motor sport stopped completely. Every time there is a fuel crisis, motor racing is hit, since it appears to be a profligate user, yet as much fuel is used getting nags and punters to a horse race meeting as a similar number of cars and spectators to a motor racing meeting. It's unfair, but it's the political reality.

In 1975, the problem was not only that money for sponsorship was scarce in Britain but British tax laws militated against it, while it made sense for drivers who came from countries with a soft currency and monetary restrictions to race in Britain. There were loopholes which involved the exportation of money for sponsorship and its conversion from a soft to a hard currency and such were dodges which were not open to British drivers (details sent under plain sealed cover for Krugerrands).

That's why British drivers faded from the scene and motoring magazines received sackfuls of 'Why doesn't...' letters from angry and puzzled fans who hadn't worked out why Galapagos Laundrettes thought it worth sponsoring no-hopers. The French had Elf, Germany had BMW, and many others had weak currencies, so while March would have liked to have had Brian Henton in the F1 team, he couldn't afford it because he was racing on his own money. Thus March ran Brambilla, who had an enthusiastic company paying his way, and Lombardi, who had a patron backing her career because he happened to like motor racing.

Meanwhile Brambilla's steady rise up the order had received a bit of a set-back as development flagged. Robin: "We were doing quite a lot of testing with Brambilla and Henton and we were making a lot of headway although the main business was going through a sticky patch. Then Max came bounding up with a grin, 'Guess what? I've sold the team spare to Stuck!' We desperately needed the money, but it set us back a lot."

By the time of the British GP there were four Marches in the field, the works cars, Stuck's, and an entry from Penske Racing for the American Mark Donohue. Roger Penske, a former driver of some ability and a first-rate businessman, had cleaned up in American racing by applying intelligence to the problem when most teams' thinking came through their drivers' backsides. In 1975 Penske commissioned an F1 car from Geoff Ferris, but when the problem of adapting to a new style of racing while developing a new car became acute, he bought a 751, which immediately proved quicker in testing. It would be pleasant to record that Penske chose to buy a March because it was clearly the class of the field, but it was a case of it being the best car a manufacturer would sell him.

Silverstone that year was the scene of carnage in a dry/wet/dry/very wet race which saw teams having to employ the then rarely used technique of tyre changes, and

One of the better March successes in 1975 was the Ford V6-powered 75A Formula 5000 car entered by RAM for Alan Jones. Here Jones is seen at Brands Hatch on August Bank Holiday Monday where he won the Formula 5000 race from Tony Brise's Lola-Chevrolet. **(Nigel Snowdon)**

Work on Brambilla's 751 in front of the pits at the 1975 British Grand Prix at Silverstone. (**Nigel Snowdon**)

Messrs Mosley and Herd in earnest conversation at Silverstone. (**Nigel Snowdon**)

very slow they were by today's standards. The weather caused no fewer than 16 drivers to crash in a mass demonstration of aquaplaning, but one man who kept his head all weekend was Brambilla.

Vittorio had a new front suspension layout with a narrower track and on the first day of practice he simply flew to record second fastest time, and even although he eventually started from 'only' fifth place on the grid he was within 0.27s of pole and that without the help of an errant pit board waved in front of a timing beam. Car and driver were going better than anyone could have expected given their budget and in the race Brambilla drove sensibly, while all around him drivers who were not rock apes slithered into the chicken wire.

Eventually the race was abandoned and Vittorio was judged to have finished sixth, while the winner, Emerson Fittipaldi, was actually in the pits having another tyre change when the race was stopped. The RAC had decided to award the race on the positions which had prevailed on the previous lap, when the bulk of the field was still on the track, but many thought the race should have gone to Carlos Pace (Brabham), who was not in the pits when the race was stopped, and that line of thought would have given Brambilla fifth, although had he known the race was about to be stopped Fittipaldi would not have thrown away his lead with a tyre stop.

Max protested vigorously, "I forget the details of the argument, but it seemed plausible to me at the time," and Ferrari protested as well, but the RAC stuck to its guns.

Brambilla has received a bad press over the years, his early reputation was justified but he deserved credit for having matured. On this occasion, as so often in 1975, he had driven immaculately, but he has rarely been given credit for it.

Mark Donohue brought his 751 home fifth, the team's best result of the year, but since it was a 'Penske', March was not credited with the points it might have added to its little score in the Constructors' Championship. There was no addition to the score at the Nürburgring, either, where the best March finish was Lombardi, who plodded around to take seventh, having qualified bog last and 16 seconds adrift of the second last driver.

The Austrian GP brought both sadness and triumph, sadness because in the untimed practice session on race morning Donohue crashed after a tyre burst. Two marshals were killed and Donohue received injuries from which he died two days later. A gentle man and a gentleman, and a very intelligent driver, Mark's accident cast a pall over the meeting and years later caused a flutter in racing when his widow successfully sued Goodyear.

The race itself began in heavy rain, but there was the possibility of a change for the better. With Vittorio eighth on the grid, Max decided to go for broke and had his car given full wet settings, while most teams more cautiously opted for intermediate settings. As it happened, conditions went from bad to worse and Brambilla found his car handling perfectly, and he drove with the same determination and sensitive car control he had demonstrated in the wet at Silverstone, So he stayed on the road and gradually hauled himself up the leader board. Eventually he dived past Hunt's Hesketh and into the lead then, with a clear road in front of him, he pulled out two seconds a lap.

It seemed almost too good to be true and March desperately needed Championship points to qualify for the special deals and discounts offered by F1CA. Max recalls, "Denny Hulme was the adviser to the Clerk of the Course and there was some discussion whether the race should be stopped. He said to me, 'Do you want to quit while you're ahead?' I certainly did, we needed the points and who knows what might have happened if the race had gone full distance?"

Just before half distance Brambilla passed the start/finish line to see the chequered flag held out, he had won his and the works March team's first Grand Prix! Vittorio raised both arms in salute, braked, and crashed; still he continued on his victory lap with his arm raised and his nose cone hanging off. As the weather started to ease some teams wheeled out their cars for a restart, but Max, rule book in hand, pointed out that since the chequered flag had not been shown with a black flag, the race was over and it could not be restarted.

At the time it was a popular win, because it catches the imagination when a man aged 37 in only his second year of F1 takes a victory, it gives hope to everybody, but over the years some wiseacres have claimed that the reason Vittorio crashed was because he was running an illegal car (what was illegal about it they do not say) and the crash was

Mark Donohue with the Penske-entered March 751 at the German Grand Prix at the Nürburgring. He was eliminated on the second lap by a puncture. **(Nigel Snowdon)**

The very able Mark Donohue who sadly suffered fatal injuries at the Austrian Grand Prix as the result of a tyre failure during untimed practice. **(Nigel Snowdon)**

engineered to disguise the fact. Brambilla's win, though, was kosher and it fitted the pattern of his other drives in atrocious conditions, while his crashing a few hundred yards past the flag showed that medical science still had not cured his red mists. Robin says, "I've heard the rumours that we were cheating, but we were too poor to make anything trick."

In fact the crashing ploy has been used but it was in 1981, when the organizers of a race, suspecting that teams were running lightweight cars in qualifying, declared that every car would be weighed as it came into the pits and any car abandoned on the circuit would be impounded and escorted back to the weighing machine. One team running a lightweight car had just gained pole position when the driver's brakes 'failed' and the car was impounded by marshals determined to escort it back to the weighing machine. Some mechanics arrived, chatted to the marshals, decided that all that was wrong was that the brakes needed bleeding and, with permission, set about to do it.

Off came the front and rear bodywork, a junior mechanic pumped the brake pedal while fluid was poured in and he kept on pumping even when nothing but air was going through the system. At this the crew chief threw a wobbly of such violence that the young mechanic burst into tears even though the whole scenario had been planned. The marshals and the rest of the crew were split between comforting the youngster and calling the crew chief a bastard, all that is except the mechanic disappearing over the horizon with the engine cover.

Vittorio Brambilla in practice for the Austrian Grand Prix. This race, shortened by heavy rain, was won by Brambilla and this was the first World Championship race victory by a works March entry. **(Nigel Snowdon)**

By the time the car was presented at the weighing machine its engine cover had been replaced by the one with the lead ballast. On that occasion it was one of the big money teams, one which could afford to build a lightweight car just for qualifying, and normally the switch of engine covers didn't require a drama. In 1975 March had barely enough money to make the start for each race let alone build trick cars.

It's a shame that some have tried to belittle March's first works F1 win because it took six years of hard graft to achieve and it had been done on a fraction of most team's budgets and with a driver who, good as he was, was not quite of the top drawer. Moreover, it meant that March single-seaters won races in every major category: F1, F2, F3, F5000 and Formula Atlantic and, for good measure, four rounds of the European Hill Climb Championship. March's real achievement that year was not its win in the Austrian GP but, as in so many other years, its ability to deliver race winning cars to the customer, on time and at a reasonable price. Robin Herd may have reservations about whether he was right to go with March rather than Rindt, but had he not done so motor racing history would have been fundamentally different.

Another point to remember is that even during the lean years in F1, 1972–5, even when it produced a disaster like the 721X, March had the resilience to dig itself out of the mire, and while its F1 cars were not world beaters they were not the utter failures that were the Lotus 76, the various Tecnos, the Maki, the Hill Lolas, the Penske PC1, the Amon-Dalton, the Fittipaldis, and all the other no-hopers which appeared and disappeared.

None of the remaining rounds of the World Championship produced much of note and, as was so often the case, the cars suffered from unreliability, largely due to the fact that money was tight, but Brambilla's glorious drive in Austria made up for so many of the other disappointments and proved that Robin and Max were right to give F1 another go. The next few months were to reinforce the decision because March had proven itself, and when Ronnie Peterson was ripe for courting again, it could point to a race-winning car.

13 Return of the Crown Prince

At the start of 1975, the big story had been Ronnie's possible defection from Lotus to Shadow. The start of 1976 saw him again ready to leave and it was not simply a case of disenchantment with an obsolete car which had given him only one fourth and two fifths in the season, there was a deeper discontent. Ronnie could get into a car and wring the last ounce from it, but he was never any good at analysing a car or making a team work for him as Stewart or Lauda could do; he needed empathy with a team which could interpret his feed-back and set the car up for him. He wasn't getting that at Lotus, he and Chapman never gelled as a partnership, yet when Lotus could give him a race-winning car, he could win in it and out-drive anyone else with the same car, as Fittipaldi had discovered. It was the relationship, rather than the car, which had made Shadow attractive, for he had remained very close to Alan Rees.

Also among those who were close to Ronnie was Googhie Zanon and he was disturbed by seeing one of the most exquisite talents ever seen in racing languishing with a team which seemed to have run out of ideas.

The crunch came during practice in Brazil. Chapman had produced the Lotus 77, which had as its thrust the idea that the dimensions could be changed to suit any circuit. It was one of those ideas which *sounds* sensible but is actually a sign of desperation. Ronnie crashed the car for all seasons when the water temperature sensor came undone and water splashed on to one of the rear tyres at a critical moment. Before the cause was discovered the driver blamed the car and the designer blamed the driver and relations between them hit a new low. Ronnie was ripe for courting.

Robin remembers, "Ronnie's car was off the pace while the 761 was going well, Chapman was rubbishing him, the relationship had gone sour and he wanted to join us. Googhie Zanon had given us £50,000 to run Lella and said that if we wanted to replace her by Ronnie we could use the money for him and he'd find her another drive.

"There was great politicking going on and we were trying to keep this away from Chapman. I was in Ronnie's hotel bedroom talking to him and we were discussing how we were going to dominate the world on our £50,000 and there was this knock at the door; it was Chapman. There were two single beds in the room and I dived between one and the wall so that it finished up with Ronnie sitting on one bed, Chapman on the other, and me on the floor just behind Chapman. There was Colin telling Ronnie that we were a load of thieving bastards who didn't have any money, and Lotus was going to be doing this, that and the other. He went on for an hour outlining all his plans with me dying for a leak but hanging on every word. I often wonder what would have happened if I'd got up and gone to the bathroom; a good talker, Chapman, very convincing."

He was obviously not quite convincing enough because at the next race, South Africa, Ronnie was back home. March had intended to run Gunnar Nilsson in F2, but a deal was thrashed out with Lotus and Gunnar took Ronnie's seat and filled it admirably. Robin: "Gunnar was always around during '75, we began to think he'd been cloned. You would open a door and there was one of the Gunnar Nilssons. He put a lot of effort into getting a drive, he was very professional, and we were ready to sign him when he got the Lotus drive, and suddenly he took all his clones away." As promised, Lella Lombardi was found a sports car drive which was better suited to her ability, although not all of her poor showings had been entirely her fault.

March fielded cars for Stuck, Brambilla and Peterson, which was as strong a driver line-up as any team had, and the 761s, some of which were up-rated 751s, were chiefly distinguished by having wider track and a wheelbase of 109 inches achieved by using a spacer between the engine and gearbox. The tubs were stiffer but remained in principle as they had been since 1971, the footwell was wider and strengthened, the rear anti-roll bar was re-sited, the oil radiator was incorporated into the left hand water cooler and 41lb had been lost. The weight shedding was essential because over the years the F2-based cars had grown heavier as components were strengthened the cheap way – they were bigger and heavier.

During the season there would be a choice of nose cones but the base line remained money. Even taking inflation into account, that £50,000 would barely pay for a top-line F3 drive at the time of writing and in 1988 March Racing's budget for its motor home was more than £50,000.

Brambilla and Stuck had run strongly in Brazil, with Vittorio battling for a fourth position, which might have become second, when he had to retire with an oil leak, but Hans came through from a mediocre grid position to finish fourth. With Ronnie back in the team for South Africa, better things were expected, especially when Brambilla recorded fifth fastest time on the first day of pre-race testing. Ronnie was due out next day, so great things were expected, pole was in sight! Then he went out and was slower than Vittorio.

In official practice he was still slower and Vittorio was fired up by the fact that he was now the ace of the team, and this led to a return of the old fiery Brambilla. In the early laps of the race he held second place using a rough-hewn driving style to keep others at bay until, under pressure from Jochen Mass' McLaren, he flattened his tyres under heavy braking. Peterson's debut was not the dream come-back everyone had hoped for, but he was running a strong fifth when Patrick Depailler spun his Tyrrell and collected the March.

Robin Herd working on Flammini's Formula Two car. This photograph was taken at Enna in Sicily in July 1976 when Flammini was eliminated by an accident. (**Jutta Fausel**)

One significant thing which happened at Kyalami was that the GPDA was absorbed into the F1 Constructors' Association and from then on F1CA became the most important force in racing. It later changed its name to FOCA because F1CA could be confused with something rude in Italian, but from then on GP racing became increasingly controlled by Bernie Ecclestone and Max Mosley though it was ironic that Max was so powerful behind the scenes while running one of the poorest teams in F1.

By the time the circus arrived at Long Beach March was represented by four cars since Arturo Merzario was entered by his own Ovoro Team, but his car was actually prepared by March Engines Ltd, which ran the 'B' team. Robin looked after the 'A' team with Dave White and this was known as the 'Over 30s' since Vittorio and Lella were two of the more mature drivers in F1. Max, assisted by Peter Hass, ran the 'B' team, which was known as the 'Under 23s', but since Stuck was 25 and Merzario was 32, he was asked how he reached 'Under 23s'. "We're stretching the point with Hans and, as for Arturo, we're talking about his mental age."

As an engine preparation business, March Engines can hardly be counted a success since it had the worst finishing record of any in 1976. In fact the March Engineering 'A' team had a 37.5 per cent rate and the March Engines 'B' team, a 33.3 per cent rate, which is feeble when compared to other Cosworth users such as Fittipaldi (53.3%), Ensign (50%), McLaren (71.8%), Shadow (75%), Surtees (73%) and Tyrrell (68.75%). Only Lotus (40%) came close to March's abysmal record, although it has to be said that March's score was depressed by the return of Brambilla's red mists.

Merzario was trying to resurrect his F1 career, which had begun with Ferrari and which had been on a steady slide thereafter, but he did not do much for his reputation by failing to qualify at Long Beach. The cars entered for Stuck and Peterson looked unfamiliar since both were white and covered with Chinese ideograms. Max had done a deal with Teddy Yip for the race and throughout 1976 the cars were to change liveries as race-by-race deals were struck.

At Long Beach Ronnie showed some return to form when he put his car sixth on the grid and was battling for fourth when his brake fluid boiled. Brakes were to be a problem throughout the year, a legacy of March's poverty, and Brambilla, wound up by having an ace in the team, was displaying none of the finesse he'd shown in 1975, just as he'd thrown away his chances at Kyalami by being impulsive, so he managed to end his race on the first lap by putting himself and Carlos Reutemann into the wall. Two laps later Stuck followed him into the wall after he rammed Emerson Fittipaldi. The red mist was contagious.

When Brambilla did not have to square himself against Peterson he drove sensibly and in a singleton entry took fourth in the Race of Champions and followed that with a strong second to Hunt's McLaren in the International Trophy. Since he also qualified second and set second fastest lap in the race, which had a good but not top-grade entry, there was no fluke involved, but being alongside Ronnie seemed to wipe his brain clean.

While the F1 team was looking promising, if flawed, the rest of the March operation was like the curate's egg. New rules in F2 allowed the use of bespoke racing engines and Renault prepared a version of its iron-block V6 sports car engine, which was to form the basis of its F1 turbo unit. March had the chance to use this and, indeed, tested extensively with it during the winter. Robin says, "Paul Rosche is one of my very best friends and he came to stay with us over Christmas, and when he left I said, 'See you next year,' and he said, 'Yes, with your Renault engines.'

"What decided us to stick with BMW was loyalty to Paul and that has been repaid handsomely over the years. I happen to believe in loyalty as a principle of life, but I've found in passing it makes sound business sense as well. The

Renault engine went very well in our car, but it was largely because it was a V6, which allowed a much better installation with increased rigidity." All the junior formulae cars also featured a new rear suspension set-up with lower wishbones replacing the former parallel arms.

Rosche responded by teasing more power from the unit by shortening the injection trumpets and modifying the inlet ports and exhaust system, but apart from the Renault engine, BMW also faced the all-alloy Hart 420R, which began life as a Ford BDA (née Cosworth FVA) and developed into a separate entity. There were, too, engines from Lancia (based on the Ferrari V6 Dino unit), Abarth, Chrysler, and Chevrolet (based on the Cosworth version of the Vega engine), but only the Hart was to stay the distance and was to be a cheeky interloper in the BMW/Renault battle in 1976. The Hart unit received its biggest boost when Ferrari, which supplied the Lancia short engine, pulled the plug on supplies and told its co-Fiatist to stick to rallying. In typical Ferrari fashion, that decision came when the motor bombed on its first appearance in Ron Dennis' Project Four Marches, which failed to qualify for the opening round at Hockenheim. Dennis then turned to Hart and the little firm was on its way.

Changes at the factory had made it become rather more businesslike in that almost everything was being made in-house and there was no more employing casual workers during the winter build season, everyone was on strength and there were about 100 employees, including the mechanics on the works racing teams. To put this into perspective, at the end of 1988 March's main rivals, Lola and Reynard, had 115 and 70 employees respectively.

March's F2 season began well with Stuck winning at Hockenheim, but, as a graded driver, he scored no points, and second-placed René Arnoux in a Martini-Renault headed the table at the start of a season in which F2 was to become known as 'Formula France'. The French stranglehold was not immediately apparent as the works 762s of Maurizio Flammini and Alex Ribeiro scored a 1–2 at Thruxton, but thereafter Renault-powered Alpines and Martinis did most of the winning, although Flammini was to win at Rouen, and Stuck won at Hockenheim (again) and Santamonica. In fact the results flatter the Renault cars because March scored a few own-goals, with cars sometimes retiring for silly reasons (throttle cable, starter motor, etc) and Flammini was inconsistent. On his day he could be superb, when the car and circuit were a good match, but sometimes his performances were mediocre and he was involved in more than his fair share of accidents. Despite early promise Flammini was never to make it to the top in racing, but is still involved with the organization of the Enna and Vallelunga F3000 races.

When the European GP season got under way at Jarama, Brambilla was well wound up and was easily the quickest of the four Marches. Starting in Spain, the 'A' team had shorter front wishbones, which gave a different roll centre, something for which the 'Under 23s' would have to wait. At the circuit the organizers had added pits of volcanic ash to stop errant cars and in practice Vittorio kindly proved that they worked very well. In the race itself

Ronnie Peterson and the 761 at Kyalami. Peterson was eliminated early in the race in a collision with Depailler (Tyrrell). **(Nigel Snowdon)**

In the Formula Two race at Thruxton in April Maurizio Flammini was the winner but, as can be seen from the way he hurls his March through the chicane, he was very hard on his car. Later in the year, the dominant marques in Formula Two became the Alpines and Martinis. (**Nigel Snowdon**)

he quickly slotted into third but was back down to fifth when he had another moment and finished up on a small mound with all four wheels off the ground and the engine revving to make your eyes water. When the back end of the car touched ground again he shot off once more, but deranged his rear suspension. All the other Marches retired with transmission problems.

All four Marches had the new front suspension and new air boxes for the Belgian GP at Zolder and the ebullient Brambilla was again the quickest of the quartet, qualifying fifth and running fifth on lap 4 until spinning to avoid someone else's accident and that probably weakened his drive-shaft, which snapped soon afterwards. Peterson who had qualified significantly slower, was running in mid-field just behind Reutemann's Brabham-Alfa Romeo when the Alfa engine suddenly tightened in the middle of a corner and Ronnie had no option but to take to the grass. The result was one badly damaged March and the revival of his career.

Robin: "In 1975 Vittorio and Lella had basically the same car, I engineered Vittorio, Max engineered Lella, but she was not happy. She would come in and say, in Italian, *Max, the car doesn't please me*. Max would put on his wise engineer's face, stroke his chin and say, 'Describe to me how the car is behaving.' She would say, 'You turn into the corner, and it understeers, and then when you put the

Ronnie Peterson in practice for the 1976 Spanish Grand Prix at Jarama with the 761. He retired in the race because of transmission problems. (**Nigel Snowdon**)

In 1976 Arturo Merzario ran a 761 under the mantle of the March 'B' team. He is seen in the Spanish race in which he retired because of transmission problems. (Nigel Snowdon)

Smiling Ronnie Peterson at the 1976 Belgian Grand Prix – but he had little to be happy about in the race; he crashed whilst avoiding Reutemann's Brabham. (Nigel Snowdon)

power on in the corner, it feels as if the back of the car falls over, and you get oversteer.'

"Max would stroke his chin and say, 'Lella how fast have you gone?' She'd say so and so. 'And how fast has Vittorio gone?' So and so, always faster, usually by about four seconds. Then Max would say, 'It's a funny characteristic of this car. We've found when when you drive it four seconds off the pace, you get this funny understeer going into the corner, and when you put in the power you get the back end falling down. If you drive it four seconds faster, you'll find the car is perfect. Vittorio, how's the car?' 'Perfetto, perfetto, Max.'

"Sometimes Vittorio would be asked to drive Lella's car, but he would only ever do two laps, never a timed lap. Max would say, 'How's the car Vittorio?' 'Perfetto, perfetto, Max.'

"Eventually Lella went on her way, we got Ronnie and went out testing in South Africa. Vittorio tested on the first day and he was third or fourth fastest and we thought 'Great, Ronnie's going to drive the next day, he'll be a full second faster, we'll be on pole by a huge distance.'

"Then Ronnie went out and was slower than Vittorio. We said, 'How's the car?' Ronnie said, 'It's got this strange characteristic, when you go into the corner it has understeer, and when you put on the power, the back end falls away and you get big oversteer.'

"We couldn't understand why Vittorio was normally quicker in the next races but at Zolder Ronnie's monocoque was destroyed so he had to have a new one – we couldn't afford a new car. Then we went to Monaco and there Ronnie, with his new monocoque, was third fastest in practice, led only by the Ferraris, and from that moment he never looked back. We eventually went through what had been Lella's tub and found it had a broken rear bulkhead, which was completely hidden. Presumably that was the cause of some of Lella's problems, so on that score we owe her a pretty big apology."

Peterson at Casino Square in the Monaco Grand Prix. His 761 was now fitted with a new monocoque and handled much better, but he spun on lap 27. (**Nigel Snowdon**)

From the moment Ronnie received his new tub, Vittorio was no longer the quickest March driver, but he still felt himself under pressure and had a lurid time in practice for Monaco, crashing quite heavily during the first practice session and spinning a lot in the second. In the race itself Ronnie immediately slotted in behind Lauda's Ferrari and stayed a secure second for the first third of the race until he spun on some oil at Tabac and crashed.

There was to be no repeat of pole position in the Swedish GP, for the cars didn't work on the twisting circuit, which had more 180-degree bends than any other, one reason being that the cars devoured their tyres on the tighter circuits, but a clue to where the 761's strengths lay came at the French GP at Paul Ricard, where Elf set up a speed trap on the Mistral Straight. Fastest of all were Peterson (182.56 mph) and Brambilla (179.43 mph) followed by Sheckter's six wheeled Tyrrell (179.28 mph), Lauda's Ferrari (178.46 mph) and Hunt's McLaren (178.19 mph).

So much for the strength; practice showed where the weaknesses were as the cars were unpredictable and were suffering endless engine troubles. Still Ronnie was a strong third when, three laps from the end, his fuel metering unit let go. There was not much to celebrate in the next two races either. None of the cars finished at Brands Hatch, although Peterson and Brambilla had a stirring scrap for fifth place, but, unfortunately, it was a little too stirring, because one of Vittorio's front wheels hit one of Ronnie's rears and he retired with a broken suspension pick-up point. Surprisingly, Merzario was the quickest of all the March drivers and in fact set third fastest lap in the race, nearly a second faster than Ronnie. In a remarkable drive he ran as high as fourth and looked set for even better things when first a wing endplate tore away and then one of his drive-shafts came loose at both ends and left the car.

Arturo's splendid performance came at an opportune moment because Jacky Ickx had had enough of

A fine view of Hans Stuck's March in the 1976 Swedish Grand Prix at Anderstorp. Here the Marches were off the pace and Stuck retired because of engine trouble. (**Nigel Snowdon**)

struggling with the Wolf-Williams FW05 (née Hesketh 308C) and Arturo was happy to take his place. This defection had a good effect on March, since preparing one fewer car made life easier, at least it would have done if Brambilla hadn't been so keen to redress the balance. Robin: "Brambilla destroyed a car at the 'Ring – actually he destroyed two and damaged a third, which even for us is a record. He had a big shunt on the Friday, we got the car back in one piece, then he had an even bigger one next day on a slowing-down lap and to this day we don't know how he managed that.

"During the race he didn't come round on the second lap and we thought, 'He's gone off again, accidents happen in threes.' Eventually he came sidling into the pits and said 'The brake pedal broke in half, it was a very close thing.' Now it was a standard F3 brake pedal, we couldn't afford special ones, so we thought, 'Jeepers, there are millions of these pedals all over the world!' The shit hits the fan and we ring up Dave Reeves at his home on the Sunday evening and tell him he's got to produce 250 new brake pedals and send them to the Argentine, Brazil, everywhere.

"Suddenly there's a production line of brake pedals and Rapid Movements are being driven mad flying them all over the world. We go to the next race, Austria, and since Vittorio had been dicing with Alan Jones at the time he crashed we say to Alan, 'We were really concerned because the brake pedal broke.' Alan just exploded with laughter, he literally fell on the ground with tears rolling down his face. When he recovered he said, 'Go and have another word with Vittorio and ask him to explain why there are four black lines from the braking point to the armco and how he managed to do that without a brake pedal.

"'What happened,' said Alan, 'was that we were having an out-braking match and he decided he was going to brake later than me. So I went absolutely to the limit and he went beyond it.' Vittorio had actually had his right foot hard on the pedal and it broke when he smashed into the barrier, which is not surprising. Of course by the time we spoke to Alan all the race reports had blamed us for the crash and so history has recorded another March cock-up."

The German GP itself saw Ronnie actually lead on the first lap, but he was then sold a dummy by James Hunt. At the start of the race parts of the circuit were wet, other parts were drying and most drivers started on wet rubber, but near the end of lap 1 Hunt realized he needed slicks and let Ronnie by into the lead. As they came up to the start/finish line Hunt dived into the pits, leaving Ronnie committed to another 14 miles with his tyres liable to go off.

Niki Lauda, way down the order, crashed on the second lap and the race was stopped when Ronnie was second to Mass's McLaren, which had started on slicks, thanks to inside information about conditions on the far side of the circuit. After the re-start he lost the car first time through the *Flugplatz*, so with Brambilla crashing on his second lap and Stuck not even completing one because he started with a broken clutch, the three Marches completed just three laps and even those didn't count since the race began afresh after Niki's accident.

It's now a matter of history how Lauda received the last rites, how he felt himself slipping off into unconsciousness and caused himself physical pain to keep himself awake until he felt that if he closed his eyes he would merely sleep, and how he was racing again six weeks later. What has not been recorded is that Ronnie was being negotiated into his seat by Googhie Zanon, who had quietly gone to Ferrari without telling March, although he would have paid a settlement, and Niki was later to admit privately that the thought of Ronnie taking his place was one of the main motivations in his recovery, not because he disliked him but because he knew only too well how fast he would be in a top car.

Ronnie showed the form which Lauda feared in the Austrian GP, where he battled for the lead with Watson's Penske and led laps 3 to 9 until the almost inevitable brake problems had him slip down the order to sixth. Brambilla had a return of the red mist and punted Emerson Fittipaldi into a barrier very hard and as some observed at the time, how Vittorio escaped serious grief at the hands of the Fittipaldi brothers was one of the mysteries of modern motor racing. There was a further March entry for the Austrian GP: one Karl Oppitzhauser, who was the lucky buyer of one of the cars with which Brambilla had had such a lurid time at the Nürburgring. It was a case of optimism over common sense and Max recalls, "Bernie came up to me and said, 'I hope you've been paid for the car because I'm about the tell the organizers he can't run.'"

Ronnie had a new sponsor for the Dutch GP, John Day Models, but as Robin explains, "We had no other sponsors and John Day is a good bloke, so we stuck his name on the car. Ronnie took pole and led the race, so John was really chuffed and immediately produced a model." Ronnie did indeed set pole and led for the first ten laps, but he was under enormous pressure as, just behind, Watson and Hunt were engaged in a titanic duel. The 761 had probably never been driven so hard for so long and its front tyres simply could not handle the treatment they were receiving and soon Ronnie began to encounter massive understeer and slipped down the order to fifth. Then his engine lost oil pressure and that was his race run, but Brambilla was having one of his clear days and came home sixth.

In 1972 it seemed that after Ronnie had decided to go to Lotus he did his best to give March a leaving present. In the week after his superb performance in the Dutch GP he announced he would drive for Tyrrell the following year, but this time there was no angst, Robin and Max taking the view they had been lucky to have had him on loan for the season and their performance hadn't given them any right over him. This time, though, Ronnie did deliver a leaving present, a superb win in the Italian GP.

Qualifying gave no indication of what was in store as Ronnie managed only eighth and even that was a false picture for the organizers had declared the fuel used by the McLaren and Penske teams illegal and they had to start from the back of the grid. Still he made a lightning start and was fourth on lap 1, third on lap 3, second on lap 4 and

In the Dutch Grand Prix at Zandvoort, Vittorio Brambilla had one of his 'clear' days and finished sixth. (**Nigel Snowdon**)

Ronnie Peterson, Robin Herd and Max Mosley at the 1976 Austrian Grand Prix. (**Jutta Fausel**)

in the lead on lap 10. It appeared from the grandstands that apart from a couple of nibbles from Depailler (Tyrrell) that he was having an untroubled race but once again his brakes were starting to fade. Then on lap 25 it rained and that slowed everyone and gave his brakes a breather.

On that lap an official held out a black square and a white square with a black cross, which was the new method of stopping a race, but most drivers hadn't heard of it, because you can't expect drivers to read the regs. A few caught the general drift, slowed, and were overtaken for their pains, some even pulled into the pits, but Ronnie kept his foot hard down. *Flags? I see no flags.* Then the rain cleared and all thoughts of stopping the race were put aside. There were other sprinkles later and again they slowed everyone just enough for Ronnie's brakes to cool, but as the race entered its final laps Clay Regazzoni's Ferrari was gaining hand over fist with the *Tifosi* going wild as the Ferrari set fastest lap. Then there was a sudden hush as on the penultimate lap the gap increased again. Brake problems or not, Ronnie responded with a new lap record and by the flag was still two seconds clear of Regazzoni. It was just as well he had not understood the flags.

It was the first time a works March had won a GP over the full distance and this time there was no muttering about luck or a bent car. Ronnie however did not suddenly find himself sorry to be leaving, he knew the score. March was never going to find reliability running on a shoestring and Robin was not going to be able to design a serious F1 car as opposed to a cheap and cheerful adaptation until he was free from the pressure of customer cars. While they could understand Ronnie's need to move, Robin and Max were concerned about his decision to go to Tyrrell. The six-wheeler was a tricky car to set up and Ronnie was not the man to do it. He needed, they reasoned, to be in a team where he was joint number one with a driver who would do most of the testing or in one, like March, where the car was simple and straightforward. They feared that going to Tyrrell would prove a disaster, and so it was, yet, ironically, March was to be another outfit to build a six-wheeler.

Even if Ronnie had any doubts about leaving March the Canadian GP dispelled them. There he qualified second and led the opening laps before gradually slipping back down the field. The reason was that the dampers on his car were knackered through over-use and they finally cried enough; it was the poverty trap. Brambilla had been on the pace all weekend too and he qualified a splendid third, and had been actually quickest in one practice session, but during the race he too slipped down the order.

Ronnie qualified third in the US GP, yet during the warm-up he found his car a handful and, uncharacteristically, spun a couple of times. Nobody could find anything wrong with the car, but in fact the front suspension bulkhead had broken and that put him out of the race, another example of the poverty trap. Having Ronnie in the team had been the best chance for years to dig a way out of it; had there been more money there could have been more wins and places and that, in turn, could have led to a different sort of sponsor.

In his last race for March Vittorio had a remarkable drive. It was the Japanese GP run in a downpour which was to see the finale of the Hunt/Lauda struggle, which had been the highlight of a season, marked by disqualifications,

The highlight of the season was Peterson's win at Monza. **(Nigel Snowdon)**

Ronnie Peterson in the pits at the United States Grand Prix. (**Nigel Snowdon**)

reinstatements, disputes, terrible decisions and, of course, Niki's crash and recovery. On the first lap Vittorio leapt from seventh on the grid into second, just behind Hunt, and he stayed there for five laps until he had to pit for a new front tyre. Then he worked his way up to second again in a matter of only eight laps and then nearly cost Hunt the Championship when he forced his way past and promptly spun in front of him. He recovered and still held fourth when his engine gave up. It was 1975 vintage Brambilla.

As for Ronnie, his last race for March ended on the first lap with a dead engine. Two years later, when he was number two at Lotus and embarrassing his team leader, Andretti, by his pace, Ronnie dropped by the March works to see his old friends. He said to Robin in his 'Swenglish', "When I come here I always feel I am coming home. When are you going to do F1 properly so that I can always feel at home?" A week later he was dead.

As always the F1 effort was only a fraction of the March story. Ian Scheckter, Jody's brother, won the South African (Formula Atlantic) Championship in a March, breaking Dave Charlton's six-year grip on the crown, and was soon in touch with Bicester talking about an F1 drive with backing from Rothmans. March had its usual clean sweep in the North American Atlantic series and top of both tables was a young Canadian, Gilles Villeneuve.

In F3 the picture was more complicated, for Chevron's new B34 was probably the best car of the year, but it seemed that Britain might have a star in Rupert Keegan, who was given a lot of press coverage as 'the new James Hunt'. Rupert began the season with a March 743 and then switched to a Chevron in mid-season, but he actually won more races in his second-hand March than he did with his new car. Britain had two F3 Championships that year, the Shellsport series, which was won by Bruno Giacomelli's works March from Keegan, and the BP Championship, which, because it had more rounds and was included in the British GP Meeting, was reckoned the more prestigious. When it came to the final round at Thruxton, Giacomelli sat on pole with Keegan alongside him and the position was that if Bruno won the race he would be Champion.

Unfortunately the spectators were robbed of a thrilling finale because at the first corner, Keegan appeared to lose his car and he took both himself and Giacomelli off. So, sitting on the armco, Keegan took the title. Robin says, "Some time later Rupert admitted to me that he had jumped the start and deliberately put Bruno into the wall at the first corner. I think I'd probably have done the same myself."

14 Drought of March

It's an odd quirk of history, but as March spent 1977 fading away it enjoyed its greatest popularity in F1. The 761 was a winner and was cheap and available, so there was soon a queue of punters prepared to buy or rent a car and no fewer than seven would be entered for the British GP, a number without parallel in the last quarter of a century. The flip side is that five of them failed to qualify, and that more or less sums up March's last F1 season in the Seventies. From winner to non-qualifier in one effortless bound, and while drivers have often received the blame the real problem was that the standard 1977 Goodyear tyre did not suit the cars, which parallels 1975, when Goodyear introduced a new tyre which happened to suit the March 751 but caused the Lotus 72 to slide down the grid. Since poor old Brian Henton had been with Lotus in '75, and ran a March in '77, it almost seemed that Goodyear was out to scupper him.

Before that was apparent March was the centre of attention when it unveiled a radical new car, a six-wheeler named the 2-4-0, after railway practice. During 1976 Tyrrell had run its Project 34 six-wheelers with four small wheels at the front and they had not only won a race but the drivers had finished third and fourth in the Championship. On top of that they had generated massive interest and soon toy shops were packed to the gunwales with model Tyrrells. The publicity value of a six-wheeler was not lost on Max and he pressed for one, for it would be an irresistible package to present to a sponsor.

Tyrrell was high in the pecking order, however, and Goodyear had been happy to make special tyres for it, while March had little clout, so if it was to make a six-wheeler it had to use existing rubber. Robin had anyway decided, rightly, that the Tyrrell P34 was a blind alley, it had increased grip through a larger contact area between road and rubber but the grip would be more useful at the rear, and the advantage of a slim front end was largely negated by the rear tyres stuck out in the air-stream, since they were responsible for 30–40 per cent of a car's total drag and anyway spoiled, and still spoil, the flow of air to the rear wing. The Tyrrell was supposed to be quicker in a straight line but as the Paul Ricard speed trap had shown, the 761 was faster. Four small wheels at the rear, all driven, would not only give superior traction and grip but the car would be so much slimmer and, hence, more slippery.

A development programme was out of the question, so one of the mechanics, Wayne Eckersley, was ensconced behind locked doors, on which there was the cheerful notice *Anyone entering will be sacked*, and he, working alone, created the 2-4-0 by using an existing 761 and raiding the spares store. As originally drawn, the gearbox casing had heavy strengthening ribs, for the stresses generated by a close-coupled four-wheel-drive system would be considerable. But cash was tight and the drawing looked expensive, so some of the ribs were rubbed out and a cheaper casing ordered.

When Wayne could see an end in sight, Max invited the press to a major launch, the workshops were tidied up and the car was presented with most of the workforce seeing it for the first time. Max went into plausibility drive, careful not to mention that it had a dummy engine, the gearbox casing was empty, and no proper engineering had been applied. Eckersley had used what he could get from spares, for example some of the uprights were from F3 cars. It was presented as a radical new F1 car, but it was really only a full-scale model.

A lot was riding on the car and Robin and Max sold it as hard as they knew how but while you can fool all of the people some of the time, this was not that time, and one of the hacks reckoned that it wasn't a real car at all and that it couldn't be made to run within a fortnight. The bluff was called and had to be answered, so, without breaking step, Max promised it would be demonstrated at Silverstone two weeks thence.

It was a situation typical of March; there was hype, but a promise had been made so it had to be kept. Now the car was common knowledge, the whole workforce could be involved and over the next two weeks it went from a publicity gimmick to a racing car. While the hype had been typical of one side of March, the response to the challenge was typical of another side and the 2-4-0 was ready within the fortnight.

Come the day of the demonstration and it hadn't completed half a lap before there was an horrendous noise and it ground to a halt; the cheaper gearbox casing had proved false economy, it had flexed and the two crown wheels had stopped meshing with the two pinions, with the result that messy things happened to them. March was left with egg on its face, but, typically, Max guaranteed a better result a few days later. The casing couldn't handle the torque from a close-coupled four-wheel drive, and there was no time to make a casting to the original specification, but not to worry, if engineering could not supply the solution then flim-flam could. By removing the rear crown wheel and pinion it became a two-wheel-drive car again with no torque loading problems, so the the rearmost

Two views of the radical, unraced but financially successful 2-4-0 Formula One car built early in 1977. (LAT)

wheels became no more than jockey wheels with dummy drive-shafts.

As luck would have it, the day was wet so nobody could expect fast times. Howden Ganley was in the car and he was told to go easy on the loud pedal but was not told why (someone might smell a rat if one set of rear wheels spun and one did not). The ploy worked and observers were soon commenting on the car's fantastic traction coming out of the corners, 'No wheelspin at all, old boy!' It was taking candy from babies and hacks beat the drum for the new car.

Flim-flam is fine for publicity, but it doesn't win races, and it was obvious that not only was a new gearbox casing needed but also a proper development programme to shed weight and fine tune the car, but the 1977 season loomed and resources were tight so the six-wheeler was put on to the back burner. Howden Ganley recalls, however, driving the car with all four wheels driven on a very wet day at Silverstone. "We went up and down the Hangar Straight and it was very wet indeed, and since there were no other cars on the track, nobody was shifting the water. The traction was incredible, you could accelerate as hard as you liked with your hands off the wheel and it would go in a perfectly straight line."

March had the palm within its grasp. The 2-4-0 could have been the breakthrough it had always sought but unable to afford the investment in the breakthrough, March limped on to the end of the year and then pulled out of F1.

In 1979, however, the 2-4-0 did appear in some hill climbs after Roy Lane persuaded Robin to lend him the current entity of the car (if that sounds enigmatic see the appendix for 1977) and he won several events even though the car's greatest asset, its advantage in a straight line, was not usable on short, twisty, British hill climbs. What it did have was astonishing traction, particularly in the wet, but it also had the inherent weakness in the transmission and was eventually abandoned for that reason.

Had the 2-4-0 been given a new gearbox casing and been raced in 1977, it might well have been a winner, for, despite a weight penalty, it had superior traction, brakes and frontal area to any other car on the grid. Had March stayed in F1, the concept could have been adapted to ground effect because it would have been possible to have put the rear wheels further out from the body to create huge, efficient, under-car air channels.

Although the idea was sound, Tyrrell's slide down the grid in '77 (for different reasons) put others off it, although five years later Williams resurrected the March concept. In testing the Williams was competitive, and the drivers said that it handled just like a four-wheeler, but it was not superior to the team's FW08s while being more complicated. Later, new regulations banned the use of more than four wheels, which knocked the Lion F1 project on the head, for that proposed 12 wheels, all of which were driven and all of which steered.

Ironically, the 2-4-0 was the most profitable car March had made for Scalextric bought the rights and royalties came in for years. Robin says, "My son's school mates had been unimpressed by what his father did for a living until they all rushed out and bought 2-4-0 models for their Scalextric sets, and then his stock went up considerably!" In addition March made what it regarded as a small fortune from hiring it (or, rather, *them*) to shows and exhibitions. Max had been right about its publicity value and Robin had been right about the concept, but it had been the right car at the wrong time.

Peterson, Stuck and Brambilla all left March, Stuck because he had severed links with BMW, who had been supporting him in F1, Brambilla because he had been offered better terms by Surtees, and in their place came Ian Scheckter and Alex-Dias Ribeiro, both selected by March's eagle-eyed talent scouts on the strength of the sponsorship each brought, about £80,000 each. Robin says, "I don't think we played fair with Ribeiro. He should have done another year in F2 because he'd gone very well with us and in '77 he would have had the star treatment. We needed the money to continue in F1 and I persuaded him to do it, which was not in his best interests. I don't think that was a very honourable thing to do, and it spoiled his career, but to my knowledge, it was the only deliberately dishonourable thing March has done."

Max says, "Robin's being less than fair to himself, Ribeiro desperately wanted to do F1 and he first tried Brabham; Bernie says he was interviewed by him rather than the other way around. He drew a blank there and then came to see me saying he'd had an offer from Bernie which he was considering, but what could I do for him? While he was with me Bernie phoned on another matter and I used a sort of code to ask what was going on. Bernie said he wouldn't touch him, so I sat there being interviewed by Ribeiro knowing what the real situation was. We took him for the money he brought, but I don't recall him needing persuading to do F1, he was desperate to do it. Unlike Robin, I never rated Ribeiro and subsequent events demonstrate that I was right."

Back to Robin, "I didn't know about that, but I still feel I let him down because I promised I would engineer his car and I broke my word. At the end of 1976 BMW severed links with us and the only way we could persuade them to continue was if I gave up F1 and concentrated on F2. I liked Alex a lot, he was a good engineer, and while he wasn't a natural driver he made himself into a good one, but when BMW issued its ultimatum I had to choose between loyalty to March or loyalty to Alex. I value loyalty, but you get these horrible conflicts all the way through."

Ribeiro was unusual among racing drivers in that he was a born-again Christian and had a *Jesus Saves* sticker on his cars. He gave out some of those stickers for the mechanics to put up in the factory and, of course, being mechanics, they put up a Green Shield Stamps sticker underneath. Alex was not amused.

Having got the driver line-up sorted out, March set to and built two new F1 cars, 761Bs. Actually they were virtually the same as the 761s but with twin-caliper Lockheed brakes, revised uprights, a Lotus-type adjustable rear anti-roll bar and a shorter wheelbase. In terms of March's long-term future the car was significant for a reason none outside knew at the time in that working on the design was Tim Holloway, who had joined three years earlier to work in the machine shop and became one of many who were allowed his head by March. In 1989 he was the mechanical designer of the F1 cars and a director of the team.

Two 771s were also built, designed by Martin Walters, and the chief external difference was a front-mounted radiator,but there was a slightly wider tub and the fuel was carried more to the centre of the car. In fact Robin said at the time he would really have liked to put all the fuel behind the driver, which would be the norm in racing as the ground effect revolution got under way. With a wheelbase of 104.3 inches, the 771 was longer than its sister cars while being much lighter (the 761B was 110 lb overweight), and all in all the idea was to build a car on what had become traditional March lines (narrow track, medium wheelbase, conventional suspension and relatively stiff springing) but without the compromises inherent in adapting F2 chassis. Ronnie's win at Monza had decided Robin and Max to have a serious crack at F1, and so they might have done had not BMW been applying a tourniquet.

In the event, despite the theoretical advantages of the new car, which was unhappy on the '77 Goodyears, the team preferred to use 761Bs. It was only after the Austrian

In the South African Grand Prix the Rothmans International entry appeared as the 'Lexington March' instead of the 'Rothmans March' and was driven by Hans Stuck instead of Ian Scheckter. Stuck retired because of engine trouble. (**Nigel Snowdon**)

GP that a 771 actually raced, because Ronnie wanted to buy his Monza-winning car (761/6), which was masquerading as '761B/1', Scheckter's car, so it was put back into 761 spec for him and Ian had to use 771/1. It was no improvement on the older car, but it placated Rothmans, Sheckter's sponsor, which was not entirely happy with its investment.

As it happened, March was not the only team to struggle with the tyres and Niki Lauda was the first person to crack the problem by having his Ferrari set up with different camber angles, so while his car was in a straight line and moving with the road (suspension systems then had movement in them) the tyres scrubbed slightly and heat was built up in them.

There's not much point in detailing the season, for there's not a lot one can say about a Did Not Qualify and March notched up 23 of them, Ribeiro accounting for eight, but the total was inflated by weird and wonderful deals done by private teams with such as Mikko Kozarowitsky, Bernard de Dryver and Michael Bleekemolen.

On a different level was the Frank Williams car driven by Patrick Neve, which was a way of keeping Frank in the game while he worked at his dream package. He'd persuaded Patrick Head to join him, so his car was well engineered, but Neve was not a Peterson and, besides, the day of the 761 was over, for the period 1976–8 saw a sudden upsurge in F1 design: Lotus introduced ground effect, Ferrari and Alfa Romeo set new standards in power output and while Cosworth strove to match them not everyone could afford the latest DFVs. When the 1978 season started Williams had backing from Saudia Arabia and a new Patrick Head design which founded the fortunes of the modern Williams team.

Then there was Merzario, who bought a 761B in another effort to revive his career. In the early part of the year he was usually quicker than the works drivers, but his little team could not maintain his car properly and after mid-season he failed to qualify for any race. In 1978 he built his own 'Merzario' F1 car using March components but this was a badly-made lost cause. As an aside, it's odd, but though March spent most of the Seventies as a makeweight team it directly spawned three other cars. There was the Hesketh 308, of course, the Penske PC3, which was a refined 751 with some of the parts being interchangeable, and finally there was the Merzario. The reason for this spawning of clones was the pragmatic one that March was always more than happy to sell cars (it had no great secrets to guard) and in F1 terms they were bargain basement. So far as Penske was concerned, team manager Heinz Hoffer summed it up: "When you're new to the neighbourhood you don't stray far from home."

Brian Henton and a friend, the playwright Don Shaw, formed the British F1 Racing Team, which was a one car, one engine, operation and when everything was fresh he managed a fighting fourth place in the Race of Champions but failed to qualify for any WC event. Although he couldn't raise the scratch to run with the March works team, he had done much of the testing in 1976 and had been sold the car on special terms. He says, "If you believe that a privateer could do F1 in 1977, you

The most promising March Formula One driver in 1977 was Patrick Neve with the 761B entered by Frank Williams and sponsored by Belle-Vue. He is seen in practice at the French Grand Prix at Dijon-Prenois where he failed to qualify as a starter. **(Nigel Snowdon)**

Brian Henton with a friend acquired a March 761B which was entered under the name 'British Formula 1 Racing'. Here he is seen at the Race of Champions at Brands Hatch in which he took fourth place. **(Nigel Snowdon)**

probably believe in levitation. March sold us the team spare for £5000, I persuaded a friend to buy us a second-hand Cosworth for £7500 and we bought an ex-Midlands Gas Board van which we did up as a transporter. We had a good result in the Race of Champions and I still have this huge trophy for best non-constructor to finish, but a bit more money would have been more to the point.

"Bernard de Dryver hired the car for the Belgian GP and it was due to go off at first light, so the night before I gave our chief mechanic £500 to cover expenses and went home. I was woken early next day by a mate who wanted to know where the car was and it turned out that the mechanic had done a runner with my £500. Thinking on my feet, I drove down the road to Bob Salisbury's house in Loughborough and tried to knock him up, but he was well away, so I climbed up a drain pipe and knocked on his window. It's six in the morning, I'm hanging on to a drain pipe, Bob is half asleep and I'm saying, 'How would you like to go to Belgium, Bob?' A couple of hours later he was on his way.

Nobody wanted to know us, with our ex-Gas Board van we didn't fit the image that F1 was trying to promote, and when we turned up at a race it was as though we were arriving at a formal dinner in T-shirt and trainers. At Zolder there are a lot of little garages which the real teams were using for their spares but we found an empty one and set up shop. Then Bernie Ecclestone came round and saw us. He had a conversation with Peter Mackintosh, who was then with FOCA, and Peter came over and said, 'Bernie wants you out of there, he wants it to store his tyres.' I said, 'If he wants us out he can turf us out, or words to that effect.' Brian is a well-built man and can be direct. Another conflab and Mackintosh came over again, 'Bernie says you can stay.' Mark you, we didn't get passes for the race...

"At the British GP we had to pre-qualify, which is Russian Roulette time, and my gearbox seized, which lunched our chances. When we took it apart we found a foreign ball bearing in it, so I think it was a case of sabotage, but I can't think who would have done it, we were no threat to anyone." Except of course to other pre-qualifiers, but all of those were above suspicion. "We might have gone better in other races, but the bottom engine mountings had broken. At first it was a case of hair-line cracks and we didn't twig until the things actually snapped in two. No wonder the car felt funny."

March showed its high regard for Brian's talent by entering him at Long Beach, when Ian Scheckter was injured in a race in his national series and came home a distant tenth and absolutely exhausted ('I've never been so knackered in my life'). At the end Max said, "You're not fit enough to be a Grand Prix driver, Brian." "Pray, try and turn the steering wheel, Mr Mosley," or words to that effect, came from the filleted Superhen, and none could. In qualifying, running with a light fuel load, Brian had been over a second faster than Ribeiro (and quicker than Peterson the previous year, when he'd been sixth on the grid), but when the tanks were filled the monocoque bent under the weight and squeezed the steering rack.

That's Brian's version, but others who were present disagree and maintain that running on a new front tyre compound fitted for the race made the car virtually undrivable and that Brian, who is a fit man, was so exhausted he simply cannot remember clearly. The trouble is that both versions are equally likely and neither reflects much credit on March, and in giving both views one must also say that the affection between driver and team remained intact, and Robin says that if he had his dream team drawn from all the drivers who have run for March, Brian would be high on a very short list.

Much of the reason for the works team's poor performance has been laid at the door of the drivers, but when Hans Stuck deputized for Ian Scheckter in South Africa he was slower in qualifying than he had been in 1976 and Ribeiro was slightly faster than Stuck, which suggests that the 1977 drivers may not have been quite as bad as their performances appear, but the new Goodyears made the car too nervous to be ideal for drivers in their first year of F1. It's interesting, though, that Stuck, who was six foot three, could fit into the same sort of car as Ribeiro, who was five foot two.

Some of the fall-off of performance was due to the fact that Robin was rarely seen at races because he was fulfilling his commitment to BMW, so there was the rumour that Max and he had had a severe disagreement, although the day that happens has yet to dawn. As Robin has said, he had not been able to fulfil his promise to Ribeiro and this helped fuel a severe lack of confidence between drivers and the F1 team, who before the end of the season regarded each other with barely disguised hostility.

Max says, "That may have been the impression from the outside, but I recall having a good relationship with Ian Scheckter, and believe I still do. I always thought that in the right circumstances Ian could have been very good and he won more national championships for March than any other driver, but the 1977 F1 team did not provide him with the right circumstances. Ribeiro was a different matter. I never rated him, we didn't get on, and the feeling was mutual."

There was, too, the matter of only eight F2 customer cars being made against 19 in 1976 and it is the way of racing that the higher the formula, the bigger the profit margin (Dave Reeves and James Gresham used to price the cars not on what they cost to make, but on what they thought the market would stand), so the situation was looking serious.

There was no problem in North America, where Formula Atlantic was dominated by Gilles Villeneuve and Bobby Rahal, but with talent like that in its cars, March would have been hard-pressed to have failed. In Formula Three, however, it was facing pressure from Chevron, Ralt and a new outfit, Argo. The Ralt RT1 in particular was gaining a reputation among drivers for being a good predictable chassis which was easy to work on, qualities which became a Ralt trademark, and when, 11 years later, March bought Ralt one reason was for the secret of those qualities: the pragmatic design skills of Ron Tauranac. Ron had been Jack Brabham's designer and partner at Brabham then, briefly, the sole owner. He'd sold out to Bernie Ecclestone and returned to Australia to retire-but a dive in the stock market had seen the trust fund he'd arranged for his old age, and his children, look shaky, so in 1974 he had returned to Britain (he is an Australian born in England) and started making cars again. It took three years before Ralt took off and in 1977 it was a cloud on the horizon threatening March's pre-eminence as the world's most prolific constructor of racing cars.

On the whole Marches were not well made and nor were they easy to work on, and even although there was a steady improvement in both areas over the years, other makers made greater strides, which was one of the contributory factors to the crisis which beset the company in 1988. It may seem odd to say that Marches were not well made when they were winning races, but the better team managers who bought them recall how they rebuilt them before use and senior March men now admit the problem, which is why production Marches are now made by Ralt and the specialized projects are carried out by March Engineering working without customer car constraints.

Speaking in 1987, when one of his Onyx Race Engineering March 87Bs, which was thought to be an impossible car to make work, was leading the F3000 Championship, Mike Earle said, "We never take a complete car regardless of the quality of the build, which has never been wonderful. For a start all the parts go through our own inspection department, and we send back anything that's not up to scratch, because over the years there has been a basic problem with quality control. March has instituted a system now, and made big improvements, but you still get, say, the odd oil cooler which comes stamped saying it's gone through quality control and there's the guy's signature to prove it, then it goes into the car and leaks oil.

"By building from a kit we end up with a car we understand, because we put it together and along the way we make our own changes and improvements, because experience has taught us that March has certain blind spots. Without giving away too many trade secrets, the gear shift has never been brilliant and that is something we always look at. If the driver comes in and says, 'That would have been a really good lap but I missed a gear change,' some teams will say, 'Hey, he did such and such a time and that was with a missed change, without that he'd have done such and such,' and they seem quite happy with that.

"If that happens to us we try to get to the bottom of why it has happened, because if a driver misses two gear changes in a race, that's two seconds lost and you have to work very hard to find two seconds. If there are 12 races in a series and he misses two shifts in every race, that's 24 seconds lost and that represents a lot of money and effort.

In North America in 1977 Gilles Villeneuve and Bobby Rahal dominated Formula Atlantic. Here Villeneuve is seen on his way to a win at Trois Rivières. (LAT)

"I think March would be better selling their cars as kits. Every year you get the odd team coming up and saying, 'Can you come and look at this, we can't make it work,' and when you go along you find something like a front suspension pick-up point has been put on upside down. When you take delivery you generally find that the bodywork doesn't fit and every panel needs hand finishing. The trouble is that the guy at the factory does not have the same involvement and pride as a mechanic in a team.

"When I was in America in 1985 I got the impression that the Indycars were much the same and people were grousing there but the point is that the car won the Championship, so it couldn't have been that bad. Listen to people in F3000 and they'll tell you that the 85B was bad, the 86B was worse and the 87B was absolutely terrible, but they still won the Championship every year.

"One thing, I think, is that most people under-estimate the product that comes out of March; our cars run closer to the standard set-up sheet that comes with the car than most. A lot of people go off on their own development programmes, but I believe that unless you know what was in the mind of the guy who designed it, you can lead yourself up the wrong road.

"Every year we have our State of the Nation meeting at Onyx and say 'Look we're getting a bit too cosy with March, it's a nice relationship, but perhaps it's time for a change, let's consider all the options.' Then we go through all the possibilities, listing all the plus and minus points and finish up by saying, 'That's decided then, we stick with March.'

"Even if March had not won a race this year I would still go back to them next year because every time they've had a bad year they come back and murder the opposition. It's the competitive instinct and it permeates down from Robin."

Robin says, "I think Mike's comments are fair and the only thing I can say in mitigation is there was a time when Ralt was even worse than we were."

That was to be the long-term crisis. Back in 1977 March could feel the first chilly blasts of a more immediate problem, the falling away of its F2 market, only eight 772s were sold and most of them went to AFMP (*Angenreri Fenoto March Pavenello*), a team ran by March's sole agent, Sandro Angeleri.

Angeleri was a charming man from a good Milanese family who had become March's sales director. He was one of those rare individuals who have a natural gift for languages, so when the Japanese market became important, he didn't turn a hair but began to learn Japanese. He was an asset, and he knew it, so began to work his corner. The F1 effort was ready to slide down the tubes, March's future clearly lay with customer cars, and Robin could see the attraction of having a multi-lingual dynamo shifting cars on his own account, especially since Angeleri was able to claim substantial backing from three Italian industrialists. It was the first of the March commercial deals in the sense that it was the creation of an outside business and not the handing over of money (sponsorship) to secure a service (run a car).

The distinction is an important one, at least it will become important in the story. We're facing here a problem of perception. March was the biggest maker of racing cars in the world, fact, but it was not a wildly successful enterprise because it was involved in cut-throat markets at a time of financial restraint. Its turnover in 1977 was £1.25 million, but it was not operating profitably by normal business standards, the emphasis seemed to be on quantity not profit and besides the F1 team was a drag on resources. The attraction of the AFMP deal to March was an improvement in cash flow, for selling racing cars is seasonal and things get tight at the end of each year.

Angeleri did not do things by halves and he set up two workshops, one at Silverstone under Tony Harvey, to run F2 cars for Ricardo Zunino and Alex Ribeiro, plus F3 cars, while a unit in Milan under Paolo Pavanello, the former March importer, would run F2 cars for Alessandro Presenti-Rossi and Alberto Colombo, Bruno Giacomelli plus, again, a number of F3 cars. All was going swimmingly, then at the beginning of 1977 Sandro looked ill – he was addicted to heroin.

March's own F2 effort was down to a single car and, under pressure from BMW to produce results, distanced itself from the customers and ran a 772P (P for Prototype), which was based on the narrower Formula Atlantic (née 712) monocoque and had a tight body with excellent aerodynamics. Patrick Neve was in it in the opening round at Silverstone and he ran away and hid until one of his wheels worked loose and the race was handed on a plate to René Arnoux's Martini-Renault. On the strength of that performance Neve was snapped up by Frank Williams for his F1 effort.

At Thruxton Brian Henton upset the form book by winning in the one-off Boxer-Hart, the first F2 win by a British driver for four years, but this brave effort soon folded through lack of money. We were back to the old problem of trying to find sponsorship in the real world of exchange rates and overseas bank accounts (contrary to popular belief, Belgium and Britain can be better than Switzerland, shame to spoil the script). With BMW anxious for results, Jochen Mass had the 772P for Hockenheim and the Nürburgring and he obliged by winning both races. A German driver winning with a German engine in Germany was the best possible result especially since BMW had hedged its bets and allowed

Bruno Giacomelli with a Sandro Angeleri-entered 772-Hart Formula Two car at Thruxton in April 1977. He retired because of a broken accelerator cable.

At Donington Park, Giacomelli by this stage in 1977 with a works car, scored his third win of the season with the prototype 782. (**LAT**)

Eddie Cheever works engines for his Ralt. As a graded driver Mass was ineligible to score points and by coming second at Hockenheim, Arnoux stretched his Championship lead.

Four races into the F2 season AFMP was wound up, Angeleri had been stopped near Heathrow and certain substances were found in his car. He was hauled before the beak, allowed bail and skipped the country. Sandro's fall from glittering personality to hunted junkie was a tragedy, but what was less well known was that he had helped a number of drivers he believed in by finding them sponsorship and easing their way, and among them were Brian Henton, Bruno Giacomelli and Gunnar Nilsson. As Brian says, "He was a great character, a super bloke, he did a lot to help us underdogs and always on the quiet." He would not have wished it, but Sandro dealt March a serious blow and without raking over the details of an unhappy story it is pleasant to be able to record that he is back in circulation, although not in motor racing.

Colombo and Zunino were able to struggle to the end of the season on their own money, Piercarlo Ghinzani was able to do the same and wound up European F3 Champion as well as Champion of Italy, while others switched cars, and this had an adverse effect on March since one of the drivers to do so was David Kennedy and he chose an Argo and helped establish the little Norfolk firm as serious rivals, while another was Nelson Piquet, and he switched to a Ralt, which did Ralt's fortunes no harm. Another of the people left in the lurch was Bruno Giacomelli, who was able to transfer what remained of his sponsorship money (only £30,000) and to last out the season in the works 772P. There was one small problem, Bruno spoke no English and Robin spoke no Italian, but Bruno was a devout Catholic and so, perhaps for the only time in racing history, driver and engineer communicated in Latin. *Festina lente Bruno. Tempus fugit Robin. Tell Marcus that the Gauls are at the city gates.*

In a season that was particularly hard-fought and featured such drivers as Arnoux, Cheever, Pironi, Surer, Patrese and Rosberg, Bruno was immediately on the pace and shrugged off an unfortunate start to his season by winning first time out at Vallelunga, crashing at Pau and then bouncing back with a win at Mugello. It was a dream start, but perhaps too good for a driver who had not got his temperament under control, and he went through a phase of trying to win races at the first corner. Giacomelli is a driver of dazzling talent who is still highly regarded at March both professionally and personally. His problem was that he did not have the depth of personal resources to help him overcome the bad times and the team had to do everything for him. He shone in F1 for a while and then his career faded and he spent most of his time in Touring Car racing, but his account was so much in credit at March that he was used for testing in 1988 and '89, years after his last F1 drive. "Bruno has added a real dimension to our testing," says Robin, "and if anything happened to one of our lads, Heaven forbid, I'm sure the team would want to put him into the car and I think he'd shake a few people. He got straight in not having driven an F1 car for six years and he was immediately right on the pace, and having had so much experience his feed-back was much broader than Gugelmin or Capelli."

At Donington Bruno ran the prototype 782, the tub of which had had a new front bulkhead and was slab-sided, the result of Dave Reeves buying new equipment to make building more efficient. In that final race Bruno found his form again and slaughtered the opposition to take his third win of the year. This meant he tied with Arnoux as the driver with most wins in a season which had seen six drivers take the chequered flag in six different types of car using four different engines, yet he still finished only fourth in the series. Had he been able to do a full season with the works car Robin thinks it is probable that he would have become the first driver in F2 to win the Championship in his rookie year.

With so many chassis and engines winning, one would have thought that the customer would be spoiled for choice, but the day after Donington March received 25 orders for 782s. There were three reasons: the economic climate was easing, in Europe if not in Britain, the Elf scholarship scheme had come to an end so the Renault engine disappeared along with the Elf and Martini cars, and *Motor Racing Golden Rule No. 3*: the most important race to win is the last one of the season because memory in the sport barely extends back to breakfast time. James Gresham, who had been in charge of the stores while helping out with the F3 operation, had been landed with sales after the demise of AFMP and when one sells the following year's production in the autumn, it does one no harm at all, so he was duly promoted to Sales Manager.

Much of the F3 season in Britain centred on a battle between Stephen South's March and Derek Daly's Chevron, with each taking a championship, although Daly won the premier series. At the beginning of the year, however, the Unipart team, which ran 773s fitted with Holbay-developed Triumph Dolomite Sprint engines, looked as though it might be competitive and Ian Taylor took a couple of pole positions, but the engine lacked torque and the effort faded, although Ian did win a single race at Silverstone to score British Leyland's first race win since Jackie Stewart had been in F3 in 1964.

As for the F1 team, not once in the season did a works car qualify higher than 17th and if Ribeiro's two eighth places do not seem so dire, it should be noted that both times he was the last classified finisher still running. March scored no WC points, had the worst finishing record of any team (33.3 per cent) and its dismal season ended on a note of farce when Sheckter landed at Tokyo and was detained because his passport had only a tourist visa.

The Japanese were very sensitive about South Africa, despite (or perhaps because of) being officially classified 'honorary white' there. Ian was escorted to a hotel room with two bodyguards and was put on to a plane out of the country 24 hours later. Jody Sheckter reckoned there were ways around the problem, but it seems that the communication line between Max and his driver had broken down, so Ian was deported.

By the end of the year Max had had enough of struggling in F1 with no money and threw in the towel.

At Thruxton Stephen South (March 773-Toyota Novamotor) chases the similarly powered Chevron B38 of Eje Elgh. (**Nigel Snowdon**))

There was no big bust up, he was simply fed up and he went off to work full time for FOCA, though maintaining links with March as a director. "We were getting to the point where some organizers were complaining that they could not afford to put on races and so FOCA said it would take over the running of some of them. That needed my full-time attention and I'd had enough of struggling. Then Günter Schmid of ATS came along with an offer to buy March's FOCA membership and the assets of the F1 team, so that let me off the hook. It meant I could move on without leaving March in the lurch.

"One thing sticks out in my memory that year. Lotus was running its first ground effect car, the 78, and was putting a smoke-screen around it; there was talk of roller needle bearings and special differentials, and I remember Bob Dance making a big thing about the diffs, covering them in cloths as he took them from the transporter to the pits. We happened to be passing the Lotus pit once and one of the cars was on trestles and we could see underneath it. Robin immediately identified its secret, the under-body venturi, but by then we knew the end was in sight for the F1 team so there was no point in pursuing it."

At the end of the season Robin bought Max's shares, paid off most of the convertible debentures, and so effectively became sole owner of the company. When March sold its F1 assets and FOCA membership to ATS, most of the F1 team members went with it, although some, like Mike Smith, soon realized that working under the volatile Günter Schmid was no fun at all and when, after the first couple of races, they had to make their minds up, they returned to March.

ATS started the season not only with the assets of March but also with the excellent Penske PC4s, one of which had given John Watson his first GP win, for Penske pulled out of Formula One at the end of the season. These were given a few tweaks by Robin, who stayed in touch with the team for the first few races, and entered as ATS HS1s.

That involvement apart, and it was more cosmetic than anything else, March prepared to face 1978 solely as a maker of production cars, so for the time being the old conflict of customer cars versus Formula One was resolved with no compromises.

15 Big Fish, Small Pond

March bounded back into F2 as the major force because the French had bowed out, most drivers opted for Marches and in truth there was not a great deal of choice in 1978, but Mike Smith, who was was chief mechanic on Giacomelli's car and later March's project Manager for F2/3000, reckons it was anyway the best customer F2 car March ever made. With the French absent, BMW became the main supporter of drivers and it had no fewer than five under its wing: Giacomelli, Marc Surer and Manfred Winklehock in works Marches, run by Roger Silman, while Ron Dennis' Project Four ran 782s for Eddie Cheever and Ingo Hoffman.

Apart from its more angular tub, the 782 sat the driver further to the front than before, and after four years of side radiators, the cooling core was back in the front again. Both BMW and Hart had teased more power from their units and there was little to choose between them, with each giving about 300 bhp.

The story of the season can be told in raw statistics: 12 races, nine wins for March plus ten seconds and nine thirds. Giacomelli took eight of the wins; it could have been ten, but an electrical fault side-lined him when he had over a minute's lead at the Nürburgring, and he tripped over a slower car when trying to make up for a poor grid position at Donington. Despite the fact that BMW engines powered around two-thirds of the cars on the grid Bruno scored every BMW win, so his was an emphatic victory especially when one considers his eight pole positions and six fastest laps.

Statistics never tell the whole story and one reason for March's dominance was the death of Chevron's Derek Bennett in a hang-gliding accident just before the season started. The ICI team running Chevron-Harts presented the only serious threat to March in 1978 and won three races, Derek Daly at Mugello and Vallelunga and Keke Rosberg at Donington; but without Bennett, the development of the car was hobbled and Chevron was a spent force by the end of the year. The only other marque regularly in the field was Ralt, represented by a few privateers, but the highest finish any achieved all season was ninth.

Although works cars dominated the season (the ICI Chevrons were works cars in all but name), Alex Ribeiro managed a win at the Nürburgring in his March-Hart and Brian Henton, running a March-Hart on a frayed shoestring, started four races from the front row of the grid, two of them from pole. Robin had helped Brian by striking a special deal but since he went to the races with only one engine, it's not surprising that he usually failed to finish and many at March think that with a proper budget he would have given Bruno a hard time; still those performances were to revitalize his career.

One significant milestone was reached at Hockenheim on 24 September in the last round of the Championship, when Giacomelli headed the fourth March 1–2–3–4–5 of the year, scored the marque's 50th European Championship win and so put the icing on March's fourth Championship title in eight years.

Bruno Giacomelli won eight out of twelve races in the 1978 European Formula Two Championship. Here he is on his way to win at Thruxton in March. **(Nigel Snowdon)**

Born again Christian Alex Ribeiro at the wheel of his Jesus Saves Racing March 782-Hart at Thruxton in 1978. **(Nigel Snowdon)**

At the races Robin was in demand by all his customers and, as Mike Earle recalls, he has an uncanny knack of keeping the customer satisfied. "Robin's secret is that he's very good with people, he works people well, he knows what makes them tick and how to get the best out of them. You watch him engineer a car; he will take a guy who's at the back of the grid and within four visits to the pits he'd have him believe he's next year's World Champion and he *will* be going quicker.

"The guy will come in and say, 'When I go into a corner it understeers a bit and I'm not getting enough grip.' Robin will say, 'Really? Now that's very perceptive, I've worked with a lot of good drivers and not many could have told me that in three laps. I can work with you.' He makes a few adjustments and the guy goes out and he's a second and a half quicker because he knows he's great, Robin's told him so.

"The guy will come back into the pits and say, 'It's funny, it feels just the same, but I am going quicker.' Then Robin will say, 'Sorry, I'm being called by my team, but it's been tremendous working with you.' You can call it kidology but the fact is the guy does go faster. I believe, and Robin agrees, that 95 per cent of a car's performance comes from the driver."

One person, a very good driver and a level-headed man, swore that Robin could adjust shock absorbers like nobody else he'd ever encountered and he marked the talent down to information known only to him. When he was told of Mike Earle's observations, there was a pause, then a chuckle, and the concession that whatever it was, it worked.

Robin says, "It's not hype, I get enthusiastic about

Bruno Giacomelli, leading Formula Two driver in 1978 and always a March favourite. **(Nigel Snowdon)**

The crash at Donington in 1978 when Eddie Cheever (Ron Dennis's BMW Challenge Team March 782-BMW) forced his way inside Ghinzani (Allegrini 782). (**Nigel Snowdon**)

Robin Herd and Bruno Giacomelli at the Formula Two race at Nogaro in July 1978. (**Jutta Fausel**)

Robin Herd and Roger Silman at the Formula Two Mediterranean Grand Prix held at Enna later in July 1978. (**Jutta Fausel**)

people who are in my cars and make a conscious effort to give each one of them some of my time, because putting the driver in the right frame of mind is important. That doesn't apply only at a circuit, for I like to talk to a driver over dinner when he's relaxed and I'm careful about details such as making sure we're not sharing the place with another team, because they will try to wind him up. Almost every driver at a certain level is worth giving time to. Very few people in, say, F2 are hopeless, and even the slow ones are quick."

Mike Smith has no doubt this is the case, "Bruno would come back from driving in F1 for McLaren and say his F2 car was impossible. Robin would tell us to adjust the dampers and he'd go away and do a real head job on Bruno. At the time Bruno still hadn't quite got his temperament under control and I don't think he'd have been nearly so successful had he not had Robin behind him. Robin squeezed every last ounce of ability from him."

While Giacomelli was covering himself in glory in F2, elsewhere the position wasn't so bright. March had made a respectable number of F3 cars but few serious runners in Britain bought one because most people thought March had lost its way, and to a certain extent it had; some of that stemmed from the fact that the previous year the development engineer, Mike Foxon, who was highly rated, had had a serious road accident and like so many people in racing made the mistake of pushing himself back to work before he was fully fit. Thus the season belonged to Ralt, which took 31 European and British Championship wins in contrast to the three apiece won by Teo Fabi in Europe and Chico Serra in Britain. In Britain most of the winning was done by Derek Warwick and Nelson Piquet, while Jan Lammers and Anders Olofsson slugged it out in Europe, and all four used Ralts.

It was not simply that the best drivers were in Ralts; by mid-season Derek Warwick had seen his huge Championship lead eaten into by Piquet, who had the luxury of being a full-time racing driver, while Derek worked in the family business, and his demon tweak for 1978 was that he no longer had to drive his own transporter. With help from BP he was put into a March, but after only a couple of races he was back in his Ralt because it was more responsive.

March got its F3 market back in 1979 when it did an aggressive sales drive and also produced a semi-ground effect car, a 783 with skirts. Suspension remained outboard all round, which is not ideal for ground effect, but was a typical March compromise, since most F3 teams at the time needed the simplest possible solution, but the track was narrower, the wheelbase shorter and there were new rear uprights as well. Ground effect had been discovered by Peter Wright at Lotus, although Colin Chapman took most of the credit, and during 1978 F1 the Lotus 79 had been the cream of the field, which immediately caused everyone else to jump on the band wagon. March 782s had appeared with short sliding skirts operated by gravity alone and the Chevrons with fixed plastic skirts. In truth they probably affected the driver's head more than the car, but then *Motor Racing Golden Rule No. 1* says that if a car wins a race and it has a purple pole sticking out the front, come the next race every car will have a purple pole.

It would be stretching a point to say that March introduced ground effect to F3, but, rather, it re-worked the sidepods and fitted diffusers which gave a degree of downforce. It did build a prototype (79C) based on the 792's monocoque, but, although it was tested, it was decided not to follow it up because it was felt not to be fair to the customers, and since March won all but one race in Britain (the exception went to Bernard Devaney's Chevron) there was no need for it. It had the market virtually to itself since Chevron without Derek Bennett was in no position to respond, but had employed Tony Southgate to up-date its existing cars to 'ground effect' spec. Since the monocoque was wide there was little he could do and most of those who bought Chevrons defected to March.

As for Ralt, Ron Tauranac says, "I went overboard to try and do a Lotus 80, as it were, the ultimate ground effect car. It took too long to build and we lost out because I told customers, 'We're doing a conventional car and we're also doing this and we're behind,' and instead of people sticking with their existing cars they switched to March." Everyone knows you can't win in last year's car, so few Ralts appeared, but there remains the mystery of why most of the lap records set in Ralt RT1s in 1978 remained intact. One RT3 did escape and it was campaigned by Eliseo Salazar without conspicuous success but on the back of its F3 successes Ralt found a steady market in North American Formula Atlantic, where the 'obsolete' RT1 knocked March off its perch.

During winter testing good reports were heard of the new ground effect 792, and given March's domination

Nigel Mansell with the works 783 at the 1978 International Trophy meeting at Silverstone. (LAT)

of the previous season few were inclined to take a chance elsewhere, so the order book was healthy but as Robin himself says, "It must be the worst car ever to win a major championship. Ian Reed did the detail work on it, and all credit to him that it won the Championship, but it was a diabolical motor car."

The trouble was that nobody, not even Lotus, then fully understood ground effect as proved by Chapman's next great leap forward, the Lotus 80 ('It will make the 79 look like a double-decker bus'), which was virtually undrivable. Everyone could grasp the basic theory: you made low-pressure areas under the car by shaping the sidepods and you prevented more air coming in by sealing the side of the car with sliding skirts, but utilizing the downforce was another matter. During winter testing the 792 had been going well with much better grip brought about by its gravity operated sliding skirts. Then a spring system was installed in the sidepods which sealed the skirts much more efficiently and at that point the programme went haywire because so much downforce was generated that nobody had the slightest idea how to cope with it.

The 792 was radically different to the long line of Marches that traced back to 1971 since it had a narrow monocoque with honeycomb inserts, inboard suspension front and rear by rocker arms, and a long (100-inch) wheelbase and wide (60-inch) track front and rear, the same dimensions as the 711. It was also unspeakably ugly, but then given its character it had no right to be good looking.

When it came to driving the beast with full downforce, drivers were all at sea as they struggled to find the right settings. Nobody had foreseen the amount of downforce which would be generated by ground effect and it took a long time to sort out basics such as spring rates. Then the early skirts caused problems, because if they did their job properly, and created a low-pressure area under the car, they were sucked inwards, and when that happened they could not slide up and down as they should. On top of that, the amount of downforce was testing the structural strength of the whole car. None of these were problems peculiar to March, but March compounded its difficulties by deciding to run a four-car team from the one truck with cars for Marc Surer, Beppe Gabbiani, Teo Fabi and Ricardo Zunino.

Roger Silman had accepted an offer to manage Toleman's new Ralt RT2s and in his place came John Wickham, formerly the BARC's press officer, who had spent a year with the Surtees F2 team some years before. Some people at March will tell you that Roger insisted on building a ground effect car knowing they would make a cock-up of it and once it was under way, he accepted the offer from Toleman, knowing his main rival would be in trouble. Actually, he didn't, but the delight some at March still express in what they perceive as a perfect example of gamesmanship gives an insight into the racer's mind; they want to believe the story is true and they like Roger even better for believing it.

The season began with four drivers to look after, and since Robin spent most of his time with Project Four, Ian Reed engineered Surer and Gabbiani, though when Robin was free he gravitated towards Surer, leaving Ian to look after Beppe. That was fine, but John Gentry, back after a spell with ATS, was left with Fabi and Zunino and it's difficult for one man to engineer two cars, so neither driver felt he was getting proper attention, bad feelings developed between them with their sponsors in the background making demands and eventually Zunino, the weakest member, quit the team.

A complicated operation was the last thing March needed as it struggled to come to terms with the new technology but it did have the advantage that all four cars could be set up differently to see which one worked best, so in effect March was running four different cars at the start of all the early races. As John Wickham recalls, "The car either worked or it didn't at a given circuit, there were no half measures. In the early races we had the problem of sticking skirts and in fact at Hockenheim as Marc Surer's car came past the pits both skirts left his car, rose about thirty feet in the air and fluttered gently down. They worked better in the air than they did on the car.

"Then we had bodywork being sucked down with the result that bits fells off, there was trouble with the undertrays as the cars hit the deck, and the tubs cracked as they were subjected to forces nobody had foreseen. You must remember we went from a spring rate of 375 lb maximum in 1978 to a spring rate of 1500 lb so there was a lot to learn and the season was spent beefing the car up." During the winter tests, which had brought such favourable reports with a gravity-operated skirt system, the spring rates had gone up to about 600 lb, itself a large increment; the leap from there to 1500 lb was a whole new problem.

There was not a great deal of opposition for March to handle, for Chevron was dying, there were the two Ralts and single cars from AGS and Osella, but in the first race, at Silverstone, Eddie Cheever put the Osella on pole and since he was running on Pirellis everyone pointed at the tyres and a tyre war began, although the real reason was that Osella had built a friendlier car which did not have as much downforce to upset things. March was in a shambles even before the start because Surer spun on the warm-up lap and Gabbiani piled into him, so half the team was out before the race began.

In the race itself, run in the wet, Cheever came home the winner, but only 0.33s ahead of Derek Daly's Project Four 792, but Daly was exceptionally good in the wet, so that helped disguise the car's fundamental problems. Then at Hockenheim, Keke Rosberg deputized for Daly, who had an F1 commitment, and a combination of the nature of the circuit plus Keke's own press-on driving style saw him take the flag. The 792 couldn't be such a dog after all.

The only problem was that in second place at Hockenheim was Rad Dougall in a 782. Rad, a South African, was number two to Henton at Toleman and the team had taken delivery of only one of its Ralts, which Brian was developing with Rory Byrne. Toleman had dusted off its obsolete car for Rad and he brought it home two places higher than Henton. He still had the obsolete car at the next round, Thruxton, and just in case anyone was in any doubt about the brilliance of the new ground

Chico Serra (Project Four, March) opened the 1979 Formula Two Season with a win at Silverstone. His was the only car to use sliding skirts. (LAT)

The 792-BMW of Swedish driver Eje Elgh at the 1979 International Trophy at Silverstone. (Nigel Snowdon)

effect cars, Rad took pole and not only led the entire race but finished it at the head of the Championship table,.

One of the main problems was 'porpoising' and the car would go into a series of wave motions at speed, something which Lotus had discovered with the 80. This unpleasantness was eliminated after two races when new dampers were tried and after some wind-tunnel work which led to taking an inch off the leading edge of the sidepods. The black art was as subtle as that. Mike Smith says, "I don't think anyone produced a particularly good car in 1979, so we were all in the same boat, and had someone persevered with a 782 and really developed it, he could have won the Championship."

Back at the shop Dave Reeves was in charge of March Engineering at Bicester while John Mardle headed a new unit at Cowley, Oxford, which bore the title *March Engines Ltd*, but it was now more of a specialist fabrication shop rather than the old engine preparation/race team outfit which had run the March 'B' team in 1975 and had undermined the main company by building rotten engines – and it's hard to build a duff Cosworth DFV. The original premises, set up by Chris Amon, had been sold to ATS at the end of 1977, but the company registration had been kept and it was thought to be Robin's private life-line should March Engineering ever fall apart.

In 1979 March Engines built a special BMW M1 around a new monocoque designed by John Gentry and with substantially altered bodywork which was intended for the Group 5 class of the World Championship for Makes but homologation problems saw it put into Group 6, where it was completely outclassed, and so at Le Mans, although it practised in mid-field, it did not qualify due to the race's 'class by class' rules. Together with a second car it later raced in IMSA and eventually both were fitted with

Teo Fabi, another favourite of the March team, who drove a works 792 in 1979. (**Nigel Snowdon**)

Chevrolet engines. It is significant, however, that these cars do not appear in March's production figures any more than the 'Orbiter' Indycars which March Engines also made.

Brian Henton meanwhile was persevering with the Ralt in testing and while he took a good second to Surer at the Nürburgring it was at the wheel of a 782. It was a win which seemed to vindicate the 792, except that the race started wet and Marc was on slicks. Jochen Neerpasch had friends on the far side of the circuit who were able to phone him to let him know that the weather was clearing and he had passed on the tip to Surer, who had driven carefully in the opening stages, while some of his main rivals threw themselves at the scenery. Surer's inside knowledge won the day, but it was noticeable that his was the only 792 in the top six. The race was also marked by the fact that Beppe Gabbiani finally completed an entire racing lap.

The season see-sawed, Surer won at Vallelunga, then it was Henton's turn in the Ralt at Mugello, and then Cheever in the Osella at Pau. Then it was Stephen South in one of Ron Dennis' 792s at Hockenheim, Cheever at Zandvoort and Eje Elgh (792) at Enna, which is where the Championship pivoted.

Cheever, Henton and Surer had been steadily piling up the finishes, so they had gone to Enna with only five points between them. There Henton had overcooked the first corner, gone straight on, and rejoined the race with a yellow flag against him. He had stormed through to win, but March lodged a protest and he was disqualified. Toleman appealed, but the matter would be unresolved until after the end of the season.

One of the sensations of 1979 was Rod Dougall, driving a 782 March for Toleman who finished second at Hockenheim and, here, won at Thruxton. (**Nigel Snowdon**)

At Thruxton in 1979 Derek Daly crashed his March badly during practice, but with a replacement car finished second for the ICI team behind Dougall. (Nigel Snowdon)

Brian could still win the title regardless of the outcome of the appeal and he won the next round at Misano and then led the final race on his home circuit, Donington, until two laps from the end he had a braking problem and spun. This let Daly into the lead, followed by Surer, and second place was enough to secure the Swiss the title, pending the outcome of the appeal. Brian sat dejectedly in his pit afterwards and swore he would never again race with a green helmet, and nor did he.

Robin says, "That was one of the few races where we were able to devise a tactic that worked. Normally tactics don't work, but this time we had a plan and a bit of luck. We knew Brian would outpace us, but we also knew that Donington would take a heavy toll on tyres and brakes and that if Brian had a weakness as a driver it was that he didn't like pressure. In the first half of the race we told our drivers to hold back so that they would conserve their brakes and tyres and then they were let off the leash and started to narrow the gap. Brian had a huge lead, but Daly and Surer chipped away at it and, of course, Toleman was hanging out a pit board telling him the position. It was the worse thing they could have done, because every lap he could see his lead disappearing and it put him under pressure and you could see him get ragged. If he had backed off in the last couple of laps he would have stayed on the track and won by a second or so."

Brian's account is different, "On the way to the race Toleman's chief mechanic was killed in a road crash and apart from the team's emotional response to the tragedy, it set us back a day. As a consequence we did not do our normal brake wear tests but had to go by guesswork and we guessed wrongly. As the race progressed my front pads wore away until we had no pads at the front and no fluid in the front brake cylinder, only air. I braked heavily in the closing stages, there was nothing left at the front, the rear wheels locked, and I spun."

Toleman's appeal eventually failed and Surer was declared champion, although it seemed an unsatisfactory way to win the title. Ten years on Brian disagrees, "I rated Surer, he was a good driver and a very brave one, he was a worthy Champion. I certainly don't feel any resentment over March protesting. During my entire career I was happiest when I was at either Toleman or March."

Had points gone with the mount rather than the jockey one of the Project Four cars would have taken the title, but Daly had some F1 commitments and his seat was sometimes filled by others, among them Keijo Rosberg, who despite a reputation for driving on his nerve ends, Robin recalls as one of the best drivers he's ever dealt with. "What a bloke! What a driver! We did only two races together and at that time he was struggling to find drives but we clicked straightaway and he won one race and dominated the other. Everyone said he was mad and wild and couldn't give feed-back, but his feed-back was excellent and he drove so smoothly in a dog of a car. I only wished I could have worked with him in Formula One. I ought to say, too, that Project Four was a very pleasant team to work in. Ron Dennis has this reputation for being hard and cold, but it was a thoroughly enjoyable experience."

It had not been a good season, but perseverance, weight of numbers and a bit of luck at Donington had told in the end. It was noticeable, however, that it was only the works and Project Four which could make the cars work; even with works feed-back privateers were all at sea, and Derek Warwick, for example, went from being an F3 Champion to an also-ran, who ended a miserable year with one fifth place.

Sliding skirts were banned in F2 for 1980 so comparative sanity returned to the formula and March again was, in terms of numbers, the dominant maker and the 802 was a neat design which was broadly based on the 792 but had side radiators and a chisel nose with separate wings. The work of Ian Reed, it was actually one of the best

F2 cars March ever made, but it came up against a superb effort mounted by Toleman.

During 1979 Rory Byrne had developed the Ralt RT2 to such an extent that it would be fair to call it a Ralt-Toleman and his new car took that development several stages further and it came with a number of advantages, not least being a special relationship with Pirelli and the fact that the car was built for the specific purpose of winning for a two-driver team, so there were none of the usual customer car compromises, although Toleman did sell examples to Siegfried Stohr and Huub Rothengatter. Toleman's drivers were originally to be Derek Warwick and Stephen South, but before the season started, Stephen accepted an invitation to test an F1 McLaren without telling the team and he was sacked. In his place, and out of the wilderness, came Brian Henton.

Against what was obviously a serious threat March lined up Teo Fabi, Manfred Winklehock and Mike Thackwell. Robin had got close to Teo over the previous year and had an enormous regard for his ability, even although a sixth, two fourths and a second were thin results for a works driver. Teo had agreed terms the previous September and added to the standard contract were two extra clauses: *21. Teo Fabi is number one driver. 22. The driver agrees to carry out three days ski teaching per year for the engineer (R.H.)* Teo did carry out the terms of his contract, but says, "Three days were not enough."

Another driver with a works connection was the Venezuelan former motorcycle World Champion, Johnny Cecotto, who had decided to invest some of his own money in an F2 drive and March farmed out the deal to Onyx, which had just been formed. Johnny took to four wheels extremely well, but he had some Formula Ford experience in Venezuela, although obviously you cannot step straight into F2. The only trouble is that nobody has ever been able to discover when those Venezuelan Formula Ford races took place.

The season kicked off at Thruxton and resulted in an effortless Toleman 1–2 for Henton and Warwick, while all the March runners, who had started the race with some confidence, had their tyres go off within five laps or so. Teo then won for March, BMW and Goodyear at Hockenheim and the Nürburgring, but on both occasions Henton was a strong second, and piling up his points score, and then he won again at Vallelunga.

At the Nürburgring Winklehock had one of the most spectacular shunts ever when he crested the brow of a hill and instead of following the road his car simply continued into thin air and into a series of backward rolls which left it looking like second-hand Bacofoil. John Wickham says, "Manfred was pleased with the balance of his car and was trying less wing, and he got slightly out of line on that particular section, the air got under the wing and he flew. He came back to the pits and said, 'I've had a little accident', but we had no idea what he meant until we got back to the hotel and saw it on television." Manfred had no real idea what had happened either until he too saw the shunt on television – and then he threw up.

With Pirelli producing tyres specifically for Toleman, Warwick was able to take pole at Pau by a full second, although the race eventually went to Richard Dallest's AGS; even without using qualifiers, Henton and Warwick were a full second ahead of the field at Silverstone and the Goodyear runners might have been in another race. At Silverstone Warwick won and Henton retired and the two Toleman drivers led the Championship, Henton by a handsome margin.

It was not just that the tyres were good. Pirelli was making a big effort and virtually producing a new tyre for every circuit, while Goodyear was losing interest in F2, but the Hart engine was at least the equal of the best Rosche units and had a better reliability record. Teo in particular suffered and lost near certain second places at Vallelunga, Pau and Zolder with blown engines. Had that not

Works March 802-ICI team driver Manfred Winkelhock in the Formula Two race at Thruxton in 1980. Here he was eliminated when he collided with Chico Serra. **(Nigel Snowdon)**

Teo Fabi's works March 802 in the pits at the Silverstone Formula Two race in June 1980. (**Nigel Snowdon**)

happened he would have led the series at the half-way point. Mike Smith is still convinced the 802 was a better car than the Toleman and that only his engines prevented Fabi from taking the title.

One other thing which helped the Tolemans was a close reading of the rule book. They were running lower fixed skirts than March and, when protested, the decision was upheld. Fabi's car was modified to run lower skirts at Zolder and was running a safe second behind Rothengatter's Toleman but ahead of the works cars when his engine blew. Tyre testing paid off for Toleman at Mugello and Henton and Warwick were an unprecedented two seconds a lap quicker.

With the Championship within his grasp again, Henton played safe and came second to Stohr's Toleman at Enna and Andrea de Cesaris' Project Four March-BMW at Misano. That race clinched the top two Championship places for Henton and Warwick and Toleman went back home to prepare for a move into F1.

Although Henton and Warwick dominated the season, both were to say they felt Teo was probably their equal, but March was not doing the same job as Toleman, and there were too many balls to juggle in the air. At this time March wasn't profitable, while Toleman's budget was huge, and then apart from the traditional markets, F1 was in the air as it so often was, there was a new sports car for BMW, and the first toe in the water in Indycar. There weren't enough resources being devoted to F2 to meet a really serious challenge.

Without the Tolemans, Teo was back in the winner's circle at the last round at Hockenheim to make certain of third place in the series, but, a straw in the wind, he was followed home by Nigel Mansell's Ralt-Honda.

Like Lauda, Mansell has had some harsh things to say about March. His version is that he *traded down* his house (some versions of his story give the impression that he exchanged his house for a drive) and sold family paintings to raise the money for the works F3 drive in 1978, but the car was junk and March was only ever interested in his money. He forgets that with the junk he set pole at the International Trophy Meeting and finished second, and his performance in his fifth race at Donington Park won him an F2 drive in an ICI Chevron. After a year running with the Unipart F3 March-Triumphs (which were never too hot) he says he was silly enough to allow himself to be taken in by March again and was let down once more. He omits to say in his authorized biography that James Gresham was instrumental in getting him the Unipart drive.

Nobody would ever accuse Mansell of being a whinger, perish the thought, but while those at March accept Lauda's most damning criticisms, they flatly deny the Mansell version. James Gresham, who was involved in the F3 team says: "Nigel did some races with us in 1978 until his money ran out. We'd wanted to run him, and had tried to find him sponsorship. Later we persuaded Dave Price to put him in a Unipart car and he did that in 1979 when he decided that the Triumph engine would never be any good and he needed to be in the works team. We didn't actually want him, we really wanted Stefan Johansson, because he was quick and we had our eye on the Marlboro

Nigel Mansell who drove a Ralt Formula Two car in 1980, had some bitter memories of his Formula Three seasons with March in 1978-79. (**Nigel Snowdon**)

money he had, but I was being pushed very hard by Nigel's mentors; they were having me up to London to tell me how wonderful he was and Nigel was phoning me regularly.

"Eventually he got some money from Pace Petroleum which was enough to do the first few races. In those days a full season of F3 was about £60,000, but we would have taken quite a lot less for him, perhaps forty or fifty thousand, so we said we would continue until the money ran out. In fact we actually went beyond because we went to Monaco and by then we were really stuck for cash and everybody was fairly demoralized. Nigel never qualified as quick as Stefan in the same car." Nigel, in fact, scored three fourths, a fifth and two sixths and his season had ended by the end of May. "We have taken a lot of bad press over that year. I don't know whether it comes from Nigel or his mentors, but certainly the Mansell camp feels we let him down. I got a two-page slagging off in one magazine and was named as the man who had chucked him out of the car, yet in fact it was the other way round. In my opinion Nigel's ability is only average, but he is the most tenacious and brave racing driver I have ever met. He is not, however, a March favourite."

No dispute is ever black and white and much of Mansell's complaint probably comes down to the fact that the 803 wasn't a very good car, at least when run on British control (hard) tyres, but it was better on the softer European 'free' tyres. It was built on the same principles as the 802, except that it had a front-mounted radiator and was a parallel case to the 723, which was not quite as harmonious a package as the previous year's car. In Europe it was no match for the Martini Mk 31 and in Britain it not only faced severe competition from the Argo JM6 but also from the March 793. Kenny Acheson, the most successful March driver, had the use of both types and generally drove the older car.

Max Mosley says that one of the problems with drivers who feel they've had a raw deal is that they have an image of 'the works' as a vast institution which is above and beyond ordinary financial rules. Despite its apparent success on the circuits March was still a cottage industry, its design staff consisted of Robin and a couple of others and it existed thanks to the good will of a succession of bank managers whom Robin had charmed into believing the same dream that he, Max, Alan and Graham had had back in 1969. That belief was going to be severely strained over the next few years because in 1980 the company recorded a loss of £123,000 and the deficit would be double that the following year. That fact explains a lot of the decisions taken at the time and perhaps puts Nigel's criticisms into a new perspective.

The main problems with the 803 were the aerodynamics and traction and it was not until mid-season that these were addressed, with rocker arm rear suspension and a new body with a narrower nose and revised sidepods, but up-date kits in mid-season are never popular and are no way to spread goodwill. Project Four, which was running Johansson, was anxious to court Marlboro and so first tried an Alfa Romeo engine and then took the plunge and bought a Ralt RT3. Since Ron Dennis went from Project Four to being joint MD of McLaren International over the winter it was an investment which paid off.

It's odd given Ralt's track record and the way Henton had made the 1979 F2 car fly, but hardly anyone had bought an RT3, the main exception being Kiwi bass guitarist/driver Rob Wilson, who was running with help from his dentist. Despite a tiny budget Rob had made the Ralt work and people started to show an interest in what was to become perhaps the greatest F3 car ever.

Johansson first raced his Ralt in early September, when the Vandervell F3 series leader board read: 1, Kenny Acheson (March) 84 pts; 2, Roberto Guerrero (Argo) 79 pts; 3, Stefan Johansson (March) 58 pts. Stefan then won his next three races and arrived at the final round at Thruxton being one of three drivers with a chance of the title. Although Acheson had had only to finish fifth to win, he was so psyched by Johansson's late charge that he tried

In 1980 Ron Dennis's Project Four team ran 793s and 803s with Toyota engines, switching first to Alfa Romeo engines and then Ralt chassis. Here at Silverstone in June Toshio Suzuki drives a Project Four 803, still emblazoned 'Toyota' (because he was sponsored by that company), although the car was fitted with an Alfa Romeo engine. **(Nigel Snowdon)**

too hard and eliminated himself on the first lap. By winning from Guerrero, Johansson carried off the palm and since the most important race to win is the last one of the season, over the winter there was a wholesale defection to Ralt.

The profit on an F3 car was slender, so there was not a depth of financial resources on which to draw in order to put things right. If you got the car right from the start, as Tauranac did with the RT3, that was to the good, if it wasn't right, you watched your market vanish. Argo, which had done so well in 1980, made a mistake with its '81 car and disappeared from the scene.

In 1980 March had built 93 cars for F2, F3, Atlantic and SuperVee, but in 1981 it built only 37 cars for the same categories. It was not just that it had had a poor year, there were other factors at play. In F2 there was a revival in interest from other makers, and Lola took over the Toleman design as Toleman undertook its first, painful, season in F1. In North America, Formula Atlantic was declining rapidly to be replaced by the lucrative SuperVee series, which attracted most of the young hotshoes, and most plumped for the Ralt RT5, while in Europe the SuperVee Championship faded away. Just as Ralt wrested the North American market from March, so too it took most of the British F3 market, and to rub salt into wounds, Ralt would take the European F2 Championship as well.

1981 would be pivotal for March as circumstances forced it to change direction, but the foundations for that change were laid in 1980 as it had its first taste of Indycar and John Macdonald approached Robin with a proposal to build a new F1 car.

Robin says, "We have been credited with great cleverness for getting into the American market, but there was nothing clever about it, it was sheer accident. We were asked to put together a group to build a new Indycar, the Orbiter, which was built at March Engines. Ian Reed designed it, John Barnard was brought in as a consultant, and it was based around a honeycomb monocoque version of the 792, which Keke Rosberg had driven in Formula Pacific at the latter end of 1979. I am afraid it was pretty disastrous though."

Les Mactaggart, who was at March Engines at the time says, "It was a terrible car. March Engineering did the front end, we did the back, and basically the two ends wouldn't speak to each other."

Dave Reeves supplies the background story: "Robin was always more at home with the racing side of the business and over the years this has led to friction between us. He has said, 'I may not be a manufacturer but I have laid everything I have on the line for March Engineering,' to which I've replied, 'Yes, but if you felt you had another option you would take it.' Anyway, in the late Seventies Robin could see that March was going to drown in its problems and he wanted to build an ark for when the flood came and that ark was the Cowley operation. I'm sure he thought if he could re-create the same sort of small close-knit team he had in the early days, March could dominate again. I took the view that the world had moved on and the Gremshek approach couldn't work any more."

Robin disagrees: "If that had been the case I could have done the usual motor racing trick, which is to liquidate and start again, but I couldn't bring myself to sack 100 people and throw away 11 years' work. It was no secret we were in trouble and a number of guys at March, including people you perhaps would not have expected, such as machine operators, offered me loans of money. I was very moved by that while at the same time noting that there were people who could have helped but who didn't make the offer. I could have got out, but I stayed and fought."

The two points of view, although opposite, are not mutually exclusive. There had been rivalry between the production side and the racing side from Day One, witness the departure of Graham Coaker, and there was also rivalry between the Bicester and Cowley operations. Dave had been Robin's staunch lieutenant for some years and if that is the impression he received then it is likely it was the one Robin gave. When Robin says that he had other options, and they included selling the business to several people who were interested in buying it, that is true as well and the fact remains he stayed and fought – and won.

The important thing is that despite its image of success, March was in severe financial difficulties which would get worse. It was a foretaste of the major crisis which faced the company in 1988/9, for when your production drops your overheads do not so each unit leaving the factory has to absorb a great proportion of the overheads and profitability drops further, while at the same time you need to have cars on the track and in the right hands or else you go into a tail spin from which there is no recovery.

Dave continues: "Anyway, the Cowley operation took on a sports car project for BMW and the Orbiter for Sherman Armstrong and I'm sure that on the face of it the business plan looked marvellous, two major projects being handled by a tiny group of people with hardly any overheads. I was convinced it would be a disaster, and said so, and the cars were awful. I'm sure we can find a million excuses. I can remember being told the BMW would have 1000 bhp, but I think it had less than half of that so it's small wonder it finished up a little gross.

"Similarly, although Sherman Armstrong had the wit to see the potential of European racing technology and he knew that John Barnard was on the right track with the Chaparral he'd designed for Jim Hall, in every other respect he was hopeless, his team was disorganized and overstretched and the difference between America and Europe in those days was if you were overstretched in Europe you worked until you dropped, while in America you cut your coat according to your cloth, although it's different now.

"After the first races with the Orbiter, Sherman cried 'Rape!' and Robin turned to March Engineering to try to sort out the problem. One of the problems was communication, for we weren't used to feed-back couched in terms such as, 'Goddam dump pipe's shit and the car's so loose my driver'll buy the farm.' We had to make up a phrase book. I still have a copy, and it has things in it like *Push = Understeer, Loose = Oversteer*." Britain and America, two countries divided by a common language.

"I sent Jim Brady to investigate and then decided to

go to the States myself. I arrived at Pocono and was horrified. Our car looked bad, but most of the rest were even worse, only Penske and Patrick seemed to have any idea at all and even their cars were poor by European standards. They put on a good show and really raced according to their lights but the cars were not at all impressive, although the motor homes and transporters were another matter. There was obviously plenty of money about and I could see an opportunity for us.

"George Bignotti came to England to help supervise modifications to the Orbiter and he and I immediately gelled. Further he could see that March Engineering had good facilities and a good bunch of people and realized that Sherman Armstrong had been on the right track. George and I discussed the ideal Indycar, and by the end of the summer we had a good idea of what needed to be done, but unfortunately George didn't have any money.

"Robin allowed us to work on initial schemes, at least I think he did, perhaps I didn't ask, but we knew that if we didn't have cash by Christmas we simply couldn't go on. The future at this point looked very bleak indeed. Robin was aligning himself with John Macdonald to build and race the March 811 and I felt that though the ark (Cowley) might not have been seaworthy it had been good enough to get Robin to the other shore."

The other thread in the discovery of America came when James Gresham, who had been on a sales trip to Japan, was flying home with Keke Rosberg. "Keke had been racing in Can-Am and he said that Paul Newman was looking for a new car. As a result of that remark we started making Can-Am cars for Newman and we found we could make far more profit on them than we could on our F2 or F3 cars, so we began to take an interest in America.

"For us it was the right move because we'd started to struggle in Europe and it was nice to go into a new market with a clean slate; nobody owed us any favours and we didn't owe any. You'll remember that in 1978 the final two rounds of the USAC Championship took place at Silverstone and Brands Hatch and it didn't escape our notice how amateurish most teams, not all but most, were compared with European teams.

"Then the Orbiter came up and we made three of them at March Engines but they were not doing anything until George Bignotti was brought in to sort it out, and he turned it round and made a moderately competitive machine from it; Gary Bettenhausen brought one home third in the final round at Phoenix. Since George is a thorough guy, he flew over to see us and was obviously impressed by what he saw because he spread a good story about us."

The contract drawn up between March and Newman Racing shows why America was very attractive, for the cars were billed at $140,000 each for two or $110,000 apiece if Newman took up the option of further cars. At the time the dollar was weak, running at about $2.40 to the pound, so the $330,000 Newman paid for his three cars was just over £45,000 apiece. To put that into perspective, a March F2 car cost £18,950, an F Atlantic was £14,950, F3 and SuperVee cars were £12,450 and a March Sports 2000 car could be yours for £9,250.

Raw figures do not tell the whole story as special jigs and moulds had to be made and the contract demanded the presence of a March engineer at all the races (salary to be borne by March, reasonable expenses by Newman), so it was not quite a bonanza, and March made only a small profit, but that was better than the loss it made in some formulae. More importantly, it's the first instance of the package deal with a third party which provided a bespoke car plus an engineering service contract and that was to become an important thread in the story because, despite appearances to the contrary, March was virtually bankrupt.

16 March Builds a Williams

While March was coming to terms with plummeting sales and the opportunities presented across the Big Pond, Robin was again courted into F1. This time the wooer was John Macdonald, who had started his career as a North London used car dealer, tried his hand at racing and then turned to team management. He'd wheeled and dealed and built up a reputation for immaculate presentation and in 1976 had run some ex-works Brabhams in F1, but a disagreement with one of his drivers over his contract had led to legal action which had wiped him out.

Whatever else John is, he is a survivor, and when he was flat on his back he took the view that the only way to go was up. It was a hard struggle, but he found his niche in the British F1 (Aurora) Championship, and after struggling for two years with uncompetitive cars he was able to put together a good package for 1980 built around two ex-works Williams FW07s. Not only did his drivers, Emilio de Villota and Eliseo Salazar, finish first and second in the Championship but the cars also appeared on a rentadrive basis in Grands Prix.

John's star was ascending once more when, in 1978, he first approached Robin with a proposal to take them both back into Formula One. Initially the idea was to concentrate on the European races only, but over the next two years they thrashed out an agreement, and what emerged was March Grand Prix Ltd, a company jointly owned by RAM Racing (1977) Ltd (John's company) and Robin Herd, in other words, the car which emerged was a March which was not a March. It was a March in that it bore the name, but it was not a March in that the company which made it was a new one with no connection to March Engineering except that, since Robin was March Engineering, it was connected.

It was one of those complicated deals beloved of lawyers and on John's side he had employed a very able one, Norman Mazure, who so impressed Robin that he would become a director of March. Norman had been hired by John Macdonald to handle his side of the altercation with the disgruntled driver in 1976, one thing led to another and he had become a partner in RAM Racing. The agreement boiled down to John running the team from a unit leased from March with Robin in charge of engineering, and with each of them drawing a salary of £250 per week, making them the lowest paid team manager and chief engineer in Formula One. There would be profit sharing and expenses, but the bottom line is that they weren't counting the pay packet.

In the background was the BMW turbo engine and a letter from BMW dated 27 January, 1981, says *after the expiration of our exclusive supplying with Brabham, we are pleased to tell you that we are willing to supply our F1 engines to the March-Team on the condition that your team and your car guarantee a successful participation in F1; terms to be determined.*

With a carrot like that dangling before their eyes the partners had unusual incentive to get it right, but what followed was a cock-up. Robin's ideal would have been a turbo six-wheeler, but time was short, money tight and ground effect had been hard to master in F2 let alone F1 but Macdonald had his Williams FW07s and since Alan Jones won the 1980 World Championship in an FW07 it was decided to short-cut the usual development programme by making a direct copy which would at least get them in the game and serve as a base line.

Copying is endemic in racing; the BRPs of the Sixties were cribs of the Lotus 25, but didn't work as well; one team once intercepted another's plans on their way to a model maker and built a replica of the original and while that was piracy it was tacitly forgiven because the ploy had style; but when employees have run off a set of drawings to sell to another team that is rightly viewed as a serious betrayal of trust. A photographer who gets clear shots of one team's secret will find a market for his pictures among others, but everyone is at it. When Lotus discovered ground effect the others didn't say, 'That's Colin's advantage, good luck to him,' of course not, everyone set to and copied.

One who did was Patrick Head of Williams and his FW07 was essentially a refined Lotus 79, so when March Grand Prix made a direct copy of the Williams, one could say it was a copy of a copy but there was an important difference, as Mike Earle, a close friend of both John and Robin, explains: "When March GP made a copy of the Williams it indicated to me that they weren't serious. In the days before the Japanese became innovators they used to copy and would always end up with something which was not as good as the original. If March GP had taken the broad outline of the FW07 and gone from there the result would have been different, but when you are making a copy you can't see into the brain of the original designer and see the process of his thinking. Sure, the FW07 had followed the Lotus 79, but Patrick Head had looked at the

Lotus very carefully and worked out what made it tick, and when he made his own version, it had gone through his own thought processes."

"I think anyway Robin had this romantic image of turning up with a car on a trailer behind a Ford Transit and blowing off the establishment." It's an exaggeration, but not much of one; when he had last engineered an F1 car it was in '76 on a budget of £50,000, then racing with Ronnie had been fun, and he had led races and won one. Robin's head knew very well it wasn't like that any more, hence the clone, but others close to him have said much the same.

There was, too, the fact that not since 1972 had March built a bespoke F1 car (the 721X), so its philosophy had been shaped by the years of making customer cars and the essential difference is that an F1 car had become a basis for development, race to race, while a customer car had to be right straight out of the box with mods developed only if a problem occurred. Mike Earle says, "John Mac was totally motivated, he'd just won the Aurora Championship and was on a high. It was a good move for him because he could get back into F1 without setting up a manufacturing facility. Perhaps at the time it seemed a good move for Robin as well but John was the driving force and there wasn't the same commitment on Robin's part."

Robin says, "If you've got a very good racing car, everyone's responsible for it, if it's no good, nobody's responsible. I'm still trying to find who designed the Lotus 40. There were two distinct early 811s, the first of which was built in Cowley. The drawings were made by John Gentry and Paul Brown under Alan Mertens and they did a nice job, the prototype was quite sensible. The fundamental problem was that there was a cock-up in the production tubs. The prototype was overweight and it was decided to take some weight off by more or less having the gauge of the panels on the monocoque lightened, which made the tub weak and flexible and I've yet to discover who took that decision."

John Macdonald's view is different, "I can't see how they could be said to have done a good job when all they had to do was re-draw a Williams, but in typical March fashion they tried to cut corners and instead of using the materials Williams used they built it like a customer car, down to a price not up to a standard, with the result it was grossly overweight, and then they tried to cut corners again by reducing weight simply by using thinner-gauge sheeting and not lightweight alloys. It was all done on the cheap and the first car never saw the inside of a wind tunnel."

The problems were to become apparent very quickly, but in tests at Goodwood the prototype produced promising results; it was overweight, sure, but the times seemed to be competitive. The only trouble was that Goodwood was no longer used for racing and everyone else was making bigger strides. Robin was keen to put Teo Fabi in the car for the season, and in testing he equalled Derek Daly's times and Derek did not add to his reputation points by crashing heavily. The final decision was John Macdonald's, however, and he went for Daly's greater experience. "I realize now," he says, "it was the wrong choice. Derek looked promising, but was not a winner as his spell with Williams and his attempts at Indycar showed. Teo would have been the better bet because of his close rapport with Robin and that might have got Robin more involved."

"I doubt it," says Robin, "I like John, he's an attractive personality, and I thought we could work together, but as everyone finds out marriage is different to courtship. I realized it was wrong for me when I went into the works with some sheets setting out what we needed to do in the season, my *Principles of Operation* document, and handed them to the crew chief, Mick Ralph (RAM Racing = Ralph And Macdonald). The document is all basic stuff like detailing when the car should have an alignment check, things like that, but I heard later from four mechanics, separately, that Mick took it into the workshop, stood in the middle and tore the sheets into shreds.

"I went to see John and told him that if we were going to be successful we had to be united in our way of thinking and that the engineer should control engineering, and he had either to get Mick to toe the line or find another crew chief. He refused and I have to say I admired his loyalty to his mate, but I knew then I had to get out and would do so as soon as I found a sensible engineer to take over. I think that John has got what it takes to succeed in F1, but he was there for six years and had some pretty good designers, Adrian Reynard and Gustav Brunner among them, and some good drivers, and during that time he failed to win a single Championship point. I don't think the weakness was in John, his designers or drivers."

The installation of the Ford-Cosworth engine in the March 811 chassis. This is Salazar's car on the model's début in the 1981 South African Grand Prix which was eventually excluded from that year's World Championship series. **(Nigel Snowdon)**

Derek Daly with the 811 in the South African Grand Prix. He finished 11th and last, three laps in arrears. (**Nigel Snowdon**)

Derek Daly, whose Formula One career can best be described as disappointing, although he has since performed well in Indycar racing. (**Nigel Snowdon**)

Max Mosley, by this time with FOCA, and Robin Herd at the 1981 South African Grand Prix. The worries besetting Herd on both the business and domestic fronts are only too apparent in his face. (**Nigel Snowdon**)

When March was last in F1 Max Mosley ran the team, now he and Bernie Ecclestone ran FOCA, which was engaged in a struggle for power with FISA which had the support of the 'grandee constructors' such as Ferrari and Renault. During the winter FOCA members had gathered in a hotel in the Austrian town of Kitzbühel and in the dining room was a mural showing a cow being painted. A local legend had it that the town was once besieged and was down to its last cow, but the wily citizens would paint the cow different colours and let it be seen by the besiegers, who assumed they had a whole herd and so gave up. Colin Chapman looked at the mural and said, "We need a painted cow!"

Thus the 1981 F1 season kicked off with the FOCA-only South African GP, which was designed to bring the others to their senses, and since it passed off successfully, with full television coverage, it had the required effect, although behind the scenes, Ecclestone and Mosley had already reached a secret agreement with Jean-Marie Balestre of FISA but both parties were continuing the 'war' until the hearts and minds of the factions they represented had been won over.

The Marches that were not Marches ran in a Grand Prix that was not a Grand Prix and while it was a low-key début the general opinion was that the team looked promising. On their début, the cars gave problems which could be put down to newness, problems which could be easily solved. One of them was that downforce sucked the sidepods down but Derek Daly was to say, "Don't worry, the March is going to be a front-running chassis before long."

His team-mate was the Chilean Eliseo Salazar, whom everyone assumed was just another Latin-American rich kid but whom John rated highly. Eliseo had a fairly low profile in South Africa because he was recovering from hepatitis caused from eating a plate of strawberries, so it was not surprising that he was not on top form for his first GP, but his condition helped disguise the fact that all was not well with the car. Apart from that, part of the race was wet, so the cars were not subjected to ultimate stresses, which again disguised their weaknesses and Daly, always superb in the wet, had hauled himself, briefly, near the front of the field.

While this was going on, Robin was in daily contact by phone with his bank manager, who was looking for excuses to allow March to continue because it was on the rocks. Apart from the bank he was also phoning the solicitors handling his side of a divorce, which was to leave him with his clothes and his shares in March, and at the time the clothes looked the better long-term prospect.

"It was not a bitter divorce but my wife's solicitors did their best for her and if it hadn't been for a loan from Teo Fabi I wouldn't have had a roof over my head. When I was in South Africa, everything looked hopeless, the company was bust, I was penniless, the F1 team was having hysterics and I went through a period of deep depression for several days and then snapped out of it and formed a two-year plan of action in which to turn everything round. I knew I had to get out of the Formula One deal if I was to save March."

1981 was a season which was so filled with politics, disputes and crises at the highest level that it seems odd to look at it from a worm's-eye view. At Long Beach, the opening round of the World Championship, there was all the fuss over the twin-chassis Lotus 88, so in the grand scheme of things the fact that both the Marches were among the five cars which failed to qualify was largely missed, but in the March pit the despondent faces told their own story, the cars were impossible to drive. Nobody could even cite the *round black driver excuses* because (another of the crises) Goodyear had withdrawn and everyone was using the same hard-compound Michelins. Daly believed that the front of the car was flexing and the team stayed on in America to test at Laguna Seca, but the results were inconclusive; still, three days' testing was a rare luxury for the team.

In Brazil the big news was that Brabham had hydro-pneumatic suspension which lowered the car once it was under way so it could use the bodywork to replace the sliding skirts which had just been outlawed while passing the 6cm ground clearance rule when stationary. This time, however, people did take notice of why both Marches failed to qualify, for the basic problem was revealed when Daly had a wishbone pull away from the tub. It wasn't just that the cars were slow, they were badly made and there was amusement at the sight of the team beefing up the monocoques by re-skinning them. John said to anyone who would listen, "The car is a pile of shit, and that's official!" Robin was in Brazil and he is a man who does not lose his temper, while John is volatile and direct. That combination makes for the worst kind of an argument, two calm people can work through their differences, two fiery ones can have a blazing row and clear the air. The trouble with a calm person arguing with a fiery one is that neither can understand the other *How can you be so calm about this disaster? It's no use losing your temper.* The relationship which, was already shaky, was irreparably damaged and Robin flew home.

John could see his dreams of the big time slipping away, but, typically, his thoughts were of his team, "They work 18 hours a day and then the car fails to qualify and the Chief Engineer runs away. But I'm not going to be beaten, one day I shall have a car that's going to win a Grand Prix and nobody will stop me from doing it." Now he says, "When things got tough and we had an eyeball, he didn't want to know. The agreement we had was that Formula One would be his number one priority (*and number two and three according to their correspondence*), but he only came to one other race and that was in Belgium. Was I left in the lurch? Ask anyone who was around at the time."

Robin says, "I had already made my decision and the fiasco in Brazil had not helped matters, so I began to cast around for another engineer to take on the job. I approached a number of people, and finally Gordon Coppuck took it on and I think he did a good job."

One of the prototype (heavy) tubs was flown out to Argentina as a replacement for Daly but neither car qualified. A month went by and they appeared at Imola and this time Salazar got on to the grid, just, but it was only because of the struggle among the big boys, since Lotus scratched its entries when its twin-chassis car was ruled illegal. Daly might have made the grid as well, but too late it was discovered that one of his rear dampers had collapsed. It was an incident which highlighted a fundamental problem in the team, the cars were beautifully turned out but there was no depth of engineering expertise.

Robin's back was to the wall and he was having to fight for the future of his company because that's all he had. His whole career in motor racing had been about fighting, but this was a different sort of battle and he chose to spend almost the entire year in the States engineering the Can-Am cars and attending Indycar meetings to look after his new customers and hustle for more. It was a complicated situation. From March's point of view Robin made the right choice in concentrating on America because it was saved and went from strength to strength but that was no comfort to John, who'd staked everything he had on an agreement which, for whatever reasons, was not kept and apart from anything else he had the right to expect a better car than the one he received.

There was an irony in the Belgian GP when Daly's car came to be measured at scrutineering and the rear was found to snag the gauge. It would have been the work of a few minutes to rectify the matter, but the scrutineers did not think to tell the team and Daly set a time which would have seen him on the grid only to have it disallowed for running an 'illegal' car. Since the next day was wet he had no chance of repeating the performance and so missed the

Jochen Mass, who joined the RAM team for 1982, and was perhaps past his best as a Formula 1 driver. (**Nigel Snowdon**)

race, but the irony was that the Marches were about the only legal cars at the race, since the rule benders had discovered semantics, and to complement their hydro-pneumatic suspension systems (which meant the cars had virtually no wheel travel) they had persuaded the authorities that rubber skirts were 'solid' as required by the rules. March GP had enough difficulty making a conventional car behave itself, without getting into trick systems. Still, by then new cars had been made which used honeycomb sections in their tubs, the work of Gordon Coppuck, who had been Chief Designer at McLaren until the arrival of Ron Dennis and John Barnard.

Gordon is not only one of the nicest and most modest men in motor racing, an activity not noted for reticence, but one of the most competent and under-rated designers in the business. He had worked at National Gas Turbines at the same time as Robin and when Robin moved to McLaren in 1965 it was not long before he had Gordon working alongside him: "Robin was the scientist, I was a draughtsman/designer. My main work at March in 1981 was on the F2 cars, but there was a gap in the middle of the season when there was only one F2 race and I agreed to move over to the F1 project for six races; by then I did not want to be involved in F1 on a permanent basis, but I must say I thoroughly enjoyed working with John Macdonald."

With only 20 cars on the grid at Monaco there was no point in the team turning up, but turn up they did and both failed to get past pre-qualifying. There they had hydro-pneumatic suspension but Derek had a drive-shaft break, which did for his chances, and Eliseo spun, which did for his. After that Daly thought seriously of quitting and trying his hand at Can-Am while Salazar voted with his feet and took his sponsorship to Ensign, where he won a lot of respect. His defection concentrated everyone's minds and, with Gordon being a temporary fixture, Adrian Reynard was called in to engineer the car.

Since his first meeting with Bill Stone on his conducted tour of March, Adrian had been engaged in a small way of business doing sub-contract fabrication and making FF2000 cars, which had been very successful for a time. During 1980 Rupert Keegan had hired one of RAM's Williams FW07s for several Grands Prix, but generally failed to qualify until he'd suggested that Adrian be brought in to engineer the car, and he had made an immediate improvement. Adrian had hoped the relationship would continue into 1981 and when it didn't he was left with his own company, which was then working a three-day week and glad to be making whelk trays for a fish merchant at £3 a time.

Adrian says, "I inherited something called a March 811. I know it was a copy of the FW07, but it was actually a different car, there were no interchangeable parts. It was overweight, but there were a lot of good pieces of engineering on it and I think it was a sensible way to start. I only ever had one meeting with Robin while I was there. He sat in on one of the debriefs I did after a test and he said, 'Fine, fine sounds great,' smiled, and disappeared and that's all I ever had to do with him. Our only other connection was in the 1982 team brochure where his picture is alongside mine and I am billed as *Chief Engineer* and he is *Chief Engineering Executive*."

Adrian's presence had an immediate effect and Daly was on the grid for the first time at the next race, Jarama. True it was only the 22nd slot and he finished 16th and last

After several dismal failures, Derek Daly qualified 22nd for the Spanish Grand Prix at Jarama and finished 16th. (**Nigel Snowdon**)

At the British Grand Prix Daly drove a shorter and lighter 811 and after losing a lap in the pits to sort out a loose gear linkage he finished seventh. **(Nigel Snowdon)**

classified runner, but it was progress. It was even better at the French GP, where he qualified 20th and so received starting money. One of the problems of the season had been a tyre crisis which had seen the return of Goodyear and the appearance of Avon. In France March GP switched from Michelin radials to Avon crossplies and the car seemed to work better on them.

Real progress came at the British GP, where Daly had a new chassis which was shorter, 58lb lighter, and had a more rounded nose, just like the latest Williams. It was, in effect, an 811B and in qualifying it featured angled skirts but these caused porpoising and it ran with straight skirts in the race, where Daly was a revelation. He had to pit after two laps with a loose gear linkage and rejoined a lap down, but be was wound up and in the end he brought it home seventh and save for that lost lap it might have been third. Car and driver could both go well, the weakness was in the team and it's not good when a gear linkage works free after only two laps.

From then on Daly normally occupied 19th or 20th place on the grid, which was a creditable performance considering that he didn't have a turbo engine or even one of the special Cosworths which some teams had. Williams, for example, commissioned a development programme from John Judd and Arrows was able to buy the tweaks a year in arrears. Nor did he have the trick qualifying tyres which the big teams were using since the return of Goodyear in mid-season had seen the return of a tyre war in which Avon was a non-combatant.

Throughout the season Adrian worked away on a weight-shedding programme and also designed a new rear suspension which was used in testing. At the end of the season Daly moved on and the team signed Jochen Mass and Raul Boesel. Adrian says, "Looking back, I think Jochen was too old to go quickly and Raul was too inexperienced. Still we were getting a good press and people were saying that we were a team who should make progress. Over the winter I re-engineered the car, made it stiffer, and managed to shed another 50lb. We didn't have too many reliability problems, the car looked good and was a lot quicker straight out of the box."

Since Adrian had applied fundamental engineering to the problem and had not come up with anything trick he had put the car into the state it should have been at the start of 1981. The times recorded by Mass and Boesel in the early races in '82 would have put them on the front row of the grid in '81, but unfortunately everyone else had made equal progress. Adrian had done very well to bring the weight down from 630kg to 580kg, the legal limit, but others had their cars down to 550kg and were making up the difference by disposable water ballast, sorry, perfectly legitimate brake coolant which just happened to get dumped on the warm-up lap if the team remembered to top it up in the first place. Further, there were more turbo cars in the field and Goodyear and Michelin had made large strides, while March GP was contracted to Pirelli, which was struggling to catch up, one problem being that its tyres were inconsistent in quality.

Just as the 1981 South African GP had seen FOCA's 'painted cow', so the 1982 race saw a drivers' strike and lock-in over a clause in their contracts. Jochen Mass earned a few brownie points with his team by refusing to join the strike and he circulated on the track alone with the mechanics of every other team holding out pit boards with ever more fantastic times on them. That was light relief in an unpleasant situation, but when the dispute was patched up, the hard reality of qualifying saw both the cars at the back of the grid (although Boesel was the quickest of the Pirelli users) and way down the finishing order.

When March GP appeared at the next race the cars were in a new livery. Guy Edwards who had had a long relationship with John Macdonald, both as a driver and as a sponsorship-finder, had landed Rothmans. Even for the uncrowned king of sponsorship it was a spectacular coup and outsiders expected March to climb up the grid, but throughout the season it remained resolutely static and from the moment the sponsorship arrived to the end of the season only twice did a March qualify in the top 20.

The problem was a little like a man close to death by starvation being shown a table groaning with food. The natural inclination is to gorge, but that can kill. When John Macdonald was shown the groaning table, he gorged and perhaps the money was not spent as judiciously as it might have been.

Adrian Reynard: "Everything looked good, I was in charge, John seemed to have faith in me, we had Rothmans money and I thought at last I've got a chance to do a good job. I was happy just to be in Grand Prix racing as chief engineer of a team which I thought was spending the money in the right direction and I instigated a wind tunnel programme and chose some more machinery. I was just about to action my wind tunnel programme, having made the model, and suddenly the programme was axed and the machines which I had hoped to have weren't coming and I was restricted on this, that, and the other. Then we had been using Pirellis, which had come free, and at Monaco we suddenly switched to Avons, which had to be paid for. I couldn't understand what was going on."

John says, "Adrian was new to F1 and had no idea how the money was spent or what everything cost and he also did not know we had lost Rothmans." The Rothmans deal was for three years and John had been in the process of setting up a three-year programme which had to have the best people if it was to succeed. The trouble was that while he was doing that he was failing to educate his sponsors in the realities of racing, that it would take time to use the money effectively, improvements this year, a new car next year and so on. They had been sold a *Give us the money and we'll be winners* sort of deal and when the results didn't immediately appear they wanted reasons. Hell, they'd provided the money, hadn't they, and money buys things, doesn't it?

Then there was politicking going on at Rothmans and some could point to the motor racing involvement as an error of judgement on the part of others. Of course, if March GP had been in the points it would have been a different matter, but since it struggled it became a pawn in corporate politics. Then again, there were those in racing who were jealous of the fact that John had landed so big a sponsor. They whispered in the right ears, 'Macdonald's hopeless, now if you came with us we could do a really super job for you.'

John knew what was going on and the switch to Avon was symptomatic of his panic. It was a desperate move because it meant offending a major supplier and giving up free tyres, but a test session at Croix-en-Ternois had shown the car worked better on them. A week or so before Monaco Avon had announced its withdrawal from F1 and John had stepped in and bought all its remaining stock.

By any normal standards it was a dumb move, because tyres do not improve by being stored in a workshop, while Pirelli was actively working at its problems, but the timing of the switch is significant. Monaco is an anachronism, but it's the place for teams to entertain the corporate fat cats and their wives or secretaries so they can strut around with their privilege passes and pretend to be part of the beautiful people for the weekend. Later they can drop it into their conversation, *When I was at Monaco overseeing one of our cars . . . that Niki Lauda, helluva nice guy . . . you ever been to Rosie's?* and all the rest of the crap which makes most enthusiasts come away from Monaco as revolutionaries looking for rope and lamp posts.

Monaco was the last chance of hanging on to Rothmans, but since neither car qualified that chance disappeared and the three-year programme Reynard had instigated had to be axed. Away from the power politics, and not taken into the boss's confidence, Adrian had a different perspective. "I felt as though I had lost engineering control and that John had lost confidence in me. As a result I was working even harder to try to catch up and I wasn't doing myself any good. I was working a 15-hour day, going in early, working late, and trying to run my own business in between. I realized I wasn't enjoying it, I wasn't in control of my own destiny. I felt John had lost faith in me and so it just sort of disintegrated.

Jochen Mass in practice for the 1982 Monaco Grand Prix with the March 821. Three cars were entered, none qualified and the RAM team lost its Rothmans sponsorship. (**Nigel Snowdon**)

Rupert Keegan at Monza for the Italian Grand Prix where the 821s were fitted with pull-rod front suspension. Neither Keegan, nor team-mate Boesel qualified. (**Nigel Snowdon**)

"The good thing is that John did give me a fantastic opportunity. Nobody else had recognized that I was capable of doing anything other than Formula Ford and I will always remember that as being a courageous move to make. I've got an incredibly soft spot for him, he's a enthusiast with his heart in the right place. Sometimes, though, his heart rules his head and I don't think he was astute enough to realize the importance of engineering. He had been successful in F5000 and British F1 by running other people's standard engineering product and applying liberal lashings of bullshit and colour to it and the standard of preparation was high, but it wasn't enough in Formula One."

John says, "I never lost confidence in Adrian, but as I've said, he was new in F1, and it's still his only period in F1, and he did not understand all the financial problems and politics. In fact I can prove I still have a lot of confidence in Adrian since I now buy cars from him."

But we have gone ahead of ourselves in the story. After the races in South and North America, where the cars were slow, shiny, but tended to finish, it wasn't until May that March GP raced again because the FISA/FOCA war had extended to a FOCA boycott of the San Marino GP. When the whole circus assembled again at Zolder there was a third March for the Spanish amateur Emilio de Villota, which was run by Onyx Race Engineering.

Mike Earle: "By 1982 John Mac was basically separate from March Engineering, but he had decided to continue and had signed de Villota. Then Guy Edwards came up with the Rothmans deal – Rothmans wanted total corporate identity on the cars but John didn't want to kick de Villota into touch. I don't think it was a matter of money, he had given his word, and he approached us to see if we would run Emilio. At the time we weren't doing much so we were happy to do it."

After running Riccardo Paletti successfully in F2 in 1981, and transforming him from a raw driver with little experience, apart from crashing, into a serious contender, Onyx had been offered the opportunity to run a car for him in F1, but Mike felt that he wasn't yet ready and another year in F2 would be sensible. Riccardo was over-anxious to graduate and took his sponsor with him to Osella, which was the reason that Onyx was at a loose end. Poor Riccardo was to die in only the second GP he started when he drove into the back of Pironi's stalled Ferrari on the grid in Canada.

Mike continues, "We did five races, but Emilio failed to qualify for any of them and he then decided he didn't want to continue. He'd won the British F1 Championship, but at the top level he was out of his depth. He was a lovely, lovely, man, the last of the gentleman amateurs, but with the British F1 title under his belt he was on a high and it caused him to make the wrong decision. Had he taken his sponsor, and his high, into sports car racing he might have had a good career.

"It was quite interesting working alongside the works programme, being part of it yet separate, seeing it not from the outside but from just inside the door. I think the problem was that not everyone was united in the same objectives, some wanted to make money, others wanted to win races. I think the Rothmans money unbalanced the team. It takes time to build a team, you have to build an infrastructure, you have to learn how to win. If you had all the money in the world you could go out and hire the most brilliant people in the world, but you would have only bought a *package*, it would still take time to make a team."

March GP had become 'Team Bullshit' and nowhere was that better illustrated than at Brands Hatch, where Rothmans brought in Britt Ekland and other starlets, who hung about the March paddock area wearing Rothmans gear and looking gorgeous. They were doubtless overjoyed to know that Jochen Mass was running with new wide track front and rear suspension and applauded his gritty drive on to the back row of the grid. A year later John Macdonald was back at Brands Hatch for the European GP and then his RAM team had one car (which didn't qualify) and there were no starlets, no freebie race gear, no tables under umbrellas with a caterer topping up glasses. A sadder, wiser, man he repeated almost word for word what Mike Earle says.

In the next race, the French GP, Jochen's car touched another and he was launched into the air and came to rest on a spectator banking, a few more feet and there would have been carnage. He sustained cracked ribs and tried practising for the German GP, but the pain was too much and Rupert Keegan took over the car; then during qualifying Didier Pironi's Ferrari crashed and he suffered injuries which ended his brilliant career. The year had already been marred by the deaths of Paletti and Villeneuve and when Pironi's accident was added to these and his own narrow escape in France, Jochen decided F1 was no longer for him.

March GP struggled to the end of the year, still trying hard to find some extra speed right up to the end. At Monza there was pull-rod front suspension and a switch to Michelins, which created more problems than it solved, for the radial tyres did not grow when hot as the Avon crossplies had, so the cars wore their skirts away. March GP faded away and RAM Racing came back, still operating in the same unit at Bicester, a stone's throw away from both Reynard and March. In 1983 a new car was built and entered as a RAM-March, but it was a March only in the paperwork; effective connection had ended in 1981, formal connection had ended at the end of 1982, when some of the personnel returned to March Engineering.

John says now, "On reflection, March GP was a cock-up from beginning to end. We did not have the right people, the right infrastructure, the right money or the right drivers. Nothing was right and eight years on I am still suffering the effects of the project."

17 March Discovers America

1981 saw March production nosedive, yet it made more models than in any year in its history with cars for F1, 2, 3, Atlantic, Indycar, Can-Am and IMSA, and a Sports 2000 model and, for good measure, a one-off hill climb car based on the 812. The size of the model range shows how desperate things were. If there was a market March was there, it was the only way to stay afloat. There wasn't much profit in a Sports 2000, but at least it kept the workforce occupied and helped pay the wage bill. During the winter of 1980/81 March Engineering was bankrupt in all but name and at Kyalami Robin had been in the depths of despair, but had formed a two-year game plan, but he is quick to say that the man who made the difference to its success or failure was Dave Reeves.

"Dave can be an awkward, grumpy, old cuss," says Robin, "but we owe him so much. When Max was with us, he basically looked after the outside world, I looked after the factory. Then, when he left, I took over his role and Dave took over mine. We worked alongside each other for a couple of years and then he was on his own, and I'm not saying he's always been super-efficient but he got things moving and injected life into the place. I tend to vacillate, but when the American market loomed Dave almost took me by the scruff of the neck, told me we were going to do it, and started to build the cars.

"He's not a trained engineer and is better for it because he brings lateral thinking to bear on problems. His input into the Can-Am and Indy cars was considerable and they were successful because of him. The critical dimensions were the same as the Williams FW07 so we knew they would work, but the difference between the cars built for March GP and the ones made for America was that Dave was responsible and put a lot of his own ideas into them.

"Doing Can-Am and Indycar meant I spent most of my time in America in 1981 and to give some idea of how desperate things were, I used to be at Victoria at seven in the morning so I could get a cheap stand-by flight in the afternoon – it was the only way I could afford to travel. Later, when I was based in the States and was only at the factory 20 days a year, it was Dave who kept things going and the company owes him an enormous debt of thanks."

Dave had formed a plan for Indycar, but nothing was happening about it and things looked pretty hopeless all round in December 1980, but as he recalls, "Just before Christmas one of those miracles happened. Alan 'Mad Dog' McCall rang to say that he had met Don Whittington and had sent him on to Bicester. None of us had heard of Don, but he duly arrived with a suitcase full of cash, just like in the movies, and by the end of that day we had the go-ahead on the project and the Whittingtons bought four cars from us. Don is a charismatic man and a very good driver, it's a pity he got involved in shady deals because I think he could have gone to the very top.

"A couple of weeks later George Bignotti arrived saying he'd got together his money and where was his car? It was a bit like '69 again, but this time I was in the hot seat. Perhaps we should have dropped the Whittingtons and concentrated on George, after all he had the knowledge, the team, and the driver, and it was his faith that had got us started, but Don had given us money which had been spent several times over and, besides, a deal is a deal. I felt we had no option but to do both and it was the best decision from our point of view, because if Sneva had gone quick in a car prepared by Bignotti everyone would have nodded and said, 'What do you expect?' As it was, when Bill Whittington went out and qualified at over 197 mph at Indy, all the pundits said, 'Wow, that must be one helluva car.'

"It was fairy tale-time for us because we'd gone from the depths of despair to the heights of elation in just a few weeks. I remember supervising a torsion test on the prototype 81C just before it was delivered and discovering that the area around the gear shift was flexing too much. I authorized a mod which delayed the car 24 hours and Don was threatening to shoot me, literally, if I didn't release it, otherwise he would miss the last possible practice day. This would have been at the end of March, because Indy is closed throughout April. The car left Bicester on a Saturday night, after we'd worked around the clock for days on end, and once it had gone we all collapsed.

"Later I had a call from the States; it was Keith Leyton ringing from Indy. I was expecting another rollicking, but instead he said, 'Listen to this . . .', he held out the phone and I could hear a car going round at high speed. 'That's the 81C,' he said. It was just 35 hours after it had left us, Bicester to Gatwick, Gatwick to Atlanta, Atlanta to Indy, and out on the track, and if that isn't a record of some sort I'd be very surprised."

The Whittington brothers were prominent in many forms of American racing and two of them, Don and Bill, had stood on the winner's rostrum with Klaus Ludwig at

Two views of George Bignotti's March 81C before shipping to Indianapolis in 1981, showing the installation of the Cosworth DFX engine and the front suspension. (**Autosport**)

Le Mans in 1979. They made their money by running a private airline which imported smokers' (non-tobacco) requisites into the USA from South America and their fleet consisted of ex-WW2 Mustangs, which they also used for pylon racing, but the business was run without official approval. When Uncle Sam found out he issued the brothers invitations to be his guests for lengthy periods.

Robin says, "The Whittingtons did a lot for us, they were good drivers and good engineers and although they made their money in an unofficial sort of way they were not the only ones. NASCAR racing grew from running moonshine and by the same token a lot of people in IMSA funded their racing by running certain substances. Quite a number of our former customers are languishing inside now, for as government agencies got sharper our IMSA market shrank. It's a funny thing, though, that when these people came into racing they were pretty straight in their dealing and behaviour, perhaps straighter than most; it's as though people leave their backgrounds behind when they enter the sport. It's the same in Europe too, there are some people in racing who have made their money outside the law, but in racing they almost fall over backwards to be legitimate, to be accepted on the same level as everyone else, because when you're running wheel to wheel, racing is pure. On a different level the same thing occurred when I was working with Paul Newman; he was not the film star he was the guy running the team."

While the 811 was a disaster in F1, partly because it was overweight, the same tub could be beefed up for Indycar, which had a higher minimum weight limit, and when Gordon Coppuck joined March his input was decisive. It was said that his major contribution was work on the aerodynamics but he says, "that part was over-emphasized, what I really did was to lay down the parameters for torsional stiffness." That's his version, but Gordon is a modest man, others will tell you that he contributed in dozens of ways. In any case, the torsional rigidity of the tub was the difference between the successful Indycar and the failed F1 car.

George Bignotti was working with Dan Cotter and their driver was Tom Sneva, who actually set fastest qualifying time at Indy with his 81C at 200.691 mph, but due to a peculiarity of the race's tradition, since it was not set on the first day it did not count for pole, but the point was made. Sneva led the race, too, until side-lined with gearbox trouble. He went on to lead most races that season, but was usually a non-finisher, mainly because of the transverse Weismann gearbox, but he did manage to win two of the shorter races. Part of the problem was that March was in a new environment with a lot to learn and here Bignotti came into his own as he 'Americanized' the design, changing the locations of ancillaries and making it stronger and better able to cope with the variety of American circuits from banked ovals to road races.

It was fortunate that the 81C had landed in the hands of a good team and driver. Sneva was pretty special at the time, because it made all the difference and explains the irony that the 81C, which derived from the 811, a failed Williams FW07 copy, was quicker than the Longhorn, which had been based directly on the FW07 via a deal with Williams. However, the March was in the hands of an expert while with the Longhorn Patrick Head and Frank Williams were dealing with a team whose level of competence was, shall we say, rather less than they were used to.

While Whittington and Sneva had established March's credibility at Indy the big breakthrough came when A.J. Foyt abandoned the Coyote he built himself and switched to an 81C. Then Foyt gave March its first Indycar win in the Pocono 500, although it was the time of the USAC/CART wars and the field was pretty thin, in fact it was padded out by eight front-engined roadsters and most of the USAC Championship races were on the old fairground ovals. Still Foyt was The Man and the fact that he had switched to March was significant, a seal of approval the other good ole boys could take note of. Also significant was the fact that, although Sneva won only two of the shorter events, one was very important, *the last race of the season*.

Paradoxically, at the time when March's traditional

Tom Sneva tests Bignotti's 81C. Note the plain white paintwork without sponsorship (although the team did have sponsorship at Indianapolis). Note also, in all the American March photographs, that most American owners removed the March name from the nose. (**Autosport**)

American market, Formula Atlantic, was rapidly drying up (although Jacques Villeneuve won the series in an 81A run by March's long-time US importer, Doug Shierson) it was enjoying a higher profile Stateside than ever before because not only was it the pace-setter in Indycar, but Teo Fabi was also setting the pace for Newman Racing in Can-Am backed up, variously, by Al Unser and Bobby Rahal in the second car. In truth there were never more than half a dozen competitive cars plus make-weights in any race, but those half-dozen were sharp and, besides, it only takes two to make a race.

Robin says, "Barry Green, an Australian who had been a designer at Chevron, was Newman's team manager and he was very good, a great guy. Teo was not doing much and I recommended that Barry took him on because I believed the car would work. Initially there were doubts about the cars because the other driver was Al Unser and he was way off the pace, and since Al is a big star the fault had to be in the car; but when Teo got into it he was about three seconds a lap faster.

"Teo won the first two rounds, retired from the third and then in practice at Elkhart Lake he lost it on a fast corner, it went backwards and because it was a wing car it took off, left the track, cleared the barrier and ended up in a farmer's field a hundred yards away. Teo didn't buy the farm, he was just looking. It was a big accident and there was massive deceleration which left him with two black eyes but he then got into Unser's car, did a lap, and stuffed it on pole. Now that left Paul Newman with a problem – who would run in the race. He nominated Al and in retrospect that helped to throw away the Championship.

"Al is a gentleman, he realized he wasn't cutting the mustard and soon he told Paul that the best thing he could do was to forgo the rest of his very large retainer and bow out for someone else. Bobby Rahal got the drive and he was comparable with Teo in terms of pace but he didn't then have Teo's stamina, so he tended to fade towards the end of races, but for Newman that drive was his first big chance.

"Teo was incredible, that year he drove as well as anyone I've ever worked with, and that includes Jackie

The Newman Racing March 817 cars of Teo Fabi and Bobby Rahal proved a strong force in Can-Am in 1981 and Fabi, seen here leading, won four of the year's eight races. (**Autosport**)

Stewart, although he has also had his off years. Mid-way through the season he had his appendix out one Wednesday, put the car on pole at Mosport on the Saturday, and won the race on the Sunday. Late in the season, at Riverside, he was called in for a tyre change and someone didn't do a wheel up properly and it fell off after half a mile; that was another 'if' of the season and, to make it worse, he didn't really need a tyre change."

As if all this were not enough, the American connection became even stronger through an unexpected source: a sports car for BMW built at Cowley by March Engines. This was a special version of the M1 coupé for the new GTP class of the IMSA series, which was taking off in a big way and was not only attracting the traditional sports car competitor (wealthy amateur or experienced journeyman) but also young hotshoes. The BMW M1C was lighter, lower and aerodynamically superior to the standard car, its body was by the French aerodynamacist Dr Max Sardou, and he came up with a design which was recognizably the sire of the March series of Group C/IMSA cars although it had the BMW twin-nostril grille

David Hobbs at the wheel of the BMW M1C, built by March and with body designed by Dr. Max Sardou. It proved largely unsuccessful, although it had immense promise. (**Autosport**)

The 1981 March 81S Sports 2000 car that proved less than successful, mainly because March was involved in so many other projects. (**Autosport**)

in the middle of the front air intake.

The BMW M1C was entrusted to the capable hands of David Hobbs, who says, "It could have been a very successful car, it handled well and was lighter than the Lolas, but it did not have the whole-hearted commitment of BMW, North America. Some there were keen, others were not, so it was done on sufferance and one sign of that was that the team running it was was obviously chosen because it was cheap, it wasn't a very professional outfit.

"We started off with the straight six 3.5 litre lump which was not the most powerful engine but was pretty reliable, and while the car was fragile in some areas, bits fell off the bodywork and things like that, it went well and I took pole at Lime Rock with Brian Redman's Lola-Chevy alongside and I reckon I would have won except for a contretemps with Rolf Stommelen which I don't think was my fault. Of course, back at base, the BMW people, who were far removed from racing, began to ask why the car wasn't winning and they decided it was the engine, which it wasn't, so we had to have the 320 turbo unit, which was nowhere near as reliable as the straight six and the inlet system wasn't up to snuff. It could have been a successful car if there'd been more commitment from BMW, but at the end of the season they decided to pull the plug on it, which in my experience is typical of BMW, North America."

While the BMW M1C was not a success, it opened March's eyes to another market and gave it a base line to work from. Moreover, European endurance racing was about to go through a fundamental change with the introduction of Group C at the beginning of 1982 and the same design could be adapted to both classes. From being a company who appeared not to understand a racing car unless all four wheels were in the open air, over the next five years March was to be second only to Porsche in terms of numbers built for Group C/IMSA.

The other sports car, the 81S built for the Sports 2000 category, was designed by Ian Reed, and was a neat little car, but was not particularly successful mainly because there was not much turnover of drivers in the formula since most were amateurs racing for fun and most preferred to stick to the makes they knew, mainly Tiga, Royale and Lola. Rob Wilson recalls: "It was the best March I've ever driven, a very pleasant car. I remember once leading a Thundersports race in one, even though it was the least powerful car in the race." Like so many March projects, though, it was swamped by the sheer range being made and did not receive much development or sales push so is perhaps an instance of a car which was better than its results might suggest.

While all this excitement was going on, in its traditional happy hunting ground, F2, March found itself facing stiff new opposition, not only from the Ralt-Honda and Lola, which made the Toleman under licence, but from other makers such as Minardi and Maurer, who had moved into the vacuum which F2 had become, for of the main 1980 contestants only March and AGS remained.

Conventional thinking has it that Ralt landed the Honda deal because the last time Honda had been in F2 it had been with Brabham, in 1966, when the combination had been the class of the field, and since the designer of the car was Ron Tauranac, he was the natural person to turn to. Tauranac believes that is the case and since he wasn't building production F2 cars he could happily take it on board because he would not be competing against customers. He says, "We built and sold cars, it's as simple as that. We'd not been running a team, but when the chance came along we took it and used F2 as a development exercise."

According to some at March it's not quite as simple as that; Ralt was virtually unknown in Japan, while March had been the regular winner of the Japanese National F2 Championship since 1973, and had often supplied the winner of the Grand Champion series as well, so it was top of Honda's shopping list. It was a tempting offer, this version says, but it would have to be an exclusive works deal, and which meant March could not maintain the front that *our cars are the same as the customer cars*. It was one thing to run special BMW units, it was another thing to run a make of engine which was denied to anyone else.

Two versions of the same story, and mutually contradictory, so one cannot take sides and say which is the right one, but the truth is likely to lie in the space between and it is fair to say, without implying preference for the two versions, that March was big in Japan and Robin became something of a star. One Yokohama Tyre advertising campaign ran a quote of his, "Robin Herd reveals why he chose race car engineering, 'I just enjoy motor racing! What better way than to spend your whole life doing what you enjoy . . . second best.'" Robin says, "I can't resist the one-liner, the same thing ruined Oscar Wilde and it's going to get me into trouble one day."

So far as F2 and Honda was concerned, another point to ponder was the long relationship with BMW, which was bearing fruit with the IMSA car, plus the fact that Paul Rosche felt that he could tease even more power from the engine. He did so, and the works motors had about 315 bhp for 1981, which was about the same as the best Harts but since Brian Hart had graduated to F1 along with Toleman, and his little factory had limited capacity, there were only two serious Hart users, Kenny Acheson and Stefan Johansson in the works connected, but under-

Swiss privateer Jurg Lienhard who led the International Trophy at Silverstone with his 812-BMW until his battery went flat and he slipped back to finish 12th. (**Autosport**)

Riccardo Paletti with his Onyx March 812-BMW. He finished second at Silverstone and third at Thruxton, but achieved little later in the season. (**Autosport**)

financed, Docking-Spitzley team. By comparison, the V6 Honda had about 10 per cent more power, or so it was rumoured, although all the extra horses tended to huddle together at the top of the rev range. Still, Honda does not do things by halves, and Ralt was not only properly funded but its drivers, Mike Thackwell and Geoff Lees, were actually *paid* to drive, something which had not happened in F2 for years. You could not get long odds on Ralt-Honda for the Championship.

Ralt seemed beyond reach as Thackwell and Lees dominated the International Trophy, with Mike winning the day before his twentieth birthday after Geoff spun, but there was very nearly a major upset when, having made the right choice of tyres in a wet/dry race, the Swiss privateer Jurg Lienhard, better known as a show-jumper, driving an up-rated 802 found himself with a huge lead at about two-thirds distance, but luck was not on his side and the battery went flat, so he slipped down the order and eventually finished 12th. It was heart-breaking to watch, for Lienhard must have had the whole-hearted support of every neutral (and sodden) fan at the circuit, but after his moment of glory he never shone again and had withdrawn by the end of the season.

A Ralt 1–2 appeared certain a week later at Hockenheim, but Thackwell started to run out of fuel, Lees spun, and victory went to Johansson's Toleman-Hart. Then in the third round, at Thruxton, Roberto Guerrero's Maurer-BMW won from Riccardo Paletti in the Onyx March. Since Paletti had also finished second at Silverstone, after three rounds he was the most successful March driver, and second in the Championship, but that was to be the high spot of his year, he was overhauled in the tyre war and a big accident in testing did not help either.

The March works team was not showing its usual form, yet it had one of its strongest teams ever: Gordon Coppuck engineered Corrado Fabi, Teo's younger brother, Ralph Bellamy looked after Christian Danner, while John Wickham paired with Thierry Boutsen, so despite the Ralt-Honda threat things looked fairly positive. Goodyear had abandoned F2, so tyre choice came down to Pirelli or the little American firm M & H, and most of the leading runners opted for Pirelli, but Toleman had progressed to F1, Pirelli went with them and as team and tyre company went through a painful learning process at the top level, F2 tyres received less attention and were a problem for many users.

March was not the only team to find the Pirellis difficult, Ralt was another, and one reason for Paletti doing well was that Onyx had opted for M & H crossplies, Mike Earle reasoning that it was better to be at the front of the queue with a small, keen, outfit than near the back with a big one which had a lot of people to please.

John Wickham had been doing a lot of liaison work for March in Japan and had formed a high opinion of Bridgestone, whom he knew was considering a move into Europe. He and Thierry had been in Japan for a race early in 1981, and the result was that each came back with two sets of tyres as hand luggage. It is not known what the Russians, during the stop-over at Moscow, made of the sight of two men each trying to control eight racing Bridgestones in the concourse.

John says, "At Thruxton I decided to run Thierry on Bridgestones, which was a big decision to take since it meant upsetting a major supplier, and I was acting in the belief, not knowledge, they would be superior. As it happened, Thierry took pole by a huge margin and led the first 15 laps until the engine gave out. From then on we stuck with Bridgestone and Christian Danner switched too." Since Fabi stayed with Pirelli, it must be one of the very few times in racing history when a works team has used two different makes of tyres concurrently.

Soon Ralt made the switch as well for, despite appearances during the first races, it was in some disarray. Not only were the Pirellis not working well on the car but the engine's narrow power band and poor pick-up were giving their drivers problems. Then during unofficial practice at Thruxton Thackwell had a huge shunt which he was lucky to survive, but it smashed his left leg, left him unconscious for three days, and was the turning point in a career which looked firmly pointed towards F1. Geoff Lees had to carry the team from then on but at least on Bridgestones the car felt safe.

Boutsen not only won the fourth round, at the Nürburgring, but set pole by an incredible 62 seconds, the second of what would be five pole positions. Eje Elgh's Maurer was the next winner, at Vallelunga, and by this time Honda was not at all happy. March-Hondas were doing well in Japan, Ralt was not delivering the goods in Europe so, as a hint, a March-Honda was parked in a unit at Slough ready to be used if Ralt did not buck up.

Ralt was in its first full season of F2 and with all the dramas of the season it was only after Vallelunga that the team had the luxury of a day's testing and from then on the picture changed, for not only did the car go better but Geoff Lees regained his confidence and the combination finished second in the next round at Mugello. First, however, was Corrado Fabi in his works March, still running on Pirellis, and it was the first indication of the form which would take him to the title the following year. It was significant that he won at a circuit he knew well; Gordon Coppuck reckons that his greatest problem was learning circuits, which is why his first year in F2 was relatively low-key.

Lees won at Pau from Boutsen, then at Enna Thierry took his second win of the year. It was Lees from Boutsen at Spa, Lees from Fabi at Donington, and with two more second places in the final two rounds (to Alboreto's Minardi-BMW at Misano, and Johansson's Toleman at Mantorp Park) he secured the title from Thierry. Although Honda had won the Championship in its first full season it was not entirely happy, for, after all, it had provided the most powerful engine but had won only four races to BMW's six and Hart's two. Thackwell's accident had contributed to the equation; he had bravely returned at mid-season but was still far from being fully fit and the man who might have walked the series was reduced to a supporting role in the final races.

Someone else who was not contented was Gordon Coppuck. After a career at McLaren, where two World Championships had been won with his M23, a car so good they named a road after it, he was restless working under the constraints at March, switching from F1, to F2, to F3, to Indycar, as needs dictated. At the same time John Wickham had enough experience to become ambitious and he had excellent contacts in Japan, where he spent part of his time. The upshot was Team Spirit, which would build and run two Coppuck-designed F2 cars, powered by Honda with Bridgestone tyres and sponsorship from Marlboro. The attraction to the firms involved was an outfit dedicated to winning the Championship with no distractions such as building customer cars and no compromises in their construction either and the drivers would be Thierry Boutsen and Stefan Johansson.

Robin says, "Halfway through the season Honda offered an *enormous* amount of money to use their engine

Phil Kerr (left), Ralph Bellamy and Gordon Coppuck (who left March in 1981 to form the Sprint team, but later returned to Bicester). This photograph was taken in 1971. **(Nigel Snowdon)**

the following year and after we took over Ralt we found out how much they were paying Ron until quite recently, and it was a real eye-opener. Had I been sensible and ruthless I'd have accepted; as it was John Wickham saw the ball bounce, grabbed it and scored a touchdown. A couple of years later, when BMW dropped out, I regretted being so loyal, in fact I was very peeved indeed." It's typical, though, that later John and Gordon would be welcomed back at March with open arms, for not every company can be that mature.

In a season which had seen March make an impression on so many fronts, although the impression it had made in F1 was not the one it had hoped for, one area of gloom was F3. The 813 worked well in the European Championship, which did not have control tyres and where the main opposition came from Martini, which was numerically superior since Ralt had not yet made an impression on the Continent, and Mauro Baldi's March-Alfa Romeo won the series by a large margin with his Michelin tyres contributing not a little. In Britain, by contrast, the year began promisingly and then March faded away and by the end of the year had announced its withdrawal from F3. Robin had even phoned Ron Tauranac with a suggestion that they should meet with a view to making an arrangement, March and Ralt would divide the racing world between them, March would pull out of the junior formulae to concentrate on America but in return Ralt would not threaten.

The meeting never took place, nor did it have to, for circumstances resolved the problem along the inevitable lines, but the intention behind the suggestion is interesting because it really did not make sense for March and Ralt to be cutting each other's throats in a tight and diminishing market. "We had so little money that we had to make a straight choice between building a car for Europe," says Robin, "or building one for British F3. We chose the former and so created a car with low drag, reasoning,

Mauro Baldi (March 813-Alfa Romeo) dominated the European Formula Three season; he is seen here at Hockenheim. **(Autosport)**

correctly, that the softer European tyres would compensate for the lack of downforce. Had we gone for downforce we would have overloaded the tyres and the car wouldn't have worked in Europe, just as it didn't perform well on the hard Goodyear control tyres used in Britain, while the Ralt package was ideally suited to them."

By the end of 1981 British F3 was Formula Ralt, but the start of the year was somewhat different. 1980 had ended with a three-way battle between March, Ralt and Argo and when Argo announced a new ground effect car, the JM8, some fancied drivers pinned their faith in it, but soon wished they hadn't. When *Autocar* published a photograph of it someone screwed up the caption, but the result was one of the most telling misprints ever: *The New Allegro*. While there were more Ralts than any other new car, some stuck to proven chassis such as the Argo JM6 and older Marches until the position became clearer.

Much was expected of the South African Mike White, who landed the works March drive, and he opened the season with a good second to Jonathan Palmer, who was using the ex-Johansson Ralt run by Dick Bennetts in his first season as an independent, an advantage which was to become apparent only later as Bennetts became the nearest F3 has had to a guru. Palmer won the first three rounds but White ran strongly and the Ralt vs March debate was by no means clear-cut, since people could point to the fact that his car had come sorted regardless of expense by Project Four, and the 813 of the Dane Kurt Thiim finished only 0.7s behind him in the third race at Silverstone with nobody else in sight.

The fourth F3 race in Britain was the Donington Park round of the European Championship, so tyres were 'free' and there, running on Bridgestones, Mike White simply ran away and hid from the opposition and the top Ralt finisher was down in eighth place. It's true most of the British Championship regulars stayed away because they didn't have the right tyre connections, but it showed Mike's class and the fact that the 813 needed only a little work to set it up for control Goodyears and it could be the equal of the Ralt. In the event, it did not receive that attention and despite a close second to Palmer at Mallory Park (by a few feet) and a win at Thruxton in early May, March's F3 operation, and Mike White's career, slid down the tubes.

In fact Mike received no testing between May and August, when he had a couple of days at Goodwood with Gordon Coppuck, but it was too little, too late. The author was present at that test and and has ever since had the most profound admiration for Gordon's skills as an all-round engineer and Mike visibly grew inches taller during the test, it was an uncanny experience to see a driver straighten his shoulders, lift his chin and be more ready with a smile than a frown, but by that time every serious runner was in a Ralt and it was common for RT3s to fill the top six places. It was slightly ironic that 813s modified by the Italian team Euroracing, and run as 'Euroracing 101s' dominated the following year's European Championship with its two drivers taking the top two places.

What Mike didn't know was that March had already decided that 1981 would be the last year it would make F3 cars, there was little money in them, the market was too volatile and was anyway shrinking due to the economic climate. It did not make sense for March and Ralt to be cutting each other's throats and Mike was caught in the middle. The author has expressed his dismay at the fact that Mike White's career was screwed by March and Robin has agreed, "I feel sorry for him, he came to us at the wrong time. I rated him highly and we tried to get BMW to allow us more choice in the drivers we used with their money, for they didn't pay us a bean for using their engines but a lot of our F2 sponsorship came via BMW. Had they agreed, I would have signed him for our F2 team in 1982."

At the time many of the decisions March made in 1981 seemed odd, but then few knew how close to the edge it had gone. Some of the decisions were hard and painful, as John Macdonald will concur, but March survived and prospered so Robin obviously made the right decisions. It's just a shame there were casualties in the fight, but the plan of action which had been born of despair in South Africa was working and starting to bear fruit.

18 The Right Package

March must be one of the very few companies where the income graph soared as the sales graph slumped, for in 1982 it made only 47 cars, fewer than in any year since its founding, but the reason for the commercial success was a change in the type of car being made. It still made a handful of Atlantics and Sports 2000s (five of each), March GP was still in F1, and Robin's photograph was in the team's brochure, but there were no real links between March GP and March Engineering. No cars were made for F3 and its share of the F2 market had settled to about a dozen cars a year, with half going to Japan, but there were two big differences: the frantic model range of 1981 had been halved and no fewer than 20 Indycars were sold. This was a record for the post-roadster era and from 1982, America became March's chief market.

It was a time of re-grouping and change within the company, but although things were looking brighter on the financial side, it was by no means out of the wood. Everyone assumed that Robin was spending half his time counting his firm's money, but although it was coming in it was swallowed by an overdraft, and it wasn't until 1983 that March would get out of the red. In the meantime, in order to service America, Robin began a period of his life which was to see him spend the bulk of his time in the States while commuting to Europe and Japan and would peak with him taking 300 flights a year. "I'd liked what I'd seen of the States and wanted to see more. It was an exciting time for me and although eventually I couldn't face the thought of one more flight across the Atlantic, let alone 30, at the time I really didn't mind. You can do a lot of work on a plane and you're never interrupted by the phone.

"Indycar was a revelation. One old-timer wore a baggy racing suit and people would call out things like, 'Hey, Beauregard, why don't you smarten up? Who's your tailor?' and he'd just smile. He was reckoned to be over the hill, but nobody could work out why he always qualified so well at Indy. I found out that when you wear a baggy suit you can strap a cylinder of nitrous oxide to your leg and nobody notices, and when you got out to qualify you can screw it into what looks like the fire extinguisher system. I'm sure I wasn't the only one who knew that, but he was one of the good ole boys, so people let him get away with it. Indycar was still pretty primitive then, he couldn't do it now."

Before the end of 1981 March unveiled its one new model for its trimmed 1982 range. Although the BMW M1C had not been successful, the chassis itself had been very good and with IMSA GTP expanding, and Group C looming on the horizon, early in 1981 it had been decided to build the company's first large sports car, the 82G (G for GTP). It was based on the M1C, but was completely re-engineered by a newcomer to the company, Adrian Newey, who was to play a major part in later March history. Built around a honeycomb monocoque its layout was conventional enough with outboard coil spring and double wishbone suspension front and rear but what was less conventional was that it was designed to use almost any racing engine known to Man and, during the run of March GTP cars, practically every sort was used at one time or another. At the time it was given out that the body was the work of Dr Max Sardou, who had created the body for the BMW 1C, but although he had a hand in it, it was not a free hand and much of the decisive detail work was done by Adrian Newey.

Still, at the launch it was Sardou who modestly conceded that wind tunnel tests 'have shown that we have an unparalleled combination of high downforce with minimum co-efficient of drag . . . I think the 82G represents the ultimate aerodynamic configuration at this time'. Litotes was catching, so Robin would only concede that the car had 'the highest quality of engineering that March has produced in its 12-year history.' He says now, "But didn't you know? That's true of every car we've ever made. I don't say things like that as a deliberate con, I just get carried away with enthusiasm and I really believe what I'm saying at the time." Had he gone further he might have added, with due modesty, that the 82G was also overweight. Given the 82G's performance, it's just as well that no great claims had been made for it, but when the decision was taken to treat IMSA seriously, with works representation, the concept would develop into a winner.

Three of the four 82Gs had 5.7-litre Chevrolet engines, the fourth had a 3.5-litre BMW unit, and the model began its career very promisingly when Bobby Rahal put Bob Garretson's Chevy-engined car on pole at Daytona. It retired from the race, but since the organizers had given out that a Chevrolet, not a Porsche, was on pole it added about 50 per cent to the usual gate. Rahal put it on pole again at Sebring, where, with Mauricio DeNarvaez and Jim Trueman, it finished a strong second and on the same lap as the Porsche 935 of Rolf Stommelen and John Paul *père et fils*.

Testing with the 1982 March 82G IMSA car with 5.7-litre Chevrolet engine. The 82Gs started the season strongly but soon faded from the results. (**Marc Sprouce**)

After a promising start, team changes and turmoil plus the sudden death of David Wilson, the factory engineer, saw that particular car off the pace and thereafter Marches took only a handful of places in a series dominated by Porsche 935s and Lola T600-Chevrolets. A 'works' 82G-Chevy also ran in Group C, at Silverstone in practice and Le Mans, but it was not quick and retired in France; it was a case of a driver trying the big time and finding that he, his car, his budget and his team were not quite up to it. After Le Mans it was converted to IMSA spec and sold to the States, where it fared a little better.

Perhaps the 82G was too much of a compromise between two sets of regulations which included such basic differences as weight and windscreen shape. It had been worth a try, though, because at the start of a new category no base lines have been set but having discovered the strength of the opposition, Dave Reeves declared that March would only be interested in Group C with a properly founded team. While it might appear that Group C Junior was March's natural market, Dave reckoned it would cost a minimum of £100,000 to develop such a car and would need to sell six to ten a year to make it a viable proposition and the market didn't look ready for it and, he might have added, March couldn't afford to take a flier to try to create a market. It was pulling itself out of the midden, but the real position was known only to two groups of people, one in Bicester, the other in Barclays Bank.

At the beginning of 1982 everyone knew that Honda was going to walk Formula Two with Ralt and Spirit, especially since BMW's F1 commitment meant that little work had been done on the engine and everyone knew how quickly Honda developed. Even BMW believed it had little chance against four Honda cars, the exclusive Bridgestone deals, and a very strong driver line-up with Johansson and Boutsen at Spirit and Palmer and Acheson at Ralt. It took a lot of persuading by Robin for them to continue and, as in 1973 and 1977, he had to agree to attend all the races, but BMW in turn persuaded Michelin to supply selected users, and that was to be decisive.

It was probably as well that Ralph Bellamy seemed unaware that March had no chance as he quietly set about creating the 822. 'Creating' is perhaps too strong a term, for it was a logical up-date of the 812 but with a narrower tub, improved aerodynamics, and new rear suspension geometry, but the result was a reliable, harmonious package which gave no headaches. Christian Danner and Corrado Fabi stayed on the strength and they were joined by Johnny Cecotto, who had spent the previous season languishing with Minardi because he had been convinced he had to have Pirellis only to find Pirelli floundering. Overall, the team was run by Peter Mackintosh, whose former credits included managing the Fittipaldi F1 outfit and the Red Arrows display team while Danner's car was engineered by Ralph Bellamy, with whom he had a very close relationship. Robin looked after Fabi and Adrian Newey engineered Cecotto.

Despite March looking strong, and Ralt and Spirit looking even stronger, after the first two rounds of the F2 Championship, the leader was Stefan Bellof in a Maurer-BMW, who had won at both Silverstone and Hockenheim, the only F2 races he'd ever entered. This was a turn-up for

The 82G cars appeared at Le Mans in 1982. This works car, which had practised but not raced at Silverstone, was powered by a 5.7-litre Chevrolet V8 and driven by Patrick Neve/Jeff Ward/Eje Elgh. It ran in mid-field, and 20 seconds off the pace, before retiring early on with electrical problems. (**Nigel Snowdon**)

In the International Trophy at Silverstone at the end of March Christian Danner set fastest lap after stopping for a new rear wing, but retired his 822 with engine trouble **(Nigel Snowdon)**

the books and the only Marches in the top six at Silverstone were Jo Gartner's private car in sixth and Sarturo Nakajima's second-placed 822-Honda, having a run in Europe before he took the car out to Japan, and that was also the only Honda-powered car in the top ten. Were our heroes downhearted? They may have been but it had become folklore at March that the opening race at Silverstone indicated the *reverse* of the rest of the season and, oddly enough, statistics tend to support the belief.

Leaving aside mumbo-jumbo, the basic problem which Ralt and Spirit had at Silverstone was that Bridgestone did not have an effective rain tyre yet Johansson had set pole in the dry by over three seconds on the field. Tyres, which were supposed to be one of the strong cornerstones of both the Honda packages, were to play an unusually large part in determining the outcome of the series.

At Silverstone it was sad to see Mike Thackwell out of a works drive, because Ron Tauranac was not convinced he was fully race fit, but running in Markus Hotz's private 822-BMW. Hotz had no special tyre deals and not much money either, and he often had to use whatever tyres were going free or at a discount, although he was sometimes able to get hold of some Japanese Dunlops, which were pretty special. By scoring thirds at Pau and Spa from the half-dozen races he entered, Mike was able to revive his career, but it was a sign of the times that he was the most successful privateer and even then could finish no higher than tenth overall. Formula Two was shrinking and just as the day of the genuine privateer had long gone, so too had the days of the private team.

Beloff won at Hockenheim from Boutsen but Fabi was third and Cecotto fourth. March was making progress and thereafter went from strength to strength, whereas, apart from the odd race, Maurer faded. Maurer had the same Michelin and BMW package as March, but used the short-stroke Heidegger version of the engine, and had a fine chassis designed by Gustav Brunner, but there was not sufficient experience and harmony in the team, and after a magnificent start to the season it could not maintain its impetus. Another thing which contributed to their early results was that while March had put in 2000 test miles over the winter, it had been tyre testing, not performance testing, so the cars were not exactly *au point* at the beginning of the season but that was soon rectified.

Maurer benefited from the information with which March supplied Michelin, and that helped them at the beginning of the year, but as the season progressed March was able to build on the foundation of its testing in a way Maurer did not because it was a classic case of the way winning can unsettle a team. You have to learn how to cope with winning and how to build on it once the champagne has been drunk, but Maurer never did learn.

Tyres played a crucial part at Thruxton, where Cecotto led until the abrasive surface of the track sent him into the pits for a new set, but he rejoined in fourth place and took the lead again from Acheson's Ralt three laps from home to score his first F2 win. Had he not won the race might have gone to Fabi, which would have been a nice present on his 21st birthday but Corrado's distributor failed with 11 laps to go. Boutsen gave Honda its first win of the season at the Nürburgring, but it was a close-run thing with Corrado only a few feet behind at the end, kicking himself he hadn't been able to find a way by, while Cecotto continued to pile up points by coming third.

Ralt meanwhile was still struggling to make its new

Johnny Cecotto won the Thruxton Formula Two race for March, climbing back from fourth after a pit stop for new tyres. **(Nigel Snowdon)**

Corradi Fabi had taken the lead at Thruxton with his March 822-BMW after Johansson (Spirit-Honda) ran into tyre problems, but retired because of distributor failure. (**Nigel Snowdon**)

car competitive. It was a repeat of the previous year, there hadn't been enough pre-season testing and so the team was always behind and Acheson's second place at Thruxton was to be the highlight of Ralt's season. While Ralt floundered, the dream package of Spirit, Bridgestone and Honda was more vulnerable than expected. There was nothing wrong with the chassis or drivers, in the right conditions both were very quick, but Honda had rested on its laurels and the power curve was still quirky but, worse, Bridgestone tried too hard and made too many variants and Dr Sodt's Law says the more choice you have the more likely you are to make the wrong one. One problem was its only wet tyres were radials, while its best slicks, the ones would last an entire race distance, were not only crossplies but were an inch larger in diameter. If the cars started on slicks, and it rained, Spirit had to bolt on radials and send them out on settings for crossplies and a different diameter of tyre, for it took about an hour to change the car. Nice one, Bridgestone.

Johansson was quick, and led races, but was plagued by unreliability and scored only 11 points all season while Boutsen was not quite as fast but failed to finish only once. Ralt never did get its act together, although Palmer and Acheson could be quick on occasion. By contrast March was consistent and reliable in all areas. It was a prime example of an integrated package and the rest of the season saw Fabi and Cecotto take command of the situation. Corrado won the fifth round at Mugello, four seconds clear of Johnny, and he followed that up with a win at Vallelunga. Then Cecotto won Pau but Boutsen took his home round at Spa, where Bridgestone provided a particularly good wet tyre, and he won what many would nominate as the F2 Championship race run in the worst conditions ever. Fabi won the next two rounds at Hockenheim and Donington and Cecotto took Mantorp Park and led the Championship from Fabi and Boutsen, but all three were still in with a chance of the title with two rounds to go.

The first of the two remaining rounds, at Enna, saw a reversal of fortune as Boutsen won, Cecotto came third and Fabi did not finish, so at the final round, Misano, the table read: Cecotto 56 points (he'd actually scored 57 but had to drop one), Boutsen 50, and Fabi, who had won four races to the three apiece of his rivals, 48 points. Before the start at Misano there was a thunderstorm and the start was delayed until it was likely that it would be a wet/dry race, which was tough on Spirit because once it had made the decision to run on wets, there was no going back, and the cars had to be set up for radials.

How could it be that Italian organizers with knowledge of local weather patterns could make such a decision? Why, if it turned out to be a wet/dry race, that would screw one Belgian and one Swede while, in the same conditions, if he played his cards right, an Italian might win the Championship in Italy. This is just wild surmise, but if the race had been started on time or delayed a further half-hour, it would have been run in consistent conditions and in that case it was likely that Boutsen and Johansson would have disappeared into the distance.

Fabi started on slicks and, no lover of the wet, he was down in eighth place trying to stay on the track as Boutsen pulled away in the lead, while poor Cecotto was chopped by Bellof on the first lap and he lost three laps and any chance of the title. At about one quarter distance, the track was dry enough for Johansson and Boutsen to come in for slicks and from then on their race was run. Corrado steadily moved up the field to win by ten seconds from Alessandro Nannini's Minardi with the Spirits down in sixth and seventh. So Fabi took the title by a single point from Cecotto although they had both scored 57 points, but since Corrado had won five races to Johnny's three, it was justice.

The 1982 F2 season remains one of the most interesting of any category, any year. Honda had four of the best drivers and the most powerful engines, but the title went to the best *team*, the best package, and BMW had made the difference by being persuaded to continue and then by speaking very nicely to Michelin, but when you make half a million road cars a year and each one comes with five tyres you can speak in a whisper to a tyre company and be heard clearly. The title had been won with the tyres and the BMW engine which took ten of the 13 rounds, not bad for a unit which had no chance.

So far as Robin is concerned that season will always be important because it was the first time he had worked alongside Adrian Newey. "It wasn't until half-way through the season that he admitted that he'd never engineered a car before the opening round and all I can say about the prick is he took me to the last bloody race with Fabi and Cecotto eyeball to eyeball. I'd been engineering cars for 13 years and this sod comes along and . . . It was the beginning of a relationship which is one of most enjoyable, rewarding and successful I've had in racing."

1982 was also March's sixth F2 title, the fifth with BMW, but it was also to be March's last win. During 1982 there was some discontentment among March F2 customers over the service they were receiving and this was one of the factors which decided March to farm out the running of the works team. That way nobody could point an accusing finger.

A deal was reached with Onyx for the usual Herd reason that he happened to get on famously with Mike Earle. Onyx would operate independently, buying its cars and having drivers and sponsors diverted its way. In effect Onyx was a favoured customer which would work in conjunction with the works on testing and so on, but there would be fine divisions. If Onyx tried, say, a new rocker arm which was worth half a second a lap, that rocker arm would be available to all other customers, but the March engineer would not tell them, "To make this work you need to do this, this and this," because Onyx may have spent thousands of pounds in testing to find that out and since expenditure is part of the competitive package, it was up to other customers to discover that for themselves. If they were smarter and spent less time finding out how it worked, that was their advantage.

Farming out the works team was symptomatic of the changes happening in March, as James Gresham recalls, "When I first joined we were running teams in F1, F2 and F3 from the factory and because we had only the three units we bought a lot of stuff in, and a lot of it wasn't very good. We designed, assembled and ran racing teams, so there was a lot going on, but there also tended to be a slight edge between the manufacturing people and the racing people as to who was making the money. Since we were all highly competitive it was not only winning races which kept everyone on a high, it was also whose side was the more important and finally it was decided that the only real way of settling the dispute was to move the racing team away.

"It was also a good way to change our personnel around because when Robin gave the team to Mike Earle, most of them didn't want to move to Bognor Regis so they moved to the production side to strengthen it. In any case F2 was in decline and running a team was becoming less profitable and we had the American market opening up so, for the first time in our history, we had no cars running from the factory. Looking back you can see how that slowly affected us; it took a long time but did have the effect of taking away the edge of competitiveness through the direct feed-back from the team and by just having it around."

It's the old racer's mentality asserting itself and it was to reassert itself in the coming years as March Engineering became a manufacturing plant operating on conventional business lines. There'd be no Ronnie to cheer after a win, or a Gunnar popping up round every corner, no one the men on the shop floor could feel was somehow 'theirs' because he dropped by and had time for a few words. Racing was going to become something which happened Out There with not much connection to the welding torch or the lathe. Nobody could think 'Good old Bruno's going to have this wishbone,' it became an anonymous component.

Roger Bailey, Director of March's North American operation says, "When March first moved into Bicester it was the only racing outfit for a 50-mile radius. Now if you live in Bicester and you want to be in racing, within a 20-minute drive you have Reynard, TWR, Benetton, Williams, any number of outfits at Silverstone and, with the motorway network, people like McLaren, Arrows, Brabham and Tyrrell are within commuting distance. The guy that wants to be in a racing outfit wants to see his upright or wishbone on a car in a race, he needs to be motivated by that contact. If you're paying only the same money and not providing the buzz, you're not going to get the best people, at least you're not going to get the ones with the racer's way of thinking." That was the long-term problem, expressed with hindsight, but from the moment there was no team around the motivation began to seep out of March, and while it didn't show for a long time in the balance sheets, the customers saw it.

March had won the F2 Championship not with the quickest car or drivers but with the best package, and the rule of the package applied to Indycar as well, where everyone ran on relatively hard and narrow Goodyears and generally used the Cosworth DFX engine. With two of the variables being taken care of, March had to concentrate on harmony and it worked hard to listen and learn. In one way it took a step back in time, to the days when an F2 field was mainly customer Marches, in another it moved forward. There had to be works engineers on site to report back to the factory, so a system was devised where you had the Bicester Indycar team and the in-place American team, with elements of both jetting back and forth. In essence it was the way it had been operating for some time, but now the logistics were different because of the distances involved; it was no longer a case of hopping on a plane from Rome or Stockholm, being home in time to catch the late film on television and being in front of the drawing board, bright-eyed, on the Monday morning. It was the only way to operate, but cracks began to appear as March stretched itself around the globe.

For 1982 March took a similar route in Indycar to the one it had taken in F2, in other words it produced a user-friendly up-date of the 81C incorporating all the lessons learned through Bignotti, but in place of the troublesome Weismann transverse transmission there was a longitudinal gearbox based on the Hewland DG400, although later it supplied a March-built transverse Weismann-style gearbox to a few teams. As part of March's new packaging a transmission department had been set up and Rob Gustafson had been promoted from crew chief of the F2 team to head it as Project Manager.

Tom Sneva was back in a Cotter/Bignotti March and Bobby Rahal was running as a rookie with Jim Trueman's TrueSports team. Rahal had struggled with an uncompetitive Chevron in the European F2 in 1979 and most of his racing in America had been in the European-

At Indianapolis in 1982 A.J.Foyt with his 82C retired after 95 laps with transmission problems. (**Autosport**)

At Pocono in 1982 Bobby Rahal drove this March 82C into third place behind two Penske entries. (**Rich Chenet**)

style classes such as IMSA and Can-Am and even, briefly, in F1 with Wolf. It was significant that CART was attracting teams and drivers from American road racing, which was something which helped March's cause, for it had good will from making successful Formula Atlantic cars, while A.J. Foyt's decision to stick with March was a message for the good ole boys from the oval tradition.

It was the old guard which opened the scoring, with Rick Mears in a Penske winning the first two rounds and then Gordon Johncock's Wildcat winning the next two, one of them the Indy 500 by 0.16s from Mears, the closest finish in the race's history. March, however, filled three of the next four places and no fewer than 17 of the 33 starters were Marches. For the typical American customer this was the really significant statistic because for many drivers and team owners just starting at Indy is enough, it makes you part of the only game in town, which is why there might be over 100 entries. Most know they can't compete with the big teams and it would have to be Hollywood time to win, but a car which can get you into the race is a car to have and March delivered that dream to guys who previously had little chance.

Progress was steady, March grew increasingly strong, and provided six out of the top ten finishers in the next round of the series, Milwaukee, with only Penskes and Wildcats in the running, and in the fifth round, the Cleveland 500, Rahal came home the clear winner from such veterans as Mario Andretti, Al Unser, Mears and Johncock. Either the kid was good or the car was, maybe both. Johncock's Wildcat led home Andretti and Rahal in the Michigan 500, but then Rahal and Sneva scored a March 1–2 at Milwaukee and there were seven Marches in the top ten.

Penske was back on top at Pocono with a 1–2 for Mears and Kevin Cogan, for in terms of sheer speed Penske had the edge and Rick Mears was more often than not the fastest qualifier during the season, but nobody could buy the latest Penskes while anyone could have an 82C like the ones which filled the next three places. Johnny Rutherford, the 1980 Champion, led a break when he abandoned his Longhorn with its unreliable transverse gearbox for the relative simplicity of a 82C and was rewarded with third at Riverside behind Mears and Sneva. It was clear that when it came to customer cars there really

Two views of the March 827 that was built for Newman Racing in 1982. Although one of the cars that March would prefer to forget, Danny Sullivan won one race and scored several good places, in the face of admittedly weak opposition.

was only one place to go and the message was underlined when first Hector Rebacque, who had been in F1 but nobody minded, and then Rahal and Sneva won the important races, the last three of the year and, as had become usual, March dominated the top ten positions.

Robin says, "We had consolidated what we had done in 1981 and it gave us a breathing space. In fact we got caught because Penske had studied what we had done, had learned from it and Geoff Ferris' PC10 was significantly better, but it wasn't a problem because we were still competitive."

The final positions seem to indicate that it was a three-way fight between March, Penske and Wildcat, but when you were thinking of buying a car for 1983, you looked at the end-of-year results and by then Penske was struggling to keep up, Wildcat had faded and, hell, if a rookie like Rahal could finish a close second in the series, and a second string driver like Rebacque could win in one, there had to be something in these Marches and a queue duly formed at Bicester.

There was one other category in which March figured and that was Can-Am, where a single 827 was run by Newman Racing for Danny Sullivan, which, oddly, does not appear in the March records, but Robin suggests a possible explanation, "I think the reason is that everyone is too embarrassed to admit to it, it was an *absolute dog* of a car, a classic March cock-up. Every so often I allow myself to be talked into things and Max Sardou did a very good job as a salesman, he certainly convinced Dave Reeves and me. Like so many engineers he's a great enthusiast and enthusiasm is catching; I believe he and Dave are still great friends. He reckoned that Can-Am came down to aerodynamics, so we gave him a free hand and said, 'Okay, you come up with the shape, we'll fit the car underneath it.' The result was the biggest racing car ever, and when you took the body off and laid it on the ground this mass of glass fibre looked like a ship. Newman's sponsor was Budweiser, the name was plastered all over the car, and the team put the body on the ground, rigged up a sail and posed for a picture as the crew of the 'SS Budweiser.'

"Thank God I was committed to F2 in Europe so was saved the embarrassment of the whole thing. Just as Niki had to put up with the 721X, which was a wonderful way of learning to drive a racing car, so Danny had to put up with the 827 and he hasn't looked back since."

19 Period of Adjustment

March, the cottage industry, had bumbled along and when, say, a driver failed to settle his bills he would receive letters from Robin like this blistering final demand after a long correspondence during which he (now a big star) had been complimented on his skills, been offered a deal for the coming season, and had had his debt reduced even though it's obvious he had been stretching his story a little. *I was a little disappointed not to receive the letter you said you had sent. My only hope is that this is not the prelude to an unfortunate legal case which will only serve to cost both of us dearly in every sense. I am sure I must be wrong!* The soft approach worked in the long run but did nothing for March's cash flow.

Until the 1980–1 crunch the company had ticked over and gave Robin a decent living, but then it had to fight for its survival, and as 1983 dawned it was still not out of the woods. With Robin spending most of his time in America, Japan, and Boeings, back home responsibility was delegated and the changes were not to everyone's liking. Norman Mazure, the solicitor who had been involved in the setting up of March Grand Prix, joined the strength and some were in for a sharp jolt, for Norman was a hard-nosed professional.

Mike Earle, who was running the works F2 team, says, "I couldn't believe it, I had never in my life encountered a more obnoxious man. As soon as he took over the writs were flying like paper darts at a schoolboys' outing. I hated him, really hated him, I'd always dealt with Robin direct over the phone, 'Our sponsorship hasn't arrived, Robin,' 'Sorry to hear that, Mike, hope it's not inconveniencing you, I know you'll settle as soon as you get it.' I don't think Robin had ever sued anyone in his life.

"Then I began to realize that Norman had two sides and operated them as though he had a switch. There was the solicitor who was doing his best for his client and then there was the guy I began to like. You'd get a call from him saying, 'My brother and I would like to go to Brands Hatch on Sunday, can you leave a couple of tickets on the gate?' So he'd turn up and sit in our hospitality unit drinking our wine, eating our food, and being thoroughly pleasant and then first thing on the Monday morning there'd be the phone call, 'I haven't got your cheque, it will be here tomorrow or the winding-up order will be in the post.' At the time it hurt, but he was right, he was being professional and it made me realize that I was running a business and had to be professional too."

Robin is not ruthless enough to be a businessman with a capital 'B', though nobody should lose sleep worrying where his next Mercedes is coming from, he's a romantic who thinks that motor racing should be fun. How many people would fly home from Monaco and miss the Grand Prix so that he could drive in a club rally at Goodwood? That's what he did, FOCA pass and all, in 1988 and the following year he was at Goodwood again while the Monaco GP was on. He's an enthusiast's enthusiast who reckons it's better to be out there doing it in a minor event than posing in the pit lane at the glamour race of the year.

As a romantic, his heart has often over-ruled his head but being an intelligent man he has had the nous to employ people who can do things he cannot. Norman Mazure is one who came in to do that and he eventually left his legal practice to become a director of March. Off-duty, he is an intelligent, charming man who is fun to be with, but as he says, "I tend to be employed when things have gone too far, when contracts have been broken, when people have not settled their bills, when you have to draw the bottom line. I think that one of Robin's problems is that you never can tell when he's saying 'No'."

So, unlike Hollywood producers, Robin employed a 'no-man' and their relationship is still successful, but then when he makes a decision on a personal level it is almost always so, one reason being that those who know him want to please him because he has the ability to make people believe in his dreams and, more importantly, to believe in themselves. When he tries to be 'professional' he tends to come unstuck because it's not in his nature, it's as though a good guerilla leader is asked to become a Field Marshal and wear a uniform and inspect Guards of Honour. As March became more and more successful it made sense to operate more like a conventional business, and he was glad to be shot of that side, but the larger March became so the further it grew away from its roots, began to lose its way, and Robin was not ruthless enough to grab it by the scruff of its neck to set it on the right course again.

In 1983 March concentrated on three main fronts, F2, CART and IMSA GTP although the Sports 2000 car remained in the catalogue. The absolute priority was CART, and by selling another 21 cars it meant there were nearly 50 March Indycars in circulation. Oddly enough, although there had been British participation in Indycar for 20 years, March made the first positive commitment to it, Lotus and McLaren had come and gone and Lola, which

The 1000th March completed in 1983 and by an amazing coincidence it was an 83C for A.J.Foyt. In the middle of the front row is Dave Reeves, now Managing Director of March Engineering and on the right of the front row is Mike Smith, now Managing Director of Leyton Engineering.

had had periods of great success, built cars only when asked to by its importer, Carl Haas, so its participation had been spasmodic, although it returned in 1983 and this time it was destined to stay. For the moment, though, March had the initiative, the differences between USAC and CART had been resolved, the position was stable and the series was gathering momentum, the sun was shining and it was the time to make hay.

During the year the 1000th March was built and, O happy coincidence, the car which posed for the publicity photograph with '1000' written all over it just happened to be destined for A.J. Foyt.

The March 83C was an update of the 81C series, but with a March transverse gearbox which bore a passing resemblance to the Weismann unit and, like it, was not entirely without its problems. That was the base car, but into the season March made it the 'Speedway' version and made a 'road circuit' kit (with Hewland DGB gearbox and rocker arm rear suspension). It was perhaps the first instance of a company making two distinct cars for CART and for some years now the speedway cars have had longer wheelbases and different bodies.

Robin says, "The 83C was the last car I'd claim to have designed as such. Superficially it was an up-dated 82C, but I'd say it was a new car, the basic parameters were different, it had new suspension geometry, it was much stiffer and Adrian Newey did a lot of work on the under-car aerodynamics. I still think of it as very much my car because I made all the basic decisions on it. It was not a major step forward but that wasn't necessary and we finished up with a bloody good car with excellent manners which worked everywhere.

The Championship did not begin well for March. In the first round at Atlanta, Rick Mears took pole in his Penske PC11 and the race was won by Gordon Johncock's Wildcat with the highest March being that of Howdy Holmes down in ninth place with five Penskes (two PC11s, the rest being privateers running the previous year's design) a Lola and an Eagle above him.

That was Atlanta. The next race was Indianapolis and the difference is the same as a soccer club winning at home and winning at Wembley. Robin says, "I couldn't then take CART very seriously, but Indy was different, Indy was what mattered. I was working with Teo in the Forsythe brothers' team, Newman Racing had withdrawn and the Forsythes had taken on most of the staff including, hallelujah, Barry Green. It was our third year in CART, the team was motivated, Teo was motivated, having just had an indifferent year in F1, we'd all worked together in Can-Am, so we were among home-town folk, and the car was super.

"They call it the Month of Indy, but it seems more like a year. In the pre-qualifying test sessions, Teo experienced the usual European reaction when first confronted with Indy, the feeling that there's no way they can drive there and then; as usual, after two days everything clicked into place. Qualifying is a science in itself, everything seems to move slowly, but the track changes enormously and not only from day to day, and after a storm, but throughout the day.

"You may get the car perfect at 6pm on the Tuesday but if it rains overnight (*And it don't rain in Indianapolis in the summer time*), when you go out again at 11am on the Wednesday you can find it impossible and have to start all over again from square one. You have to duck and dive to match the car, track, fuel load, driver, temperature, wing settings and so on, but it's intellectually fascinating, like trying to do a moving crossword. You have to get the basic work out of the way by Tuesday night and then discipline yourself not to make basic changes but to follow the track and fine-tune the car to it and it can change in half an hour without rain; if there's a storm it changes so much that unless you have belief in your basic settings you can get horribly lost.

"Qualifying is so fascinating that I wish F1 would do it the Indy way, it's not only safer but is a marvellous spectacle, which is why they get a quarter of a million spectators to it. You draw for a place in the queue and when

Teo Fabi with the 1983 March 83C car. (**Autosport**)

it's your turn you either go out or go to the back of the queue if you don't want to go out because the wind is up, for example. You have to guess your settings by watching how the other cars handle (there are always plenty of journalists ready to give you expert advice) and once he's out the driver has to adjust the balance of the car with his roll-bar control. Some have even put an extension on the front bar control so it adjusts the front wing in harmony. It's illegal, and we were too naïve to do it, but it seems to me to be a perfectly sensible arrangement and I can't see why it shouldn't be allowed.

"When Teo went out and broke every record the crowd went wild. They're so sporting, they didn't mind if it was an Italian in an English car and I couldn't help but wonder if we would be so generous if the Americans came over here and put one over on us. There was this archetypal American sports commentator: *Ladies and Gentlemen, hooold onto your haaats. That was two-o-eight miles per hour.* Teo said he could actually hear the cheering all the way round the track.

"If you get pole in a Grand Prix you hold it for 20 hours, at Indy you hold it for two weeks and Teo became an instant American hero. Later that day we all went to an Italian restaurant, where, of course, we were fêted and we had a great evening, in fact by the time we were through it was more like two great evenings."

Teo averaged a record 207.395 mph for the four qualifying laps and to prove it was no fluke he stormed off into the lead and after ten laps he was so far ahead that when he looked in his mirrors he thought there'd been an accident because nobody else was in sight. At about quarter distance, though, his race was run and he was out with a leaking fuel, tank but Tom Sneva came home to give March its first win at the Brickyard. Looking down the list of finishers, every car in the top ten is a March or a Penske with an even split and March had filled 18 places on the grid.

The next two races saw Penske 1–2s with, a straw in the wind, the increasing competitiveness of the new Lola T700 in the hands of Mario Andretti, who went on to win the fifth round. Despite all the logistical problems March responded and so did Penske as it dumped its PC11s and made up some PC10s for Rick Mears and Al Unser Snr. Teo then took the Pocono 500, finished second to Bobby Rahal's 83C at Riverside, and then won again at Lexington to lie second in the Championship. Mears and Andretti won the next two races for Penske and Lola but meanwhile Al Unser had been quietly totting up his score, and when it came to the last two races, Laguna Seca and Phoenix, Teo

At Indianapolis Fabi with the 83C was fastest in qualifying and fastest in the race, but was eliminated by a fuel leak. (**Rich Chenet**)

could win the title if he took pole, a win and fastest lap in both end Al did not finish above fifth in either. It was a tall order, but Teo did just that at Laguna Seca, where Unser retired. On the first day at Pheonix though, the car was dreadful and was on row eight.

Robin recalls, "Teo and Barry had a long heart to heart then I took a flier on the settings and next day he was on pole by half a second. Mario got the jump on him at the start, but Teo simply drove round the outside of him, and you can only appreciate what that means if you've been to Phoenix. He did everything he needed to, he set pole, won, got fastest lap – but Al Unser finished fourth and took the title."

That was the last time Robin was to engineer a car, the last time there would be that intimate triangle between engineer, driver and machine, and since all his talent had been channelled into that for so long instead of fulfilling his potential as a designer it was a wrench. Despite its success, March was not yet out of trouble, so he gave up the thing he did best to become a salesman, and he hated it.

During the season March took pole nine times out of 13 (Teo taking five), and the 83C typically dominated the top ten places and made some drivers look better than they had previously. Since, too, there were works engineers on hand, a quicker response to problems than the typical American team was used to, and a massive truck filled with spares, it made sense to buy from Bicester. Fabi's pole and Sneva's win at Indy had generated disproportionate interest and that a rookie had nearly taken the crown did March's cause no harm either. It is a curious statistic (Americans are as keen on statistics in racing as they are in other sports) that a driver has more chance of leading Indy in his rookie year than at any other time in his career.

There was also the fact that Teo took four wins, Al Unser won only once, so was the moral Champion and moreover had won the last two races of the season. It all seemed to represent a fairly cast-iron case and before the end of the season Roger Penske had bought an 83C for evaluation and then ordered two 84Cs as a fall-back position in case his new PC12s did not come up to snuff. When Penske did that it was as though everyone had received 24-carat inside information on the Stock Exchange and no fewer than 47 March 84Cs would be sold.

Three years before Robin had been fighting for the survival of his company, now the main problem was fulfilling all the orders and dealing with the headaches which success brings, like expanding the home base. In 14 years March had gone from John Thompson interpreting Robin's sketches and fabricating bits and pieces in his spare time, the drawings would come later, to Project Managers, Project Engineers, on-site engineers, and design *departments*. It became Big Business. Long gone were the lunch-time karting sessions round the workshop (all the best March stories come from the early days, when it was a struggle, Robin calls the recent part of the story 'The Boring Eighties') and the easy familiarity of a small workforce, you could no longer be sure of knowing everyone by name and with hindsight while it was entering its period of greatest success it was planting the seeds of its own downfall.

This is not to suggest that mechanics were carrying brief cases or the factory was becoming glitzy, for while McLaren has a waterfall in its foyer and a reception area larger than most people's homes, when you visit Bicester you enter a space the size of a box-room, with a couple of chairs, a few magazines, mostly in Japanese, and a friendly receptionist and the Managing Director can be seen at work through a plate glass partition. Everything remains on a friendly scale but you can't keep the vital spirit going when you expand.

On 23 September, 1983, the staff of Barclays Bank, 24 Cornmarket Street, Oxford, received a case of champagne because March was in the black but on the same day Robin received a 'seriously worded letter' from the manager which had crossed in the post, things had been that tight. Robin says, "I dealt with four managers at Barclays over the years and became good friends with them all. It was they who kept us going when by any sensible standards we were bankrupt, and of course as soon as we started to make money we were told we needed a proper financial director so we appointed Malcolm Shaw, who arrived at a very good time. Until then I'd looked after all that, drawing up the cash-flow charts and negotiating with the bank and I must say I missed all that."

Shortly afterwards Ralph Clarke, who acted as the company's part-time non-executive chairman, left, there had been an argument between he and Shaw and people had taken sides and dug their heels in and with hindsight was again a case of a conflict between March as it had been and March as it was trying to become. Ralph had dealt with people over the phone, giving his guarantees and standing by them, but perhaps that was not appropriate as the company grew larger and had to be be structured on a more professional basis.

CART was not the only happy hunting ground in 1983, for despite the relatively disappointing performance of the 82G, five examples of its successor, which had been tidied up and lightened, were sold, four of them going to the States and the fifth to Nissan, which was the beginning of a not altogether smooth relationship. Robin says, "We ran one as a works car in IMSA GTP and contracted Al Holbert, the '76 and '77 IMSA Champion, to run it and he mainly co-drove with Jim Trueman. I have my heroes in motor racing, Adrian Newey is one, whenever we've worked together the result has always been a successful car, Paul Rosche is another, Leo Mehl of Goodyear is one and two others were Al Holbert and Jim Trueman, both of whom are now sadly dead. They were bloody good blokes."

The first IMSA car was sold to Ken Murray, who fitted it with a 5.8-litre Chevrolet unit and entered it in the Daytona 24 Hours, where it was joined on the grid by the Cowart/Miller, 82G which had a flat-six 3.2-litre Porsche 935 engine, but it was a bit of a bodge and lasted only 14 slow laps. In qualifying the 83G was not particularly quick and started from 15th place, but while the faster Porsche, Lola, Jaguar and Aston Martin Nimrod drivers fell by the roadside the March held together and Randy Lanier, Terry Wolters and Marty Hinze held the lead for 269 of the 618 laps. Eventually they had to give best to a Porsche 935, which pulled out six laps by the end; but since the Porsche had lost a considerable amount of time having its turbochargers changed, that second place was a little plodding.

By the second round of the series, the Miami GP, Al Holbert had the works 83G-Chevy, which incorporated a number of subtle improvements, and he and Jim Trueman put it fourth on the grid. The race started in a downpour and while cars spun everywhere or spluttered around with damp engines and misfires, Holbert drove superbly and was still in the lead when the race was stopped at half-way through its scheduled three and a half hours. He was so delighted with the handling of his car that he promptly sold it to Pepe Romero, but replaced it with another 83G-Chevy.

None of the three Marches in the field finished the Sebring 12 Hours, although they were quick in practice, which was surprising given how ponderous they'd been at Daytona but tweaks to the suspension geometry and aerodynamics had wrought a transformation. Pepe Romero and Doc Bundy put their 83G on pole for the Road Atlanta 500 Km, but problems saw them finish only seventh, while Emory Donaldson and Bill Whittington brought their car home second to Bob Tullius' Jaguar. There were no fewer than five Marches in that race and the 82G-Porsche of Cowart and Miller finally worked and they took fifth.

Riverside saw an interesting entry, an 83G entered by Giampiero Moretti, which had a Porsche 935 engine, but which did not finish. Holbert and Trueman, however, took pole and came second to the Porsche 935 of John Fitzpatrick and David Hobbs, who declined to mount the podium at the end of the race because their team-mate, Rolf Stommelen, had died in an accident caused by his rear wing coming adrift.

Holbert took pole and won the Laguna Seca 100 Miles sprint and that more or less announced that the day of the Porsche 935, for so long the mainstay of IMSA, was nearly over. A number of owners began to look at the Porsche 956, which had won the first Group C Championship and was sweeping all before it in 1983, but the governing body of IMSA rejected it on the grounds that it did not comply with its rules on frontal protection. One way round the ban, however, was to fit a flat-six 2.6-litre Porsche 956 turbo unit into another car and which better than the March which was leading the series?

Thus Holbert had a works engine, with a single turbocharger to comply with IMSA rules, in his 83G for the Charlotte 500 and he and Jim Trueman set pole and won the Charlotte 500 with the Cowart/Miller car second. Co-driving with Doc Bundy as well as Trueman, Holbert went on to win a further four rounds and had put the title out of reach long before the end of the season. Not to be outdone Bundy, Trueman and Rahal also won a round in an 83G-Chevy and in fact all the IMSA Marches ended the year with top three finishes and they won eight of the 17 rounds to the four apiece of Jaguar and Porsche.

Nissan's 83G was delivered in Group C spec, was fitted with a four-cylinder 2.1-litre turbo engine, prepared by March's importer, Tom Hanawa's the Le Mans Company, and appeared as a 'Nissan Silvia'. It also underwent some bodywork changes including a higher

A March did win at Indianapolis in 1983, the Theodore Racing car of Tom Sneva. **(Rich Chenet)**

At Thruxton in April 1983 Beppe Gabbiani scored his second of four wins that year with the Onyx-entered 'works' 832 Formula Two car. **(Nigel Snowdon)**

rear wing and air intakes all over the rear of the car. Kazuyoshi Hoshino had some success with it in Japan but its sole appearance in an international race was the Fuji 1000km, where he and Akira Hagiwara qualified seventh and finished seventh, but they were only just ahead of one of the three March 75S entries. These had been undergoing continuous development in Japan and one had received a Mazda engine, another a Toyota unit, and they were now all known as March MCS1s. Strange but true, those seventh and eighth places at Fuji were enough to see Nissan-March finish third equal with Aston Martin in the World Endurance Championship (Makes) and Toyota-March equal fifth with BMW-Sauber. The reason was less exalted, so complete was Porsche domination that another make rarely finished in the top ten, but since only seven Porsches were entered at Fuji, some points places were up for grabs and it should also be said that the two Marches each covered only 198 laps to the winner's 224.

Even as March handed over its F2 team to Onyx the category was going through a crisis and as the season wore on, so the grids became thinner and there were only 16 entries in the final round at Mugello, yet March sold 25 cars, which was almost its record for a season. The two statements are not contradictory for most 832s went to Japan, where F2 was growing (and some of the Japanese cars were used in the Can-Am style Grand Champion series), while in Europe where an economic crisis was peaking F2 was going into a sharp decline. The wider situation affected sponsorship, but that was only part of the trouble. More serious was that F2 did not receive much television coverage and nor did it attract many spectators. While Formula One increased in popularity, the junior partner declined and F1 team managers were not queuing up simply because a driver was F2 Champion. Perhaps it had sunk in that no ungraded driver who had won the F2 Championship had ever gone on to be World Champion. By contrast, at the end of 1983 Martin Brundle and Ayrton Senna went from F3 into better F1 teams than any of the Formula Two Class of '82 drivers managed.

For 1983, Ralph Bellamy came up with an entirely new monocoque with honeycomb bulkheads, to meet new survival cell regulations, and it was slimmer and tidier than its predecessor. With Onyx taking over the works team, Peter Mackintosh, whose official role was 'motor racing consultant', looked after March's customers, especially Mint Engineering, which ran Dave Scott under ex-Lotus crew chief Glenn Waters, and James Gresham Racing, which looked after Enrique Mansilla, while Onyx strengthened its management team by hiring Peter Gethin, who took Beppe Gabbiani under his wing. Gabbiani was a surprise choice to defend Corrado Fabi's crown for he'd been in F2 since 1979 and was regarded as something of a rock ape, but Gethin applied his 'drive like an Italian and think like an Englishman' therapy and the result was a transformation. It is another instance of engineering the driver rather than the car. Beppe was supported by Thierry Tassin and Christian Danner in the 'works' team and much was expected of Scott and Mansilla.

Ralt was happy to keep Palmer and welcome Thackwell back into the fold, but just to make sure there would be no repeat of the tyre disadvantage, switched to Michelin, which also covered most of the field. Just as everyone thought that was the smart thing to do, Dave Scott set pole on Bridgestones at the streaming wet International Trophy race. That created a sensation and from the pit lane it looked as though Bridgestone had cracked it, but out in the freezing cold at Stowe, the reason was obvious, Scott was one of only three drivers (the others were Gabbiani and Streiff) who were using their heads and driving on the less wet parts of the circuit even when they were off the normal racing line.

Scott's moment of glory was not to last as he bodged the start and was away last and from then on his season spiralled, and even a switch to Onyx later in the year

Mike Earle who runs the very successful Onyx team. **(Jutta Fausel)**

when Tassin's money ran out did not help. The race itself seesawed as the weather changed and eventually it was Gabbiani who came through to win from Thackwell and Danner to the astonishment of all. Beppe then compounded the amazement by winning three of the next four races at Thruxton, the Nürburgring and Vallelunga and the only mistake he made all season was at Hockenheim, which was taken by Palmer's Ralt. His secret was simple, by driving with infinite finesse he was able to run a softer tyre than his team-mates and a much softer one than Ralt, which had a heavier car, and in the early part of the season the 832 was a superb car, but it was not to remain so.

Then things started to go sour, he spun at Pau and re-started without losing his lead, but immediately a drive-shaft snapped, and since in the team truck there was a set of stronger drive shafts brought along to cope with the rigours of a street circuit, it was shoot your foot time. Then he suffered a series of retirements and he had to watch Palmer first chip away at his commanding lead and then watch the Ralt disappear over the horizon.

Mike Earle recalls, "Beppe was magic and when Ralt got the Honda engine working and he saw his huge lead whittled away he was very un-Italian about it and simply said, 'I've got to come in the best BMW runner.' About mid season, though, the car started to go backwards because of chassis flexing. We sent our cars back to the factory and they added carbon fibre inserts round the top of the tub, which cost us a bomb, but our drivers could feel no difference, and since no more ideas were coming out of the factory we faded away."

In fact the carbon inserts served to highlight a basic flaw in the chassis rather than improve matters. The problem stemmed from the fact that the 832 had a conventional sheet aluminium twin tube monocoque, but in order to fit it into an optimum aerodynamic package the bottom of the tub sloped inwards and this proved not to be enduringly stiff over a season. With hindsight, the position might have been retrieved had every 832 been re-tubbed half-way through the year, but by the time the problem was understood it was too late and apart from the fact that March had a major problem, Ralt had made a lot of progress.

At the start of the year Ron Tauranac's relationship with Michelin was new and there were what were described as 'communication difficulties' between Ralt and its supplier. With Honda breathing down his neck, Ron felt the need to make his point forcefully and from then on the position improved, aided by the fact that the RH6/83 went on a diet and the engine made a visit to John Judd's Engine Developments at Rugby. Judd goes back a long way with Tauranac, back to the Brabham-Repco days in the late Sixties (and the Brabham-Honda F2 days) and although John will only admit to giving Honda personnel the use of his dynamometer (they were a long way from home, poor chaps) in fact he greatly improved the engine's quirky power curve.

Jo Gartner scored a surprise win at Pau with his private Spirit-BMW (the last win by a privateer in F2) and at Jarama March was nowhere, well actually it was down in sixth place thanks to Enrique Mansilla, who like everyone else was struggling with terminal understeer caused by his flexing chassis. Ralt, Maurer and AGS had all been using double springs, which, it was alleged, allowed the cars to clear the ground clearance bar in the pit lane but allowed them to run closer to the ground at speed. Prompted by Ralph Bellamy, and it can be no coincidence it was after a race where March received a drubbing, Onyx slapped in a protest and a messy F1-style controversy followed with the decision first going to March and then being overturned on appeal.

Ron says, "I'd never been involved in protests at race meetings so I didn't have the yellow book with me which would have given me the ammunition to sort things out there and then, so basically I went along to listen to the protest and I was found guilty. I came home, found out what you had to do, went over to Barcelona with a solicitor and was cleared." While Maurer and AGS continued to use double springs, Tauranac's response was to shrug and run his cars with single springs – and they won every remaining race. That's style. "When we went to single springs we concentrated on racing instead of being clever.

"The book said that the cars had to have 4cm ground clearance on a flat metal surface. FISA decided that this didn't necessarily mean it couldn't be measured somewhere else as well so they placed observers around the track at Misano and said: 'If your car is seen to touch the ground you'll be out of the race.' How you can race without touching the ground, I don't know, but we painted the bottom inch of our bodywork black so against the black tarmac you couldn't tell if it was bottoming or not, and we'd had steel skids which sent up sparks and we changed them to brass overnight and you couldn't see any sparking."

When Palmer clinched the Championship Ralt placed an advertisement thanking all who had contributed to the success and generously included Ralph Bellamy for designing the March 832.

20 Wearing the Business Suit

In 1984 Robin ceased to be an engineer and became a salesman. Richard King, the bank manager with whom he had come closest, and who had been transferred to Preston on his upward progress in banking, received a letter in April 1984 which said that March's net balance at Cornmarket Street had risen to over one million pounds, the Kyalami game plan had finally paid off. "People started telling us that if a load of ignorant racers could make so much money, think how well we'd do if we had professional management advice, and that is where I think we started to go wrong. All our troubles in 1988 come partly from losing the edge of having a racing team at the factory, but mainly when we started to become a big business and lost flexibility and speed of response." There'd been a time when March was like a nippy speedboat, but it was becoming more like a tanker which took two miles to make a turn.

Robin had engineered his last car and had become your friendly neighbourhood March salesman and says he hated it but despite that was superb at it, for apart from knowing how people work, he has an astonishing memory. When Robert Synge was a schoolboy at Stowe a couple of miles from Silverstone, he spent a lot of time watching testing at the circuit and would normally manage to hitch a ride to school from someone there, Peterson, Lauda, Bell, Hunt, some hack or another. Years went by, Robert built up his team, Madgwick Motorsport, the time came to move into F3000 and he went shopping at March. Robin had not seen him for about 12 years, but he greeted him with, "I often wondered how long it would be before you came to buy a car from me." With a start like that to the negotiations it's no wonder that Madgwick became a March customer.

For the next three years Robin lived out of a suitcase, his accountant had pointed out that he was spending so much time abroad (he'd even bought a house in America) that if he slightly varied his routine and spent just under six months in America and just under two in England, it would result in not paying tax anywhere, so he became an exile, checking his diary, adding up the days, and spending the odd spell in Jersey to keep on the right side of the tax line.

His life now is a complete contrast: he's a Fellow of his old college, St Peter's Hall, and vice-president of Oxford United Football Club and he is as likely to be seen at Covent Garden watching the Royal Ballet as Lord's watching cricket. Whenever he has the chance he's at the wheel of a rally car, receiving tuition from Bill Gwynne or driving in club events. Bill rates him highly as a pupil, and having been his co-driver the author knows from first hand why, we're not talking ace but he's good, and is very perceptive about the car. In fact part of his pleasure comes from engineering the machine, so by 1989 his Metro 6R4 was reckoned to be the best around. As always he surrounds himself with pleasant people so when he goes rallying everyone has fun and there have been deserving but less well-heeled drivers who have quietly received his help.

Robin's enjoyment of rallying goes back a long way, indeed when he was working at McLaren and Alan Rees was living nearby they did a number of rallies, Alan doing the driving and Robin as passenger. Alan says, "We used to use Robin's car and it's a funny thing but every time we crashed. Then once we used my car and we won without a mark on it. That received a mixed reception from the rest of the team, but I suppose I was more careful when I was driving my own car."

Living in a village, being involved with your old college, cheering your team, and taking part in sport is an Englishman's idea of an Englishman and it's something which can't be done from seat 34F in a Boeing.

In between jetting around the world and glad-handing customers, at the back of his mind was still the unfinished business March had in Formula One, and one of the persistent rumours of 1983 and '84 was that BMW and March would combine to build an F1 car. It didn't happen, but there was no smoke without fire, and while the March-BMW F1 car became a theme on the gossip market (sometimes it was an Onyx-March-BMW) the two sides were in fact talking about such a project. At the same time there was another F1 project in the air, a collaboration between March and Lola to build a car for Carl Haas, Lola's long-time American importer. Haas would be team owner and race director while Robin and Eric Broadley, Lola's founder, would make up the rest of the board. An alternative plan was that March alone would provide Haas with cars, but when Haas set up FORCE in 1985, he decided to go with Lola.

March did eventually make it back into F1, but in 1984 there was still the matter of F2 in what was to be its last year, and there Ralt was almost invincible. Tauranac was as good as his word and after helping Jonathan Palmer to the '83 title Mike Thackwell did indeed take the last F2 title with his team-mate, Roberto Moreno, second. March built a much stiffer F2 chassis, a one-piece honeycomb monocoque designed by Ralph Bellamy, which turned out 15 lb lighter than the tub it replaced, and F1-style, the top section of the body was made of carbon fibre to add extra stiffness. The engine was tilted up four degrees to the horizontal to increase the size of the venturi area, the wheelbase was slightly reduced by moving the front axle line back, the track slightly increased and at the front, pull-rod suspension similar to that on the Indycars replaced the previous rocker arm system.

On top of that a team spent ten days in the Imperial College wind tunnel, so there were a lot of subtle alterations to the shape. All in all, it represented a big advance. Mike Smith, who by that time had graduated to F2 Project Manager, reckons it was one of the best F2 cars March has ever made, a particularly good customer car, and he was still getting potential buyers enquiring about them two or three later for use in hill climbs and so on.

If March had advanced, so had Ralt, which made a very stiff and well-balanced car and had gone wind tunnel testing in the Williams facility. "I fluked into something on the aerodynamics," says Ron. The result was that the car was so good that had Ralt been using BMW engines it would probably still have taken the championship, but then Tauranac was building only cars for his own works team and did not have to make the compromises that March had always faced.

There was one other decisive factor and that was at the end of 1983 BMW had pulled the plug on the supply of works engines, partly because it felt its days were numbered, partly because of its F1 commitment. Robin still admits to being hurt at the way his loyalty was rewarded by the firm, not by Paul Rosche, who remains a very close friend, after all, he'd passed up the Honda V6 and the large bag of gold which accompanied it. "I don't think Honda has ever quite forgiven us for that," says the man who has since been trying to get his hands on a Honda F1 engine.

Ralt-Honda steam-rollered the opposition and the works March team ended the year without a single win for the first time since 1970. Onyx had decided to go with Bridgestone to try to get an edge since Michelin was prepared to supply almost anyone, but there was to be no advantage. Mike Earle: "Bridgestone's learning curve was almost vertical, but we were still behind Michelin all the way, so were stretching in every direction to make up ground."

For Onyx the withdrawal of BMW works engines was a shock to the system, it had become used to the best equipment and having a works engineer make a choice of perhaps ten engines for each race. With that element missing from its package and not having a big enough budget to come close to being able to reproduce the standard it had set itself in 1983, it perhaps ran its engines longer than it should have done and Heini Mader, knowing the position, cut things finely to accommodate the available money. As a result Onyx suffered nine destroyed engines, which came close to wiping it out.

One sign of the cut-back was that March was without BMW's protégé, Christian Danner, for the first time in three years. Christian finished up with Bob Sparshott's B.S. Fabrications team, where, it was reasoned, his experience would be beneficial to the junior drivers. Thierry Tassin should have established a similar role at Onyx, but seemed to lack the character to do it, while the junior drivers, Emanuele Pirro and Pierre Petit, simply lacked experience and if the entire points of all three were added together they would have just made second place in the series.

March's only win came at Hockenheim, where Moreno crashed and Thackwell had problems which let Pascal Fabre (in a B.S. Fabrications car running on Michelins) win from Tassin, while the only other non-Ralt win came in the last race of Formula Two at Brands Hatch, where a deluge equalized the field, the extra power of the Honda became an embarrassment (Thackwell anyway retired) and Philippe Streiff won for AGS. Danner finished the season as the highest scoring March user, so perhaps the presence of Richard Davila as the Sparshott team's engineer was significant, but even then Danner was only fifth in the series behind Thackwell, Moreno, Michel Ferté (Martini) and Streiff.

It was a low note on which to end a 15-year presence

Thierry Tassin on his way to fourth place with his March 842-BMW in the Formula Two International Trophy at Silverstone. (**Nigel Snowdon**)

in Formula Two, during which time March had not only won considerably more races than any other marque but had kept the category going by supplying race-winning cars year in, year out, and abysmal as 1984 was by March standards, there were still a number of outfits which had come and gone over the years which would have been pleased with it. F2 was anyway at its natural end, strangled by Honda, which had not quite grasped the notion that in a junior formula a supplier with a distinct advantage has a moral obligation to offer it to the field because all junior formulae should be centred on drivers rather than technology. Still, waiting in the wings was F3000, which would give everyone a fresh start.

Elsewhere things were rather brighter and in Japan not only did Satoru Nakajima's 742-Honda win the Japanese F2 Championship but March users filled the next seven places, while on the strength of Holbert's '83 Championship win, March sold six 84Gs to the States. Four had Chevy engines, one a turbo 3.4-litre V6 Buick, while the sixth had a Porsche 962 unit developed by Andial and went to the South African Kreepy Krauly team. Kreepy Krauly ran the ex-Holbert 83G-Porsche at Daytona and the all-South African driving crew (van der Merwe, Tony Martin and Graham Duxbury) brought it home first. It was significant that it was an endurance race, for while it made sense from a sponsor's point of view to field three national drivers, van der Merwe stood head and shoulders above his team-mates (in his spare time he was jetting home to clinch his ninth national rally championship), so he led races but watched his cushion disappear when a co-driver took over. In fact the only other race the team won was the Lime Rock 100 Miles sprint in which van der Merwe drove single-handedly.

Although a March 84G-Chevy was to win the Championship for Randy Lanier, it was a close-run thing, for Porsche was in the field with a new car. Having been excluded from IMSA GTP because its 956 did not meet the safety regulations, it responded by building the 962, which was a 956 with the driver's feet behind the front axle line, a steel rather than alloy roll cage, and a single turbocharger. To underline its determination Porsche arranged for Al Holbert to be paired with Derek Bell and at Daytona the car showed its potential in no uncertain way when Mario Andretti put one on pole, but they failed in the race and were taken home to be sorted out, so there was an hiatus before their return which was to make all the difference.

March made the most of its numerical superiority in the meantime and there were seven cars on the grid at Miami with Emerson Fittipaldi making a return to the sport in an 83G-Chevy and shaking off the moth balls by setting pole. Emerson would also be seen in CART at the wheel of a March, and since the USA is such an insular place the double World Champion would qualify for the 'Rookie of the Year' award, which is like the girl in the *New Yorker* cartoon who said, "I'm thinking of moving to another town and becoming a virgin again."

Miami turned out to be a catalogue of disaster for all the Marches, but a couple limped round in eighth and ninth. History was made at the Sebring 12 hours when a Porsche 935 scored its last win in IMSA GTP from Lanier and Bill Whittington in their 83G-Chevy, but then March came back on stream and took the next five races, with Lanier drawing away at the head of the points table in his Blue Thunder car (Blue Thunder makes high-powered speedboats which are very popular among racers and some sorts of businessmen in Florida).

In May, however, Porsche returned with the 962 and after a couple of races took its first win, after the Californian outfit, Andial, made a 3.2 litre version of the engine which provided enough torque to make it competitive. From then on the season seesawed with Holbert and Bell taking five of the remaining nine rounds to March's four. Although he was not the quickest driver around, Randy Lanier worked hard on his learning curve and held on to his points lead. Later he looked destined for higher things (he was Indy Rookie of the Year in 1986) until the abrupt ending of his career, for he was another whose idea of a free market economy (smokers' requisites and sinus highballs) did not have Uncle Sam's approval.

While IMSA GTP remained the main thrust of the March sports car effort, the March Buick which had been supplied to Pegasus Racing and whose engine was developed by the American branch of McLaren Engines, appeared at Le Mans, which was a little odd since it had never shown well in the States. While the drivers weren't stars, it appeared to be a serious effort and it was not hard to detect the hand of Buick itself using the race as a low-profile evaluation exercise. The car proved very quick in a straight line, but was slow overall, due to its drivers, and it qualified half a minute off the pace and retired with engine trouble after 95 laps. That made a change because in IMSA GTP it retired in every race because the transmission failed for it could not handle the Buick's torque, and that led March to make its own sports car gearbox the following year.

An altogether different class of effort was Mazda, which bought an 84G late in the year, fitted a turbo-charged twin-rotor Wankel engine and entered it in the Fuji 1000 Km for Yoshimi Katayama and Takashi Yorino, who qualified it 16th overall and finished eighth and the second Group C2 (née Group C Junior) car home. Thus March-Mazda (the nominal priority had changed) finished ninth equal in the Group C2 Manufacturers' Championship. After so promising a start one would have thought the success would have been built upon, but the car was never raced again. It had been built to set in motion a turbo development programme, but then Mazda had a change of policy and came out firmly in favour of banning turbos from Group C, which may have had something to do with the fact that while its turbo unit had 550 bhp it also had poor torque and a heavy thirst.

One of the most impressive statistics in motor racing history is that 29 of the 33 starters in the 1984 Indianapolis 500 were Marches. It would have been 30, but Jacques Villeneuve had an accident in practice and failed a medical, which allowed Chris Kneifel's Primus PR 84-Cosworth to take 33rd place on the grid to become only the second American car in the race. Not only that but every classified finisher, first to 14th, was a March.

In 1984 March still listed a Sports 2000, the 84S, but few were sold. (**Autosport**)

It takes no time at all to write '29 out of 33' but to grasp what that means requires a leap of imagination. On the one hand there's a little factory on an industrial estate in Bicester and it's not one of the smart new high-tech estates, it's showing its age. On the other hand it is the biggest one-day sport event in the world and since it's also one of the oldest in the world, it has its own traditions and mystique. It's the biggest, the brightest, the brashest, and it's very, very, important – no other race has a 220-page annual devoted to it. You can't even say that the Launton Road Industrial Estate is 4000 miles from Indianapolis, they're light years apart.

The quality of any win in sport depends on the opposition; if you stepped into the ring with Mike Tyson and he flattened you with his first punch it would not add to his reputation, in fact he'd probably be booed, but if you teased him for four rounds and then drove him into the canvas with a whirlwind combination of punches you'd be a hero. Those 29 cars did not just happen to arrive on the grid, there were 117 entries, a record, and each one represented someone's best shot. Even the worst car team and driver of the 117 was not a complete wash-out, so to dominate the grid as March did with the only opposition coming from two Lolas, an Eagle and a Primus was a considerable achievement.

It was actually the only time that Robin watched the race from the track. With typical self-deprecation he says, "I had to turn up to see if we could be such a load of wankers as to have 90 per cent of the grid and then blow it." Blow it March did not and in first and third places were the Penske Marches of Rick Mears and Al Unser with 'Rookie' Roberto Guerrero splitting them after a number of dramas including a spin and overshooting his pit. Penske had bought 84Cs as insurance and after running its PC12s in the opening two rounds it abandoned them and switched to March. At about the same time Pat Patrick stopped making Wildcats (which began the year with March bodywork) and bought Marches. As A.J. Foyt, who once built his own Coyotes, said at the time, "Racing has gotten so damned expensive I can buy three or four Marches for what it would take me to develop one car."

First to 14th, all the finishers, it is a unique achievement and if you study the whole season's results you see occasional oddities like an Eagle-Pontiac, a second-hand Penske, the Primus, the Shierson, even F1 names like Ligier and Theodore, but most would either collapse or turn their faces towards Bicester, so as the season wore on it was wall to wall March except for the incursion of two cars, and both were Lola T800s.

Lola had begun making cars almost exactly ten years before March was founded and they vie for the title of the most successful production racing car maker ever, but until March went to America it had never taken on Lola in any major category, which was top priority for both. March had been in F1 when Lola hadn't, Lola had been successful with 2-litre sports cars when, for March, they were a means of mopping up extra BMW engines. The first real head-to-head confrontation between the two firms was in IMSA GTP, and March had eventually won, but now Lola was back in Indycar, this time as the under-dog but with the advantage of a fine team, the result of pooling the resources of Paul Newman, Carl Haas and Mario Andretti. Then, after the first race, Dough Shierson, who had once been March's North American importer abandoned his own Shierson DSR1, a March derivative designed by Ian Reed, and bought a Lola for Danny Sullivan, who had returned home after a year in F1 with Tyrrell.

The 84C was still recognizably a March, but was a completely new design, and the honeycomb monocoque (with aluminium bulkheads machined from solid billets) was five inches shorter than the 83C, which gave an extra seven inches to the crushable nosebox area to increase driver protection and the foot box was widened and strengthened by carbon fibre. Despite these changes the wheelbase and track remained the same, but the engine was canted at an angle of three degrees. A lot of work had

In 1984 March won again at Indianapolis and the winning car was this 84C-Cosworth driven by Rick Mears. (**Rich Chenet**)

At Indianapolis in 1984 Al Holbert drove a fine 'rookie' race finishing fourth, two laps in arrears, but on the same lap as the second and third-place finishers. (**Autosport**)

been done on the aerodynamics and a team of six had devoted five months to the body, with the result there was less drag and more downforce and particular attention had been paid to improving traction out of slow corners, which had been a weakness on the 83C and one which Andretti's Lola T700 had been able to exploit. As part of the new package the March transverse gearbox was replaced by a longitudinal one which used Hewland internals in a new March casing which incorporated the oil tank and shock absorber mountings. Pull rod suspension was retained at the front and as part of the aerodynamic package, rear suspension was by rocker arms, just as in the 83C's road circuit kit.

Nobody would have put money against a March steamroller, after all, at the beginning of the season there was only one serious non-March in the field, a new Lola, the T800, which had an aluminium/carbon fibre monocoque drawn by ex-Lotus and Theodore man Nigel Bennett. March may have had numerical superiority, but only one car can win a race and in the opening round at Long Beach that one was the Lola T800 with which Andretti took pole and won by over a minute: sharp intake of breath all round.

Wins by Sneva at Phoenix and Indy in a March, run by ex-McLaren men Teddy Mayer and Tyler Alexander, restored the balance, but only after Andretti had set the pace in unofficial practice at Indy, his car having problems in both qualifying and the race. Sneva then headed a March 1–7 at Milwaukee and Al Unser Snr headed another March 1–7 at Portland. Then Lolas won the next eight races, five going to Andretti, three to Sullivan.

March's former travelling salesman says, "During March's golden period in CART, 81–86, the 84C was our least good car. The trouble was it was a committee effort and you know the definition of a camel, a horse designed by a committee. We only got back on course when Adrian Newey took overall responsibility and came up with the 85C, which was a superb car, but in 1984 Lola had a very good year and administered a kick to our backside."

Tim Holloway says, "We lacked overall direction with the 84C, Robin made an input, Adrian, Ralph, Alan Mertens, and myself. I'd done the front suspension on the

Yet another March victory, at Phoenix, where the winner was Tom Sneva with this 84C-Cosworth. (**Rich Chenet**)

842, so I did the front suspension of the 84C, but nobody was in charge of deciding whether my front suspension would work with someone else's rear suspension."

He might also have added that the car was grossly overweight – by nearly 200lb – and that there were many crown wheel and pinion failures. As a result of that confusion March devised a pattern whereby one man would be the concept engineer and would work at the trackside with a particular team gathering the information for the following year's car while another would take the concept, the overall parameters, and create the mechanical design.

Nigel Bennett, on the other hand, built a car which was not only about 100lb lighter but he had devised a clever turbo installation which allowed a lower centre of gravity, a lower rear deck and lower rear wings and the combination of weight and aerodynamics produced a car which would work almost anywhere. One further reason for Lola's success was that the two cars were run by teams which would be recognized as 'professional' by contemporary mid-to-back of the grid F1 standards (even the best CART teams do not do anywhere near the amount of testing a middling F1 team does).

Thus while both firms were in the hands of their customers there was no doubt that Newman/Haas was a works team in all but name, while March's flagship team, Penske, lost the services of Rick Mears after 11 of the 15 rounds when he crashed in practice at Quebec and broke both his feet. Until then he had been perhaps the class of the field over all types of circuits although too often he was side-lined or slowed by niggling and inconsistent problems more to do with the engines than the car.

Mears' crash marked the 13th time in two seasons that an Indycar driver had received serious leg injuries following a crash. It was to take him nearly two years before he was able to drive on all types of circuits, and it led to new frontal safety regulations in 1985.

Robin's position in 1983 with the Forsythe team had been clear-cut so there was no conflict of interests, but Herd the engineer having to wear a salesman's hat was less comfortable. "My trouble is that I get enthusiastic about anyone driving a March, so when I had time I'd go down the pit lane and try to help all the March runners, but even this created problems. In those days the competence of some teams left a lot to be desired, but even so they knew it all and it was a battle to get them to do even fundamental things right. Then people would get paranoid in case you were passing on their secrets to the other teams. I'd try to be scrupulously fair because most of the drivers were worth believing in, there were very few wankers, and you can find much more time by making a driver believe in himself than you can by playing about with the car.

"When I started to talk to a driver, you could see his rivals starting to count the seconds. *Spending a lot of time with Rick Galles today, ain't he? Spent a lot of time with him yesterday as well. Probably went to bed together if the truth be known.* It's amusing to look back on but, it wasn't fun at the time. It's always much better to work with one driver."

March had tried to improve exit speed from slow corners, but Lola had done even better in that respect and the T800 was particularly at home on the road circuits which made up half the series. This was food for thought, but the better March teams retaliated and Bobby Rahal won two of the last three races in his Jim Trueman (TrueSports) car which, was helped no end by the arrival of Adrian Newey in the team. Adrian not only managed to shed a lot of weight from the cars (140lb in one case) but he also applied F1-style thinking and came up with new components and set-ups to tailor the cars to each circuit.

It was Tom Sneva who won the last race, and his third of the year, to finish runner-up in the series with 163 points to Andretti's 176. The season thus ended in a tie so far as buying for '85 was concerned, because although the two Lolas took nine wins to the six of the umpteen '83 and '84 Marches in the field, March had won the last three of the season. Orders rolled in for '85 Lolas, but, for the time being, March was to hold on to its numerical superiority.

Whither Teo Fabi in all this? Having been the class runner in 1983 Teo spent the first part of the year flitting back and forth between Indycar and F1 to the detriment of both sides of his career. The adjustment between the two classes was too much and by mid-season he had quit the Forsythe team to concentrate on his Brabham F1 drive. Attempting to do both types of racing cost him the chance to do well in either, as by 1984 Indycar was emerging from the Dark Ages and was becoming a specialized category and not even the best driver could have done both F1 and Indycar simultaneously. Mario Andretti had managed to bridge them with equal success in the same season and he had tried when neither was as specialized.

As for the constructors, March and Lola had managed to spend most of their respective careers managing to miss each other in single seater racing, but 1985 would see them not only locked in a struggle in Indycar but, for the first time ever, they would be meeting on two fronts, for both would be in F3000 as well.

21 Sports Car Interlude

Although the Porsche 962 had put the writing on the wall for the 82G series, and in block capitals at that, six 85Gs were sold to the States, three with Buick engines, two with Porsche units and one with a Chevrolet. Because of the problems encountered with the '84 Buick car's gearbox, March's Alan Mertens designed a new transmission based on the Hewland DG, but the internals needed wider cogs and Hewland could not supply within the deadline (not many people know this, but the longest lead time on any part of a racing car is the crown wheel and pinion). Rob Gustafson, Project Manager of the transmissions department, chose that time to leave and set up Roni Developments with another former March man, Nick Wasyliw. A former driver and mechanic, Derrick Worthington, took over and found he had a gearbox and no gear supplier. After a frantic hunt through a trade directory Derrick found that Staffs Silent Gear was willing to talk business at the price and within the deadline, although it had never before been involved in racing.

The new transmission worked perfectly, one thing led to another, a Staffs/March gearbox for the lower formulae was designed by Ian Ashdown and other joint projects were planned. In the end, Derrick went to work for Staffs and for other reasons the joint range of transmissions never materialized, but the March sports car gearbox was sold to Jaguar, Toyota and Nissan.

So far as IMSA was concerned the 85G was almost a dead issue despite a refreshment programme led by Peter Vennick, which included a slimmer gearbox which cleaned up the under-car aerodynamics. Its only performance worth mention was at Miami, where David Hobbs and Darin Brassfield brought their 85G-Chevy home second followed by a similar car driven by Emerson Fittipaldi and Tony Garcia, but then it was early in the season before most of the new owners of Porsche 962s had come to terms with their cars. In any case the 85G was not reckoned as good a car as the 84G, for it was unstable under braking, one of those instances where a good car is developed but loses its harmony.

Even that's not the whole story. In '83 and '84 the only categories March had to worry about were IMSA GTP and CART, the F2 team had been farmed out to Onyx, so IMSA received proper attention. In '85 there was the advent of F3000, with things to learn, and the chance to use the GTP car in conjunction with a major manufacturer in Group C, so IMSA suffered and apart from that flattering early-season performance, March became a make-weight, but it was different for a maker looking for a car in which to stick a new racing engine. Nissan was such a one and the choice basically came down to Lola and the 85G, but March had an inside track as James Gresham explains, "I'd been travelling to Japan since 1978 and had got to know our importer, Tom Hanawa, very well. He's a man I've a lot of time for as both a businessman and as a friend. He'd told me he could arrange a liaison with Nissan and was as good as his word. Our idea was a future partnership, but initially we scored hits with Formula Atlantic cars and various things with Nissan engines.

"I tended to push this along a bit; I wouldn't claim to be very active just making sure that we didn't miss out, and eventually they ordered an 83G to which we fitted one of their straight-four (LZ20B 2083cc) engines. I was then running a Formula Two team so I couldn't put as much background energy in as I would have liked but the job got done and the car was used; then early in 1984 we had a visit from Electromotive of California, who were looking at purchasing a car to do IMSA with their version of the V6 Nissan VG30 engine, which was being used by Paul Newman in America.

"I was very keen that we got this job because it was Nissan but the meeting didn't go very well, the personalities didn't gel, and Lola got the order. Then Hanawa did a very good job at pulling sales for us with the same engine, so we could at least get in there to make our point, and if our car proved better than the Lola then we thought maybe Nissan would use it for the World Endurance Championship. Time went on and eventually Electromotive co-operated quite well with us and we built three 85Gs for Nissan, two with V6 engines and one straight-four.

"Nissan was delighted with our car and I had built up a reasonable relationship with their star driver, Kazuyoshi Hoshino, who'd run for me in F2 in 1983 at Donington Park. We managed to make sure that Hoshino said that the Lola was junk and that the March was great, so Nissan were converted to March, but we were helped by the fact that the Lola broke things all the time whereas ours was a pretty well-proven old bus.

"The three 85Gs were entered for the Fuji 1000 Km and on the first day of practice, God knows how, Hoshino put his car on pole and Porsche were crapping themselves, but then so were we because we were running out of engines. In fact one of the qualifying engines had to be used for the race because they had wired the boost so high they had started detonating. Overnight Porsche fitted their qualifying units with big turbos, etc, but we couldn't improve because we had no spare engines left."

Hoshino had to be content with a place on the second row of the grid, but it had been the first time in four years that the works Porsche team had been seriously challenged by a Group C car which was not a Lancia or another Porsche and the stage was set for a great race, and then before the start there was a monsoon and most of the European contingent refused to start in it. "Hoshino did a magic job in very difficult conditions, he won by a lap or something, including a spin half way through which gave us all a heart attack."

That was March's first Group C win, and it was aided immeasurably by the rubber Bridgestone supplied, but like the works' first GP win it was a shortened race so only half-points were awarded. By 1985, however, points were awarded to teams rather than makes, since almost all the serious runners were using Porsches, so the ten points went to NISMO (Nissan Motorsports International Co. Ltd). Since it was the only race in 1985 which Porsche didn't win, it put James in a strong position to make a bid for 1986, when Nissan was considering entries at Le Mans.

Nissan was not the only firm in the chassis market, BMW North America bought a car to take another shot at IMSA. This was a modified 85G with the rear suspension lowered and given new geometry, while at the front a twin-blade anti-roll bar replaced the previous single solid beam. Rebodied by McLaren (North America), it had the radiator intakes on either side of the cockpit and was fitted with a 2-litre turbo unit; it did not make a race until December, when David Hobbs put it on the front row at Daytona, but the engine gave up in the race; still it was an encouraging performance and just as Nissan was interested in extending its involvement with March, so too was BMW. As for March it was the old story, the opportunity to get into bed with a major manufacturer on a joint programme, especially since, just down the road, Tom Walkinshaw Racing had become a manufacturer in all but name, as Tom autonomously handled Jaguar's racing operation with Roger Silman as team manager.

Gordon Coppuck had returned to March in 1985 when Team Spirit gave up the unequal struggle in F1 and he was put in charge of designing the Nissan 88G. The only part of this car which was interchangeable with the BMW car was the tub and he drew it in a very short time: from start to finish it was less than five months, although perhaps 'drew' is not the right word because the 86G was the first March to be created with Computer Aided Design and Computer Aided Machining (CAD/CAM), which he undertook at NGA in Coventry. The resulting car finished up 100kg lighter than the 85G so had to be ballasted according to the class in which the car ran.

Although all the '86 cars had consecutive chassis numbers, there were two distinct types, BMW and Nissan, the former deriving from the 85G and the latter being the new Coppuck design, for most of the decisions on the IMSA cars had been made by the time Gordon arrived on the scene, which is why the Nissan cars were sometimes designated '86S'.

Now March was Big Business, it was more interested in other, bigger, businesses and of the 11 cars made only one (an 85G derivative with a V6 Buick unit) went to a private customer, Conte Racing in the States, while six were bought by BMW (North America) and another four went to Nissan. BMW had originally ordered just four cars, but a couple of unfortunate fires destroyed two – 'BMW Barbecues' – and so provided March with extra business. All used a 2-litre turbo engine prepared by McLaren Engines, North America, and once again David Hobbs was on the driving strength along with John Watson, Davy Jones and John Andretti, Mario's nephew. David says, "It was a bit like the BMW MC1, there was not full commitment from the parties involved. Ultimately the car was unbelievably competitive and if they'd stuck with them I think they could still be winning races today (1989).

"One of the problems was that it was a last-minute decision by BMW North America, who, as usual, did not give the programme whole-hearted backing. The engine had inherent vibration problems which caused other problems, wires fell off and oil lines broke, which led to a spate of fires. The car itself was extremely good, particularly after we took it to the Lockheed wind tunnel and did a bit of basic work; it was well balanced, had very good downforce, and amazing grip, and you wouldn't believe the speed we came out of corners. Bob Tullius who was running his Jaguars reckoned we had a power advantage, but it was all down to the grip, at Watkins Glen his cars were 8 mph faster than us on the straight, but we were four seconds a lap quicker."

Early in the season the cars had a small BMW-style twin nostril 'radiator grille' in the nose and had nose splitters but after the wind tunnel testing a smoother, sharper nose was adopted. Although it was improved aerodynamically the special body was one of the problems with the car; at least one fire was caused by the rear bodywork being forced down on to the exhaust system at speed, and during testing at Daytona, Bobby Rahal had a fortunate escape when the rear bodywork detached and the car was wrecked in the subsequent shunt.

"As with the MC1, the team running the programme wasn't very bright, we'd started the season behind the game because it was all decided too late, so after Atlanta in early April we took a break of seven weeks to get everything sorted out and I persuaded BMW to take on John Dick as team manager (we'd worked together in TransAm in '73 and I knew he was good) and he brought in new people and new thinking. John had a lot of work to do and he did a bloody good job, Wattie and I would have won Elkhart Lake by miles – he was just coming up to lap the eventual winner, the Holbert/Bell Porsche, when the engine died, a wire had vibrated off putting it to full rich. We could have won at Portland if Wattie and I hadn't completely messed up our change-over and got into a tangle over the seat belts, and Wattie was catching the leaders hand over fist at Sears Point when he was punted of by a normally reliable driver who was struggling ten laps down with problems.

"Davy Jones and John Andretti won the second Watkins Glen race and Wattie and I were second in qualifying only 0.3 seconds down, but for some reason we had overheating problems. As I've said, the car could still be winning races today with a bit more development with the same team but at the end of the year BMW North America pulled the plug. They decided their future lay in stressing that they sold luxury cars so what happens but their two main rivals in the luxury car field, Mercedes-Benz and Jaguar, come back into racing. BMW couldn't have made a worse decision." There speaks a man who had BMW agencies in the States.

At the end of the season Gianpiero Moretti bought two of the cars and fitted them with Buick engines, one a 4.5-litre normally aspirated unit, usually driven by Jeff Andretti, and one with a 3-litre turbo engine for Moretti himself, but only the latter made any top ten finishes up to the end of 1988 and then only rarely.

March's first full-blown attempt at Le Mans was with Nissan in 1986 and James Gresham's account of the sorry tale indicates why for all the technical ability of all the Japanese firms, only Honda has cracked motor racing. "After Hoshino won at Fuji in a March-Nissan at the end of '85, I made a presentation to Nissan for the '86 car and persuaded March to let me use Gordon Coppuck. We got the go-head on 1 December and the car ran in March and I think for a brand new top to bottom Group C car that was going some. In the meantime Nissan asked us how we should organize running at Le Mans and since we'd made the proposal they said they were going to use us and wanted me to be team manager. I thought, 'Crikey, I don't even know where Le Mans is,' but Tom Hanawa was saying, 'You must do it, it's Nissan, you're my friend,' and all that sort of thing.

"Now one bloke who was bloody impressed by the performance of the cars at Fuji was Keith Greene and since he had nothing else on he said he'd run the team. Nissan wasn't too happy. It was a case of 'We thought you were going to run the team,' so I said, 'I am, and I've decided to hire Keith.' It threw them, but they could see the logic of it. We eventually built the first 86G, but we were late and it had to be shipped to Japan before it was really finished.

"We had some cooling problems in testing, so we fitted extra radiators and a mechanic didn't tighten an oil pipe, the car went out, did half a lap, oil squirted over the turbo and the car was set alight. Gordon was out there and he had to take all the flack, 'We spent the money' and all that and on top of that we had a press launch in London, we hadn't finished the second car and all we had to show was this wreck.

"We flew it back home and had the idea that we could cut out a large piece of board which would go round the back of the cockpit, like one of those seaside photograph booths where you stick your head in the hole. The wreck arrived at Bicester at six o'clock in the evening and we had that evening to get out all the fire extinguisher foam and clean it all at the back end, make the board to go round the cockpit and get the car to a hotel in London, where it had to go in through a window.

"So we have the press launch with the front end of the car poking out through the board, and Robin making speeches and all that sort of thing, but people wanted to see the engine, so we took away the board and showed it. We got through that drama too because we'd cleaned it up and most people don't notice missing pipes and that sort of detail.

"We took it back to Bicester, did a proper job on it and went testing at Donington a couple of weeks later prior to it being flown back to another race in Japan and this was the test where everybody's jaw dropped, we talk about it to this day. Keith had managed to get some jungle juice, Mobil Formula One fuel I believe, and the acceleration out of the hairpin was just *stunning*. People talk about the 1000 bhp F1 cars, but this was *so* impressive because it's got lots of grip, lots of traction, no wheel spin and real acceleration. James Weaver described driving it as 'Picking the gears as fast as I can without looking at the rev counter.'

"When you've been round racing a long time, racing cars don't accelerate, they do of course, but it's a matter of perception, you get used to them and become blasé. But this thing *accelerates* so we thought, 'No problem, pole is definitely on at Le Mans.' Nobody thought we'd finish, but we could sit on pole since the opposition was weak, Jaguar was struggling since it was its first year there and Porsche weren't interested, so there was a good chance.

"We then started a test programme and the engine never ran properly again. The electronics screwed up, the engine blew up, you name it, it was terrible. We went to the Le Mans test day and the thing misfired all day, but we were only just off the pace so we knew this was the biz. Eventually we arrived for the race and I reckoned Hoshino would do a good job for us. I really rate him as a driver and as a bloke, and had sold Keith on the idea he was good. Hoshino got into the car in practice and we wondered where he'd got to he was so slow. It was four minutes thirty seconds, four minutes twenty nine, well over a minute off the pace.

"We called him in: 'Anything wrong?' 'No, no problem.' 'But what about the time?' 'Don't worry, second practice will be no problem.' 'But 4 mins 20 doesn't get you into the race.' 'Oh? Okay.' 'Can we put Weaver in the car to see that the car is all right because we have done some mechanical changes and he will be able to tell us straightaway if it's all right (us Brits knowing that Weaver can give it a bit of a plug and sling it on pole).' 'No.'

"He then went out in the 85G and carried on with practice and it was terrible, miles off the pace. Eventually they were just under the four-minute mark so they had all qualified, but we're thinking, 'This car with a misfire has done 3 mins 25 and now it's pushed to break the four-minute barrier. What's going on?' Then it gradually dawned on us that the Japanese were frightened, a couple of them said they were frightened, there was something strange going on. By this time Keith was jumping up and down and we were getting so frustrated, so Weaver took the old car out and by the time he got to the Tetre Rouge down the hill the engine was on the limiter in fifth so he had to back off.

"He came straight back into the pits and said, 'I'm on the limiter in fifth – put a bigger limiter in.' 'No, no,' said Yasuharu Nanba, the head of NISMO, 'this is how we are going to run it in the race.' James said, 'I can't drive it like this, if I pop down Mulsanne at 170 mph everybody will laugh at me.' 'Just go out, qualify, and forget about it,' said Keith. James went out and did his three laps, but the car was undrivable because they've eased off on the downforce."

It was all very mysterious but nobody on the March side knew that testing had revealed a tendency for the crankshafts to break and to have run the engine as it had run in testing at Donington would have resulted in an early bath for the drivers. NISMO had committed itself to running at Le Mans so there was a lot of face at stake. It was Nissan's first attempt at a major endurance race, it had previously confined its activities to races at home, so there had to be something to show for it. NISMO knew it couldn't run competitively over 24 hours, but to run slowly and finish would be regarded as a good result back home, for Le Mans has as much magic there as anywhere else in the world.

Someone with a lot of experience of Japanese racing expresses the attitude, "If the British or Italians go down a particular route and find it's not working they have no problem about saying 'Oops' and doing a 180-degree turn, they've goofed so they go back to square one and start again. Not so any other nation in racing, if they come across a problem they pretend it isn't there or they can find a way around it. The Japanese are worst of all in this respect (the Americans aren't much better), with the exception of Honda. Most Japanese outfits operate with committees where everyone has to mind his back, but Honda groomed Nobuhiko Kawamoto, sent him over as a mechanic with the F2 Brabham-Hondas in the Sixties and as a result he has the type of thinking and the individual power of a British or Italian racing boss and you can see the result. Kawamoto and Honda are exceptions, though, which is why apart from them the British and Italians dominate racing."

Someone else with experience of Japanese racing, and neither British nor Italian, says that they are so set in their ways that if a driver complains of oversteer and suggests adjustments to the car to dial it out they will take on board the fact that the car has oversteer but will ignore the suggestions. They will then go through a set programme to deal with the problem but will not try the short cut even though the driver is employed to know it.

One team working with a Japanese company had to choose between two drivers, both European, and driver A was the hot favourite with everyone. Then A turned up to a test session with his girlfriend, as drivers do, but she was Japanese and immediately all the Japanese personnel moved to one side because it was taboo to bring a woman into a working area. The seat went to driver B. *East is East and West is West.*

James Gresham continues, "There was a big argument going on, and a lot of toing and froing, but eventually we got to second practice and they had just got down to the four-minute mark when we saw soft tyres being put on the car. Keith asked, 'What's this?' and the Japanese said, 'Hoshino says full boost and soft tyres now.' 'But he hasn't broken four minutes and with a misfire and a race engine we can do 3 mins 25. This is stupid, I'm leaving.' The Japanese pleaded with him, 'Please don't.' They got it down to 3 mins 30 in six laps, but the engine was finished, the tyres were finished, it sat there, a bundle of junk. In the next pit lane the same thing was going on, but the engine blew up.

"Meanwhile we were all demoralized. Gordon wanted to fly home, I didn't want any more to do with it because we'd put ourselves on the line and told everybody we were going to be on pole, but we were only doing 170 down the Mulsanne straight and everybody was saying our car was draggy, but the engine was on the limiter by the restaurant at about 200 hp, it was ridiculous. Then we were told that all they wanted to do is to finish the race, so Keith said, 'Okay, if that's your plan what we do is we fit the race engines, we run them carefully and briefly, and then park them. You'll have to qualify Weaver at night, but he only does three laps and then parks it.' Fine, it was all agreed and they did it with the first car, they qualified it, and parked it. Then Weaver came over and said he had been told to drive the bloody second car again and they'd made it even worse by taking even more downforce off it and it was undrivable first time around.

"There was nothing I could say except, 'Just drive it, qualify yourself and see what happens.' So he climbed in and there was this bloke bending over the dashboard playing with the rev limiter and this time the engine was not on the limiter by the restaurant, it's on it 200 yards before because they'd taken off another 500 rpm. James still set a faster time than any driver except Hoshino, who did it on full boost, qualifiers, the whole bit, and James was driving a hobbled car to qualify himself at night.

"At this point Masahiro Hasemi, the lead driver of the 85G, was getting worried because his job was on the line. There's a big loss of face, because he's been blown away by this little erk from Newbury. Keith could see what was going on, he leapt across the front of the car, opened the door, pulled the rev limiter out and showed it to Nanba with, 'Your drivers are cheating you.' You can imagine what loss of face that was, a Japanese driver was cheating a Japanese manager and a European finds out. Keith said, 'I refuse to work for you a minute longer,' and threw the rev limiter on the floor and we all left them to it. Apparently the car went out and blew its engine.

"James, Gordon, Keith and I went into the motor home and started on the wine. There was a knock on the door, Keith opened it and there was Nanba. 'Yes?' 'Er, could I see you please, Mr Greene?' 'In a few moments, wait outside.' Slams the door. After a while Keith ushered him in. 'Please Mr Greene, would you continue to manage this operation?' 'I'll continue to work here because I respect Mr Gresham and Mr Coppuck, but it's only under these circumstances I'm doing it, I'm not doing it for you. The way you have treated Mr Weaver is disgusting. If you want Mr Weaver to drive please will you double his fee?' Nanba said, 'Yes, no problem,' and walked out again.

"In the race the 85G was going really well and the drivers were setting times faster than the 86G, faster than the qualifying times, and that was on race tyres and race boost. We were even starting to climb up the leader board, but at six hours 86G came into the pits with a broken crankshaft and all the Brits said, 'Oh dear, what a shame, but it's over.' Then Nanba came over and was pleading, pleading, with us to take the engine out and repair the damage. We told him that even if we did that it wouldn't qualify as a finisher but, no, we *must* finish. It wasn't until the engine builder told us how long it was going to take that he accepted that we were right. He thought we were giving up but the English mentality is you don't give up and when you realize the position is hopeless you turn to the next page. Not so the Japanese, they wanted to continue to the chequered flag even if they had to push it round the circuit.

"Anyway they wheeled the car away and because Aguri Suzuki, one of the 86G drivers, hadn't had a drive and he's a rising star, a terrific guy, incidentally, and easily the best driver they have, they wanted him to drive the 85G, so Keith rushes up to the organizers, he has a very good relationship with them having being going there for years, and says, 'Can I put Suzuki in the other car?' and they say, 'Yes, if you nominate him, no problem.'

"Ten minutes into the Suzuki stint a marshal comes up and says, 'You've had four drivers in the car, the rules say there shall only be three drivers in the car.' Keith has a fit, so legs it up the pit lane to see the organizers and says, 'You haven't seen Suzuki driving car 32?' They give him an old-fashioned look, but remember Keith managed Rondeau, the last French team to win Le Mans and they say, 'No Keith, we haven't seen him.' Keith then charges back to call Suzuki in and sends for James, who went out and drove the fastest laps of the race for us.

"We finished 16th on 284 laps to the winner's 367, but the Japanese fêted us as world heroes because we'd finished the first time Nissan had been to Le Mans. That finished me; so far as I was concerned they had finished the 18 Hours of the Le Mans, since the distance they covered in 24 Hours is what the leader had done in 18, so they hadn't really finished, but to watch them celebrate you'd have thought they'd won.

"I felt so let down, and the experience has coloured motor racing for me ever since; that was my blow-on-the-head job. I was blitzed at the prize giving, I couldn't cope with it at all; they didn't tip up to the official prize giving, they had their own and slapped each other on the back and

There were two March-Nissan entries at Le Mans in 1986. This 86G driven by Hoshino/Matsumoto/Suzuki was beginning to climb up the leader board when the crankshaft broke. **(Nigel Snowdon)**

The second car, an 85G, seen here in practice, driven by Weaver/Hasemi/Wada eventually finished 15th. **(Nigel Snowdon)**

stood up and made big speeches about what big heroes they were. Keith and Gordon coped very well, but I just wanted to go away and hide. We had a really super bit of kit and I'd spent years working on the project, there was a lot of me in it, and they'd thrown it all away.

"I suppose a lot of it was due to the fact that it was their first go at Le Mans and they didn't understand European racing, but watching them now, they've got their act together and there's no hard feelings because Keith is currently managing the team. I count a lot of the people involved as personal friends, so if the opportunity arose to work with them again, I'd jump at it because I think they've learned a lot."

Later that year four March-Nissans ran in the Fuji 1000 Km, but none showed much pace largely because Nissan had not learned how to optimize its use of fuel, or so it was given out, but who knows what the truth of the matter was? The crankshaft problem had not been solved and the best finish was Hoshino and Hamesi in tenth with no apparent problems, the car was simply slow.

Apart from the 86G-BMWs, which were entered as 'BMW GTPs', IMSA was pretty thin so far as March was concerned, even although the Porsche 962 was by no means invincible, with wins going to Lola and Jaguar as well as that 'BMW GTP' win at Watkins Glen. Still, an 85G-Buick driven by Whitney Ganz finished second at Atlanta (with John Paul Jnr) and third at Charlotte and Lime Rock with, respectively, Bob Lobenberg and Jim Crawford, which suggests there was still life in the car, though most people apparently did not believe it and had switched to others.

Nissan bought three more cars the following year, which was March's whole production run. The 87Gs were slightly updated 86Gs modified to take the new three-litre VEJ30 V8 engine (which was ineligible for IMSA) and two cars were run at Le Mans. They did not run well because Nissan still hadn't cracked the fuel consumption problem and, further, a serious flaw in the engine was revealed, its own cooling system was inadequate. As a consequence the cars were extremely difficult to start after a pit stop and would frequently not run on all eight cylinders. Both gave up the ghost around dawn. Apart from the NISMO entries, the Le Mans Company ran an 86G with one of the V6 engines and this proved extremely impressive during qualifying, but during the race the third driver, Patrick Gonin, crashed.

As usual, the only other major race NISMO entered was the Fuji 1000 Km, and while the V8 cars were slow, the fuel problem was still present, although the position was much better on the V6 engine, Takao Wada put the Le Mans Company's V6 car on pole, but a blown tyre ruined its chances and it could finish no higher than 13th. Of the two 87Gs, one lasted three laps before a tyre blow-out and the other was simply slow and finished a lacklustre 16th.

After redesigning the V8, Nissan modified its 87Gs by extending the wheelbase and redesigning the rear bodywork and these were run as Nissan R88Cs, but these 'improvements' were a backwards step. March itself made one 88G, which was a new design by Paul Bentley which had a lower monocoque and a brand new body created by Nick Wirth, while an 87G was updated by the factory. Both were built for the Le Mans Company, which fitted V6 engines, and Bentley made regular visits to Japan to oversee the cars. That single 88G was the only sports car made by March in 1988, whereas only two years before it had made 11.

Only Le Mans and Fuji were contested on the International scene and at the former an R88C finished 14th, 50 laps down on the winning Jaguar, while various other March-Nissans failed to last the distance, the two V6 cars both retiring on lap 74 for the same reason, the electronic engine management system had not been correctly mapped for four-star petrol, or so it was said, but some believe that the real reason was the old Achilles' heel, broken crankshafts. Even although the problem had been ignored, it had not gone away. At Fuji all the cars were outclassed and the best result was Hoshino, Kenji Takahasi and Allan Grice, who finished ninth in an R88C.

One of two 87Gs entered by NISMO at Le Mans in 1987 this car was driven by Hoshini/Takahashi/Matsumoto. Both retired after a slow race. **(Nigel Snowdon)**

Dave Scott drove an R88C in the six-hour races at Fuji and Suzuka for the typically Japanese reason that Kenji Takahashi could not drive at his usual pace because of an injured back, but, since he had been signed, he had to run, so Scott and Grice were brought in at the longer races to support Takahashi so face would not be lost. Dave says, "There were a lot of reliability problems with the engine, particularly with the turbos and inter-coolers. I think we never ran more than 15 laps without trouble, while the fuel consumption was ridiculous. In fact the best result they got all year, even in Japanese national events, was sixth at Suzuka and that was helped by some of the faster cars retiring, and at Fuji they seriously considered turning up the wick to make a good showing knowing they'd run out of fuel.

"The car itself suffered from brake problems, but it had huge downforce, it was very quick in fast corners, but I don't think they got the balance between downforce and drag right, so it wasn't very quick on the straights and it was incredibly heavy to drive. Team organization was complicated. NISMO prepared the cars, another outfit ran them, and having raced in Japan for two years I have to say the overall standard of professionalism is not very high. They could never sort out a seat belt to make me comfortable, for example. They have their own way of doing things and I don't think the communication with March was very good."

By the end of 1988 March was going through a period of reorganization and crisis and it decided it had had enough of supplying cars to customers who might or might not have the competence to run them properly. As part of the reorganization at Bicester a workshop was prepared ready to return to Group C, but not with customer cars, it would be a joint effort with a major manufacturer with March in charge of the racing side (Nissan would be welcomed on those terms) and negotiations were entered into with a number of possible partners.

Existing cars continued into the 1989 season and since Nissan's '89 car was not ready NISMO entered two 3-litre V8 'Nissans' (March 87Gs) and a 3.2-litre V6 88G at Suzuka in the opening round of the FIA World Sports-Prototype Championship. They were not on the leading edge of the pace except in a wet practice session, where Wada (V6 88G) set third fastest time, which suggests there was still life in the car. In the race itself, Hoshino and Toshio Suzuki had a troubled run to finish fourth behind two Sauber-Mercedes and a Porsche and ahead of the leading Jaguar.

The 88G with a V6 engine, further detuned to try to make it last, was entered at Le Mans under the umbrella of the French Cougar team and ran as the Cougar-Nissan C22. Driven by Takao Wada, Akio Morimoto and Anders Olofsson it had transmission problems and couldn't top 190 mph on the Mulsanne Straight (a Sauber-Mercedes topped 250 mph) so could qualify no higher than 14th. It was running in 19th place close to the 18-hour mark when an oil leak ruined the engine.

That appeared to be the effective end of the line for the old-style customer Marches, not that the name featured on the car, although at the time of writing it is expected that the 88G will appear in later races in 1989. It did not go unnoticed that in the pit lane at Le Mans were James Gresham and Dave Reeves, who were not there to sample the local cuisine . . .

At the end of 1988, in a different context, Eric Broadley, the founder of Lola, was talking in general terms about a team tying in with a major manufacturer and specifically about 1963, when Ford hired Lola as a consultancy to produce the GT40. "It wasn't a very comfortable time, but then working with big companies is rarely comfortable. It was a lesson of the importance of maintaining one's own independence and keeping the company self-contained. It was our fault really, we allowed too much involvement from Ford. They were too deeply involved with everything and the consequence of that in a big company is that certain individuals will take advantage. To make a project like that work it is necessary to maintain the two sides, they must work closely together but they must maintain their separate identities, because the big company has come to the specialist to do a job for it. If they get themselves too involved they must screw it, otherwise there is no point going there in the first place."

A few yards away work was progressing on a new Group C project – with Nissan.

22 March Versus Lola

Everyone knew that F3000 was going to replace F2, the idea had been kicked around for long enough and been found good. F1-style cars, F2 budgets, West End quality, East End prices, the only trouble was that it was not officially announced until December 1984, with the first race slated three months later, and the final regs were not issued until half-way through the first season. Given the uncertainty of the launch of a major new formula, it's not surprising that there was equal uncertainty among teams and manufacturers. March and Lola, however, were so convinced that it was going to work that each laid down a production run on spec. Had they not the series might not have got off the ground, so even though March had orders for only three cars three weeks before the first race there were nine 85Bs on the grid.

Some reasoned that using proven F1 designs was the way to go, Lola adapted its T900 Indycar, AGS built an entirely new car, and Ralt stuffed Cosworth DFVs with their Glen Monk limiters (to 9000 rpm) in the back of its 1984 F2 car. March went the Ralt route in broad terms and Ralph Bellamy and Tim Holloway's 85B was a stiffer 842 with slab sides and two inches longer.

The first race at Silverstone showed who had taken the right route and from the start the season was between March and Ralt. By adapting an Indycar design Lola, like those who had chosen F1 cars, had overlooked a basic parameter, weight distribution. The space for the fuel cell was considerably larger than needed for a restricted DFV running in 100-mile races, so in F3000 trim there was a lot of air between the driver and the engine doing absolutely nothing except redistributing weight to where it wasn't wanted. After the first two or three rounds you could pick up up a slightly used Lola T950 at a bargain basement price and most of the F1 cars had disappeared by mid season.

Emanuele Pirro nearly won the opening race for March, Onyx and Avon, but a late spin in the wet wiped off his nose cone and allowed Mike Thackwell and John Nielsen to score a 1–2 for Ralt and Bridgestone. Before the season Ralt had an exclusive deal with Bridgestone and the only other tyres available were Avon crossplies. There was nothing in the rules against such a deal because the final regs didn't appear until June, so the formula was running on the good will of all involved and since all wanted it to succeed, it was agreed that any tyre company in F3000 had to be prepared to supply at least 30 per cent of the field.

Pirro made amends at Thruxton, where he led home Thackwell, who had had to stop for a new nose cone, then Nielsen took the round at Estoril, where Thackwell's rev limiter failed completely. Thackwell was unquestionably the class of the field, but Ralt wasn't selling cars, so newcomers and those junking their Lolas and F1 cars turned to March and by the end of the season 85Bs were about three-quarters of the field. Robin thought he'd better take a look at F3000 so went to the Nürburgring, where Thackwell sat on pole, but the race was abandoned because of snow and that remains his only contact with the formula.

Pirro won again from Nielsen at Vallelunga and then, after five years of driving Marches, Christian Danner took his first win in Bob Sparshott's car at Pau. He had scored points in the early races when he had run on Avons, but a change to Bridgestones transformed him, not because they were superior, there was little difference between them, but he had spent his entire single-seater career on radials and had more confidence when using them. Thackwell won at Spa on a track which was breaking up and caused the postponement of the Belgian GP, and he deserved it since he was the only driver not to have an incident; then it was Danner at Dijon, where the Ralts had to run very hard tyres to last the distance, Thackwell at Enna and Ivan Capelli at the Österreichring.

What was remarkable about Capelli's win was that it came from only his fourth F3000 start, he was one of the few in the field not to have F2 experience, and his team, Genoa Racing, couldn't afford its own truck let alone testing. In fact Genoa had three mechanics, two engines, and was run from Cesare Gariboldi's garage – not a motor dealership, the garage alongside his house.

Danner won again at Zandvoort, so at the start of the final round at Donington three drivers were in with a chance of the title and the points table read: Thackwell 45, Danner 43 and Pirro 38. Mike sat on pole by half a second with Christian and Emanuele back in fourth and fifth slots, but with the title at stake everyone was fired up. Pirro make a great start, but at the first corner he and Thackwell went for the same piece of road with the result that Danner merely had to finish in the first three to take the crown. He came through to win in fine style and Marches filled the top 12 places apart from Streiff's AGS in fourth. For the second year on the trot Danner and Sparshott was the most successful March combination and the performance was the more meritorious because 'Bucko' was running his

The Onyx March 85B of Johnny Dumfries in the pits at the first Formula 3000 race at Silverstone. He spun off in the wet on the second lap. (**Nigel Snowdon**)

Emanuelo Pirro scored a fine controlled win for March in the second Formula 3000 race at Thruxton in April. (**Nigel Snowdon**)

team on a much smaller budget than most of the other front-runners and did not have an official works connection. He'd also found a clever tweak; the car worked better when the rear anti-roll bar was disconnected, which does not speak highly for the basic design.

The fact that a privateer had taken the series did F3000 a power of good because people had stood back to see what would happen before they made a commitment, so Sparshott's performance plus the fact that Gariboldi did a good job on peanuts was very encouraging and as a result there was a stampede to join in. Since March was the successful customer car most people pointed their cheques at Bicester, but as Robin says, "To be blunt, the 85B was probably the *least bad* of all the cars that year, but the Lola and Ralt were even worse so we won by default more than anything else. After that our cars got steadily worse and the 85B was the best of a bad bunch."

That would become clear over the next few years, but the records say when March and Lola had their first confrontation at a serious level in Europe, March wiped the floor with its rival even although its customers were complaining about the poor build quality and how difficult it was to set the cars up. All was not entirely happy either between the works and Onyx and Ralph Bellamy found himself the odd man out, and he left March and went to Lola, where he designed a car which was not unlike the 85B but as a result of different constraints was a superior product.

Although March had frequently been blown off by the two Lolas in CART in 1984, the order books were still healthy and 44 cars were delivered in 1985, and those who bought them had their faith justified because Adrian Newey had taken hold of the project and in place of the committee car came perhaps the best of all the Indycar Marches.

It retained the same method of construction, aluminium honeycomb with a composite fibre top, but CART rules ban tubs made entirely of composites and the suspension outline was as before, although the days are long gone when the term 'rocker arm rear' means much, it only signals a direction, it tells the lay man nothing at all, for the geometry was completely revised. There was, too, an extra bulkhead of honeycomb and machined-from-solid aluminium to protect the brake master cylinders, and comply with new regulations, and Adrian removed 20lb from the tub alone while at the same time giving it twice the torsional stiffness of the 84C.

On top of that, by using a lower fuel cell he cleaned up the overall shape and the entire body was new. He also managed to lower the centre of gravity and the final car was 50lb underweight so had to be ballasted. Since the better teams in CART had already adopted completely different suspension set-ups for each type of circuit (road, street, long oval, short oval) the ability to move the ballast around was an added advantage. All in all, the 85C was a honey.

Lola hadn't been standing still either and the T900 was another step forward, but perhaps not quite such a big one as March had made, and they were still relatively thin on the ground, since Lola made 'only' 25 cars and fewer reached good hands. Adrian Newey continued to engineer the TrueSports cars, which had taken the lead among CART teams in the technical race in that it was the most experimental, it made many of its own pieces and Adrian developed a new under-car shape for the team. He also began to share information with Peter Gibbins, the engineer at Patrick Racing. Robin says, "It's an interesting concept, the downside is that you don't gain in relation to the team you share information with but you don't half gain in relation to the others. I think that philosophy is going to have to come in F1, because no one team is able to do the amount of development it needs to do. It's rather like the Airbus, no one group can do it all." March did in fact form such a relationship at the end of 1988, but it led to unforeseen problems.

Mario Andretti (Lola) won the opening round at Long Beach from Fittipaldi's Patrick Racing March. World Champions first and second, CART was starting to become serious. Penske, which was now an established

At Monaco in 1976 Bruno Giacomelli won the Formula Three race with this March 763-Toyota/Novamotor. (Nigel Snowdon)

Ronnie Peterson with the 761 was fastest through the speed trap at the Paul Ricard circuit, scene of the 1976 French Grand Prix, and was holding third place when eliminated by failure of the fuel metering unit. (Nigel Snowdon)

At the 1976 Dutch Grand Prix Peterson was 'sponsored' by John Day models and Ronnie took pole position and led the race until his tyres went off. (Nigel Snowdon)

Alex Ribeiro with the 772-BMW at Thruxton in 1977. He finished third behind Brian Henton (Boxer) and Eddie Cheever (Ralt). (Nigel Snowdon)

The March 792s of Ricardo Zunino (BMW engine) and Juan Traverso (Hart engine) in the pits at the International Trophy at Silverstone in 1979. (Nigel Snowdon)

Andrea de Cesaris at the wheel of Ron Dennis's Project Four March 802-BMW, the best of the Bicester entries at Thruxton in 1980; he finished third behind the Tolemans of Henton and Warwick. (Nigel Snowdon)

Eliseo Salazar during practice for the 1981 Brazilian Grand Prix with the March 811. (Nigel Snowdon)

A picture of despondency: Eliseo Salazar (left) and Derek Daly (right) at the 1981 Brazilian Grand Prix where both failed to qualify with their 881s. (Nigel Snowdon)

Tom Sneva during qualifying at Indianapolis in 1981. He was sensationally fast with George Bignotti's 81C and led the race only to retire with gearbox problems. (Rich Chenet)

Thierry Tassin with his March 832 Formula Two car at Thruxton in April 1983. He was eliminated by an accident on lap 11. (Nigel Snowdon)

The March 85G-Nissan of Weaver/Hasemi/Wada which eventually finished well down the field in 15th place at Le Mans in 1986. (Nigel Snowdon)

Michel Ferté with his ORECA 85B Formula 3000 car in the pits at the International Trophy at Silverstone in 1985. (Nigel Snowdon)

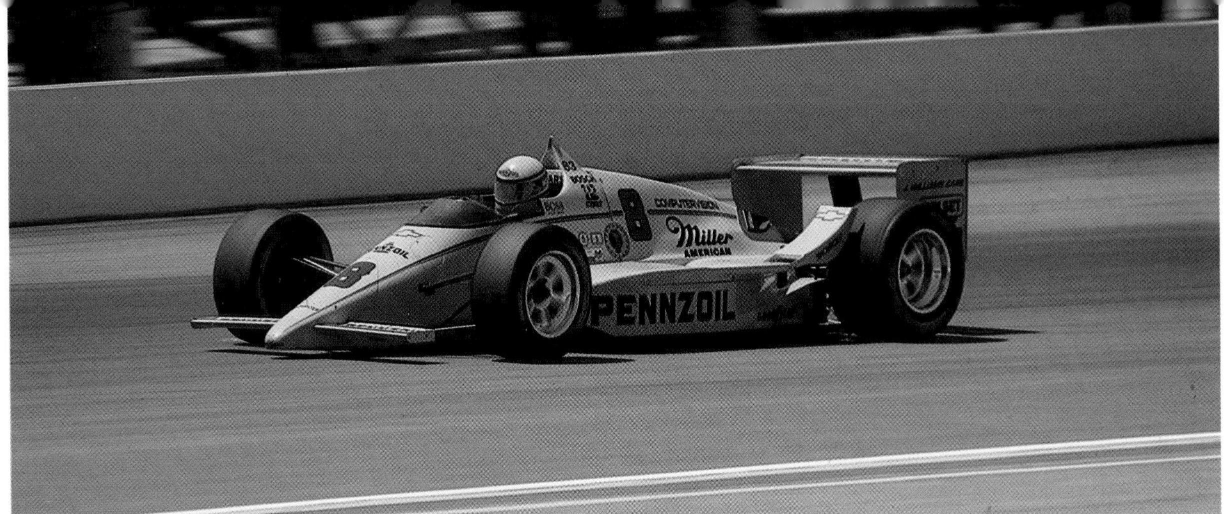

At Indianapolis in 1987 Al Unser, Snr scored a fine win with his Penske-entered March 86C. (Rich Chenet)

Former World Champion Emerson Fittipaldi finished second at Indianapolis in 1988 with this March 88C. (Rich Chenet)

Ivan Capelli with the March 871 at Monaco in 1987. He finished sixth, two laps in arrears. (Nigel Snowdon)

At Brands Hatch in 1988 Pierluigi Martini (March 88B) leads the Lola T88/50 of Gregor Foitek. (Nigel Snowdon)

Capelli's March 881 overheated while waiting for the start of the 1988 Brazilian Grand Prix. It resulted in his retirement with engine problems early in the race. (Nigel Snowdon)

Mauricio Gugelmin and Ivan Capelli (second and third from left) at the 1988 Portuguese Grand Prix. (Nigel Snowdon)

Ivan Capelli with the March 881 at the 1989 Brazilian Grand Prix. (Nigel Snowdon)

Mauricio Gugelmin (March CG891) leads Eddie Cheever (Arrows A11) in the 1989 Hungarian Grand Prix. Gugelmin retired because of an electrical problem. (Nigel Snowdon)

The 1989 March-Alfa Romeo 89CE, still to prove itself.

March customer, had taken on Danny Sullivan with Al Unser standing in for Rick Mears, who was still injured, and Sullivan then gave March its hat-trick of wins at Indy, with Mario's Lola second, but it had been a close-run thing, for just after taking the lead on lap 120, Danny had spun immediately in front of the Lola. He might have hit the wall, he might have been T-boned by Andretti, he might have stalled his engine, but he did none of those things, kept second place and lost very little time. He had to pit to change tyres, but then found that the fresh rubber made his car work even better than before – it was almost as though the script said he had to win.

Even although it could not repeat the utter domination of 1984, March still provided 24 of the 33 starters at Indy, and 51 of the 99 entries. Just as Group C manufacturers produce special bodywork for Le Mans, so in CART there are two packages, one for the tracks, one for the road circuits, and March was able to come up with the better package for Indy. A win at the Brickyard is worth any number of wins elsewhere and, as Robin says, it was the only CART race he personally takes seriously. It was just as well March took that view, for Lola won the next four races with two going to Andretti and two to Al Unser Jnr in Doug Shierson's car.

Andretti looked to be on his way to another title, but he crashed a couple of times, and one caused him to miss a race through injury for the first time in his career; he also had a fire in his car while leading at Cleveland and in general had more than his fair share of retirements. Sullivan too faded, he was quick in qualifying, and led races, but had a terrible run of reliability, unusual for the Penske team.

Emerson Fittipaldi won his first CART race at Michigan (oddly, given his background, he seemed more at home on the diminishing number of ovals than on road circuits) and since he'd been picking up points all season he was in contention for the title and headed the table (with Andretti) for a couple of weeks in August, but others who had been picking up points all season were Al Unsers, Senior and Junior. Jacques Villeneuve (85C) was the next winner and then Rick Mears was back on top at Pocono. Al Unser Snr had been drafted into the Penske team to do the three 500-mile races, but Mears found his feet would not stand road races, so Al did the full season and after Pocono led the series, although he'd not taken a win. Then Johnny Rutherford (85C) won his first Indycar race in five years when he won at Sanair and at last Bobby Rahal came on stream in the TrueSports car and he took the next two rounds. Rahal had been on the pace all season, he took seven pole positions with a further six front row starts, ran with the leaders on all sorts of track (some teams had different drivers for road circuits and ovals) but he too had rarely finished.

As the series progressed it was developing into the most closely fought in American racing history, eight different drivers had won the first 13 races. There was, too, a lot more overseas interest in CART and among the drivers who raced were Alan Jones (three World Champions!), Bruno Giacomelli, Rupert Keegan, Raul Boesel and Michael Roe, who joined established exiles such as Derek Daly, Roberto Guerrero, Geoff Brabham and Jim Crawford. Fittipaldi's challenge began to fade mid way through the season as he encountered a spate of unreliability and his cause wasn't helped by the fact that he lacked pace in qualifying so had a lot of overtaking to do in the races.

Just as CART reached its peak, so there were worries about its future, for there started to be squabbles and Rutherford had won at Sanair only after protests. There had been a lot of crashes in the race, the yellow lights were on during the last lap and then the race restarted with only one corner to go and Pancho Carter had won the drag race to put his March ahead at the line. There was a growing split between the big teams and the little guys and some of the small teams were struggling. Most team owners in CART are businessmen who dip into their own pockets and find it hard to compete against what are works teams in all but name.

After 13 rounds Al Unser Jnr held a narrow lead over his father, then Dad put one over on the kid by leading him home in the penultimate round at Phoenix and he went into the final round at Miami with a three-point advantage. As was usual in the latter part of the season, Rahal set the pace but had to concede victory to Sullivan and in third place came Al Unser Jnr, but since his old man was right behind him he took the title by a single point, with Rahal third in the series, Sullivan fourth, Andretti fifth and Fittipaldi sixth.

Despite the fact that March had been dominant at Indy since 1981 and had won more races than any other maker since it had arrived in CART, that was the first time that one of its drivers had taken the Championship. True it was by only a single point, but it was enough.

Thus the season ended with March taking Indy, the series and ten wins to Lola's five, but all was not rosy. Apart from Sullivan's win at Indianapolis it was not until late July that a March won a race, a pattern which had become familiar. While Lola delivered cars which worked straight from the box, it took time and effort to get a March to work. Roger Bailey, March's man in America, says, "Bicester took a hard line on the balance sheet and a lot of our later troubles stemmed from this. To give an example, at Indy in 1985 the Rick Galles crew was trying to put a body on a car, but it wouldn't fit, and then they found that painted on the inside was 'reject', and that sums up the attitude at the time, any old crap was good enough for America, yet these guys were paying nearly $200,000 for a car. While we were winning, they would put up with that sort of thing, not willingly and not without a fight, but we were not generating good will and when the crunch came in '87 and there was a horrendous mismatch between the car and the tyres, people weren't prepared to listen to any more excuses and they left us.

"American team owners are different to their European counterparts. In Europe a guy starts off as a mechanic, say, he saves up, buys a car and runs it for someone so he becomes a team manager and he builds from there. He knows all the problems he's going to get and accepts them. In America the team owners are all successful men in their own right. A few like Carl Haas and

Doug Shierson have built up their businesses through racing, but mostly they come from outside, they're all successful men and they expect to be treated as special, but March failed to distinguish between the two types of customer and this caused our downfall." Another way of putting it is that European team owners are professionals and most American owners are amateurs.

That was the gathering cloud on the horizon, but before the CART season was over March had moved in deeper into the American racing scene when Robin and Pat Patrick announced the 'Mini-Indy' American Racing Series. It had been proposed to CART's governing board and rejected, but they decided to go ahead anyway. "America doesn't produce many drivers because it hasn't got the right racing sub structure," says Robin, "so Pat Patrick and I came up with the idea of an equivalent to F3000." The plot was a March 85B chassis, although the cars are known as 'Wildcats', a Buick V6 engine and control tyres, a package which was engineered by Gordon Coppuck while the business package included regulated engine rebuilds (at fixed cost) and a race hire facility. "The 85B is an easy car to maintain and drive, it's basically simple and safe, and because you cannot change the car it cuts down on testing and the cars keep their resale value. The series was badly marketed at first, but is taking off nicely now (early 1989) with good prize money and every race televised."

Although March had been going through a period of huge success it was still dependent upon volatile markets and just as it had wiped out constructors in the States so it was possible for someone to do the same to March and Lola was having a damned good try. Long gone were the days when if a car didn't work you knitted up another, the lead time on a new design was long, complicated and very expensive. A Concept Designer (Adrian Newey in the case of CART) laid down the parameters of the car then oversaw the integration of the aerodynamics produced by one team, and the mechanical design produced by another.

There had been a time when a guy bought a car, prepared it with friends, and trailed it behind a Caravanette with a mechanic, and unless he was a complete no-hoper, he could cover his expenses and perhaps come home in profit. Then the car was his biggest single expenditure, so once he had made his choice he was committed and did his best to make it work. Now, when even little teams have sponsors, a motor home, many mechanics, a team manager, an engineer, and lots of testing, the price of a car drops to perhaps 15 per cent of the budget and when re-sale value is taken into account it drops to single figures. If a car is now not quick straight out of the box it makes sense to junk it and buy another which won't consume so much time, effort and money.

To illustrate how volatile the market has become consider the ratio of the entries at the first races of the F3000 Championship, 1987–9.

	1987	1988	1989
March	17	7	5
Lola	8	14	7
Ralt	6	6	0
Reynard	0	6	19

Within a week of the 1989 opening round two runners had switched from March to Reynard and by the third race, Pau, only two Marches were entered and only one made the start, yet some impartial observers thought the 89B potentially was the best car on the grid.

If you make washing machines, you can be big by making the fifth best in the world, but nobody wants the fifth best F3000 car and moreover the product is put to the test a dozen or so times every year and there are guys whispering in your ear, 'You've got to dump that heap of junk and buy a Larchard or you'll lose your sponsor.' That's the reality of the customer car business, yet you can stay in F1 and attract seven-figure sponsorship for year after year without ever looking like winning a race; look at Osella, Minardi and Zakspeed.

March had been making hay while the sun shone, but knew only too well that it didn't shine for ever and it made sense to lay down the foundations for a future which was not so dependent on fashion and whim. A new factory was built at Brackley, eight miles from Bicester, one part of which would house a new 0.4 scale wind tunnel facility custom-built for cars while the larger part would house Composite Technics Ltd (Comtec), an outfit devoted to supplying March and the commercial exploitation of March's knowledge of composite materials. Dave Reeves was put in charge of Comtec, and owned 10 per cent of the shares, and early Comtec projects were the development of the Panther Solo sportscar, parts for a French space satellite and the 'Aerotech'. This latter was an 85C with an all-enveloping, closed body and a twin-turbo quad-cam Oldsmobile engine with which A.J. Foyt set a world (unofficial) record for a closed circuit lap at just over 251 mph.

Porsche and Lotus had been making most of their money from consultancy and there was a growing trend for road car makers to farm out work to freelance studios and some predicted that before long they would be assemblers and marketers, buying in the designs. 'Consultancy' became a buzz word among racing car makers, especially after Cosworth landed major contracts with Mercedes-Benz and Ford to develop new engines and make cylinder heads using its patented vacuum casting technique.

There had been a time when industry had supported racing, then cars became mobile billboards, now the position had turned full circle and racing had lessons to teach industry. "We were getting an approach almost every day which we were having to refuse because we hadn't the people or facilities," says Robin. The idea of consultancy had been at the back of March's collective mind from the start, and one manifestation of it was that in 1986 of eleven 86Gs made, only one went go to a private buyer, the rest were bought by Nissan and BMW. The beauty of such deals was that one could negotiate a service contract to provide on-site engineers, in effect to run a works team without financial risk.

As March took its first steps to becoming what would be described as a 'multi-disciplined engineering design consultancy' (*all singing, all dancing*) at the end of 1985 Charles Towns was head-hunted from outside racing to bring his professional expertise to bear on the new style of

The Panther Solo seen in its later form, reflecting the development input of Comtec.

The Oldsmobile-powered Aerotech with which A.J.Foyt set an unofficial closed circuit lap record of just over 251 mph. **(Autosport)**

company which March was hoping to become, and Robin said, a year or so later, "March has become a sensible business as well as a racing company and we may be following in the footsteps of, say, Louis Chevrolet or Henry Rolls or Ferrari. I'm not saying that we are in the same category, but I can see how people start out with bunches of enthusiasm in their late twenties to build racing cars, and then branch out into doing things outside that. I am sure in the future the racing will become purely a flagship and the major business side will be our special project work. I can remember the time when Lotus built Formula Ford cars – and now their main business is as a specialized consultancy. I can see March going the same way."

The shift in emphasis made perfect sense, nobody could fault the logic, but the key people who worked at March, who were prepared to work all hours, who spent their time jetting back and forth across the Atlantic and Pacific, were racers. They worked for March *because* it was a racing car maker, any one of them could have earned as much money elsewhere and have a quieter life – if you design Bogmobiles and Joe Punter's X5i does not come up to scratch, you do not get Mr Punter on the phone to you personally. Sorting out the Bogmobile's handling, or designing a composite front bumper, might be an amusing part-time exercise but it wasn't the reason one joined a racing car maker.

It was not something peculiar to March, the whole of motor racing had been going through a process of tightening up and being run on more professional lines. Many fans look back to the old days and bemoan the disappearance of the 'great characters' like Hawthorn, Schell and Ireland, by which they mean the great pranksters. All that changed when sponsorship became a serious business. Time was when a team on a 'fly away' would have cushion fights on the plane and goose the stewardesses, but now a team flies out wearing its sponsor's uniform and not so long ago one hapless mechanic was sent home at the airport because he wasn't wearing his team tie and so missed the Brazilian GP. There are still great characters in the cockpit and in the pit lane but they are constrained by the need to represent a company's corporate image.

During the 1970 Canadian GP meeting Robin played a round of golf with Graham Hill and Jackie Stewart and to put some ginger into the game he'd made a bet with Stewart – if he won Jackie would drive his March 701 and not the Tyrrell 001 in the race. Robin recalls, "We had just finished the fifteenth hole, I was ahead and the final practice session was just about to start, so I said, 'I think you can concede the game, don't you?' Jackie said, 'No way, nobody's ever had more incentive to win a game of golf.' So we finished the game, Jackie won and then we drove into the circuit. The session was already under way, but Jackie got into the Tyrrell and started from pole."

This is real 'Can you imagine that happening today?' time, for one thing it's hard to imagine being able to drive straight into a circuit for final practice these days. When the opportunity arises, however, the spirit is still there, just as it's always been in racing. During the winter of 1986–7 for example, Bicester was under snow for some weeks and someone noticed that the car park at March Engineering, combined with the one next door and a section of road, made a decent Rallycross course. So while there was snow and ice on the ground if you'd gone down Murdock Road at night you'd have seen respected citizens squirting their company cars between the walls and managing to miss them – most of the time.

There was a time when the arrival of the motor racing circus was a signal to lock up your wives and daughters (and granny if you wanted to be safe) for it was like a plague of sexual locusts descending. Now if drivers have any spare time at all they are smiling at sponsors' receptions and it's considered bad form to hump the sponsor's wife. The same goes for mechanics. In the days when there were two men to a car there was more free time to get up to mischief, now there are eight or ten to a car yet every individual works so much harder. There are more parts in a car and each one has a designated active life, so the amount of work has increased out of all recognition. Alan Rees says, "You talk about how hard we worked when we set up March, I can tell you it was 60 per cent of how hard we work today and it's harder every year. You see our boys fly out to a race and everyone's lively, they fly home and they're all asleep."

Some of the fun had gone at March when there was no longer a racing team in Bicester, that had blunted the competitive edge, now there was a new management which did not think as racers thought. When Honda went into F1 in the turbo era it was with Spirit, a partnership between a huge company and one which had 12 employees. At the time John Wickham said it was an exercise by Honda to expose some of its bright young engineers to thinking the English *racer* way, solving problems on their feet. March was starting to put this process into reverse.

A rift would develop between the racers and the new professional management and, like the rift between Ralph Clarke and Malcolm Shaw, it was a conflict between March as it had been and March as it was trying to become. One cannot take sides in this, but simply present the problem, if there is any blame it lies at the door of Robin Herd, who made the decision, but it's hard to fault the logic of his thinking, especially when you consider he had to think of not only the company's future but his responsibility to 140 employees. The trouble was that March Engineering was a winning team, but in setting up Comtec and the wind tunnel, the team began to be fragmented and when the F1 team was set up it tore the heart out of March Engineering.

"I think that's a fair analysis," Robin says, "we needed Comtec and the wind tunnel for our own purposes and Dave was the obvious person to set them up, he'd done such a fantastic job on building cars and I thought it would be good for him to have a change of scenery. I had also been told that we would be better with a professional production engineer in charge of building the cars and at the time I believed that, hence Charles Towns.

"Racing is different to other industries because it's so competitive and demands the willing exploitation of the people in it. Unless you have that you're not going to be successful no matter how good the people are, and outsiders coming into racing just do not understand that. If we'd kept Dave in charge of production, and got someone else to run the wind tunnel and Comtec, I don't think they'd have done it as well, but it would have been the right thing to do. I made the wrong decision and am paying the consequences, for it was the beginning of the crisis we had in 1988."

At the time, though, it seemed that everything was going forward and the year ended with some pleasant surprises. "At the end of 1985, the accolades started rolling in. There was the Duke of Edinburgh's Designer's Prize – each area of industry has an annual award for design presented by the Design Council and the Duke of Edinburgh's goes to the top of the top, and they very kindly gave it to us. Ironically it was mainly for the 84C, which was probably the worst Indycar we did until 1987.

"Then there was an award from the Worshipful Company of Coachmakers and Coach Harness Makers (now the City of London's automotive and aerospace guild) for our outstanding contribution to automotive engineering and that brought with it the Freedom of the

Robin Herd and team proudly display the Duke of Edinburgh's design award.

City, which means I am entitled to drive my geese over London Bridge free of charge and without obstruction, so if you have problems with your geese, I'm your man. On top of that came the CBE, which was most unexpected. I remember picking up this envelope marked '10 Downing Street' and thinking, 'Oh damn, Mark Thatcher's after a drive.'"

The honours were fine and well deserved, but there was still the matter of Formula One. March had done everything except hack it at the top level and it was still at the back of Robin's mind. There'd been the relationship with John Macdonald, the idea of a deal with Carl Haas, and for years there had been contact with BMW, with whom March had just signed the deal to do IMSA. In 1985 the idea of a BMW F1 car was gaining ground among one faction of the board, and a number of teams, including Brabham and Benetton, were asked to submit proposals to build a car for the company. Since Brabham had been BMW's main team in F1 for some years, Mr Ecclestone was not amused.

On 10 December, 1985, Robin submitted a proposal to Munich which includes the following profile . . . *March now employs over 140 people. Though still based at the original factory at Bicester, Oxfordshire, this has been expanded to 17,000 square feet, including a well-equipped, modern machine shop, fabrication department, gearbox and chassis assembly shops, model-making facilities and an inspection/quality control department.*

As the visible face of March there's a great deal of emphasis on Robin himself and then, significantly, he steps out of the spotlight and introduces Adrian Newey as The Man: *he is undoubtedly joining the small group of world class designers*. Another interesting point the document makes: '*Despite scoring several notable victories in Grand Prix racing . . . March has had only a passing interest in F1 since its main task has been building cars for sale. Its success in this field has meant it has developed the facilities and philosophy associated with being a manufacturer of production racing cars. It is unlikely, therefore, that March as an organization could or would wish to return to Grand Prix racing.*' Within a year March was to do just that, but when those words were written they were true.

Everything at March seemed to be going

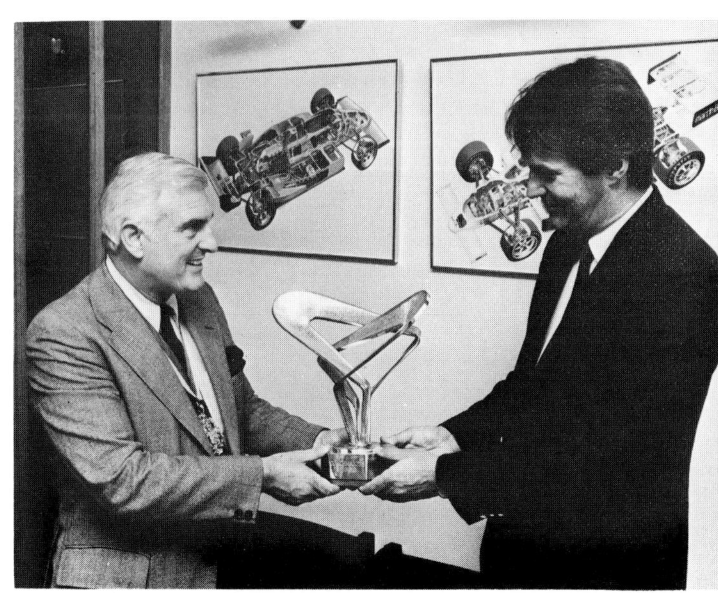

Another award this time from the Worshipful Company of Coachmakers, also presented in 1985.

swimmingly, the new management team was in place, Comtec and the wind tunnel were taking shape, the orders were rolling in and it seemed as though there was nothing it could not do. It was a bit like the early, heady, days of 1969–70 except that now everything was going forward on a secure basis. There was CART, F3000, a healthy market for F2 cars in Japan (all 15 cars in the 1976 Japanese F2 Championship were Marches) and the tie-ups with Nissan and BMW which would surely lead to other things, and both were being wooed along with others.

The BMW F1 deal was nicely on the boil and March's tender was the least expensive partly because Adrian Newey was prepared to take a relatively modest salary but would own the manufacturing company together with Robin. By May 1986 the March-BMW IMSA programme was under way, however, and was proving an expensive disaster and although the weak links in the project were BMW itself and McLaren (North America) the IMSA experience was threatening the deal. Another problem was that Peter Flöhr, who was handling BMW's end, had had too many dinners with Max Mosley and had heard too many hair-raising stories from 'the good old days at March', so the Duke of Edinburgh's Award and Robin's CBE were useful antidotes to present March as a respectable, reformed, outfit.

BMW seemed to be favouring March when John Barnard entered the equation. He was restless at McLaren, where he had designed the cars which were to win three consecutive World Championships and was ripe for courting. Just after he emerged as the clear favourite, company politics within BMW scotched the idea of an F1 car and Barnard went to Ferrari.

After an initial year which had seen all the bugs ironed out and all the important questions answered, F3000 got into its stride and at the opening round at Silverstone there were 37 entries, more than double the average of 1986. Most runners chose March and the 86B was an up-date by Andy Brown of the 85B (née 842) with revisions to the aerodynamics and rear suspension. The broad mechanical layout remained as before, but the sidepods were moved eight inches forward and received new profiles and there was a new high engine cover. After testing Onyx, the main works team, showed its enthusiasm for the new body by running without the engine cover.

Nineteen Marches would be sold against eight Lolas, a new design by Ralph Bellamy with a carbon fibre tub which overall followed the thinking of his designs for March, and Ralt sold four cars, although the works team had exclusive use of the Honda (Judd) V8. To keep costs down, FISA stipulated control tyres and the contract went to Avon, who are probably the best in the game at supplying a standard product.

Despite its numerical supremacy, March did not have a happy time at Silverstone, where Pascal Fabre put his Lola on pole and scored a narrow win from Emanuele Pirro in an Onyx 86B, and five of the top seven places were filled by Lolas with John Nielsen's Ralt-Honda in third. As so often happens, the International Trophy was beset by bad weather and turned into something of a lottery; it was stopped after two laps when the heavens opened, and after everyone had changed to wet tyres, it ran only another 24 laps before an accident on the start/finish straight caused it to be abandoned, so only half-points were awarded.

Capelli then won at Vallelunga in his Genoa Racing 86B; as in 1985 this was a tight-budget effort with little chance for testing so the team was running the car virtually as it left the works, which suggests that the basic car wasn't as bad as some have made out. The win also led to a significant development because Akiri Akagi had come to Europe looking for a driver and on the strength of that race invited Capelli to run in his cars in Japan. There he acquitted himself well and soon the name 'Leyton House' began to appear on the car in Europe although few had any idea who Mr House was. Had they known they might have taken more interest, for Leyton House is the leisure activities division of Marusho, a huge Japanese company specializing in industrial real estate and Akagi is reputed to be one of the 20 richest men in the world.

Mike Thackwell guested for Ralt at Pau, and won, and Pirro took the next round at Spa, although by coming third, Capelli shared the head of the points table with him, but the next three races all went to Ralt-Cosworths run by the Pavesi team, Pierluigi Martini winning at Imola and Mugello, and Luis Sala at Enna. With seven of the eleven rounds completed Martini led the series by a point from Capelli with Sala third. Ivan then repeated his '85 performance at the Österreichring and led from pole to flag, while neither Sala nor Martini scored.

Lola's promising start to the season had not been maintained, neither of the works Ralt drivers, Nielsen and Satoru Nakajima seemed capable of winning, and Pirro had become disheartened at mid-season and was not giving of his best. Sala and Martini then led a Pavesi 1–2 in the Birmingham Superprix, but the race was abandoned just after half-distance due to heavy rain and accidents so only half-points were awarded.

Pirro, cheered up by the offer of an F1 drive if he did well in his next race, led all the way on the Bugatti circuit at Le Mans and then won the closing round at Jarama after Martini, who had led across the line, was disqualified because his team had worked on the car during the period when the race had been stopped due to a shower and that promoted Capelli up to third, but in fact he had needed only fifth to clinch the title. The Pavesi team's goof, plus the fact that he had scored only half-points for a superb drive in terrible conditions at Birmingham cost Martini a Championship he would have deserved equally as much as Capelli.

The records say that March and Ralt each won five races and Lola one, but Martini's disqualification played its part and not only did March enjoy numerical superiority but Marlboro was backing Onyx and Oreca. Thus the two most experienced teams were able to choose their drivers and not be dependent on people buying seats and both were receiving works technical support, so a fair report on March would have said, 'Could do better'. The trouble was that it didn't, there was too much complacency pervading the place now that it had been reorganized to become more efficient.

So far as Capelli was concerned he had done a superb

job for Leyton House both in Europe and Japan and at the end of the season Mr Akagi asked him what his plans were. When Ivan told him he wanted to go into F1, Akagi more or less said, 'Fine, find the team and I'll back you.' His willingness to become everyone's dream sponsor was partly to take Leyton House into F1, partly because Ivan is one of the very nicest men as well as one who had done a good job, and partly because Akagi had come to value Cesare Gariboldi on whom he could rely for sound, straight advice, which was apparently a refreshing contrast to some of those around him.

Across the Atlantic 1986 saw March peak in CART despite a strong Lola presence and the 86C was an Adrian Newey up-date of his superb 85C with particular attention paid to frontal protection, aerodynamics and weight distribution. New rules had tightened the aerodynamic envelope which Adrian reckoned would have removed 30 per cent of the downforce of the 85C. Even so his work in the wind tunnel reduced this deficit and the 1986 car was quicker than its predecessor. Most distinctively it had a longer, slimmer, nose cone partly as a result of extending the nose box and under the skin was thicker honeycomb and aluminium sheeting. As part of the aerodynamic package the engine was canted 2½ degrees from the horizontal and while rocker arm suspension was retained at the rear, the spring units were horizontal and parallel to the gearbox.

It was another large advance, but even so, as it was delivered it still needed rebuilding, de-bugging and developing, so things had not improved greatly and Lola scored in these areas. March still had the initiative since it placed cars with six of the better teams to Lola's three, and the 86C was probably the better car. CART was becoming really rather serious (i.e., closer in content to F1) and one manifestation of this was that there were two new engines in the field, both British V8s, the Ilmor (Chevrolet) and the Judd (Brabham-Honda).

The Judd, a 2.65-litre turbo version of the 3 litre normally aspirated unit which Ralt used in F3000, had been conceived by Engine Developments. Honda had put up the money, cast the blocks and supplied the engine management technology and the name Brabham was used because Sir Jack is both a shareholder in Engine Developments and a consultant to Honda, and on its entry into CART Honda did not wish to maintain too high a profile. Later, Honda would pass over the major castings, all the engines would be known as 'Judds' and in October 1987 the first F1 3½-litre example would be collected by a driver with 'March' writ large on his van.

Ilmor came about when Mario Ilian and Peter Morgan, who were both working for Cosworth, felt they would like to branch out on their own, for both could see ways of making a superior engine to the DFX but were being frustrated. Peter Morgan made a phone call to Roger Penske, found they were talking the same language, Roger spoke to General Motors and within a very short time Peter and Mario were installed in a new factory eight miles north of Cosworth to build 'Chevrolet' engines for, at first, Penske's exclusive use.

Penske bought 86Cs and also commissioned former McLaren engineer Alan Jenkins to design a new car, but, while the March would take any engine the PC15 would accommodate only the Ilmor, which was shorter and narrower than the DFX and had tidier ancillaries. One can see Penske's thinking; a bespoke car for a smaller engine can have aerodynamic advantages, but developing a car and an engine together can be fraught with opportunities to shoot oneself in the foot. So it turned out, the PC15-Ilmor was very quick, but suffered engine failures, and while everyone blamed the lump the problem was in the car's oil system, something which only became apparent when it was run in a March.

As for the season itself, from March's point of view, it's simply told, 86Cs won all but three races, one of which was won by Al Unser Jnr (Lola T86/00) while two were taken by Mario Andretti's Lola, and one of them, Portland, he took when his son Michael (86C), made a slight mistake on the run to the line which left Dad winner by 00.05 second, but then it was Father's Day. That was a rare mistake by Andretti Jnr because he led 11 of the 17 races (28.7 per cent of the season), but he was often let down by his engines (his team, Kraco, built its own Cosworths) and sometimes he was let down by youthful exuberance.

The season threw up a number of winners and it was only late in the year when Bobby Rahal strung together a series of wins that the Champ emerged. Rahal had shown his class all season and had scored a famous victory at Indianapolis, where, late in the race, the yellow lights were on and the pace car out so the entire field bunched up and Kevin Cogan (Patrick Racing 86C) saw his advantage disappear. With two laps to go the pace car pulled in and there was a frantic dash for the line with Rahal pulling out nearly a second and a half over Cogan and Rick Mears. March was experiencing its peak in Indycar and filled all but one of the top 11 places (Al Unser Jnr's Lola came fifth), and provided 24 of the 33 starters. It's true it was not March's most dominant win at Indy, but in 1986 the in-depth competition from Lola was much greater.

It was also a poignant win because Jim Trueman had been fighting a losing battle against cancer for two years. He was obviously very ill as he joined Bobby Rahal on the victory parade and ten days later he died. Trueman's death had some effect on the team and all the commitments which sprung from winning Indy threw Bobby Rahal off his stroke for a time, but both sides gathered their act together and came on strongly later to clinch the series.

In '84 and '85 TrueSports had been the March works team, but then Jim Trueman had started to woo Ferrari and Ferrari made it known it was interested. There's been an on/off war between F1 and CART for years and it may have been a political move to make FISA reconsider a plan to limit F1 engines to ten cylinders when Ferrari has long preferred 12-cylinder F1 engines. A V8 was actually built and it seems more than likely that this lump now has 'Alfa Romeo' cam covers (both firms are part of the Fiat empire) and is sitting in the back of a March Indycar.

As a result of this wooing of Ferrari, Adrian Newey moved over to engineer Michael Andretti in Maurice Kraines' Kraco March 86C, which was managed by Barry Green, so Kraco became the March works team. Before

Mike Andretti testing at Laguna Seca in 1986 with the March 86C and the biggest rear wing in the world. (**Marc Sprouce**)

Emerson Fittipaldi on his way to second place with his March 86C-Cosworth in the Dana 200 race at Phoenix in 1986. (**Rich Chenet**)

At Phoenix Danny Sullivan took fourth place with this March 86C-Chevrolet. March took the first five places. (**Rich Chenet**)

Pit stop for Bobby Rahal (March 86C) at Pocono in August 1986. Rahal had locked up avoiding Rutherford's crashed March, suffered four deflated tyres and damaged the wing end plates when he ran over Rutherford's nose cone. He made three stops while the yellow flags were out. He climbed back through the field to second place but was eliminated at a late refuelling stop when debris in the fuel vent caused a flow back into the engine bay and a resultant fire. (**Autosport**)

the end of the season, when it was clear that BMW was not going ahead with its F1 project, Adrian agreed terms with Newman/Haas to engineer Mario Andretti.

In the summer of 1986 Gerard Larrousse approached March with a proposal to set up a new F1 team, the idea being that he would look after the financing and running of it while March would supply the cars as a contractor. The home management was keen on the deal and it looked as though it might go ahead, but as Robin says, "By the end of the year I was absolutely knackered after six years averaging 300 flights a year. I wasn't having a nervous breakdown, I'm not that sort of person, but I was completely exhausted. I was on a plane to Miami for the last race of the year when I thought, 'Dammit, I'm not going to do this any more, I'm going to do Formula One, now's the time.'"

That decision knocked the Larrousse deal on the head and he went to Lola instead. "I didn't have a sponsor, a designer, or anything, but it's one of those funny things. I got off the plane at Miami and Cesare Gariboldi came up and said, 'Look I've got a sponsor for F1, you must come and meet him.' I'd had a number of people who had been talking to me but, Cesare was the right sort of person, so I said, 'All right, let's give it a go. Leyton who?' We flew straight from Miami to Japan to discover that Mr Akagi had just suffered a heart attack, but we went back later and he was as good as his word."

23 Back to Formula One

March was riding so high that it seemed anything could happen, you made a decision on a plane and when it touched down somebody came up and offered you the money to do it. Cesare could have taken the Leyton House sponsorship to any number of teams, but he and Robin were kindred spirits and what better for Ivan than he should start with a team built around him. Robin says, "I think I'm lucky. To a certain extent you make your own luck, but I've had more than my fair share. You know, the first thing which Napoleon always asked officers he was interviewing for possible promotion was, 'Are you lucky?'"

Robin had made his decision in November 1986 and there was the little matter of there being just 22 weeks from the idea of going F1 to running a car at the opening round of the 1987 season for, while it was then still possible for a new team to field only one car, it had to attend every race. It was an even tighter schedule than March's first season, and that had seemed a near-miracle, to repeat the performance when the sport had become infinitely more sophisticated was an achievement which bears comparison with 1969–70.

Robin says, "I vowed this team would do it the proper way, the way March GP should have been done, to start with people of ability with the right attitude. In any team the two most important elements are the guy who gets the money and the guy who makes the cars go quickly. It was my job to set it up, get the money and select the right team. I tried to get Adrian, but he was committed for 1987, but I was lucky enough to get Gordon Coppuck and Tim Holloway, who is another of my heroes in racing. Tim's been very important in the success of the F1 team, he's very quiet and unassuming, not a glory boy but a mature, rounded person and a real source of strength to that team."

Tim was head of the drawing office at March Engineering, so essentially occupied the same position that John Thompson had in the early days. He was the man who made practical the designer's ideas and his own input had been considerable, which is why he had a credit on the Championship winning 85B and 86B F3000 cars. Gordon, of course, had been in charge of the 1986 sports car project, but moving two key men weakened March Engineering, although the parent company built the 871 and Gordon and Tim, with others, were employed by one branch of March to service another.

Les Mactaggart recalls, "Charles Towns took the view it was just another project, I said, 'No this is Formula One, it will be like a cancer which devours everything around it.' Charles wouldn't be persuaded, it was just another project. I said, 'We should have this conversation again in nine months' time, it will be interesting to see if you still hold the same view.'"

Given the time scale, there was no way that Gordon could design an original car, so he adapted Andy Brown's new F3000 design off the drawing board before any parts were made. It had to have a longer tub to accommodate the larger fuel cell and the rear suspension had to be

Ivan Capelli in practice at Rio in 1987 with the 87P, a modified 87B Formula 3000 car powered by a Cosworth DFZ engine. It non-started because of engine problems in practice.

redesigned to take the larger tyres, so it was a compromise car but one which was good enough to win WC points in the odd 1987 season when normally aspirated cars had their own Championship as they ran in the same races as the turbo cars.

By a coincidence, March entered F1 at the same time that Lola fielded an official works F1 team for the first time for a quarter of a century. It wasn't run from the factory and there had been other tie-ups along the way (Honda, Embassy-Hill, Beatrice-Ford), but it was the first time since 1962 that Lola had fielded cars under its own name. Thus Lola and March met for the first time at the top level as well as in F3000 and CART.

Robin had decided that his job was to set up the team and give it its head without breathing down everyone's necks. "Initially I wanted to do it with Onyx and fought the case very hard, but Cesare was against it." There was no strife between Gariboldi and Earle, they remained good friends, but Cesare had just won the F3000 Championship with a private outfit run on less money than most, and he had beaten the Onyx 'works' team in the process and had been instrumental in promoting March into F1, so he naturally wanted to be involved in the team in a way which would not be possible if a Herd-Earle alliance was formed.

"My next choice was Roger Silman, another of my heroes in racing, but he turned us down on two grounds: he'd had enough of being at the back of the grid when he was with Toleman and he was told he'd be answerable to Charles Towns and not to me. One thing I've found is that if I've taken on a guy who wasn't a team manager and asked him to become one, he's always done a first-class job, and we've had a long list, including Roger, of course, Ray Wardell, Peter Briggs and John Wickham. John could have done a good job for us, or Keith Greene, and then I thought I'd always liked Ian Phillips and felt there was more to him than met the eye, so I picked up the phone one evening and said, 'How would you like to be a Formula One team manager?' and the next day he was.

Ian had been editor of *Autosport* when he was only 22 until he left to run Donington Park in its first year, and he'd later turned freelance and had become very close to March because he lived nearby and used to drop in, and he also acted as the part-time PR adviser. He says, "I was working in Japan for Philip Morris as well as covering F3000 so I'd got to know the people at Leyton House as well as Ivan Capelli and Cesare Gariboldi and knew roughly what the plans for F1 were. Robin asked me for suggestions as to who should be in the team and then one night suddenly phoned up and said had I ever thought of being a team manager and if I fancied the idea I had 12 hours to make up my mind. I had a quick conversation with my wife and that was it. I thought I'd put my typewriter in my drawer and if it doesn't work out I can always take it out again, it was a far bigger gamble on Robin's part than it was mine."

Once most enthusiasts have realized they are not going to be a Grand prix star a phone call like that must rank as Fantasy Number Two, but the reality is turning up to a bare factory with no experience and not even knowing where to hang your coat; since Robin was hand picking his people he was picking the sort who would work together. There's all the difference in the world between a package and a team, that had been shown by the March Grand Prix fiasco, but since Robin was starting from scratch he gathered around him people who thought like he did, so there was unity from the start and he held Ian's hand in the early stages and then was rarely seen at a race.

Robin continues, "Ian's done a fabulous job of keeping the attitude right in the team. We didn't set out to make an impression, we set out to be successful by having the right people and the thing is that has created an image of the team which is quite different from any other apart from Benetton, which is anyway March Old Boys. They're a good lot of blokes and we have cricket and darts matches against them." The team was going to be the nearest modern equivalent to turning up with a car towed behind a Transit, the parameters had changed but the essential spirit was to remain.

As the '87 season loomed it was clear that the 871 would not be ready in time and since there was no way that the team could avoid attending the Brazilian GP, an 87B F3000 car was fitted with a 3½-litre Cosworth DFZ engine, a March 6-speed gearbox, 871 rear suspension and

The 871 made its début at Imola and was distinguished by a very tall air-box. Capelli retired because of low oil pressure. **(Nigel Snowdon)**

modified aerodynamics with side air exits in the sidepods. Since it had only a 26.6-gallon fuel cell it had no chance of completing the race, so building the car was really an expensive entry fee into the F1 club.

The team's début as even more of a nightmare than the '81 Brazilian race with March GP and Ivan Capelli did not actually make the start because two of the team's three engines were destroyed during practice, one because not enough oil was put in, the other because the engine builder, Heini Mader, supplied a sub-standard piston ring package which consumed all the oil and hampered March for the first three races. Still, the team put in its appearance even though it knew it couldn't finish the race because of the fuel cell and Ivan knew a tyre change would take ages because there simply were not enough people to do it; March Racing had just six employees at the time, all were in Brazil and there was nobody at home minding the shop.

The term 'character building' is often used when a team is having a hard time but is frequently misapplied. In March's case, however, it was literally true and as a result of the experience, the little team welded together with Ivan Capelli playing a large part. Ian says, "He basically carried us through with his humour and general enthusiasm for life."

Capelli had the 871 for the San Marino GP which was chiefly remarked on for its very tall air-box, something which hadn't been seen in F1 for some years but which would become a March trademark and one which was widely copied. It was too new to shine at Imola, for there had been very little testing due to the shortage of engines and the inexplicable oil consumption problem. Six DFZs had been ordered at the beginning of the year, but delivery was slow and the sixth did not appear until the Mexican GP in October and in the meantime spares for the engine were also slow in arriving, for Cosworth had over-committed itself. Thus the team was hampered and Capelli had to use a 3.3 litre Cosworth DFL sports car unit at Spa, but he was leading the normally aspirated race until side-lined by low oil pressure.

After that an additional three-gallon oil tank was installed and March was told by Mader that its oil system was to blame, which was unlikely to say the least given the experience both Gordon and March had of the Cosworth engine. In fact the problem went away when different piston rings were fitted.

Ivan finished sixth overall and second normally aspirated car at Monaco, which was a pretty good result for a driver in only his fourth Grand Prix and was a good result for a car cobbled together in a rush which was having only its third race. Gordon Coppuck is not regarded as one of the tiny group of superstar designers, but he had shown he could still cut it in F1.

Tim Holloway recalls, "During practice there was hardly a session when something hadn't gone wrong so Ivan was always having to walk back to the pits. On the grid, Cesare gave him a 2000-lire note so he could get a taxi back. At the end of the race Ivan gave it back and you can imagine the state it was in since it had been in one of his gloves all the time. We were delighted to have won a point so soon and our number-one mechanic was overwhelmed. He said, 'That's the first car I've worked on that's ever finished a race.' That's no recommendation for a mechanic, but he had been with RAM for three years."

After that highlight the team then hit a spell of unreliability which saw four consecutive DNFs but at least by the French GP one problem had been solved. Ian Phillips: "We were following Cosworth's wiring diagrams exactly when we bought an extra engine and had it looked after by Brian Hart. He checked over the installation and said, 'You're not using that diagram, are you? It was wrong when it was new and is now four months out of date.' Meanwhile we were being branded a bunch a incompetents, but Brian helped us out and we finished the season in good shape. We were good on quick tracks, horrible on slow ones, except at Adelaide where we went well, because the car was too small to take a lot of wing downforce. From early on we decided to make our big step in the second year and we were fortunate in that Leyton House agreed to back us and the March board had enough confidence in us to allow us the facilities to progress."

Among the normally aspirated brigade, Ivan was emerging as a serious driver. In Detroit he retired with a broken battery caused by Nakajima's Lotus thumping him, led the 'atmo' class in the French and British races until his engine blew in the first and the gearbox broke in the second, so was showing promise but not finishing races. One problem the team had was with engine temperature, which led to modified bodywork, but when the Hart-prepared engine was finally fitted at Monza (it had a different engine management system) it ran 15 degrees cooler, at which point the original body was fitted again.

In Hungary the team was joined by Adrian Newey, who took a long hard look at the car, went away and spent some time with a calculator and came up with different settings. That was the turning point and Ivan led the 'atmo' class until his tyres went off and then dominated in Austria to take his first class win of the year.

Soon after the Austrian race March was able to do its first proper testing, which was a novelty for Capelli for never before in his career had he known such a luxury because his previous teams couldn't afford it, so it's no wonder that his feed-back had not been 24 carat. As March Racing grew, however, and he had more opportunity to hone this particular skill, he emerged as a good tester. Even so it was not until the end of the year that it was possible to maintain a separate test car or team, because, by the end of the year, March Racing was still only 18 men strong, less than a quarter of even a mid-field team such as Arrows and not much more than a tenth of McLaren's strength.

A string of good 'atmo' finishes followed the Austrian GP, which were more meritorious when one considers how small the team still was and how tightly things were being run. Adrian Newey agreed to join for 1988 and before the end of the year two important decisions had been made for '88, the number two driver and the engine.

Ian says, "We had a short-list of about half a dozen drivers and we were going to go testing after Hockenheim, but Ivan was not available and nor was Andy Wallace, who was the official test driver. Mauricio Gugelmin happened to be at Hockenheim when we were casting around for someone to test for us and we all knew him since he had been through the British School of Motor Racing. He came in and did a good job for us and he fitted the bill all round so it was a case of him being in the right place at the right time."

As for the engine it would be the new Judd unit for, as Ian explains, "John phoned me up early in 1987 to wish me luck in my new job and during our chat he mentioned he was hoping, with Honda's permission, to build an F1 version of his engine and perhaps we might be interested in testing it. The reason he chose us was that we had engine mounting systems on our F3000 and Indy cars which would take either a Cosworth or a Judd engine, so it was not too difficult for us to fit one of his engines; in fact, we were the only outfit able to do it.

"At Spa we were disenchanted with Cosworth, apart from the fact that we were low in the pecking order with both Cosworth and Mader, our engines were late being delivered and so were the spares. The F3000 people were at Spa so I went to see John to discuss using his engines in '88. At the time he still did not know whether he could get Honda's go-ahead on the deal, but we mentioned the problem to Leyton House and they went to see Honda, who gave their blessing almost immediately, although the decision took longer to filter down to John, who naturally did not want to proceed until he had permission in black and white.

"Around the time of the British GP John was in a position to say he was going ahead and needed deposits to get the ball rolling. First on board was Ligier, for whom John built Cosworth engines, then we joined and later, when Williams lost the Honda deal, they became Judd customers. While we were the junior team, the fact that Williams was in the deal was good for us because they could bring so much more pressure to bear than we could. Basically we were the number three team except that we were the only outfit to be able to test the engine as soon as it was ready because of our engine mounts."

Thus Judd became the first engine maker in the history of F1 to supply three established two car teams in his first year. It was a slightly over-ambitious programme but John was under no illusions that Williams would be other than a short-term customer because as a top team it was in the running for any engine from a major manufacturer which might appear and in the event Williams soon did land a deal, with Renault, so it was important to make an all-out effort to place as many engines as possible. March Racing took delivery of the first engine in late October and the team first tested it soon after the Mexican GP by which time they had a designated test car.

Adrian Newey's presence had an effect from Hungary on, but he missed the late races since he was hard at work on the 881, so Capelli and March ended the year on a slight down, but the important thing was that everything was in place for a proper assault on a second season: designer, sponsor, staff, drivers, engine. Despite some of the dramas of the year March had not exactly disgraced itself in 1987 and given better reliability Capelli might have finished third in the Jim Clark Trophy for 'atmo' cars, but on the first occasion when March and Lola had met with works teams in F1, the Huntingdon outfit had finished narrowly ahead.

Gordon Coppuck stayed with March Racing until the following July, when March Engineering desperately needed his expertise on the 88B. He stepped down graciously when Adrian appeared for he had no further ambitions in F1, but contributed his own breadth and depth of experience to the F1 project. He became, if you like, a moderator rather than an originator.

The F1 team, however, was only one aspect of March's new direction, and at the start of 1987 it was decided to become quoted as a public company on the Unlisted Securities Market. "We decided to get really stuck into consultancy work," says Robin. "Comtec and the wind tunnel were on stream and we were getting lots of offers to do racing consultancy work. We set up a new division, March Engineering Projects, under Dr Laclan Fergus-Shackleton and we needed the share issue to expand. I'd make F1 my baby, Charles Towns would oversee production and Dave Reeves would look after the consultancy market, Charles and Malcolm became joint Managing Directors and I moved upstairs as non-executive Chairman. The idea was that the managing directors of each section should be responsible for the profitability of the section and they would keep me informed with all the figures, unfortunately not all did that. We went public on 6 April, 1987, and it was a very successful issue."

Robin was persuaded to go public after experience with a property company (with startling originality it was named April) which he had formed with Norman Mazure and which was making his money work for him in a most satisfactory way. It was the first time in history that a company whose main business was making racing cars had gone public and since its pre-deductions profit in 1986 was £1,648,000 it looked a good bet and surprised a lot of people who did not associate racing cars with success of that order. March Group PLC was valued at £14.5m (11,860,000 shares were placed at £1.20, with Robin remaining the biggest single shareholder). One block of shares for which Robin was offered £1.2m was made over to employees who had played a key part in the company over the years and had stuck with it through thick and thin.

Nothing, it seemed, could stop March from soaring ever upwards, but even as the company rode higher, things began to fall apart in North America. March still sold 33 cars and while that was a downward increment in its sales graph, the fact was that the Indycar market was shrinking, the gap between the big money teams and the little guys was growing too wide, the board of CART was in some disarray, sponsors became harder to find for anything bar Indy as spectators voted with their feet and the on-off switches of their television sets and made it quite clear that when it came to American racing, NASCAR was the thing.

TrueSports, now managed by Steve Horne, an Englishman raised in New Zealand, ominously switched its allegiance to Lola and more than a few other teams wished it had followed its lead, because when the 87C was delivered it was found to be a handful. Designed by a team led by Alan Mertens it followed the broad layout of the 86C with new profiles in the sidepods and a rear structure which was 33 per cent stiffer. Its most unusual feature, however, was a new transmission which re-introduced the hypoid differential to racing after an absence of many years in order to get a lower drive train and, hence, centre of gravity.

It seemed fine in pre-season testing and had sold well on the back of the superb 86C, but the cars did not work on the new Goodyear radials and an up-date kit had to be rushed out. That did the trick, but confidence was dented more fundamental damage was also done.

1987 was the first time that no new American built cars appeared on the scene; the Penske PC16s were up-rated PC15s (which were anyway built in Poole, Dorset) and in the early part of the season Penske ran them in conjunction with his 86Cs and then, in July, junked his own cars, fired Alan Jenkins, who went to work for Onyx, and soldiered on with his March 86Cs.

Rahal's switch to Lola changed the balance of power in CART because TrueSports had emerged as the team to nudge Penske off its perch as the most professional around and it became the first outfit in CART to run a separate test team. That had long been the practice in F1, of course, but for all its glitz and grand titles, CART had really been operating on the lines of F3000 with customer cars, customer engines, control tyres and private teams and it was this sort of move, and the edge which came from it, which began to open up the gap between the big buck teams and the smaller outfits.

While March still dominated numerically, some of its regular customers were finding things a struggle. Doug Shierson's outfit, for example, had to cut back on testing, so, although Al Unser Jnr finished third in the series, it was without a single victory. Les Mactaggart, who was then the March Indycar Project Manager says, "The 87C was a Lola in disguise in that it was an effective road circuit car, but there were problems on the speedways. We had brought Shierson back into the March fold and then did to him in '87 what Lola had done to him in '86. When we faced the switch from crossply to radial tyres the car had problems; for instance it became unusually sensitive to pitch, but at the same time for a number of reasons we had lost the ability to cross the barrier presented by the problem."

Les does not say so, but the reason was to be found in the Newman-Haas pit. Adrian Newey is one of the handful of designers who can oversee the entire problem and square the concept with the work of the teams of engineers producing the mechanical design and the aerodynamic design and make the inevitable compromises between each group's ideas work in harmony. Some designers have made their reputations in one area or the other in the past and today's 'superstars' are those who can straddle all areas.

It was left to Mike Andretti in the works-assisted Kraco car, run by Barry Green, to be the main March runner and he might have taken the title but for the fact that he was using Cosworth's new electronic management system, which was not always reliable. It was one of those chances you have to take when an outfit such as Cosworth offers you a possible edge.

Undoubtedly the fastest man of the year was Mario Andretti in his Newman-Haas Lola, which used an Ilmor engine, and he took more poles (eight) and led more laps than anyone, but he finished only five times. Often he was the victim of engine problems and twice he crashed. Mario opened his score in the first race, at Long Beach, and led home five Marches, so things weren't looking too bad for Bicester and anyway Lola had tended to make Long Beach its own.

Many people in Europe had felt that F1 had let an exceptional talent slip through its fingers when Roberto Guerrero had failed to get a seat with a good team and after three mixed seasons in CART he finally managed to get a competitive drive when Vince Granatelli, son of Andy, bought Dan Cotter's team. Roberto stormed to a superb win at Phoenix, despite having to start from the back of the grid when his car was found to be 2lb light and then was the quickest March runner throughout the Month of Indy, although Mario Andretti took pole.

Lola was definitely the class at Indy and filled four of the top six places, with two of the drivers being Dick Simon, who has never been more than an honest journeyman (he was 35 before he even saw a motor race) and A.J. Foyt, who had not had a full season, nor been on the pace, for some years. Guerrero was leading Indy until his final pit stop when an overheated clutch saw him struggle to get back into the race, so handing it to Al Unser Snr's 86C, who scored his fourth win and March's fifth in succession. At Indy March took the first five places and ten of the 12 finishes so it looked like business as usual especially since '86 and '87 cars dominated the results all season.

Guerrero, who finished second at Indy, set pole at the next two races, but he failed to finish either; at Milwaukee Mike Andretti led home Rahal and then the positions were reversed at Portland. Mike then led the series, but Rahal took the top spot by winning at Meadowlands at the end of June and from that moment was never off the top of the table as he strung together a number of good place finishes and another win at Laguna Seca (the Marlboro Challenge Race at Miami which he also won was a non-Championship event).

Rahal was probably the best driver of the year on all types of circuit and TrueSports the best team, but it would be fair to say both were assisted by the fact that Mario and Mike Andretti both suffered reliability problems; Mike certainly led and won more races than the Champion. Al Unser Jnr wasn't getting enough testing, Penske had fallen back to running last year's equipment and there were enough good March drivers to share the points and wins. Emerson Fittipaldi took a couple of races (Cleveland and Toronto) for Patrick Guerrero won Lexington before receiving head injuries in an accident which he was reckoned lucky to survive. Rick Galles' March-Judd showed well and impressed with its torque and while Geoff Brabham perhaps wasn't quite up to using it to its utmost, he often filled high-scoring places.

Rick Mears was back in the winner's circle at Pocono

and his fight back to form after smashing his feet three years before must rank as one of the most remarkable in racing history. Not only that but he was looking increasingly good on road circuits, and team-mate Danny Sullivan was another March driver who was also picking up places and helping to spread the points.

Rahal with a well-run Lola using a non-trick Cosworth DFX thus took the series, a triumph for the excellent package and it was, too, the 11th year in succession that a Cosworth car had won the American Championship. Since March had won ten races to Lola's five, and apart from Rahal and Mario Andretti, every driver in the top 14 at the end of the season had been in a March, everything looked hunky-dory from the outside, but the reality was a little different. The customers were not at all happy and the person who had to take the brunt of their displeasure was Roger Bailey.

"What did for us in North America was the March management. I've already said that they didn't know how to treat the American style of customer and were only interested in the balance sheet, and while we made cars that worked people were prepared to put up with it. Not willingly or happily, I became known as Mr Ninety Per Cent and that galled me. Things didn't fit properly, the cars were late arriving, the customer would be told 'Your car's in the paint shop, it'll be with you on Friday,' while the truth was the tub was still in the curing oven, meanwhile the owner has told all his mechanics they're going to be working over the weekend, the car doesn't arrive, the crew sit around twiddling their thumbs and the guy's got to pay them and he's already paid out $200,000 for the car.

"When we cocked up in '87 we hadn't enough good will among our customers for them to stick by us and weather the storm. We rushed out an up-date kit to put things right and then I received invoices that I had to send out to the owners who had had the up-date kit. They had spent $200,000 per car, and many of them had bought more than one; we cock-up and then expect them to pay more for us to rectify our mistake. It got so bad that we were accused of changing things on the cars just so we could make more money by selling up-dates.

"At the first race of '89 Lola found it had cocked-up on its gearbox, but by the second race had sent over 27 new 'boxes, f.o.c. That's the sort of treatment the American team owner appreciates, because that's the treatment he receives in his business life. Off the record, this is just one letter from a team owner . . ." He reads out a horror story which would appal you if it had been written by the buyer of a third-hand Cortina.

"When we had our problems in '87 Robin was not around and that was a severe blow, because until he came out here things were pretty primitive, they'd never heard of an engineer, the crew chiefs did everything. Suddenly there's an engineer telling them, 'You're a really good driver, now just take a tiny amount of wing off the front, and slacken off the rear dampers a notch and a half, not too much, you'll find that makes all the difference.' And of course it does and suddenly Robin's the Messiah, he can walk on water, everyone's got to have an engineer and when things have been tight during the Month of Indy we've had practically anybody from March who can hold a pen coming out and being 'engineers' – and it didn't do us much good in the long term.

"Robin was absent and Adrian Newey, whom everyone regarded as the Golden Boy, was working for Newman/Haas running Lolas, so the 87C was perceived as a committee car and no matter what the reality was, that was the perception, and who wants a committee car? This very morning (June 1989) I got a call from a team owner about to make a decision for 1990 and his question was, 'Who's going to do the car?' He wanted a name he recognized. We'd lost our two biggest assets, Lola was beating us on quality and price, and all that the management could say was, 'You've got to sell harder.' One of them came out to a race with a sack of wishbones as hand luggage, yet he turned up at the track empty handed. 'Where are the wishbones,' 'They're back at the hotel, they were a bit heavy for me to carry, send someone to get them.' I couldn't believe the man's arrogance. The management screwed us up in the eyes of our customers and when you don't respect the guy driving the bus you get out and walk.

"On top of all that March was suddenly back in F1, so everyone assumed, perhaps correctly, that CART was no longer a March priority. In the meantime, Eric Broadley was attending all the races and his presence was noted and appreciated by everyone. He's not as out-going as Robin, he's never claimed to be a brilliant race engineer, but in his quiet way he probably did a better job promoting Lola than Robin did promoting March. Eric was never billed as the Messiah, whereas Robin was everywhere one minute, nowhere the next, and people felt badly let down. If he'd spent one week out here he could have generated a year's work."

"In the middle of '87 we had the chance of signing Nigel Bennett, who had designed Lola's cars." Nigel had left Lola to set up on his own in partnership with Ray Wardell, but their backer pulled out leaving them stranded, so if he was to continue in CART he had limited options. Roger continues, "We could have used Bennett, but our management offered him floor sweeper's wages so he went to Penske and built a kick-arse car. If the management had had its brain in gear the PC17 would have been the March 88C and that would have put us on Broadway. Penske buys six cars at a time, so by not employing him we straightaway lost six orders and those alone could have made enough money to pay him what he was asking."

Customers were to leave March in droves, sports car production was already down to the odd car and having won the first two F3000 Championships, and dominated the entry lists, March was heading for trouble on that front too. The root problem with the cars in both Indy and F3000 was that the general consensus of feeling within the factory was to build cars for all-out performance, in other words, within the constraints of making customer cars to build machines which could go well in the right hands, with the right engineer, but which would be less user-friendly. A smaller number of teams would be able to wring

Stefano Modena scored a fine win, despite the loss of third gear, in the 1987 Birmingham Superprix with his Onyx March 87B and went on to clinch that year's Formula 3000 Championship, the first rookie to win a F2/3000 title. (Nigel Snowdon)

the last ounce from them, but at least some would be winning.

In F3000 everything looked fine at the beginning of the season and March made 37 cars, about half of which went to Japan. It has been said that Andy Brown was allowed a new sheet of paper, but although he came up with a much smaller car than before, it used the same basic layout as the 1984–6 cars built around a new slim monocoque made of aluminium honeycomb reinforced by composite fibres. Far from being a clean sheet of paper, there was a new tub and bodywork, but much of the thinking of the old car had been transferred directly across to the 87B and just as in CART the car could deliver the performance if understood, but fewer teams had the depth of experience and/or expertise to understand it.

Once again March was the numerically superior marque, but although the new car won the Championship, and March won more races than any other *marque*, the car was extremely tricky to set up and drive. It would transmit to the driver the feeling that it was on its limit before it was actually there and the driver had to screw up his courage and drive through that feeling. Then it was possible to get the best from it, but not every driver was prepared to make that commitment.

The Ralt-Honda (Judd) works team was probably the cream of the field in F3000and Mauricio Gugelmin and Roberto Moreno between them took pole six times, but reliability problems (brakes, gearbox, engine) ditched their chances although both drivers ended the season with their reputations intact and a win apiece, Gugelmin at Silverstone, Moreno at Enna.

Various Lolas also won races but these were split between Michel Trollé, Luis Sala (two wins) and Julian Bailey, so it was one of those years where the right package

***The installation of the Cosworth engine in the March 87B. This is Gabriel Tarquini's FIRST car seen at Birmingham.* (Nigel Snowdon)**

won and that was provided by Onyx for Stephano Modena, a man who had done less then 20 races, not counting karts, before the beginning of the season. Modena proved an exceptional driver not least because he was honest with himself and knew when he had more time in him, so if he was a little off the pace he applied logic and didn't ask his team to make unnecessary adjustments in an attempt to find time in the car. He came fourth in his first race at Silverstone, where it was clear that the car was not quite right.

Works-generated modifications were initiated and he then led from start to finish at Vallelunga, failed to score in the next two races (he crashed both times while in the top three), and then a second at Donington, despite severe vibration caused by him flat-spotting his tyres, saw him take the top of the table because the points had been spread around and he was the first driver to emerge. From then on he was never headed and wins at Birmingham (minus third gear) and Imola clinched the title for him. It was the first time a driver had ever won the F2/3000 Championship in his rookie year.

Thus March won its third successive F3000 Championship, and Onyx at last took the crown after five years of close March association (it was by then a works-*related* team, just like ORECA, rather than the actual works team). So once again March sold more cars, won more races, and took the crown, but just as in CART below the surface success there was an unhappy position.

The story has already been told of how Robert Synge was sold his 87B. He was riding on the crest of a wave and Madgwick Motorsport had just guided Andy Wallace to an emphatic win in the 1986 British F3 Championship, so, though both team and driver were new to F3000, they came with a solid record and on a high. At the opening round at Silverstone Madgwick suddenly found itself dumped from a champion team to one struggling to qualify. Nothing they did seemed to improve the handling of the car and there was talk about there being a fundamental fault with the tub which was making it flex.

Madgwick struggled, made the car work on some circuits and picked up a few points, but failed to qualify on others. It then threw away the March and leased a Lola. Immediately Andy Wallace was on the pace, which suggests that neither he nor his team were the prats they'd appeared to be earlier in the season. Robert says, "We never did get the car sorted out and we asked, we begged, for help from the factory and got none. We were not the only team all at sea either, but nobody at March wanted to know; we still don't know what the basic problem with the car was, we finally suspected a flexing tub.

"When we switched to Lola it was chalk and cheese; instead of fighting to get on to the grid Andy was suddenly fighting for pole and Lola couldn't have been more helpful. We had guys from Jean Mosnier's works team coming up and saying, 'Anything we can do to help, just ask. We don't care who wins so long as it's in a Lola.'"

That was one team's experience, but it was the team running the driver who had been pencilled in for the March F1 test contract. Other teams also made the switch to Lola during the year and it's clear from internal memos that Onyx and ORECA were none too happy with the service they were receiving either and had called upon the intervention of their main sponsor, Marlboro, to bring pressure to bear.

In fact the root problem, as Madgwick and others had suspected, was a flexing tub and Onyx only found its way round it by running on very soft settings and dispensing with the anti roll bars. Once Stephano Modena, who was engineered by Mike Earle, had found a basic set-up which worked reasonably well, he had the strength of character to stick with it bar fine tuning at each circuit and settled for a consistent package which he knew well rather than trying anything trick in the pursuit of ultimate performance. It was a remarkably mature thing to do, and one can think of very few drivers who would have the confidence to do it, but he took the view often expressed by Mike Earle and Robin that the greater part of a car's performance comes from the driver, so while everyone else slagged off the car, he won the Championship with it. By contrast Pierre-Henri Raphanel, his team-mate, worked with Andy Brown and got lost in a plethora of mods and new pieces. Mike Earle reaffirmed his faith in March at the end of the year, but Hugues de Chaunac, boss of ORECA, was actively considering a change for 1988.

ORECA's main driver was Yannick Dalmas, another F3000 débutant, but one who had made his F1 debut with Lola before the season ended, and he was quickest of all the Marches in qualifying for the opening round at Silverstone, but crashed on the first lap. Then he set pole at Vallelunga, but crashed when lying second when a rear pull rod lever pivot broke; it was a big accident from which he was lucky to emerge with only slight injuries. ORECA blamed March, but March believed the breakage was due to poor maintenance; they replaced the offending part on all Marches and could find no fault on any of the returned pieces. No matter who was at fault, the incident further soured relations.

Still, after missing Spa, Dalmas won easily at Pau, had a tyre delaminate at Donington, crashed whilst avoiding a spinning back marker at Enna, took fifth at Brands Hatch and then suffered a string of DNFs, but then drove magnificently at Jarama to score his second win.

Between them, Onyx and ORECA won five of the 11 races, with the works Ralt-Hondas taking two and various Lolas the remaining four, so, despite the flexing tub, it took the lion's share of wins, but the trouble was that only two teams could make it work consistently and then only the number one driver in each seemed to be able to wring performance from it. An ominous statistic is that 17 Marches were entered for the first race of the season against the 16 of all other marques, but only Stephano Modena (Onyx, Champion) and Yannick Dalmas (ORECA, fifth) finished in the top six of the Championship table. March, which had built its reputation on making user-friendly customer cars, was losing its way.

Mike Earle says, "I think part of the problem was a matter of perception and degree. Everyone says what a terrible car the 87B was, but the fact is it won the Championship so it couldn't have been that bad. If Andy Brown had designed that car for Onyx, after we'd won the

Championship everyone would have said he was a superstar, but because it was a March it was a heap of junk."

True enough and considering how technical and professional motor racing is supposed to be it's astonishing how little rational thought is often applied to decisions and how much comes down to 'perception', which is another way of saying rumour, gossip and superstition. It works all ways, of course, the '86 Lola F3000 was a better car than the '86 March, as anyone at March will tell you, but superstition had it that the March was the one to have. By the end of the year nobody was sure of that any more and a new maker, Reynard, was about to come in having cleaned up in F3.

The problem was that March was riding on its reputation and had no reserves of strength to respond to the calamity which was about to hit it in its main markets. One crisis came at the end of 1987 when the dollar plunged against the pound, American customers took fright and projected Indycar production took a dive. Fourteen men were made redundant and others were transferred to other work. Too many good people had already transferred to the F1 project, Robin's baby, which was not making any money for the company. The new management at Bicester could not cope with the challenge of re-asserting the company in the customer markets which were sliding away, it lacked both flexibility and the special sort of commitment which only racers have. Worse, the company was being operated without proper control and there was anarchy as individuals were left to their own devices to make their own decisions. Despite its rising share value on the market, it was soft at the core and it did not need much pressure from outside to make it collapse.

That pressure came in 1988 from March's dwindling band of customers and when it came March very nearly did collapse and the fact that it didn't, quite, was not due to anyone who was there in 1987.

24 Decline and Fall

At the beginning of 1988 Robin was talking about March pulling out of the production racing car market to concentrate on special projects with other manufacturers, of building a supercar, something which would see off a Ferrari F40 or a Lamborghini Countach, and even about buying a large design studio in the States, one which had an expanding contract with one of the Big Three American car makers. It was a company listed at ten times March's Stock Exchange value, which was then at its height, and the take-over would involve funding by a merchant bank, but at the time the future had no limits.

March's share in its traditional markets had shrunk (it made 103 customer cars in 1986, 73 in 1987 and only 56 in 1988), but in March 1988, the money men were predicting a profit of £1.5m, the wind tunnel was operative and attracting customers, Comtec was engineering the Panther Solo and was talking to a very prestigious maker about a short-series production model. There was, too, a suggestion that Comtec might explore ways of automating composite materials, just as Lotus had patented injection-moulded glass-fibre techniques.

As the racing season started, however, came the first sign that beneath the optimism all was not well and the crunch came at the opening rounds of the F3000 Championships in Europe and Japan. Only seven Marches were entered at Jérez (most of the 30 cars went to Japan), just five qualified, and the highest finisher in an 88B was Pierluigi Martini, who came eighth in one of the FIRST cars. Since both team and driver were known front-runners it was not hard to find the fault and, besides, Onyx and ORECA were likewise all at sea. Although the tub had been beefed up, traction was poor, the car rolled in the corners, was unstable under braking, and the aerodynamics were severely flawed, which made the cars slow in a straight line and difficult to trim – the 88B was completely out of harmony.

Had the grid been wall-to-wall March as in previous years, perhaps the problems would not have been thrown into such sharp relief, but apart from a large number of Lolas, which worked particularly well on tight circuits such as Jerez, there was a new contender, the Reynard 88D. Not only was the 88D quick straight from the box, but Reynard had adopted an aggressive attitude in its marketing. Further, it placed examples with the two stars of the season, the very experienced Roberto Moreno and young Johnny Herbert, whom some were calling the next Senna and who strengthened that view by winning his, and Reynard's, first F3000 race. Reynard had two secrets, one was excellent aerodynamics, the other was a very long wheelbase (109 inches to the 101.5 inches of the 88B, which was the average of the opposition), which made it very stable and easy for drivers to wring the best from it.

The telephone lines to Bicester were soon humming with calls from Italy (FIRST), France (ORECA) and Littlehampton (Onyx). Quite apart from the fact that established customers were unhappy, de Chaunac and Earle jointly oversaw the award of Marlboro sponsorship below F1 so were able to select those they believed to be

Pierluigi Martini's March 88B in the 1988 Birmingham Superprix. (**Nigel Snowdon**)

the best drivers for their teams and those teams did not have to use Marches.

In Japan the position was much the same, for whilst there had been 11 new Marches at the first race, there would be one at the third. Tom Hanawa, March's agent, had been bought a Lola for his team by his sponsor and was told that the sponsor would withdraw if he didn't run it. A works Honda engine deal and a Bridgestone tyre deal also went from March to Lola. Akiri Akagi was sponsoring the March F1 team yet also having to run a Lola. Not only that but a number of other March negotiations in Japan, including talks with major manufacturers about F1 and other work were being adversely affected by the car's performance.

Robin wrote a memo to all concerned and it is still spoken of at March with awe, for it was *angry*. Robin is a man who does not lose his temper, he can be annoyed and let you know it in the nicest possible way but as one senior man commented, "The memo was written in the way an angry man speaks."

The basic problem with the car was that the concept was past its natural life and the 1988 updates had made it even worse. and instead of the new car which was needed a barely adequate one had been patched up. The 87B had been touted as a new design, but really was a re-tubbed and re-bodied version of the 85B series and should have been regarded as an interim design instead of the first of a new generation of F3000 cars. Normally the decision to create a new design more or less arrived as the result of a groundswell of opinion, an atmosphere in the works. Someone would say, 'the old bus is getting tired' and someone would comment that, say, Lola was set to overtake and what could be done about it, so an idea would snowball with everyone contributing ideas and a step forward would be taken.

On this occasion there had been complacency, for everyone knew that Reynard was about to come into the picture but nobody thought it could win first time out or even make much of an impact. March had been winning F2/3000 races for nearly 20 years, it knew the score, a brash newcomer could not possibly hope to come in and wipe the floor with the opposition. Yet that's what did happen and as one senior man put it, "Reynard moved the goal posts and we were caught completely unawares, whereas in the past if there were goal posts to be moved Robin was normally the person to do it."

More fundamental was that Reynard was young and hungry and although their paths have only crossed once, Robin senses in Adrian a younger version of himself with the same drive and belief. By contrast, March had been taken out of the hands of the racers, the competitive edge had been dulled, Robin had become distant from March Engineering as he concentrated on March Racing and too many key people had gone there. In 1986 Robin had said that he was amazed just how many first class youngsters March was able to attract from the universities, but even the best young talent needs both experience and direction. Malcolm Shaw and Charles Towns had become joint Managing Directors and Robin had moved up to Chairman, so, while it is easy to blame the newcomers, the buck ultimately stopped with RJH.

The memo indicated that Robin was not satisfied with Charles Town's leadership but he had been appointed to make March operate on a sensible, conventional basis and there was a fundamental conflict between that brief and the way in which racing car makers operate. Conventional factories operate on a 9–5 basis, or whatever, whilst racing car makers operate on adrenalin and all-nighters when necessary and March Group PLC, the publicly quoted company with anonymous shareholders, was trying to operate as an ordinary business.

As the season went on, Reynard went from strength to strength with Moreno being the first driver in the four-year history of F3000 to dominate rather than become Champion by picking up a couple of wins and points finishes. There was soon a queue of customers at Reynard, whose factory is a stone's thrown from March Racing, and among them was ORECA. About the only thing which can be said in March's favour is that it at least won one race, for Ralt failed to win any.

From mid-season on Gordon Coppuck came out of March Racing to work with Onyx, Andy Brown moved to March Racing, where he did an excellent job engineering Mauricio Gugelmin's car, FIRST had Richard Divila making modifications to its cars and Ralph Bellamy, who had parted company with Lola, was back with March and working at the problem. Of all the March F3000 cars Pierluigi's Martini's FIRST 88B-Judd alone was a consistent points scorer with a third at Pau, a win at Enna, second at Brands Hatch and third at Birmingham, to take fourth in the series. The general feeling at March is that he might have done even better but towards the end of the season FIRST was preparing to go into F1 (it built the car but found itself without the money to run it) and as a result its performances tailed off although Martini said after Birmingham that the car had come to the end of the line, there was no more development left in it and it couldn't compete with the Reynard aerodynamics. Still, before Birmingham he had been holding second in the Championship and had he come first or second his chance of taking the title would still have been alive so FIRST might have made more effort.

Onyx had begun the season with two drivers, Volker Weidler and Alfonso Garcia de Vinuesa, but after three DNQs de Vinuesa left and took his sponsorship with him. According to Mike Earle, when Gordon Coppuck arrived on the scene he didn't know where to begin on the car, but once he arrived things began to improve aided by a test session at Snetterton with Stephano Modena, who also found the car hopeless at first but who was able to point the team in the right direction with his excellent feed-back.

Gordon's modifications included a new floor, a fresh profile on the nose section, different rear upsweeps and new front and rear wings. By the time he was through he'd made something like the 88B Mk X. From the moment Gordon arrived on the scene Weidler became more competitive and started to pick up points finishes and he was further helped when Bernie Marcus became involved, because although Wielder spoke excellent English his feed-back was even better when he and Bernie were able to talk in their native German. These late-season performances showed that March could still respond and take decisive action, but by then it was the under-dog swamped by Lola and Reynard and in that position improvements were not enough, there had to be the sort of long stride forward which could only come with a new car.

March, the all-singing, all-dancing, multi-disciplined engineering consultancy was not only heading down the tubes but doing so without many friends, although Onyx would have stuck with it had it continued in F3000. It would have been a case of Mike Earle using his long association, his friendship with Robin, and the clout of his Marlboro sponsorship to have got everyone round the table to talk sensibly about 1989, but Onyx went on to F1, so while Mike's faith in March's ability to turn things round remained it was of no practical help.

March had lost face in Japan and in CART the position was much the same. Alan Mertens had produced a car which was potentially superb but which was beyond typical CART team. Some of the problem came down to the fact that proposed rules intended to limit the size of the front and rear wings, and to cope with this a much smaller car was built, in effect a 7/8ths model of the 87C, although the critical dimensions remained much the same as before. Those rules did not come into force, but March was left with its concept even although it was able to claim that when run with 1987-size wings the car had 13 per cent more downforce and 8 per cent less drag. The trouble was that it was caught between two sets of rules and was out of harmony. Its aerodynamics were rather like an engine with a peaky power curve; if you could catch it at the top it was fine but just as it's so much easier to use an engine with less power but a flatter curve, so 98 per cent of the 88C's ultimate aerodynamics over a wider range would have been preferable for customers. A similar situation existed with the 88B except there was no exciting peak in the aerodynamics.

Les Mactaggart says, "It had a knife-edge performance curve. If it was set up properly it could be quicker than anything, but the velocity ratios were so high that it could sustain its performance only for a lap or so, while you could run a Lola with a range of set-ups and while it would not be as quick over the odd lap it would maintain its performance, while our car, which was over-sensitive, would fall away and not be as good over a series of laps. It was the ideal conceptional engineering car but wasn't so good for the customer."

There was a different rear end with pull rod suspension and a new transmission casing, but unfortunately the casing flexed, which threw the rear suspension out of kilter when cars used the Ilmor engine. Ilmor used a smaller bell housing than the Cosworth round which the casing had been designed and that detail, together with the choice of material, had caused the problem.

One of the less publicized aspects of engineering a car is the work which can be done in the shop (remember Dave Reeves refusing to release Don Whittington's first 81C after discovering that the tub around the gearchange was flexing?). This basic contribution to a car's engineering had been overlooked at Murdock Road. Another problem was that the rear suspension was so finely tuned that unless the bushes were replaced after a very short active life the minute amount of play in them created a secondary damping system.

Yet another problem was that the car did not make the tyres work properly and this was not because it was poor, it comes down to a paradox in tyre supply. In Formula One, tyre companies work with the very best teams and produce tyres in conjunction with them, so the second and third division teams have to use the rubber developed, say, with McLaren and one of the things which makes a third division team what it is, is the fact that it cannot use the tyres as effectively as a top team. When it comes to providing a control rubber for a series, companies generally go for the lowest common denominator, so instead of making tyres for the best team it makes them for anybody. Tyres have been a recurring theme in the story, for good or ill, but March Indycars had always been light on tyres and in 1988 could have run with a much softer compound, which would have given 88C users a distinct advantage, but with control rubber it was only on the twisty circuits that enough heat was generated in the tyres to make them work properly.

Leaving aside that very important factor, and the flexing of the gearbox casing, which was a cock-up which was soon fixed, the 88C was a car which could work provided it was run by a wholly professional team, it was too uncompromising to be a friendly customer car. Unfortunately the number of wholly professional teams in CART was tiny and while, in the past, March had managed to corner most of the better teams (its impressive list of victories has been achieved by a handful of outfits) the operative word is 'better', F1 standard they were not. March could no longer maintain the interest of those better teams, Lola's superior build quality and after-sales service had paid dividends and, after the collapse of the dollar, only 20 88Cs were sold. There had been a time when 20 Indycars had lifted the company out of the mire, now it was a sign of decline because the home base had expanded and there were more salaries to meet every month.

Penske found itself with its first competitive own-built car for years and it cleaned up with the PC17, which could have been the 88C, and Ilmor had overcome the vibration problems which had beset its engine in the previous two years and was clearly the unit to have – it finally finished Cosworth's 11-year run of CART Championship wins. Mario Andretti (Lola-Ilmor) won the opening round at Atlanta after Rick Mears appeared to have the race in the bag until he tangled with Randy Lewis, who was notorious for such incidents, then Al Unser Jnr (March-Ilmor) won Long Beach for Galles Racing, which had become the official March team, and had Alan Mertens on the strength. Al Jnr's win was a clean one with no excuses or hard-luck stories involved and for once March showed it could build a car which could win on the tricky road circuit.

This was the pointer, the 88C went well on the slower circuits because they worked the tyres hard and put heat into them, but it was difficult to dial in properly on the quick ones while the Penske PC17 was competitive everywhere (between them, Danny Sullivan and Rick Mears took all but two of the year's pole positions and led over half the total number of laps) and the Lola was the best all-round car which anyone could buy. Penske dominated Indy and Rick Mears won his third '500' from Emerson Fittipaldi's March-Ilmor and Emerson followed that with a couple of third places, but his team, Patrick Racing, had switched to Lola by July.

Emerson wasn't the only one to switch, Mike Andretti and Raul Boesel followed soon after, despite both drivers racking up strong points finishes in their 88Cs. It was too difficult to make the car work and for 'difficult' read 'expensive', for running a car a mile in testing costs as much as a mile in racing and nobody wants to persevere with a car with which the works team can win but the customer can't. The 20 cars March had built at the beginning of the season soon looked an academic figure and its fortunes basically rested with Al Jnr. While everyone was saying what a dog the 88C was, and voting with their feet, Al Jnr won four races (Long Beach, Toronto, Meadowlands and Miami), which was as many as the Champion, Danny Sullivan. People's perception of March was so poor, however, that everyone said 'What a driver!' instead of 'That car must be good'.

The truth lies somewhere between the two extremes and the fact remains that Al Jnr was runner-up in the series, although one of the reasons why his car went so well was that it used the 86C underbody, designed by Adrian Newey. This became public knowledge in 1989 when the Machinists' Union team bought the cars and ran them for Kevin Cogan and some observers felt that these cars were sufficiently special for Cogan to have returned to the winner's circle had he had Ilmor rather than Cosworth engines. The trouble was how people perceived Alan Mertens, an ex-March man working for Galles; was it a case of a March secret being withheld for a selected customer? It wasn't, it was simply a clever thing to do, and an admission that the basic 88C was not all it should have been, but March's ex-customers didn't see it like that.

One other thing which helped the Galles team was that it had dumped the Judd engine, while Rahal, who was third in the series, spent the year developing it in the back of his TrueSports Lola, so one major contender was slightly hobbled.

Another driver to be hobbled was Teo Fabi, who drove a March-Porsche for Al Holbert, Porsche's North American Director of Motor Sport. The trouble was that the engine lacked torque and it has to be said that for all its success in sports cars, Porsche has never cracked single-seater racing and had switched to a March chassis after its own '87 effort had proved an embarrassment, but then Porsche has never been too hot on chassis design. Teo could occasionally make the car go reasonably well despite the engine, but a fourth at Pennsylvania was his only top six finish, although CART's scoring system had him equal tenth in the Championship. The Fabi/March/Porsche combination was to continue into 1989, but the architect of the team, the much respected and liked Al Holbert, was not to see it, for he died at the controls of his private aircraft as he left Pennsylvania having just seen Teo demonstrate that the combination had promise.

March had fallen apart in its four markets, only one sports car was made in 1988, few had wanted to know the 88B in European F3000 at the beginning of the season and fewer still by the end, and customers in both Japan and America left the company in droves. Paradoxically, while it was in deep trouble on the customer car front it grew ever stronger in F1, but then Formula One was only intended to be a flagship, not a money-making operation. It was also absorbing a lot of talent and Les Mactaggart, the Indycar Project Manager, was one who moved down the road to March Racing during 1988.

There has been a lot of emphasis on finance in the latter part of the March story, but the fact is that if a company is not making money, before long it is also not making cars. It had been with this in mind that it had reorganized so as not to be dependent on the volatile customer car business, so there was the fall-back position of the money-spinning consultancy operations: Comtec was engineering the Panther Solo, working on a new March Supercar and speaking to other companies; March Engineering Projects had been formed to sell the Group's expertise and was floating ideas; the wind tunnel was operational and it was predicted that it would make a million pounds a year. It seemed that the forward planning had saved, the day but a rude shock was waiting.

In July 1988 the Group's half-year interim profit had slumped from £828,000 (1987) to £113,000 and things were obviously going to get worse, sales had fallen but overheads had not, so each car made had a higher unit cost and that in turn prevented the recovery of overheads. Then, the fewer cars which go out through the door so fewer spares are sold and spares represent 25–30 per cent of a racing car maker's turnover. Desperate times call for desperate measures and shortly afterwards, on the recommendation of Peter Leach, March's auditor, John Cowen arrived on the scene and the entire senior management, except for Robin Herd, was sacked. From the moment of John's arrival, Robin handed over the reins of the company and he too began to drift out of the picture in terms of making day-to-day decisions. Norman Mazure remained a non-executive director.

John's background includes Jensen Cars. In the Sixties, when it was successful, he'd been a merchant banker and then had gained a reputation for being a first-rate crisis manager with the ability to turn companies around. He came to March on a part-time basis by personal recommendation, Robin relinquished the title 'Chairman' to him, but retained the position of Managing Director of March Racing and became 'President' of the Group. It was an unusual title for a British businessman, but was apposite since he had the contacts and presence to walk into any boardroom in the world and make a case for March. He became like an MP who goes to the House of Lords – he remains in the game but loses his vote, because from the moment of his arrival John Cowen was in charge and within a fortnight he had the situation in hand, if not quite under control.

John says, "I asked all the key people to submit their ideas on how we should proceed and the result was . . ." – let's just say he could control his enthusiasm without difficulty. John Cowen's appearance at March was followed by the departure of Towns and Shackleton-Fergus (Shaw left in October) and Dave Reeves was called from Comtec to become Managing Director of March Engineering.

March's wind tunnel had been touted as *State of the Art, the Most Advanced in the World, blah, blah, blah*, but there was a slight problem, it didn't work to expectations. It had been designed by Bill Marshall, who developed terminal cancer, and Bill's illness was the root of some of the trouble. There were severe problems with the boundary layers, for example, and March Racing had been using the Southampton University facility, although the two statements are not connected. The wind tunnel was a profit centre and March Racing had to give way to customers' bookings rather than have total freedom of access, which, properly, was unacceptable to Adrian Newey.

Although March Wind Tunnels Ltd took space at the 1989 Racing Car Show to promote its services, and predicted it would soon have a second tunnel in use, shortly afterwards it changed its role from commercial operation to in-house facility. Ken Burgin had been given a year's sabbatical from Southampton University in September 1988 and he, with Adrian, Robin and, especially, Nick Wirth, had sorted out the problems, at which point it lived up to its publicity and became a very useful tool for March Racing. Robin now says, "Beyond any doubt it is now the best, the most accurate, rolling road wind tunnel in the world. Bar none." As soon as that happened it made no sense to allow rivals to share it, in any case it was unthinkable that Adrian Newey had to find a gap in a queue. Apart from anything else, it had been forecast that the wind tunnel could make an annual profit of a million pounds, but it was soon clear that a tenth of that was a more realistic figure.

Comtec's involvement with Panther Cars had lost it £300,000. March Engineering Projects had made a proposal to Lamborghini to design a supercar and that had cost £170,000 with no result. John Cowen says, "The presentation was beautiful, but March has always built prototypes, the car which leaves the factory is a basis for development, nobody at March had engineered a production car the specification of which is set. The people at Lamborghini had said, 'Fine, nice car, but who's going to engineer it?' they were right, we had nobody."Despite that, John had a lot of time for Shackleton-Fergus, but was concerned that he didn't quite appreciate the reality of Comtec's position.

Comtec had been playing about with a March supercar which had reached the stage of a 0.4 scale model photographs of which appeared in magazines as the real thing, but as Dave Reeves says, "There's a market for supercars, but you need a provenance, the Ferrari F40 and the Porsche 959 have it, everything is made by Ferrari and Porsche and there's a history behind them. What engine could we put in our car which would have the same connections? Had there been a successful March-Lamborghini F1 car a March-Lamborghini road car might have worked, but you can't sell a car as a thoroughbred, at thoroughbred prices, if it's a cross-breed. The proposed McLaren supercar is a different matter because of McLaren's success in F1."

March Engineering Projects was put into limbo and the deal between Comtec and Panther was terminated with Panther receiving the moulds and technology. For the time being Comtec would revert to being a March supplier, although expansion into other areas in the future was not ruled out, after all it had made parts for a french space satellite due for launch in 1991, but whether Comtec will ever expand outside of being simply a March supplier is problematical.

As soon as the basic decisions had been made, in August 1988, negotiations opened with Porsche to build an Indycar for 1989. Less than a month later separate negotiations opened with Alfa Romeo for another Indycar programme. Both sets of talks were successful, wholly due to Dave Reeves.

Dave went to America to speak to March's customers, and former customers, who did not welcome him with open arms as you would expect if you represent a company where a customer once phoned to demand, 'Where's the car you promised me? The race is in two days' time,' and he had been told 'Your car would have more chance of being

Dave Reeves who became Managing Director of March Engineering in 1988. He played a major role in reorganising the company and negotiated the 1989 projects with Porsche and Alfa Romeo.

finished if I'm not constantly interrupted by phone calls like this.' "In Indycar," says Dave, "you're dealing with 20 or so team owners, a little club, and if you want to be accepted as a member of a club you have to abide by the rules."

Roger Bailey says, "When Dave came out here a lot of people found him a bit blunt and black and white, but they soon found they could trust him and if he said such and such would be ready Friday, you could bank on it. Now he's in charge I think March has a chance of bringing it all back, people are relieved to be dealing with someone who talks straight, but we're well past the days of 'Tell me', now it's 'Show me'."

John Cowen flew out to Miami for the last race of 1988, "Kicking March was the popular sport, but when I suggested that we might withdraw altogether they did not like that at all, they wanted us back so that they would not be wholly dependent on Penske and Lola. In rubbishing us they were getting their own back, and who can blame them, but they would have been sorry to see us go. Not only that but there had been two special contracts in the air, Porsche and Alfa Romeo, and we weren't the only people bidding for them. It did not go unnoticed that we had landed both." A March 89C customer car was announced, but John decided not to go ahead with it on the open market, it would be supplied only to Alfa Romeo, 1989 would be a time of regrouping ready for a fresh start in 1990. Dave says, "If you're in a rowing boat in a gale and you've only got a broken oar, it makes sense not to try to row against the wind."

While all that was going on, March Racing had gone from an outfit of six people running a modified F3000 car to one of the most admired teams in Formula One. In recent years the raw specification of a car has told one very little about the car itself; regulations are now so closely defined that the designer has to work within a very tight envelope and in essence every chassis on a grid is the same. Although a designer such as Colin Chapman could work in bold strokes in the early Eighties, the designers of the late Eighties had to apply a subtlety of thought undreamed of only a few years previously, for not only is so much of their work dictated by regulations but the parameters of performance are common knowledge, so the overall level of competence is so much higher and what marks out the handful of star designers is their ability to do basically what everyone else is doing but do it that bit better.

Just as once Bruce McLaren designed his 'Whoosh Bonk' Special in a note pad and John Thompson built it up, so the modern F1 designer operates on parallel lines. The concept designer can put all his parameters on half a sheet of paper; it may have taken him a year working with a computer program to reach those decisions, but the overall layout and dimensions can be expressed simply. The mechanical designer, in this case Tim Holloway, had to make the car work within the concept's parameter, so such vital decisions such as the design of the uprights and the location of the pick-up points were down to Tim.

When a car is driven over a road, deflection transmitted from the wheels is energy which has to be absorbed and normally it is absorbed through the springing. In order to optimize the aerodynamics of the 881's suspension set-ups were very stiff indeed so that the car would present a constant profile to the air stream and the generated energy had to be absorbed through the entire system, uprights, etc, instead of just the springs and dampers. It was in this area that Tim's work was decisive.

Adrian pioneered a new shape in F1 with a very narrow monocoque which was given the ultimate accolade – almost everyone copied it in 1989. The layout was conventional enough but the reason why the 881 became regarded as one of the two best chassis on the grid (the other was the Benetton 188) was its supreme stiffness and the cleverness of its aerodynamics. It had a waisted monocoque towards the front of the cockpit resulting in the front of the footwell being only ten inches wide, a feature which was to give the drivers some problem, for there was little room to rest their left feet with the result they had to 'ride' the clutch, which led to an unusual number of clutch failures. The sidepods were noticeably lower in height than most of the opposition and were sharply waisted with a complex-curved rear diffuser which provided a lot of ground effect downforce.

At 112.4 inches its wheelbase was among the longest of the class of '88, while its 70-inch front track was narrower than all but the recalcitrant Tyrrell 017 and its 66-inch rear track came second only to the Benetton 188 in width. Every car on the grid had double wishbone suspension front and rear operated by either pull or push rods and Newey opted for the latter, while the Judd CV engine delivered its power through a new 6-speed March gearbox which derived from the Indycar unit.

One thing on the agenda was the new V12 Lamborghini engine, but March's commitment was only to install one in an 881 chassis, which would have sapped resources, but there was a proposal to link up with Onyx, which was looking for a way into F1. March would lend Onyx an 881-Lamborghini which Onyx would test while sharing its information with March. This was an extension of the 'know how' agreement Adrian Newey had had with Peter Gibbins in CART, it would keep March warm should the engine turn out to be something special, and if the subsequent Onyx F1 car turned out to resemble the 881 that would be a remarkable coincidence.

The Onyx connection did not happen because if it had arrived at the 1989 Brazilian GP with a car which too closely resembled the 881 it might be deemed to have broken the rule which insists that each team must create its own cars, and had that happened it would have been the end of Onyx. So far as March Racing was concerned it did not happen because the cost of using the engine was $3m, or twice what the Judd engines were costing, while the power figures were no better. On top of that it was a much longer unit which to have installed properly would have required a lot of extra work on the aerodynamics, so it would have been an expensive distraction for no apparent gain.

March Racing was growing to a sensible size due to large injections of cash from its sponsors, there were nearly 70 employees by the end of 1988 and the number was steadily increasing (it was about 105 by mid-1989). It had become completely separate from March Engineering and was no longer dependent on its parent to design and build its cars. One other advantage from its increased size, and bigger budget, was the amount of testing it was able to do during the season, but that was something which would come later, however, for the cars were still being finished in Brazil at the first race where several mechanics had to receive medical treatment for heat stroke as they worked in violent temperatures.

It was not only the cars which were brand new, for Adrian Newey himself had not been to most of the circuits so was having to learn as he went with only limited help from the previous year's settings. The fact that he established himself as one of the élite designers at the age of 29 with his first F1 car and in his first year of being on the F1 scene (most designers serve an apprenticeship at least as a race engineer) speaks volumes.

In the opening round in Brazil Capelli put his car ninth on the grid with Gugelmin only four places behind on his F1 debut. Both performances with a car which had not previously turned a wheel were the more creditable when one remembers there were still eight turbo cars in the field and Capelli was quicker than three of them. The dream start was not to last, however, for on the warm-up lap Ivan had a water rail detach and he drove to the pits in a cloud of steam to switch to the spare and had to start from the pit lane. Mauricio's race was run on the first lap when his transmission broke and Ivan was out after six laps with his engine overheating, a problem which afflicted Judd units in their first few races, although Williams was to

The mechanics work on the Judd engine in the March 881. (Nigel Snowdon)

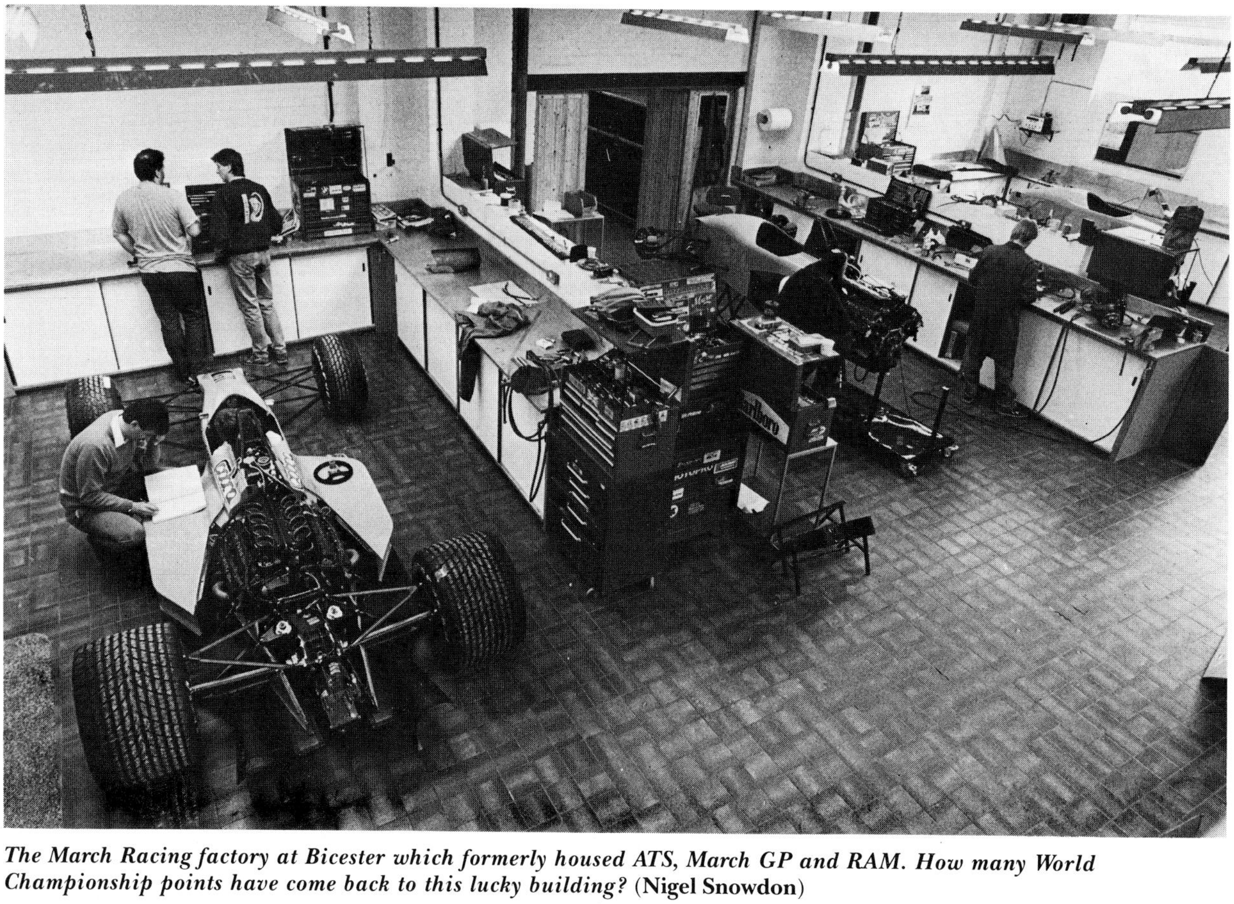

The March Racing factory at Bicester which formerly housed ATS, March GP and RAM. How many World Championship points have come back to this lucky building? (Nigel Snowdon)

suffer more than March. Even when the engine did not overheat terminally it often ran sufficiently warm for it to lose power, but Judd had the problem cracked by the end of the season.

One thing which Judd was not able to overcome was the supply of engines and March's allocation of 12 meant it was sometimes short of units with which to go testing. Thus with a car which was not only brand new but had a new aerodynamic concept, the young team did not make as much progress as it might have done in the early part of the season, but once the mid-way point was reached it went from strength to strength.

Larger front wings at Imola were designed to increase downforce and so they did, with such effect that the team lost four nose cones in as many laps in qualifying. Stronger bobbins solved the problems and Capelli qualified ninth again, but was out after two laps of the race with transmission problems, while Gugelmin struggled with an ill-handling car and was not helped by the fact that his radio unit fell into his lap.

The root of the transmission failures was that the angles on the teeth of the crown wheel and pinion were all wrong and this caused overheating, which led to other problems. Since a crown wheel and pinion has the longest lead time of any component in a racing car it was not until Silverstone that replacements would be delivered and the team could race without worrying about its gearboxes, but from the beginning a small oil radiator had been fitted to cool the transmission oil. The discovery of the problem was fortunate because, after the early failures, the team was working on a new gearbox, which was draining effort.

Neither Monaco nor Mexico saw March in particularly good shape, the cars were not so happy on tight circuits because their main advantage lay in their aerodynamics and that presumed stiffness of chassis, on tight circuits a softer chassis would have been preferable and later March tried to make one by cutting holes in an 881 tub, but, alas, it was so well designed that it would not flop as required. By 1989 the thinking was that an F1 team might have to consider making two types of car, one for road circuits and one for speed circuits, with the softer chassis for the former. This would not be an entirely new idea, but an extension of Indycar practice with its different wheelbases and bodies but the thinking as regards CART had already extended to considering four distinct cars, for road and street circuits and for long and short ovals.

Although the 881 was not at its best on the slower circuits, Adrian beavered away at the problem and at the Canadian GP Capelli opened his 1988 points score with a fifth. He was unable to add to his total at Detroit because he crashed heavily in practice, as the result of a puncture caused by debris left by an argument René Arnoux had had with a barrier, and he broke a bone in a foot. Mauricio, however, charged in the race and was up to fifth and looking for better things when he retired with overheating caused by a split radiator, but it had been a terrific drive by someone in only his sixth Grand Prix.

New front suspension pick-up points were used by Capelli at Paul Ricard and these were one of the keys to the cars' subsequent storming performances, but neither driver had a trouble-free practice and eighth and ninth at the end were disappointing; Mauricio had an overheating engine and Ivan had not recovered from his Detroit shunt. Silverstone would be a different matter, the turning point of the season, and on its home circuit March gave notice of its intention. Capelli had the first of the new high-compression Judd engines and qualified sixth, but the sensation was Mauricio, who put his car in fifth spot, the fastest non-turbo. In an extremely wet race Capelli was an early retiree with an electrical fault, but Gugelmin brought his 881 home a splendid fourth to score his first Championship points.

Gugelmin's performance perhaps illustrates the difference between the two drivers. Capelli is an all-out racer while his team-mate approaches the problem in a different way, he knows when the car will work and when it will not so tends to be much slower than Capelli on a circuit where he knows the car's a lost cause, but he had mentally prepared himself for the quick circuits.

At Hockenheim Capelli came home fifth and the first non-turbo finisher having taken a gamble on wet settings, while Gugelmin had run 'dry' and finished three places behind. March had come alive on the quick circuits and was challenging Benetton as the best non-turbo team, although Benetton, with its favoured link with Ford and the Cosworth DFR engine, seemed to have a power advantage.

Since the Hungaroring had a mixture of fast and

Mauricio Gugelmin (March 881) leads Alessandro Nannini (Benetton B188) in the 1988 British Grand Prix. Gugelmin took a fine fourth place. **(Nigel Snowdon)**

slow sections prior to the race the team split up, with Mauricio going to the tight little circuit at Pembrey to dial in the car on tight sections, while Ivan ran at Silverstone and the two parts of the team swapped notes over the phone. More modifications resulted and Ivan qualified fourth in Hungary, though retired with a misfire, and Mauricio scored March's third points finish with a fine fifth. Then Capelli made it four points finishes in a row at Spa, where both drivers had a troubled practice session, and while Mauricio lost his clutch and spun out of the race, Ivan charged up from 14th on the grid to fifth at the end. More troubled practice sessions followed at Monza, with Ivan's best chance of a time on the quicker day being spoiled by a leaking tyre valve and Mauricio's by a blown engine but Ivan came home fifth again, despite vibration from a wheel caused by a brush with Patrese early in the race.

All this was very promising, the team was learning, the problems were being ironed out, the car was constantly changing and the drivers were growing in stature with every race. Nothing, however, prepared the racing public for the sight of Capelli and Gugelmin in third and fifth places on the grid in Portugal. As usual the McLarens of Prost and Senna occupied the front row, but only Berger's Ferrari prevented it from being an all-March second row. Just to prove that the timing had not developed a glitch Capelli hounded Senna in the early part of the race, unable to pass on sheer power until his fuel load lightened, and he swept by and began to chase Alain Prost, who led. It's true the McLaren-Hondas were having to drive with an eye on fuel consumption, but Ivan closed to within 1.6 seconds of Prost when his engine temperature went up, and seeing his team-mate parked by the side of the track with his engine blown, he eased back to finish second and less than ten seconds down. It was the first indication that Capelli might be a very special driver and it gave him an enormous boost of confidence; he'd taken Senna and hounded Prost and Prost was his hero. In post-race interviews he referred to 'Mr Prost', a touch of modesty rare in motor racing, but anyone who knows him will say it was typical of him.

Being a tight circuit, Jerez did not suit the Marches quite as well, but still Capelli qualified sixth, only to retire from the race with engine trouble, but afterwards March stayed on to test and Robin can tell an interesting story, "We bribed someone at Benetton to let us have some of their fuel, which we put in the car, and Ivan went out and was a second faster. He came back to the pits saying, 'What have you done to the engine? Why has it taken 14 races to get it to go like this? We've been using a turd all year and suddenly we have a decent engine.'

"There's only one thing to do at a moment like that and that's to stroke your chin in the Max Mosley fashion and say, 'It's very interesting you should say that, because that's the point of the exercise. We'd now like you to do another test,' and we filled up the car with our usual four star. Ivan came back to the pits saying, 'What have you

Ivan Capelli and the 881 during testing at Jerez after the 1988 Spanish Grand Prix. (**Nigel Snowdon**)

done to the engine? You've turned it into an old dog again.' The next day FISA announced it was stripping Benetton of the points it had won at Spa because its fuel had been found to be irregular." There was no question of Benetton deliberately cheating; there was an innocent miscalculation of the octane rating by an outside party which had interpreted the regulations too generously.

The race in Japan was more than usually important because it was the home of Leyton House. Ivan was going fairly well in practice when Ian Phillips bet him £1000 he couldn't break 1m 43.8s. Ivan couldn't resist that, he set a time two-tenths under and Ian paid up with a smile because it had been an excellent investment. Capelli had put the car fourth on the grid, the fastest non-turbo runner, and Leyton House had many corporate guests at the circuit who were naturally delighted by the performance of 'their' man.

In the race itself Senna fluffed his start, Ivan slotted in behind Prost and Berger and on the sixth lap moved up to second. Then he strung together a series of fastest laps and was snapping at Prost's heels and he actually led across the start/finish line on lap 16. It lasted for only about 400 yards, but it was the first time a normally aspirated car had headed a race since 1984 and it had Leyton House writ large on its side, no bad thing in Japan. Prost regained the lead, but Ivan held second until an electrical fault sidelined him after another three laps.

Some people thought that Capelli had been sent out on light tanks to put on a show for Leyton House. Tim Holloway says, "McLaren was one outfit which thought so, but that was fine by us, it meant they hadn't taken us seriously and had to look for excuses. You know you have the opposition worried when they accuse you of cheating.'

In fact Capelli's tanks were topped up on the grid and he was actually running with about three gallons more fuel than he needed and the real reason why the car stopped has never been found; all the systems were checked and found to be working so it might have been a glitch in the telemetry caused by something as innocent as a couple of crowd marshals talking to each other on walkie-talkies.

In the final race at Adelaide, March was back on a street circuit for the first time since the front suspension modifications were introduced at Paul Ricard and there was a lot to learn. Mauricio had an unhappy time and his race ended when he was thumped by Nakajima's Lotus, while Ivan brought his car home sixth, minus its clutch.

The March Racing team of 1988 was a different outfit to the one which had made a tentative appearance the previous year and in the seven months of the season it had gone from being a promising newcomer, being in most people's reckoning one of the top teams, with drivers and engineers who were still new to F1. Its success had had its downside in that it had helped drain March Engineering, but in a troubled year it had been the one bright point. At the beginning of 1989 Robin was predicting that it would be the team of the Nineties in the same way that McLaren had been the team of the Eighties, but, on the day he said that, he also confided that he had decided to sell it to Akiri Akagi.

At the time it was a surprise, but it was almost inevitable, since Akagi wanted in and the team was not really appropriate for a publicly quoted company. It was known that March was re-grouping after a lean period, but the company seemed bullet-proof after all it had been through. It was far from that and was about to enter a period that Robin would call *Dynasty II.*

25 Dynasty II

The crisis of mid-1988 had shown that the March game plan had become seriously flawed, none of the money-making operations had worked and the one bright spot had been the F1 team, but as John Cowen says, "One had to question whether a public company should be involved in Formula One because the primary motive of an F1 team is to win races, the motive of a public company is to make a profit for its shareholders, and the two aims are not always compatible. There is no proper cost control in F1 and even if a team has a profit margin built into its budget, if it needs to spend that money to be successful then it does so, the sponsorship is there to win races not to make money for shareholders. In any case it was soon clear that the cost of mounting the Formula One challenge in 1988 would exceed the funds provided by sponsorship." As they say at Indy, *Speed costs money, how fast do you want to go?*

Having stemmed the haemorrhage, John was left with the problem of regrouping on a firmer base before the position had to be made public and he received unexpected assistance in September, less than two months after his arrival, when he heard that Ron Tauranac might be prepared to sell Ralt. It was an ideal opportunity and he quickly concluded an agreement to buy for £1.25m.

The acquisition of Ralt came as a surprise but Ron Tauranac explains, "My business was becoming too seasonal; there had been a time when Formula Three, SuperVee and Atlantic had dove-tailed into each other, because the build season for Atlantics 'Down Under' came in our summer. In SuperVee we'd been a victim of our own success because we had no one else to beat, we were getting down to just F3 so we had a problem in keeping people occupied.

"Apart from that, I think some of the problem was the way customers perceived us; everyone had decided they had to have carbon-fibre tubs without realizing that some carbon-fibre construction in F3000 was a way short of F1 standards. I have seen a car break up just because it bottomed and everyone said 'Wow, look at the strength of carbon fibre, the driver's unhurt', but it should never have broken in the first place. Part of the problem was business ethics. I've always built a car and said, 'There it is, if you want one that's fine, if you don't, that's fine too.' We came up against people who'd wine and dine the press, who'd phone up drivers and tell them they had to buy their cars, who'd offer them special deals, lease arrangements and so on, anything to get the right people into their cars, and I wouldn't do that.

"I'd been making a profit of £750,000 a year, but had re-invested in machine tools, so I think I can say that the difference between our product and other people's is that we make things to such tolerances that if you buy something from our parts store it will fit, whereas if you bought almost any production car in the past you'd buy parts and then proceed to make 'em fit."

That's no idle boast and it is the reason why March jumped at the chance to buy Ralt, that and the pragmatic design skills of Ron Tauranac himself. As Robin said at the time, "Nobody builds production cars as well as Ron," and as some senior March men said also at the same time, "We really shouldn't be building production cars because we're no good at it."

Ron continues, "In 1988 we were down to 35 cars from the 80 we'd been used to making and our profit disappeared when two drivers in F3000 didn't find things to their liking, and instead of waiting for me to sort out the

Ron Tauranac who sold his Ralt company to March in October 1988. **(Nigel Snowdon)**

car they decided to take their sponsorship, £400,000, elsewhere. For a number of reasons, then, our market had shrunk, March needed the extra capacity and we needed more work to keep our people occupied, so it worked out nicely."

The plan was emerging, Bicester would pull out of the production market to concentrate on special projects such as the one with Porsche, which would be hand built rather than semi-mass produced, and would tout for other work, a Group C car, perhaps, or even a rally project. All the customer cars would be built at Weybridge with the two companies retaining their identities in their traditional markets, Ralt in F3, March in CART.

At the time Robin said, "I have a lot of time for Messrs Tauranac, Reynard and Broadley. In some ways it's a bigger challenge to build production racing cars than doing F1: your budget is tighter, your time scale is much tighter, and you have to give away all your secrets. The most difficult job in the world is to be the chief engineer of a production racing car company because the compromises you have to make are so great, it's much easier to do an F1 car because you don't have to consider cost. I think to run a successful production car firm, the chief designer has to be the owner, because nobody else is going to put up with all the aggravation. That's why we'll leave Ron well alone but give him back-up on composites, aerodynamics and sales."

Soon after that deal became public March agreed to sell its F3000 operation, which was losing money, to Leyton House and henceforward the cars would be known as Leyton Marches. This was possible because F3000 already operated as a separate project under long-term March man Mike Smith, and the attraction for Akagi was that he would have his own marque with which to contest the Japanese F3000 and Grand Champion series.

In order to keep Porsche and Alfa Romeo equally happy, the former was based at Bicester under the engineering control of Gordon Coppuck and the latter at Ralt under Tauranac and Maurice Philippe, who had just left Tyrrell. While the March F1 car was setting new standards in aerodynamics, neither project could take information directly from it for Adrian Newey had secrets to protect, on the other hand, there might be a limited amount of shared information in an indirect way, through Comtec, for example.

A March production man, Pat Selwood, was placed at Ralt to install systems compatible with a branch of a public company and he says, "Ron has been running things as a one man-band. I think he's basically looked at his bank balance and if it looked okay he carried on as before and if it was showing a drop, he did something about it. Once you become a public company, you are accountable and you have to have things like two signatures on a cheque. Ron's impatient with this, he's always operated on the basis that his signature alone is enough, but you can't operate like that when you're a public company."

Ron shrugs his shoulders, smiles, and says it will work out, but he can afford to be relaxed, he's unlikely to want, and he's needed. At the time, in May 1989, his own F3 cars were back on top of the heap having been overshadowed by Reynard for the previous two or three seasons. As for the future and the possibility of March regaining its lost markets, "I don't know. It comes down to efficiency, and I don't know whether a PLC can be efficient enough to build cars and put the amount of engineering quality which will go in if I'm involved. I rather doubt it, they want accountants involved, two signatures on a cheque, costings and projections because when you're a public company you have everyone trying to cover their backs, you no longer operate just on trust, and the overhead costs of doing all that are fairly great. If the whole business can be made more efficient so you dovetail production and build your ARS cars at odd moments, because they're not going to change, you might cover your overheads, we will see. You've got to do Indy-type cars at their sort of prices to cover the extra overheads, it's difficult to do it making Formula Threes."

While March was coming to terms with a massive loss looming on the horizon, and its own restructuring, in November 1988, Akiri Akagi paid £4m for 19.9 per cent of March's stock (137p per share) and took his place on the board. As a director he had access to the books, so discovered the true position, and within a very short time he was negotiating to buy a majority holding in the Group, although, in fact, his main interest was the F1 team and the F3000 project. Had the deal gone through, and agreement was reached in principle in January 1989, it would have meant that less than two years after being floated March would become a private company again, but this time Akagi would be the majority shareholder.

The plan was that he would inject more cash into the company which would have reduced Robin's share, which then stood at 43 per cent, to 20 per cent and there was also an arrangement for him to take over Robin's share in the future. At the time Robin put on a brave face and reasoned that it was the right thing to do, "When you get a patron of a team you usually get a three-year cycle. In the first year they spend a small amount, in the second they get more serious, but the third year is the big go and if it doesn't work they get out. There are three types of sponsorship: those teams sponsored by major companies, Fiat with Ferrari, Honda with McLaren; those which are sponsored by very wealthy companies which in the third year want an involvement, the power as well as the glory, such as Arrows and Benetton; and the third type is exemplified by Frank Williams, who has a group of sponsors every year until the day comes when he can't put a package together.

"Akagi buying in more or less guarantees the future of the F1 team. On a personal level I'd rather not do it because it has been my project, even though I haven't profiled in front of the pits, and I shall be sad not to have seen it through but I was torn between recommending the bid to the share- holders or going the Frank Williams way and looking for sponsorship every year but the team deserves more than that, it's too good. I wouldn't swap the engineering team there for any in the business. McLaren has been the team of the Eighties, March will be the team of the Nineties. Now I have done my job I can make sure that the rest of the Group works sensibly."

On 5 January, 1989, the board of March Group PLC

John Cowen, Chairman of March Group PLC, who has done so much to transform the Company's fortunes.

warned shareholders that the year to 31 October, 1988, would likely show a loss of £4.5m (March Engineering accounting for £3.5m) and that Mr Akagi was offering 50p per share, except for Robin's holding, and would inject cash into the company in the form of equity and loans. Shareholders would be advised to accept the offer.

It was a bombshell; less than two years before the shares had been 120p each and they'd risen to 180p, not only that but there had been the purchase of Ralt, which, of course, took £1.25m from the profit sheet and put it in the asset column. Something was obviously seriously wrong, but nobody outside of a tight circle knew about all the bright plans which had crumbled. The outside world had not been told about the temporary abandonment of the Indycar customer market and the fact that very little cash had come in after August 1988, which precipitated a severe cash-flow problem.

What happened next is told by John Cowen, "We had floated at 120p per share and our talks started at 110p per share, but came tumbling down until eventually it was 50p. After a lot of heart-searching the board recommended our shareholders to accept, although we thought the company was worth a lot more, but the reason why we recommended it was we had a ferocious cash problem, so severe there were many instances of employees paying off creditors so that we could get raw materials coming into the factory, and Robin supported us with considerable personal loans.

"We recommended selling at 50p per share because the only alternative was liquidation, in which case our shareholders would have got nothing and it was anyway important to avoid that since March has loyal and highly skilled employees and it was not acceptable to let them down." It might also be said that many of those employees were also shareholders because of their loyalty and contribution over the years. On 10 February, which was a Friday, Akagi withdrew the offer at 5.30 in the afternoon. De Zoete & Bevan, March's financial advisers and joint stockbrokers, resigned – their official reason being they had lost confidence in the board, so March had no stockbroker and no financial adviser on the evening of 10 February.

"By 8 o'clock the same night De Zoete & Bevan had been replaced as stockbrokers by Smith Keen Cutler, a Birmingham firm which had been joint brokers, and First Independent Corporate Finance Ltd came in as financial advisers, and both supported March at a time when they didn't know if they'd get their fees paid and when there was the possibility that there might be a lot of adverse comment in the press. Robert Kitzinger of First Independent and Philip Shepherd and Bill Melly of Smith Keen Cutler, in particular, supported March through thick and thin.

Next morning John Cowen met with one of Akagi's advisers and asked why the bid had been withdrawn and why it had been done at 5.30 pm on a Friday. According to John, the adviser answered, "We're going to buy March. We're not going to buy it at 50p a share, we might buy it at 40p, we might buy it at 20p, or we might buy it off the receiver, but buy it we will."

On the Monday morning John went to Oxford and negotiated a loan of £600,000 with Lloyds Bank, which Robin personally guaranteed with no security, and in the afternoon Smith Keen Cutler called together March's institutional shareholders and told them what was happening. Robert Kitzenger and John laid the whole position on the line and asked for their support. John says, "Our institutional shareholders agreed in principle to support us but asked to be able to think about it overnight. The next morning, every one of them phoned and pledged support." On that day, Monday 13 February, March shares were suspended, at the company's request, at 50 pence each.

John continues: "On Tuesday morning the phone rang at my home at eight o'clock; it was one of Akagi's advisers, who said, 'You've still not announced in the press that the bid is off. Does the bank know that the bid is off?' Since Akagi was on our board and this man was his alternate, he had a legal right to the information, so I had to tell him that the bank didn't know. In fact we had permission from the Stock Exchange to delay making the announcement and, of course, the previous day, which was the first working day since the offer was withdrawn, had seen me up in Oxford arranging the Lloyds loan and then back in London for the meeting with the institutions in the afternoon. There hadn't been a great deal of time to talk to the bank and, in any event, the priority was to organize the financial support.

"However, I thought if he's asking about the bank, I'd better tell them so I picked up the phone at a minute past nine and got a very frosty reception from the manager, who said, 'I've had a letter faxed to me and on the strength of that information I'm afraid we've had to freeze your account.' On the Friday before we had received our first payment from Alfa Romeo for the Indycars, which meant that our overdraft was at an artificially low level, but it had been frozen at that level. They also refused to give us permission to draw on the loan we'd arranged with Lloyds and that worsened our already perilous position and it looked as though we would be driven into receivership."

When the news broke that negotiations had broken down, the press speculated that the stumbling block had been a deal March had entered with another team to sell them technology and, in fact, it had entered a 'know how' agreement with another team, similar to the one Adrian Newey had had with Peter Gibbins in Indycar, but the other team cannot be named for there was a confidentiality clause in the contract. Akagi objected to this arrangement and as Robin says, "It was a double-edged thing, one could well understand a team owner might object to it, but I thought it was right for us at the time, and I still do." One of the reasons why it was right for March was that behind Team X were connections which might have been helpful, but the story was a smokescreen.

John Cowen says, "It was an objection but one I could have sorted out in 48 hours but at the time I was not given 48 hours. It is ironic that, but the 'know how' agreement was terminated on very amicable terms shortly thereafter. I then requested, and got, a meeting with the area director of the bank and was able to tell him we had full support from our institutions. This persuaded him to thaw the account and to allow us to use the Lloyds' loan facility."

On that meeting had ridden the future of March. Had not John managed to persuade the area director to reverse the bank manager's decision, which was a proper and reasonable one, then the game would have been over. It was as if the house manager had over-ruled the croupier and allowed John to return to the table. He still had a weak hand, but at least was back in the game.

In the meantime Robert Kitzinger had scored a major coup in the he had opened negotiations with a Swiss bank to underwrite a Rights Issue and this allowed John to go back to Akagi's advisers and say, "You had us running. You have told us that your aim is to buy us for a fraction of your original offer. I want you to know we have the solid support of our institutional shareholders, and of our bank, and we have a large standby credit facility with Lloyds. Now let's sit down and talk sense. The sense we are going to talk is that we are going to sell March Racing, the wind tunnel and the F3000 project to you for £6.5m and we are going to buy your shares for £1. Those terms are not negotiable, take it or leave it."

This put things in a different perspective. Leyton House was not interested in March Group as such, only in parts of it, and that had been the reason Akagi had bought into the group. The price for those three elements was on the high side, but Akagi was anxious to buy and while selling shares acquired only three months earlier for £4m for just one pound looks a poor deal, it would save Leyton House having to worry about March Engineering, Comtec and Ralt. Moreover, what remained of March Group could be put on a new footing and be free of outside interference. For all his confidence, though, John was playing the game with markers, not chips, for his financial security was a bank overdraft and Robin's guarantee on the Lloyds Bank loan.

Thanks to meetings and the phone lines humming between various City institutions, March's position had changed dramatically and this time the response was appropriately different. The advisers said that Akagi was in New York and one caught a night flight, had breakfast with him next day, and phoned John to say, 'Akagi accepts, at £6.25m.'

Robin maintains that he has remained on excellent terms with Akagi. "I will not hear a word said against him. He has been 100 per cent open, honourable, straight and generous with me in all our dealings." The parties might, however, have reached an understanding more easily if Cesare Gariboldi had been there to act as honest broker, but he had died in a road accident in December, 1988.

Negotiations resumed on 22 February and a fortnight later, on 7th March, Mr Akagi resigned from the board of March Group PLC.

John continues: "During the negotiations which followed, which were protracted, they continually tried to beat us down and I continually said, 'The terms are not negotiable and they never have been. Take it or leave it.' It was brinkmanship, because if they had said, 'Forget it,' we would have gone bust."

The money which Leyton House owed us was connected with F1 sponsorship and F3000 and sales ledger items going a long way back and at one point it reached £1.3m, which was accounting for a lot of March's cash problems. One Wednesday during the negotiations John phoned one of the advisers and told him that if the money was not in March's bank account by noon on Friday he was going to shut down the F3000 operation, sack the staff, end it. Mr Akagi had cars entered in a race at the weekend and would lose much face if he had no cars to run. On the Thursday he received a call to say, "The money will be telexed to your account tomorrow," and he retorted, "Fine, so long as it's there by noon because otherwise the F3000 operation is no more." By ten the following morning the whole £1.3m was in March's account.

Final agreement, on John's terms, was reached on 13 April, documents were signed on 2 May, and press statements issued on 4 May, the day John told his story.

As a result, March Group PLC was not only saved from liquidation but from being close to bankruptcy. It emerged financially secure if somewhat smaller. Akagi's shares were bought for £1 and were liquidated and since that holding was 19.9 per cent it meant that the value of shares in other hands increased by 25 per cent, which put Robin Herd back in charge of his company since his holding then tipped over the 50 per cent mark, but he had put himself entirely in John Cowen's hands so John was running the war, Dave Reeves was fighting the battles, and

Robin was making the diplomatic missions. Roger Young, formerly with Bank Julius Baer, was appointed Chief Executive and while the significance of appointing a banker was missed at the time, it became clear later.

Before the deal became public a new logo was designed to announce that March had changed, the old style had looked forward to the Seventies the new one towards the Nineties, but it remained possible that the old logo might be retained for some purposes.

Robin's majority shareholding made the Extraordinary General Meeting of March Group PLC called for 30 May a formality but as part of the package all the other shareholders were offered, on a one new share to two shares held basis, further shares at 40p (they had an asset value of 50p so it was an attractive deal) to raise an extra £2.8m and since Robin renounced his right to this offer, his holding went down to 33.3 per cent. As President he remained a director of the company, but a non-executive one.

At that point March Group PLC relinquished the right to use the name 'March' in F1 and F3000 for ten years (in effect it licensed Akagi to use the name in those areas, but could still build cars for a third party or make, say, a Ralt F3000 car) and announced that in place of the March wind tunnel it had bought a new wind tunnel from British Aerospace for its own use. Since all other companies, including the optimistic March Merchandising Ltd (to exploit the name and image), were in limbo, the Group effectively consisted of Ralt (production cars), Comtec and March Engineering (prototypes).

Almost immediately March Racing changed its name to Leyton House Racing Ltd with three executive directors, Ian Phillips, Adrian Newey and Tim Holloway. After some heart-searching Mike Smith decided to stay with the F3000 operation as managing director. Although Mike had been with the March F1 team as a mechanic in two stints, he had always preferred F2/3000, but after nearly 17 years with the company it was a wrench. "I've always tried to give 100 per cent to March," he said shortly after making his decision. Some of those who dealt with him over the years disagree, they say it was 110 per cent. On its transfer from March Group PLC, the F3000 outfit changed its name to Leyton House Engineering Ltd and it was planned to move to premises close to the F1 team before the end of 1989. All of Leyton House's operations, including the wind tunnel, were expected to move to new premises on a green-field site before 1992.

Compared to the wild optimism of only a year or so before, when anything was possible, just like it had been in 1969–70, what remained was a sadder, wiser, slimmer, company. A sense of reality had returned but, in truth, it should never have gone.

Some of the problem comes down to the fact that Robin is a bit like Micky Rooney in the movies he made with Judy Garland, *I got it, we'll put on a show right here, in our own back yard . . .* but who can blame him for being an enthusiast? It's one of his most attractive traits, but before Rooney started filming a script writer had already decided that the back yard show would end on Broadway: there's no script in real life. Part of the problem stemmed from another of Robin's attractive qualities, he is prepared to give people their head and then expects them to perform, which is why Dave Reeves started out as a bracket basher, and Mike Smith as a junior mechanic, and both are now managing directors. Depending how you look at it, you could say he was a slack manager or an enlightened one whose trust was betrayed. Perhaps the truth lies somewhere in between.

As for John Cowen, if ever a distinguished-looking gentlemen introduces himself and suggests a friendly hand of poker, find an excuse to be elsewhere, for it might be he. If you take on one of the richest men in the world from a position of virtual bankruptcy and you come out of the game with all your objectives achieved, you have beaten four aces and a king with a pair of twos. The drama being played out in offices and on the phone was every bit as exciting as a motor race and March was lucky to get the right man at the right time because nobody who was in place in July 1988 could have played the game as he did. He has not had much interest in motor racing, but you can see why, when he came to March, the racers welcomed him and he gave the racers their head because under the urbane air and the well-cut business suit there beats the heart of a racer.

Robin says, "I often wonder what would have happened if John had been with Max and me from the beginning, he would have kept us under control and we'd have missed some of the fun and the wild times but . . .

26 La Ronde

Since the 1989 racing season was far from reaching mid-point by the time this book went to press, it would be silly to comment on it, for Dr Sodt's Law decrees that if one said, for example, that Teo Fabi's 89P appeared to be the best handling car in the Indy field but was let down by a poor engine from Porsche, by the time those words appeared in print something would have happened to render them obsolete. Still, that was the general opinion at Long Beach, where he headed two of the four practice sessions, and at Indianapolis the car was the second fastest through the bends but only 28th fastest on the straights. Then Fabi took third at Milwaukee and set pole at a record speed at Portland, so Porsche's learning curve was in upward mode at the time of writing, but what is beyond question is that Gordon Coppuck, with Tino Belli looking after the aerodynamics, produced the most compact car ever seen in CART (it was designed around its diminutive driver unlike the customer cars which have to accommodate anyone) and many of those on the Indycar scene reckoned it was the most advanced and best-handling car ever seen in America.

Although Gordon did not have the freedom he might have had in F1, the parts list for the car was 50 per cent greater than any other March ever made and while one would think that with only four 89Ps to produce during 1989 the workforce at March Engineering would have had time on its hands, Dave Reeves commented that they were saying they had never worked so hard. Such is the difference between the run-of-the-mill customer car and a special project made for a specific client with sensible funding.

This perhaps indicates March Engineering's future plans in racing, the servicing of a few select clients who want cars built up to a standard, not down to a price, and for them to receive the very best effort of the company without the compromise inherent in making customer cars.

In June 1989, Roger Bailey said, "If I had 89Ps to sell, I could shift ten over the phone right now. There are a number of factors, one is that Lola has found itself with the market and has over-extended itself, just as we did. Then every team has its speed guns, so they know the score about who's quick round the bends and on the straight and, most importantly, there is a name on the car. People are looking at the 89P and saying, 'Gordon's still got his touch.' Gordon designed the McLaren M16 series of Indycars, which made everything else look old hat and twice won Indy and people here remember that."

The March-Porsche, driven by Teo Fabi, seen at Indianapolis in 1989. After a disappointing start to the season the combination came on song and took its first win at Mid-Ohio in September, its ninth top-four finish of the season.

The March-Alfa Romeo 89CE seen before it was raced. To date the car has shown considerable promise but has yet to achieve success.

Nobody can buy an 89P, but Porsche was so delighted with its early showings that before the middle of 1989 it extended its contract with March until the end of 1991. Porsche is a name which is not unknown in motor racing so such a commitment says something for the Bicester product.

At the time of writing, the 89CE-Alfa Romeo had only just made its racing début, so there is no way of knowing whether it might be either a winner or a disappointment. Initially three 88Cs were re-engineered for Alfa Romeo to use as test beds and then another two 89CEs were made. Originally, these were to be the '89 customer cars, then they were to form the basis of the 1990 cars but March bought back the technology of the 89P in July 1989 and this will form the basis of customer cars if any are built in 1990.

Although it was not sensational on its début, it eventually finished eighth, the Alfa car seemed to have a good base line for development, for the engine had covered many thousands of miles without serious faults, so one important parameter seemed covered, but who knows what next week, next month, next year, will bring?

One thing which might affect the car was that on 5 June, 1989, Maurice Phillippe, the designer of the 89CE and a man who had a history of depression, took his own life. Men of his experience are thin on the ground, few in history can surpass his record of designing cars, which won 37 Grands Prix, not to mention the American Championship. Maurice's outstanding record as both a

The V8 Alfa Romeo engine that may have originated as a Ferrari design in the mid-eighties.

Robert Guerrero never achieved the breakthrough in Formula One that he deserved but enjoyed a good record of success in CART racing before he was signed up to drive the March-Alfa Romeo.

creative designer and a pragmatic engineer seemed the best guarantee possible for March's future in CART but. . .

Nick Wirth, who had left March to set up his own design consultancy, was contracted on a part-time basis to continue development and later it was announced that former Lotus designer, John Baldwin, would take charge of the project.

In Formula One, the March Racing CG891 was given its designation in memory of Cesare Gariboldi, a man who had influenced the team by his humour and honesty. It was said to be the most expensive racing car ever built and featured a new narrow-angle Judd engine, exclusive to March, as part of its package. It was sensational in qualifying in Mexico in Capelli's hands, less impressive at Phoenix and Montreal, but one cannot know what the future will hold.

It followed the broad lines of the 881 except that some of the rigidity had been taken out of the tub to make it a better compromise between fast and slow circuits, and the rear springs and shock absorbers were mounted over the gearbox instead of alongside because in 1988 the dampers had become too warm in their original location (due to heat from the engine's exhaust pipes) and had lost performance after a few laps. The real advance, however, was in the aerodynamics, and while the layman could see the difference if the 881 and CG891 were side by side, he would not know why the CG891 was superior. It suffered from unreliability in its early races, in particular the oil reservoir/gearbox casing was not strong enough, but that was soon fixed. As in 1988, the team was expecting to go much better on the speed circuits which predominate in the latter part of the season, for its strength is in its shape.

In June 1989, the models for next year's car were being built and work was proceeding with John Judd for a new engine, and while that was the team's 1990 base line, if, say, Honda offered an engine deal it might be accepted. That is no reflection on John Judd's ability, for despite his diplomatic silence on the subject, he has been a consultant to Honda, not the other way around. It was Judd who made the Honda V6 engine into the dominant force in F2 but his main constraint is money and, given Honda resources, most feel he could do at least as good a job.

The Leyton March 89B, drawn by Ralph Bellamy, was probably the best engineered car in F3000 in 1989, but an early-season misunderstanding with FIRST over Bellamy's availability for direct consultation led to the Italian team switching to Reynard, but Mauro Monti stayed with Leyton March and his car was run direct from the works. While European F3000 was basically about Lola, Reynard and petty protests (teams once had to have an engineer, now they have to have a lawyer) so depending on the outcome of wrangles, it may or may not have won a race in Europe. Fabrizio Giovanardi's second place at Vallelunga became a win when Martin Donnelly's Reynard was disqualified for an alleged technical infringement and at the time of writing it's still a win, but the appeals procedure has not been exhausted. Despite that by mid-season there was typically only one Leyton-March in European races, a works car for Gary Brabham.

In the two main Japanese series, F3000 and Grand Champion, the cars began the series on the pace and were regular top three qualifiers in the early part of the season, the Grand Champion car taking its first win in July. Since Akiri Akagi is determined to win, and has the wherewithal to back his aims, it is likely that the F3000 project's future is assured for some years to come.

A couple of weeks after *Dynasty II* was resolved, I drove to Robin's house, arrived a little early, and was asked to wait in another room while he finished a meeting. Dave Reeves' car was parked in the drive, so I assumed it was a routine conflab, but when Robin reappeared he explained I had been present at a significant moment in March's history, the end of one era and the start of another. "It was quite an sentimental meeting because I was more or less handing March over to Dave; the time has come for me to stand on the touchline and be available if required, just as Max was there if I needed him, although I shall retain my shares and remain a non-executive director. If I stayed around the place the mere fact I was there could screw things up, as Matt Busby did at Manchester United after he'd retired as manager. The time has come to give everyone a clear run without me hovering over them.

The installation of the narrow angle Judd V8 engine in the 1989 March CG891. **(Nigel Snowdon)**

Front suspension of the March CG891. **(Nigel Snowdon)**

Mauricio Gugelmin at the wheel of the March CG891 in the 1989 French Grand Prix. **(Nigel Snowdon)**

"From here on March will diversify, probably more into the financial services sector with Roger Young as chief executive, while maintaining its motor racing links, of course. As for me, the first thing I did when I decided to move on was to phone Max. . . One thing which is fairly certain is that I shall be involved in a City project outside of racing which, to use the well-worn cliché, will give me a chance to re-charge my batteries."

It appeared at one stage that this story might cover March from 1969 to its liquidation in 1989. Instead it covers the Herd era, and from May 1989 March Engineering entered the Reeves era and March Group PLC the Cowen/Young era. At the works there was a natural feeling of uncertainty surrounding the change-over; the general mood was one of qualified optimism, but everyone had been too close to the edge of the precipice to be certain any more.

It does seem, though, that in five or ten years' time there will still be a racing car company called March Engineering, but, given the changes of direction of both March Group PLC and R.J. Herd, one should not put money on it still being part of the March Group. Things moved at a rapid pace in the two years between March becoming a public company and Robin's departure and it is not difficult to see how, in the future, March the financial institution might be open to a management buy-out of the racing side. Who knows? Who at the beginning of 1987 could have predicted the events of the next two years?

At the end of June 1989, Robin spoke of his options and mentioned one possibility which would enable him to set up a new F1 team for a major manufacturer and he listed the personnel it might involve. He said, "If we set it up, we can't guarantee results, although with the package I have in mind I have no worries on that score, but if I can get the people I want to do it with, it will be *fun* . . ."

This is where we came in, there's a deal in the air, there are possibilities, there's the chance of bringing together Melmoth Motors, Gasper Tobacco, Danny Doodle, Harry Hotshoe, and all the rest. It's the courting ritual which is still much the same as it was in 1969, when four guys each put £2500 into the kitty so they could go racing.

27 Endgame

Nearly 12 years have passed since the previous chapter was written and March now exists only on paper. However, March still exists very prominently in people's minds, and perhaps the reason for this can be found in the sub-title that was used for the first version of this book: *Four Guys And a Telephone*. That is how the story of March began, as a great adventure which still has the power to capture the imagination.

In 1969, four friends each chipped in £2,500 (roughly $4,000) and the following year built 10 Formula One cars – in those days almost anyone could have a go at Formula One. Thirty years on and Robin Herd headed a consortium which wanted to secure the 12th, and last available, Formula One franchise. Robin's consortium was beaten by Toyota by two days in the rush to place a deposit of $48 million in order to secure that last entry ticket to the modern-day F1 arena. As the Lionel Bart song says it: *Fings Ain't What They Used To Be*.

From mid-1989 the story of March divides into several strands. There is the Formula One team, which was renamed Leyton House in 1990 but which, for the purposes of clarity, I will call LH March – that separates it both from March and from Leyton House, the leisure company which owned the team. Besides, the team was renamed March F1 when Leyton House crashed. There is the Leyton March Formula 3000 project, which was run separately from LH March. There are the two Indycar projects, one based in Bicester, the other in Weybridge. There is March Group PLC, the holding company which was diversifying into financial services; there is Ralt and there are other projects which have used the name of March.

The latter includes the March 'superbike'. Not heard of that? Well, nothing much happened, though seven engines were built by Al Melling's company, MCD. This project was originated by a March company owned by Robin and based in Bicester at the old factory.

The problems with the March Wind Tunnel were rectified and it is now owned by Jordan Grand Prix.

In 1989 March was still devoted to production racing cars, even if they were marketed as Ralts. In fact, for Ron Tauranac, the founder of Ralt, life carried on much as before; apart from the fact that he was now part of a larger unit, on the technical side he was left to his own devices.

However, he was not quite left to his own devices all of the time, and he is still scathing about all the pointless management meetings he was asked to attend. You can bet your house on the fact that Ron will never enrol for an MBA. His idea of managing a motor racing company was not to call committee meetings, but simply to design more good racing cars than anyone else in history. I wonder how that theory would go down at the Harvard Business School.

The Weybridge (ex-Ralt) factory became the production centre for March from early 1989, and from that point on March production figures cease to be statistics and become a matter of debate. To give an example, March had made four Formula One cars at the time of the Leyton House takeover. Overnight these became Leyton House Marches and, later in the year, March built a fifth car for Leyton House. Is that a March or is it a Leyton House? We could discuss this from here to eternity.

Though there are clear strands to the story, there is also a lot of confusion. March owned Ralt, and any Formula 3000 car it made had to be sold as a Ralt since Leyton House had the rights to the March name in F3000 for years, and so it goes.

In the summer of 1989, it became known that the motor racing side of March was for sale, and that included Ralt and the Indycar projects. Eddie Jordan was one who took an interest, Chip Ganassi was another, but even more serious was Adrian Reynard, who was also based in Bicester.

Adrian wanted to enter the Indycar market, and buying March, with its exclusive contracts, seemed to offer a good way into what, in 1989, could still be called Indycar. If you use the term Indycar today, unless you are referring to the Indy Racing League, you will be receiving letters from men in suits, but history is history.

The plan was for March Group PLC to divest itself of anything except money or assets, such as buildings, which would generate cash without having to make or sell things in a volatile market. This money would be invested wisely, nay, brilliantly, and make more money. Robin had already had a taste of this through his contacts in the City.

Adrian Reynard wanted March for its Indycar contracts and also because Ralt was the main thorn in his side in the junior international single-seater categories. What he would have done with Ralt had he bought it, not even he knows. Reynard had the backing of Carl Haas, the North American importer of Lola, who was also attracted by the contracts with Porsche and Alfa Romeo. Haas had taken on March in Indycar and had won. His relationship with Lola was not all sunshine, however, and he was ready to back Reynard's takeover in order to compete against Lola.

Documents were exchanged and, to prevent any outsider from guessing what was going on, the names were changed. In this correspondence there was a racing car company called 'Radiant', which was based in Telford Road, Bicester, and was interested in buying 'Magenta', a racing car company in Murdoch Road, Bicester. Reading the documents, you almost expect a man in a trilby to siddle up, ask for a light, and say *'The pink parrot flies tonight'*.

Reynard reached an agreement, subject to the usual safeguards. The clock ticked by, and 24 hours before contracts were due to be signed, Reynard's accountants reported that the product for sale did not square with the product as advertised. Reynard and Haas pulled out and, by then, there was no other buyer in the queue.

If nothing else, the problems at March assisted Reynard, which was soon hiring ex-March personnel. Adrian was able to take all of March's mistakes on board and avoid repeating most of them. When March had returned to Formula One everyone in the works wanted to be involved, and that ripped out the heart of the production side. When Reynard became part of the BAR Formula One team, Adrian told his workforce that anyone could apply for a job with the new team, but only after they had tendered their resignation from Reynard.

Dave Reeves, for one, was secretly relieved when the deal with Reynard fell through. As Managing Director, he was charged with selling the company and he had found a buyer. As a March man for most of his adult life, however, he wanted a different future for the company.

March Group PLC was therefore stranded with making racing cars, though only the two Indycar projects bore the March name. Volume production, on which the company was founded, was in the hands of Ron Tauranac and while Ron was pushing the ironware through the factory doors, and winning races everywhere his cars appeared, profit on a Formula Three car is modest compared to an Indycar.

Ron had been making a comfortable living from his Ralts and, in 1989, 37 Ralt RT33s were made. That's terrific for a small company, especially when you add the profit from the spares, but it's not so good for a PLC. In effect, Ralt's contribution to the coffers represented the sale of no more than four or five Indycars.

March Group PLC, the bright new financial arm of the company, bought a private stockbroking company. It appeared to be doing well and it took the interest of a major bank, which proposed a takeover. Negotiations were successful and contracts were written. The decision to turn the holding company into a financial services centre looked as though it was the right one.

Whereas Reynard had pulled out of buying March's racing car division 24 hours before the contract was due to be signed, the bank pulled out of the deal just 60 minutes before there was to be ink on the dotted line. One of the directors of the stockbroking company, a man who had been in position before March had bought the firm, had been skimming so much money that the business was virtually worthless. John Cowen was forced to perform one of his acts of wizardry and was able to sell the business on.

During March's decline in America, Dave Reeves went over to check out the market. He says, "I found a residue of goodwill towards a March, but it was too late to build a new production car. Then along came Al Holbert, who won the '83 IMSA Championship in a March-Porsche and was then involved with the embryo Porsche Indycar project. He felt that Porsche lacked sufficient single-seater experience to design a top-class chassis, and Porsche obviously agreed because we got the job.

"Then I got a message from Robin to go to Milan to speak to Cesare Fiorio about a Ferrari Indycar. I set off with lovely renderings of the car in Ferrari livery – it was an open secret that Ferrari had built a V8 Indy engine. I arrived at Milan to be met by someone from Alfa Romeo – Robin was *nearly* right. In the car I used a red pen to obliterate the Ferrari badge and Cesare liked the picture so much that he hung it on his wall. It was after we got the deal that I pointed out the modification.

"At the end of 1988 my master plan was:

'89 Porsche Indy + Alfa Indy + F3000 + F3
'90 Porsche Indy + Alfa Indy + F3000 + F3
'91 Alfa Indy + Customer Indy + F3000 + F3

"I always thought the Porsche contract would come to an end in 1990. We had a mixed relationship; we were on the pace in '89, won a race, and Teo Fabi came fourth in the championship. Most people thought the performance was due to the chassis, not the engine, and all the speed traps confirm that.

"In 1990 Teo got only one pole position and one third place. We had gone through a loophole in the rules and, after receiving agreement from CART, had designed an all-composite monocoque. In December 1989 we were told that we could not use it. Basically we had to cover it with aluminium sheeting, so we finished up with a chassis which was too heavy and we were already having to cope with a Porsche engine which was too heavy, too long, not a good shape and not as powerful as the very best Chevy engines.

"Because of a disagreement between a key figure at Porsche and one in the American team, Robin was brought in to engineer the car in 1990, but the last time he had done that was in 1983 and things had moved on a lot in Indycar racing since then. There were some very good racing men on the Porsche side, but they were restricted by being part of a big company. A couple of their men, who were really keen to get on with the job, exceeded 35 hours work in a week, which broke German law and the company was fined."

Dave says that he always thought that the Porsche deal would last only two years, but working more directly with the team, Robin believes otherwise. "In 1990 we had to cover a carbonfibre chassis with aluminium, we had two chassis. Porsche knew that, and also knew we would have a head start in 1991 when we could have an all-composite chassis.

"What killed the project was economic recession."

In 1990, the bottom fell out of the exotic and classic car markets. Porsche's sales took a nosedive, particularly in America, and for a time the company looked to be in serious trouble. Under those circumstances there was no point in running an expensive racing programme aimed at America.

The Alfa Romeo project was somewhat different. Whereas the Porsche chassis programme was exclusive to Porsche, the Alfa Romeo car was intended to become a production March Indycar. Dave Reeves recalls, "Alfa had proposed what seemed like a sensible programme. We would have a learning year using a Phase 2 engine (Phase 1 was its Ferrari parent, the one which is always denied as being originally a Ferrari unit), followed by two years with an all-new, compact, state of the art Phase 3 engine. Cesare Fiorio seemed to have the right attitude, 'Of course we expect to win every race we enter,' he said, 'but we know it takes time to get to that position'."

The running of the Alfa Romeo engine was entrusted to Patrick Racing. March had long supplied cars to Pat Patrick for his American Racing Series so there was a solid foundation there. Or so it seemed, but a lot of the glue in the relationship was the personal friendship between Pat and Robin – Pat is godfather to Robin's daughter.

Dave Reeves tells the story this way: "I am certain that Patrick became jealous of our contracts with Porsche and Alfa Romeo and tried to displace us. Porsche did not fall for it, but Alfa did. Once on the inside, he tried to cut us out, he persuaded Alfa to make changes to the programme which put us at a disadvantage; he interfered with arrangements we had made with sponsors; then there was his switch to Lola chassis at the 1991 Indianapolis 500 and his refusal of our request to do a properly conducted back-to-back test, and so on.

"We desperately needed the Phase 3 engine, but it never appeared and, so far as I know, it was never built. Our deal with Alfa Romeo ruined any chance of us being able to build customer Indy cars."

Pat Patrick seems to agree that the Alfa Romeo engines were sub-standard because he sent two Chevrolet (Ilmor) engines to Italy to show Alfa how an Indy engine should be made. Mario Ilien, one of the co-founders of Ilmor, knows this to be the case because one of the engines was not reassembled when it was returned to Ilmor.

This act on Patrick's part meant he was not able to get his hands on an Ilmor engine once the Alfa project folded at the end of 1991, and he had intended to run Ilmor engines – which were leased, not sold – in 1992. With no engine the Patrick team folded.

For March, the position was further aggravated by the fact that Alfa Romeo did not pay its bills. Dave says, "The two deals which were supposed to put us back on top again went sour for completely different reasons. Worse, we had expanded to cope with the Alfa project so we had either to cut our overheads or else expand our business."

The prestigious Indycar projects had made it seem as though March was going to need larger, more swish, premises in order to impress the sort of people that it hoped to deal with in the future. The hope was that Porsche and Alfa Romeo would be merely the first in a line of prestigious clients.

In 1990, March moved into a smart factory near Heathrow, a factory, indeed, which had once been home to the Beatrice Lola-Ford Formula One team. The original factory at Bicester became used for projects in which Robin Herd had an interest, the Larrousse Formula One team, for example.

With backing from the Japanese March agent, plus key members of the management team putting in their own money, and even putting their houses on the line, the company became March Cars Ltd. At the time it seemed to be a reasonable gamble if only because 81 Ralt RT34 Formula Three cars were made in 1990, and Ralts would occupy the top six places in the British Championship. Outside of Britain, however, Reynard and Dallara tended to have the edge.

Ron Tauranac says, "An accountant put together a package which said that to survive they had to build 15-20 Formula 3000 cars and 50-60 Formula Three cars. They were never going to do it but, because that was the target, they thought they were going to build that number of cars and so they bought in all the stuff to make them. There was a massive amount of spares on the shelves, doing nothing except losing value."

The new management team had lost the thread of the story and were acting as though they were employees of a successful PLC who needed only to put in an expenses sheet for the expenses to be paid. They had not taken on board the idea that the money first had to be earned. Salaries were top-whack, people were flown around the world, and further, there was worldwide economic recession, which is no atmosphere in which to try to sell racing cars.

Clutching at straws, March Cars decided to change tack. Early in 1991, Dave Reeves said, "The obvious market for us is sports cars, for both the World Championship and the Japanese series. In the 1970s we introduced a new type of customer car in Formula One, we did the same for Indycar in the 1980s and we are ready to do it for sports cars in the 1990s. We did have some success with sports cars in the 1980s, only Porsche built more Group C/IMSA cars than we did. We won the IMSA Championship in '83 and '84 and also built cars for several major manufacturers.

"I wish we could afford to build some cars speculatively, but we are at the stage where the next step will eat cash and we can only make that step when someone makes a commitment to us. We have designed our car around the Judd GV10, which is the very best engine available. The March 92S has been designed as a complete turn-key car which will fill the gap vacated by Porsche. We have in mind the private team which wants to be able to buy a fully developed and integrated package; we have not made compromises in the design and technology but it comes with the combined experience of

March and Ralt so it is practical and user friendly. I think it will be hard to beat." Unfortunately, there was no such market for the concept and the March 92S was stillborn.

Only the Ralt side of the company made money, but as has been noted, a Formula Three car does not make a huge profit. Besides, the annual rent on the smart new factory was £350,000. March Cars was bleeding money and before the end of 1992 had been sold.

In order to keep some sense of chronology, we will pick up the story of March Cars after first considering the Grand Prix team. Strictly speaking, this has no place in the story from mid-1989, except for the fact that the team was called March. It was a Japanese team, based in England, albeit at a former March factory, employing mainly English personnel.

As part of Akagi's ambitious plans, it was proposed to build a new, state-of-art factory on a greenfield site. The Bicester connection would be severed and the split from March was emphasised by a change of name from the beginning of 1990. Japanese name, Japanese team, because apart from motor racing Leyton House had no visible commercial interests in Britain.

March Grand Prix had an indifferent season in 1989, the season which saw a blanket return to non-turbo engines. The position was not helped by a severe shortfall in cash over the winter of 1988/89, nor was it helped by the inevitable ripples which follow a takeover.

The March CG891 was a car which worked well on fast and smooth circuits, and was hopeless on others – it was such a contrast to the 1988 car. Nick Wirth, who was number two to Adrian Newey on the 1988 and 1989 cars, reveals why. "The 881 was intended to have a transverse gearbox, but time was against us so we fitted a conventional longitudinal 'box. That meant that there was a pronounced hump at the rear of the undertray and, though we didn't know it at the time, that played a significant part in our success."

It's not the only time that a racing car has been good by accident and it's not the only time that the accident has baffled the design team. At the time Adrian Newey was quoted as saying of the 1990 car, which would be a development of the CG891, "There's no point in building a new car until we fully understand this one." It took time before they did understand it.

The 1989 season had begun brilliantly, with Mauricio Gugelmin taking third in his home Grand Prix, Brazil. That was with a lightly updated 1988 car, however, and it would prove to be the only time in 1989 that a March would finish in the points. More often than not the cars retired, and there was no pattern to the cause of retirement. If your gearbox keeps breaking, you know that you have a problem with the gearbox, but the CG891 would go out in one race with an electronic fault, the next with suspension failure, then an electrical fault, a blown engine, and so on. Worse, the cars were slow in qualifying and at some races could be found on the back row of the grid.

It is fair to assume that the uncertainty surrounding the team contributed to the retirement rate, but that does not explain March's dismal record in qualifying. As Adrian Newey said at the time, the design team did not understand the car. They were not helped by the fact that the usually reliable people at the Southampton University wind tunnel went through a wobbly period.

One understands that it was a blip on the chart of the university's competency and it is understandable. Newey and Wirth had pushed back the envelope and the technology in Formula One was developing at an unprecedented rate. Though it took a little time to realise it, the difference between a car which won and a car which finished just outside the points was due not so much to horsepower, or the talent of the driver, but to how far ahead was the aerodynamic team.

Not long into 1990, Adrian Newey left to head the aerodynamics team at Williams Grand Prix Engineering. Newey's departure was in part precipitated by the team's dismal showing in the early races of the year – neither car even made the grid for round two, the Brazilian GP.

There were other individual DNQs, including one at Monaco, which is not the way to impress a sponsor; sponsors arrive at Monte Carlo expecting to have their egoes massaged.

In Mexico, both cars again failed to make the grid. It should be remembered that the return to normally aspirated engines and the ready availability of Judd and Cosworth units meant that, typically, there were 10 more entries than places on the grid. Unlike today, when teams buy a franchise, with the limit set at 12 teams, in 1990 anyone could turn up and try for a place. Even so, LH March's failure to qualify its cars was humiliating.

Newey's replacement was Gustav Brunner, who was not a superstar, as Adrian has since proved to be, but Brunner was and still is a talented and reliable engineer who is much respected and liked. Towards the end of 1989, Brunner, acting as a consultant, had come up with a new front suspension layout for the CG891 and this had made a dramatic improvement to the front-end grip of the car.

Brunner is a pragmatist, and he drove a straight line through Newey's complex aerodynamics. In the 1990 French GP, Ivan Capelli came close to a victory but was denied it through disintegrating baffles in a fuel tank which caused the engine to cut out through the right-handers. Gugelmin had held second place until his Judd EV engine gave up the unequal struggle with its oil consumption.

The French GP was the highlight of a thin and ragged 1990 season. Brunner was generous in the praise that he gave to the legacy he inherited – which is a clue to why he is so well-regarded. Before he left for Williams, Newey had designed the bits which had made the car work so well on the ultra-quick Paul Ricard circuit, having screwed up on the design overall, but not every designer would be as generous to a predecessor as Brunner was.

Apart from that single race, LH March cars failed to perform at just about every other circuit; the French GP was a blip. Only one more World Championship point was scored when Gugelmin and Capelli were 6th and 7th in the Belgian GP.

John Judd's Engine Developments had provided

Mika Hakkinen at Thruxton in 1990, the year he won the British Formula 3 Championship in his Ralt RT34-Mugen.

Leyton House with units tailored to its needs (the narrow-angle EV engine was exclusive to LH March) but, for 1991, Leyton House would go for a new V10 engine built by Ilmor, which now designs engines for McLaren-Mercedes. A car was run with the new engine before the end of 1990 and on the cam covers the name was not Ilmor, but Leyton House. The team had bought the design.

There were internal problems in the team as certain individuals fought to promote themselves. Ian Phillips, who had been team manager from the start, was absent for a time through illness. When he returned to work, he found that he had been engineered out of his job. Some key personnel left in sympathy. LH March was not a happy place.

According to someone who was close to the team, from the moment Phillips left, LH March became slack. "It quickly became scruffy, you'd even see mechanics smoking in the pits."

Chris Murphy was lured from Larrousse to head the design team, but it was not Murphy's fault that the season was a disaster. There was a new six-speed transverse gearbox and the design was sound, but the components supplied by a subcontractor were not.

As if that was not enough, there was a new engine to run in and develop – it was Ilmor's first foray into Formula One. Add to that all the internal problems in the team, and it is not surprising that LH March did not perform well.

No sooner had the gearbox been sorted than the fact dawned on the team that the front suspension had a fundamental flaw in its design. It was so basic an error that it should never have been drawn, let alone allowed to leave the drawing board.

The CG911 was not quick in a straight line, but it liked fast corners until it reached Estoril. There Capelli had a problem which is probably unique in the history of Formula One – the nosecone fell off. We are speaking about one disheartened team.

Then in September Akiri Akagi was arrested by the authorities in Japan. It was said that he was involved in a 2-billion – not 2-million – dollar fraud. Naturally, he spent time eating prison food, but Robin remains adamant that he had nothing but honourable dealings with Akagi. "It was a hugely complicated fraud and, frankly, I do not believe he was bright enough to have thought of it himself. I believe it was the work of his key advisers and Akagi was the fall guy."

With its main sponsor in the hoosegow, it is a wonder that the team did not collapse immediately, but help arrived in the corporate person of Mercedes-Benz, which was promoting the careers of the drivers in its Junior Team. Michael Schumacher had already been found a seat in Formula One and Karl Wendlinger was eased into the LH March team, in place of Ivan Capelli, for the last two races of the year. It was tough on Capelli, round whom the team had been based from the beginning.

Ken Marrable, Managing Director of the team, took charge and from the beginning of 1992 Leyton

House was renamed March F1. The world economy was still not out of recession, sponsorship was thin on the ground and, no matter what it was called, the team had no great record over the previous three years.

One thing which Marrable did was to sell the Leyton House engine back to Ilmor so that Ilmor could supply other teams, though March remained a customer. It had, however, to defer to Ilmor's number one team, Tyrrell.

There was no money to build the CG921, on which work had begun, so March F1 continued with the 1991 cars. Though there were sponsors' names on the car, the team was largely kept going by the money that the drivers could bring. As soon as their money ran out, a seat was offered to someone else who could pay, which explains why there were four drivers during the season.

Marrable also pulled off some unusual sponsorship deals with businesses local to an individual race. Thus it was that, to the envy of the F1 paddock, the March mechanics lodged in one of Canada's top hotels in Montreal and why, in Hungary, they arrived at the circuit in stretch-limos.

That sounds fun, but the week-by-week reality was that the workforce did not know when, or if, they would be paid. When the team had Leyton House backing there had been 161 employees; in 1992 there were 45.

Testing was almost non-existent, and whereas most teams will throw parts into the rubbish bin after a given 'life', March F1 kept them going as long as they were considered safe.

In Canada, Wendlinger drove superbly to finish fourth, but that was largely because he had all the makings of a top-rate Formula One driver. That March F1 lasted to the end of the season was remarkable, that it then folded was inevitable.

We left March Cars in 1991 with Dave Reeves dreaming about building an off-the-peg sports car. We now come to the endgame.

When March moved into the new factory it unveiled two cars. There was the RT35, which was one of the best Formula Three cars that Ron Tauranac ever designed, and the RT23 Formula 3000 car. The RT23 was the car which was intended to generate the serious money, and initially it looked as though it would fulfil its objective.

Twelve RT23s were sold, a remarkable number for a new car, and it won its second race, at Pau, which is widely regarded as the jewel in the crown of Formula 3000. Jean-Marc Gounon, who won at Pau, also took the flag at the fifth round, at Enna. The organisers there, however, decided that he had jumped the start and issued a one-minute penalty which dropped him to sixth. Gounon's penalty allowed Italian drivers to fill the top four places, yet video evidence shows that Gounon did not jump the start. On the other hand, Enna is in Sicily, where in 1982 the Formula Two Championship had been decided in favour of an Italian – the story is told on page 156. One would never dream of suggesting that the Mafia has influence at Enna, but nevertheless wise team managers tend to collect their prize money in cash.

In the first six races of the year Gounon took two poles, three fastest laps and twice took the flag first. Mike Earle, who ran Gounon, said at the time, "If anyone else came into Formula 3000 and won its second race everyone would say how good it was, but because it's a Ralt they're not impressed."

Ron says, "I was working on the RT35 Formula Three car, the Atlantic car which became the RT40, and also the RT23 Formula 3000 car. There's a limit to how much one person can do, so John Baldwin finished off drawing the Formula 3000 car. When I first went testing with it I discovered a big problem. The bottom of the carbonfibre monocoque had been made with a curve in it so when you tried to fit the flat floor it distorted and so the car was very difficult to set up.

"I went back to the factory and said that the problem had to be rectified, but the production manager said that it was okay, and that it had been passed by John Baldwin, but I'm not sure that John knew this. Basically everyone was in a panic. To rectify the problem would have cost money and held up production, and they were desperate that neither should happen."

What could have been a consistent winner, which could have put March Cars back on course, was reduced to being a car which worked sometimes, unlike the Reynard 91D which was fine everywhere. An update for 1992, the RT24, was engineered by Nick Wirth's new company, Simtek, but only two were sold and only one of those raced – it failed to win a single point.

March Cars built 12 F3000 machines in 1991 and two in 1992. Reynard built 30 F3000 cars in 1991 and 38 in 1992.

The cause of the RT24 was not helped by the fact that after the first round of the European Formula 3000 Championship, the management announced that it was withdrawing from F3000. March Cars was occupying a factory large enough to house a Formula One team, yet hoped to be saved by building cars only for junior formulae.

In Formula Three in 1991, Ralts took first and second in the British and French Championships and the top three places in the German series. Great though these results were, March Cars was facing ruin. Enter Andrew Fitton.

Fitton, once an amateur rally driver, had made his name, and his money, as a company doctor, turning around ailing businesses in return for a stake in them. He built up an impressive reputation in the City and in 1990 *The Sunday Times Business News* had nominated him as one of 'Ten To Watch In The Nineties'.

Fitton had long showed an interest in March, indeed in 1989 John Cowen had even employed him as a consultant for a month. When Cowen had told him that March was going into financial services Fitton's reaction was that he was mad to be thinking of that and that he should be building a group of engineering companies using March as the flagship.

Cowen dismissed the suggestion, but the idea did not go away and Andrew thought that he would like to do that himself. Since the economy was in recession, there

Mika Salo, seen here at Thruxton, made 1990 a Finnish 1-2 season when he became runner-up to Hakkinen in the British Formula 3 Championship, also in a Mugen-powered Ralt RT34.

David Coulthard and Rubens Barrichello fought a season-long battle for supremacy in British Formula 3 racing in 1991. Here is Coulthard in the lead while Barrichello takes a tight line in third place during one of the Silverstone rounds.

were plenty of small engineering companies having a rough ride. As a skilled company doctor, Fitton could buy them cheaply and return them to profit. His businessman's brain also knew that March Cars would soon be on the market.

On top of its other blunders, March's management team had become focused on the company's image and decided that it needed to project a youthful one. Ron Tauranac had just designed the hugely successful RT35 Formula Three car but, with its fixation on image, the management dropped Ron from the F3 programme and brought in Andy Thorby.

Thorby was a bright young designer whose TOM'S Formula Three car had won the four races in Britain in 1991 which a Ralt had failed to win. He seemed a likely candidate, if you were silly enough to drop the most successful designer of production racing cars in history.

There are other points to consider. One is that Tauranac had built a massively loyal following in what was then a 30-year career. Another is that Andy's design for TOM'S, though very clever, was beyond the capability of most F3 teams to run at its optimum. Design of a production racing car, like any product, needs to bear the consumer in mind. The most clever computer program is not necessarily the best for most users.

Ron did not endorse the RT36 and some team managers lost confidence in Ralt, yet the RT36 was still a pretty successful car. The problem was that it was not a good customer car.

One team manager says, "It was okay if you were running a Formula One-style operation, but you can't run a customer car if it takes half an hour to change the battery. You don't get many words out of Ron, but he does know how to engineer cars for customers. The Ralt RT36 should have been billed as 'Ron Tauranac *with* Andy Thorby.' Andy could have done the main work, with Ron just helping him out, showing him how to make a customer car that works within the limits of the testing available, the expertise of the teams running them, and so on. Instead, we finished up with a reasonably good car, with no name to it, which was not a customer car."

Among the Formula Three team owners who defected from Ralt was Glenn Waters, who had been a long-time customer. Glenn says, "I think that the management put up Ron to getting me to visit the factory to look at the car. He looked a bit uncomfortable and quietly said, 'I don't think it's any good'."

Using an RT36, Phillipe Adams was a distant runner-up in the British Formula Three Championship, and that was its only achievement. It was the car which was to send Ralt into a nosedive in the Formula Three market.

One of the constraints which Thorby faced when designing the RT36 was the management's instance that its carbonfibre tub should be made using a male mould. The reasoning behind this was that they could pop out a monocoque every day because it was easier to lay up the material than when using a female mould.

McLaren used a male mould for its monocoques, but the difference was that the March mould was solid and the McLaren mould could be dismantled. Using a solid mould meant that in order to be able to remove the finished tub, the mould had to be tapered. In turn, that meant that the tub was too wide behind the driver's shoulders so the aerodynamics were compromised.

While chasing an imaginary market in a time of recession, the management hired a designer and then put a constraint on the most important elements of any racing car, the chassis and the aerodynamics. It was clear to everyone that fewer cars would be sold in 1992 than in 1991 – the economy was in recession, Ford sells fewer cars when the economy is in recession. In fact, 56 Ralts were sold in 1991, 30 in 1992. The comparative figures for arch-rival Reynard were 36 and 26.

Ron Tauranac's first bespoke Formula Atlantic car, the RT40, came just in time to compete in the last three races of the 1992 Toyota Atlantic series, and it won immediate approval. March Cars Ltd had put their most experienced designer on the North American Formula Atlantic market and he won it, in fact his cars won the Toyota Atlantic series in 1993-4-5-6-7. That was Ron's personal triumph; March Cars Ltd did not survive to see it.

Andrew Fitton re-enters the story. He says, "I kept myself informed of March's situation and eventually received a call from one of the directors suggesting a meeting. He was surprised that I did not ask why he wanted to speak to me. 'How many cars have you sold?' I asked. He told me. 'You've lost £800,000,' I said. He was flabbergasted and said I was spot on. 'I wasn't expecting the call for another two months', I said.

"I enjoyed the cut and thrust of the City, and the thrill of the chase, but something was missing. One of my companies makes air conditioning units and, believe me, when you've seen one air conditioning unit, you've seen them all. I had not really enjoyed a single day at work since I had left motor sport in 1981."

Fitton enlisted the aid of his old rally co-driver Steve Ward. Steve had sold carpets from the back of a van and had parlayed that into the Steve Ward chain of carpet warehouses. He had sold his business at the peak of the market and had gone off to California to live a life of leisure. His old friend's suggestion that he might like to run March and Ralt appealed to the romantic in Steve and he returned to England.

Fitton made some sound decisions. For a start he moved the company to a smaller unit in Wokingham and saved more than £250,000 in rent. Since he bought March Cars lock, stock and barrel, he also bought pictures and trophies which had once decorated the reception area in March's Bicester factory. Walking into the Wokingham factory was like stepping back four years in time.

Then he trimmed down the design staff. He inherited no fewer than three chief designers and whittled them down to one, Chris Radage, while keeping on Ron as a consultant. He also decided that he would not make spares for previous cars built by March, the deal was that if anyone wanted a spare part, they could buy a copy of the original blueprint. That was a clever move – March had made nearly 1,500 cars and many were reappearing in

Rubens Barrichello in the process of adding more championship points at Donington Park on his way to the 1991 Formula 3 Championship with his Ralt RT35-Mugen.

Historic racing.

At the beginning of 1993, Ralt suffered its biggest humiliation ever. Ron was given the task of designing the RT37 which actually came down to putting together whatever components were in the March spares bin, which included the unloved monocoque of the RT36.

Ron says, "Steve Ward insisted that I had to use the RT36 monocoque because they had eight in stock. I told Steve it was a loser in the first place, the composite work wasn't good enough on the leftovers and they weren't properly engineered."

Ward insisted, but predictably the RT37 was a disaster. For a start, only four were sold, and possibly only two raced – three times apiece. Had Ron been given a free hand, there is no doubt that old customers would have returned. The word got out, however, that Ron was merely a consultant designer to an outfit which had bought the March name, but whose principals were known to nobody.

Edenbridge Racing ran two RT37s in the British Championship, but sent them back as soon as the Dallaras they had ordered arrived. Team boss Pete Briggs – a member of the March workforce in 1970 – refused to pay for them.

In North America, however, the position was different. The RT40 was winning races and 17 would be sold. Fitton thought that he'd got the situation cracked, and even spoke of taking March back to Indycar, nor did he rule out Formula One at some time in the distant future. He seemed not to have grasped the fact that the Formula Atlantic market is small relative to Formula Three and that many drivers use the same car for more than one season.

Buoyed by the reception he received in America, Fitton set Chris Radage on the design of a new Formula Three car, the Ralt 94C. Ron Tauranac was told that instead of being a year-round consultant, he would become part-time. Ron elected to go six months on, six months off.

Radage had a good reputation, he'd worked in Formula One and Tauranac had employed him and rated him. Consider, though, Fitton's decision. He had made March/Ralt a leaner outfit in some ways, but old habits die hard. There were fewer people designing and making cars, but the office staff was disproportionately large, there was even a full-time accountant on board. He brought City mentality to the problem, just like March had done when it became March PLC, but he had only one small market.

Radage had never designed a complete car before, yet he was expected to take on the might of Dallara, which had ousted even Reynard from the Formula Three market. Fitton also had to find customers, a lot of them, to see a return on the £350,000 which he invested in the 94C – at least 60 cars a year would have to be sold just to break even. He is not the only cool businessman so infected by the disease which is motor racing as to lose control over his reason.

In the event, the 94C did not work, it was too pitch-sensitive. Initial testing, in late 1993, proved that

Although David Coulthard won the first of the three F3 Championship rounds to be held at Donington in 1991 with his Ralt RT35-Mugen, he failed to score points in the other two races, both of which went to Barrichello, and had to settle for being runner-up to the Brazilian in the final points table.

the car was impossible over bumps. Fitton had got to know Jacques Villeneuve, who was driving an RT40 in the Toyota Atlantic Championship, and he hired him to run in the prestigious end-of-season Formula Three races at Macau and Fuji. Even Villeneuve could do nothing with the new car.

Despite that, a two-car works team was announced for 1994, a move which, at best, could be described as stretching optimism to its limit. Four races into the British Formula Three Championship it was obvious that there was nothing to be done within the competence of anyone involved with the RT94C, though Ron, who had been edged out of the picture, reckons that the design was retrievable.

March withdrew the cars, leaving two very aggrieved drivers and some very aggrieved sponsors. Had the product been a washing machine rather than a racing car, it would have fallen foul of the Trade Description Act, which says that a product must be fit for the purpose for which it is sold. It was a sour note on which to end what had once been an illustrious history.

Soon afterwards, March was wound up. Andrew Fitton took the March brand and the blueprints. Steve Ward took the Ralt brand, moved to modest premises near Oxford and continued to make and service Ralt RT40 and RT41 Toyota Atlantic cars. There could not be an RT42 Atlantic car because, from 1997, Toyota Atlantic became a one-make series. The contract went to Swift, though existing cars were permitted to race provided they were run in their original specification. As it happens, Ron's 1994 RT41 trounced Swift in 1997, and still won races in 1998.

This edition is sub-titled *The Rise And Fall Of A Motor Racing Legend*. The rise came when the company existed only to race, the decline began when that simple objective became blurred, when March was launched as a public company. March was the first racing car constructor to be launched on the stock exchange and, in fairness, nobody at the time said it was a bad move, in fact the motor racing community was quietly proud that it had happened.

Unfortunately, it was the worst move March could have made, and from then on the decline was hastened first by racing people who did not understand

The Ralt RT41 for Formula Atlantic racing, one of Ron Tauranac's last efforts for his former company, subsequently brought under the March wing, and a car which was still winning races in 1998.

management, then by managers who did not understand motor racing.

March still exists as an icon, however, and early in 2001, Robin Herd told me that hardly a week goes by unless he receives a proposal to use the March name. He is not interested.

Of the three survivors of the original four guys with a telephone, Alan Rees remained with the Arrows Grand Prix team for many years. He is not happy to be reminded of the early days of March. Max Mosley went on to become President of the FIA, international motor sport's ruling body, and there found the ideal outlet for his negotiating skills.

Robin now is far from motor racing. He is a director of Wastec, a company which is developing technology to recycle household rubbish. It has massive financial backing from the United Nations because it promises to solve a crucial problem. Presently most waste is burned, put into landfill sites or piled on tips, none of which is ecologically desirable; measures such as bottle banks merely scratch the surface.

Wastec has apparently found a way of taking mixed rubbish: plastic, glass, paper, waste food, etc, sorting it out and using 90 per cent of it. Robin says, "The Chinese had a proverb a long time ago, 'Waste is something for which you have not found a use'."

It is remarkable when looking back at the 1970 March workforce to find how many went on to become very successful. But of course they did; they were the type of men who were up for the adventure which was to turn a bare factory into the home of one of the most successful constructors in motor racing history. Such men will succeed at almost anything they do.

In fact, one could say that March's real achievement was not so much building racing cars as in offering people a remarkable adventure.

Mike Lawrence, assisted by Robin Herd, who provided the Metro 6R4 and looked after details such as driving the beast, stormed to second overall (quickest on the road but handicapped) in the Mid-Sussex Car Club's stage rally at Goodwood on May 7, 1989.

INTRODUCTION TO APPENDICES

In preparing these appendices, the problem has been not what to include but what to omit. I have had at my disposal March Engineering's chassis list and the period of the company's participation in motor racing is so well documented that it would have been possible, for example, to give the chassis number of a car which finished 19th in a Formula Ford race at Snetterton in 1970 (708/1 went to Mike Spence Ltd for Ian Taylor, 708/2 was Mike Endean's car, while 708/3 was bought by Sonny Eade).

One has to draw a line somewhere and I have given the most detailed coverage to Formula One, listing the race, chassis number, driver, qualifying position, and finishing position or reason for retirement on every occasion a March raced in an International F1 race. I stress 'International F1' for Marches appeared in the (Aurora) British Championship, John Love raced his March 701 in the South African series, and Skip Barber's March 711 ran in Formula A (F5000) in North America.

Coming down a level, in the case of Indycar and European F2 and F3000 I have restricted myself to race wins achieved by March together with the final top six finishers in each championship. The sheer number of cars built for each category (402 F2/3000 cars, 236 Indycars) would make a chassis-by-chassis, race-by-race, record impossibly long, and would fill this book with pages of data which would only be of interest to the sort of person who regards the Albanian telephone directory as a good read.

I hope readers agree that this selection gives a taste of each season without an excess of data. For the same reason, when we go down to such as Formula Three, I have contented myself with the top six in each year's main championships, with comments where appropriate, which should provide a ready guide to the overall season. I have exercised qualitative judgement when giving such as Formula Atlantic results, giving greater emphasis to North American championships than to some British ones which came and went in the Seventies. Additional notes list March's performance in categories which were low on the company's list of priorities.

Specifications of cars are meant as a rough guide only, to help the reader 'place' cars, the art of the designer is such that a car cannot be understood from its spec sheet, had that been the case the March 811, which was a direct copy of the Williams FW 07 might have worked rather better than it did.

To simplify things further, I have not included type numbers except when they do not correspond to the year. In other words, if an F2 March won an F2 race in, say, 1982 then you may assume it was a 1982 model (i.e. a March 822) except when told otherwise. In practice, this happens very rarely because few drivers can win in last year's car, even if the only difference between last year's car and this year's car is the colour of the air-box. If cars with orange air boxes are winning this year then you've got to have an orange air-box to win, which is one of the perennial problems which face makers of production racing cars.

March's early chassis records were compiled by an enthusiast working at the factory and are therefore not official. In preparing this guide I have drawn on March's records, contemporary reports, and as yet unpublished material compiled by the Formula One Register.

In publishing a year-by-year list of production, together with a roll-over total of each type of car made, I have used the March records, but have made my own adjustments and my conclusions vary slightly from the March list. For example, March records state that ten 701s were made, which leaves us with the problem of Mike Beuttler's 1971 car, 701/11, which appears to have been built up from spares using parts from Ronnie Peterson's car, 701/8. There were also, by my calculation, two March 701/6s, which gives us 13, not 11, 701s, while 701/4 ran only in practice with its original tub and had a lightweight (i.e. new) monocoque on the occasions it raced, so this is arguably two cars as well. Where a car has retained its original chassis number but received a new tub I have indicated it thus: 701/6 is the original car, 701/6-2 has the new tub. More complicated combinations are indicated in notes in each year's appendix.

March's own records say four F1 cars were made in 1973, but since these were merely modified 721Gs I maintain no F1 cars were built in 1973, so while they were entered as 731s no such animal existed in the metal, only in the paperwork. The picture become more complicated as, say, 741s were stripped down and rebuilt as 751s, and 751s became 761s, and as a 771 became a 781 and, just to make things really difficult, various 761s were converted into six-wheelers and then converted back again to four wheels.

There is another anomaly and that is the 'unnumbered' tubs which appear in the March records from time to time and which presented a problem until I cracked the code. An 'unnumbered' tub is one which had previously been numbered but had been damaged and later repaired. Thus imagine the surprise of the Frank Williams team in 1977 when it discovered under the black paint of the tub of its March 761 a layer of orange paint which indicated a tub previously used by that great devourer of tubs, Vittorio Brambilla. Does this mean that in 1977 Williams was palmed off with a 1976 tub? Of course not, it was a 1975 tub!

Such riddles disappear when it comes to more recent cars because in the period between March leaving F1 in 1977 and returning in 1981, things had changed so much that monocoques were no longer salvaged, they were junked.

When it comes to the junior formulae I have decided to stick to the March records, which list *entities* (or chassis plates) rather than chassis made, for many of the cars, especially in the early days, had new tubs and frames after being crashed. In the case of the works March 703s, for example, not even the team manager cares to hazard a guess how many frames were used in the season. Damaged frames went back to Arch Motors and serviceable frames were returned, end of story. There is now no way that anyone can discover how many 1970 March F3 chassis frames were made and how many were repaired. There was, too, an exhange deal operating in the early days of the monocoque cars: you took your damaged tub to Bicester, paid the estimated cost of repair and came away with another tub while yours was repaired and entered the exchange pool. It was an imaginative scheme from the customer's point of view, but it does demonstrate some of the pitfalls of placing too much emphasis on chassis plates.

March Production 1969

Type	Description	Number Made	Running Total
693	Formula 3	1	1

693. Square tube space-frame with outboard springs, unequal double wishbone front suspension and rear suspension by radius arms, top links and lower wishbones; one-litre Ford engine, Hewland Mk 8 gearbox; glass-fibre body built by John Frayling; numerous Brabham parts used (seat, pedals, gearshift, steering, etc); front wheels F2 Lotus (Alan Rees spares), rear wheels F3 Brabham (Graham Coaker spares).

This car ran in only three race meetings at the end of 1969. Its best performance was on its début, when, in a top-class field, Ronnie Peterson brought it home third in the F3 final at Cadwell Park on 28 September. It is often written that he might have won save for a puncture, but the puncture occurred during his heat, when he finished fifth. He crashed at Montlhéry and late in the season James Hunt finished tenth in a race at Brands Hatch.

March Production 1970

Type	Description	Number Made	Running Total
701	Formula 1	10	10
702	Formula 2	6	6
703	Formula 3	16	17
705	Formula B (Atlantic) 5	5	
707	Can-Am Sports	3	3
708	FF1600	8	8
709	FF1600 (USA)	2	10
	Total	50	51

701. 'Bath tub' aluminium alloy monocoque with cast magnesium bulkheads; front suspension; outboard coil springs and double wishbones; rear suspension; outboard coil springs, reverse double wishbones, tranverse upper links, twin radius arms later, twin parallel arms replaced bottom wishbones; front track 59in; rear track 59in; wheelbase 95 in; Cosworth DFV engine; Hewland DG300 gearbox; outboard disc brakes (later, rear discs mounted inboard).

707. 'Bath tub' aluminium alloy monocoque with cast magnesium bulkheads and tubular support for engine; front suspension: coil springs and double wishbones; rear suspension: coil springs, parallel bottom links, tranverse upper links, twin radius arms; front track 59in; rear track 59in; wheelbase 95in; 7.6-litre Chevrolet engine; Hewland DG300 gearbox; outboard disc brakes.

All other cars based on March 693 with new bodywork by Specialised Mouldings and all parts made specifically for the range.

March Formula One Racing Record

Team Tyrrell had three cars (701/2, 701/4, 701/7), and in most races all three were tried during practice. From the Spanish GP on, March had 701/6 as the team spare, but see notes after the F1 race results.

South African Grand Prix, Kyalami, 7.3.70

		Q	race	
701/2	Stewart	1	3	
701/5	Siffert	9	10	
701/1	Amon	2	rtd	broken radiator pipe (equal pole)
701/3	Andretti	11	rtd	broken radiator pipe
701/4	Servoz-Gavin	17	rtd	engine

Race of Champions, Brands Hatch, 22.3.70*

701/2	Stewart	1	1	first March F1 win
701/1	Amon	7	rtd	engine

Only 12 starters

Spanish GP, Jarama, 19.4.70

701/2	Stewart	3	1	first March GP win
701/3	Andretti	14	3	
701/7	Servoz-Gavin	12	5	
701/1	Amon	6	rtd	clutch
701/5	Siffert		DNQ	unsatisfactory qualifying system

New rear suspension layout with parallel arms replacing inverse wishbones; Andretti's car was fitted with a new monocoque after this race.

International Trophy, Silverstone, 26.4.70*

701/1	Amon	1	1	fastest lap
701/2	Stewart	2	2	

Monaco GP, 10.5.70

701/8	Peterson	12	7	GP début (Antique Automobiles)
701/5	Siffert	10	8	
701/6	Amon	2	rtd	rear suspension
701/2	Stewart	P	rtd	engine
701/7	Servoz-Gavin			crashed in practice

Peterson's car still had Mk 1 rear suspension

Belgian GP, Spa, 7.6.70

701/1-2	Amon	3	2	fastest lap, new monocoque
701/5	Siffert	10	7	

701/8	Peterson	9	running, but not classified	
701/2	Stewart	1	rtd	engine

Dutch GP, Zandvoort, 21.6.70

701/4-2	Stewart	2	2	new 20 swg monocoque
701/8	Peterson	16	9	
701/7	Cevert	15	rtd	engine, first race for Tyrrell
701/5	Siffert	17	rtd	engine,
701/1-2	Amon	4	rtd	clutch

French GP, Clermont-Ferrand, 5.7.70

701/1-2	Amon	3	2	
701/4-2	Stewart	4	9	electrical problems
701/7	Cevert	13	11	
701/5	Siffert	16	rtd	crash
701/8	Peterson	9	rtd	final drive

British GP, Brands Hatch, 18.7.70

701/1-2	Amon	17	5	
701/7	Cevert	14	7	
701/8	Peterson	13	9	
701/4-2	Stewart	8	rtd	oil line
701/3-2	Andretti	9	rtd	rear suspension
701/5-2	Siffert	19	rtd	rear suspension, new monocoque

German GP, Hockenheimring, 2.8.70

701/7	Cevert	14	7	
701/5-2	Siffert	4	rtd	ignition
701/1-2	Amon	6	rtd	engine
701/4-2	Stewart	7	rtd	engine
701/3-2	Andretti	9	rtd	gear selection
701/8	Peterson	19	rtd	engine
701/9	Hahne	DNQ		private entry

Austrian GP, Österreichring, 16.8.70

701/1-2	Amon	6	8	
701/5-2	Siffert	14	9	
701/3-2	Andretti	12	rtd	crash
701/4-2	Stewart	4	rtd	split fuel line
701/7	Cevert	5	rtd	engine

Italian GP, Monza, 6.9.70

701/4-2	Stewart	4	2	also practised Tyrrell 001
701/7	Cevert	9	6	
701/1-2	Amon	14	7	
701/8	Peterson	11	rtd	engine
701/5-2	Siffert	7	rtd	engine

Canadian GP, St Jovite, 20.9.70

701/1-2	Amon	6	3	
701/7	Cevert	4	9	
701/8	Peterson	16	14	
701/5-2	Siffert	14	rtd	engine

Stewart used Tyrrell 001 from Canada on.

United States GP, Watkins Glen, 4.10.70

701/1-2	Amon	5	5	
701/5-2	Siffert	23	9	
701/8	Peterson	15	11	
701/7	Cevert	17	rtd	lost wheel

Mexican GP, Mexico City, 25.10.70

701/1-2	Amon	5	4	
701/7	Cevert	9	rtd	engine
701/5-2	Siffert	16	rtd	engine

Drivers' Championship:

1,	Rindt (Lotus)	45
2,	Ickx (Ferrari)	40
3,	Regazzoni (Ferrari)	33
5=	*Stewart*	*25*
7,	*Amon*	*23*
15=	*Andretti*	*4*
19=	*Servoz-Gavin*	*2*
22=	*Cevert*	*1 pt*

Constructors' Championship:

1,	Lotus	59
2,	Ferrari	52
3,	*March*	*48*

NB March's own chassis records disagree with contemporary race reports and there is disagreement, too, among contemporary race reports as to the occasions on which Stewart used 701/2 and 701/4. In fact, 701/4 was never raced in its original spec, although it appeared in practice, but its racing history was undertaken with a 20 swg monocoque, thus I have chosen to give it the designation 701/4-2.

After Siffert crashed in the French GP, 701/5 was given a new monocoque, but this was the tub which had been originally fitted to 701/1, which had been repaired after Amon had damaged it in practice for Monaco. 701/1 received a new monocoque for the Belgian GP and this has been designated 701/1-2. Siffert's car with the tub from 701/1 has been given the designation 701/5-2, but it could be argued that 701/5 disappeared and that the car which Jo Siffert drove after the French GP was actually 701/1 and 701/1-2 was a new car.

European Formula Two Championship

1,	Clay Regazzoni	Tecno-Cosworth	44
2,	Derek Bell	Brabham-Cosworth	35
3,	Emerson Fittipaldi	Lotus-Cosworth	25
4=	Ronnie Peterson	March-Cosworth	14
	Dieter Quester	BMW	14
6=	François Cevert	Brabham-Cosworth	9
	Tetsu Ikuzawa	Lotus-Cosworth	9
	Robin Widdows	Brabham-Cosworth	9

No driver of a March car scored an outright win, the best finish of the year was Peterson's third at Hockenheim in October, where he took pole position. He also finished sixth at Rouen, fifth at Tulln-Langen-Lebarn and fourth at Imola. The best private effort was Stommelen's sixth in the April Hockenheim race.

Apart from the eight Championship rounds, there were many other F2 races, with some of them attracting top-class fields. The only March win came in the F2 German GP, when Xavier Perrot (March-Cosworth) won from Hannelore Werner (March-Cosworth), which remains the highest place a female driver has achieved in an international F2 race. Despite the title, the 1970 F2 German GP did not attract a top-class entry.

Formula Three

No March won an F3 race in 1970. Wolfgang Bulow, Harald Ertl and Wilheim Deutsch came second, third, and fourth at the Nürburgring in April and Deutsch took a couple of third places later in the year in Germany.

In Britain, Dave Morgan took three second places and three thirds, and Tom Walkinshaw in a works car also scored a third place before injury cut short his season.

Sports Cars

Helmut Kelleners drove a 7.6-litre March 707-Chevrolet in the Interserie Championship, won at Croft and Hockenheim and finished third overall behind two Porsche 917s. In was on the pace, and often led races, but was dogged by unreliability. Kelleners also won a combined Groups 5, 6 & 7 race on the South Circuit of the Nürburgring and a race at Neubiberg. Chris Amon had a 707-Chevrolet in the Can-Am Championship for the last three rounds and took a fifth and two fourths.

Formula Ford

March owners had a mixed season with the most successful driver being Ian Taylor in a car loaned to him (he was a friend of Graham Coaker's) and entered by Mike Spence Ltd. Taylor won an international event at Hockenheim and half a dozun races in Britain, but his wins tended to be at minor meetings. Bill Stone won three races in his modified 708.

March Production 1971

Type	Description	Number Made	Running Total
701	Formula 1	1	11*
711	Formula 1	7	18
712M	Formula 2 (Monocoque)	20	26
713M	Formula 3 (Monocoque)	11	28
713S	Formula 3 (Space-frame)	9	37
717	Can-Am Sports	0	3**
718	FF1600	4	14
719	FF1600 (USA)	3	17
71B	Formula Atlantic/B	13	18
	Total	68	119

* 701/11 built up from spares and bits and pieces from Ronnie Peterson's car (701/8) for *Mordaunt Clarke Racing with Alistair Guthrie* who entered Mike Beuttler in F1.

** March's records have the 717 as a new car, but in fact it was Kelleners' 707 given an up-date.

711. 'Full' aluminium alloy monocoque with steel and Dural bulkheads; front suspension: inboard coil springs, double wishbones, rocker arms; rear suspension: upper trailing arms, short tranverse links, lower wishbones, outboard coil springs; front track 60in; rear track 60in; wheelbase 96in; Cosworth DFV or Alfa Romeo T33/3 engine; Hewland DG300 gearbox; 10½in disc brakes, inboard all round (later outboard at front) with Girling AR calipers.

Junior formulae cars. Choice of either improved space-frame or 'bath tub' monocoque except for FF1600 which had to use a space-frame; front suspension by outboard coil springs and unequal length double wishbones, rear suspension by outboard coil springs, top links, lower wishbones and radius arms; gearbox, Hewland Mk 8 (F3) or Hewland FT200 (Atlantic and F2); outboard brakes; foam-filled fuel cells to meet new regulations; choice of engines, but in practice most used Ford units with the notable exception of Dieter Quester's 712-BMW; engine a semi-stressed member supported by a tubular structure.

In Formula Three, 1600cc engines with 20mm air restrictor replaced previous one-litre 'screamers'.

Space-frame cars had improved frame drawing from Bill Stone's revised 708 which used both round and square tubes.

March Formula One Racing Record

#Alfa Romeo-engined cars *non-Championship race
++mixed F1/5000

Argentine GP, Buenos Aires, 24.1.71 (run in two heats)*

		Q	race	
701/6	Pescarolo	7	2	(Frank Williams)
701/1	Bell	8	5	(Tom Wheatcroft)
701/5	Siffert	6	6	entered by driver

South African GP, Kyalami, 6.3.71

711/2	Peterson	13	10	
701/6	Pescarolo	18	11	
711/1#	de Adamich	22	13	
711/4	Soler-Roig	25	rtd	oil pressure
701/10	Love	21	rtd	differential

Race of Champions, Brands Hatch, 21.3.71*

701/6	Allen	12	6	
701/11	Beuttler	13	rtd	fuel metering unit (Clarke Mordaunt)
711/3	Peterson	DNP	rtd	broken inboard brake-shaft (Frank Williams)

Questor GP, Ontario, Calif, 28.3.71 (run in two heats)*

701/3	Cannon	15	12	
701/6	Bell	20	15	not running at finish
711/2	Peterson	18	18	
711/3	Pescarolo	14	rtd	collapsed sub-frame after 'incident'

Rothmans International Trophy, Oulton Park, 9.4.71*

701/5	Rollinson	12	5	(Jo Siffert)
701/11	Beuttler	8	rtd	radiator mounting
701/6	Williams, C	crashed in practice		

Spanish GP, Montjuich Park, 18.4.71

711/2	Peterson	13	rtd	ignition
711/1#	de Adamich	18	rtd	c/w pinion
711/4	Soler-Roig	20	rtd	fuel line
711/3	Pescarolo	11	rtd	car would not start after pit stop

International Trophy, Silverstone, 8.5.71 (run in two heats)*

711/3	Pescarolo	21	6	(Frank Williams)
701/11	Beuttler	20	11	
711/1#	Peterson	6	rtd	crash, throttle linkage

Monaco GP, 23.5.71

711/2	Peterson	8	2	revised rear suspension, copper brake discs tried in practice, Peterson's first WC points finish
711/3	Pescarolo	13	8	
711/4	Soler-Roig		DNQ	lost wheel in practice
711/1-2#	Galli		DNQ	combination of driver and engine, new tub
711/5	Barber		DNQ	gearbox problems

Jochen Rindt Gedächtnis-Rennen, Hockenheim, 13.6.71*

711/6	Peterson	7	2	first race for this car
711/1-2#	Galli	10	5	
711/5	Barber	13	6	Gene Mason Racing
711/4	Soler-Roig	16	8	
701/5	Perrot	18	11	Jo Siffert car
701/11	Beuttler	14	13	
701/6-2	Allen	17	rtd	metering unit and fuel leak

Dutch GP, Zandvoort, 20.6.71

711/2	Peterson	13	4	
711/3	Pescarolo	15	13	
711/5	Barber	24	14	
711/1-2#	Galli	20	rtd	crash, revised 'Monaco' rear suspension
711/4	Soler-Roig	18	rtd	engine, 'Monaco' rear suspension

French GP, Paul Ricard, 4.7.71

701/5	Mazet	23	13	(Jo Siffert)
701/6	Max	22	14	(Frank Williams)
711/1-2#	de Adamich	20	rtd	fuel pump
711/3	Pescarolo	18	rtd	split gearbox casing
711/6#	Peterson	12	rtd	engine, high air-box
711/4	Soler-Roig	21	rtd	split gearbox casing

British GP, Silverstone, 17.7.71

711/6	Peterson	5	2	
711/3	Pescarolo	17	4	
711/4	Galli	21	11	
711/1-2#	de Adamich	24	running but unclassified	
711/2	Beuttler	20	rtd	oil pressure, works car on loan

German GP, Nürburgring, 1.8.71

711/6	Peterson	7	5	
711/4#	Galli	21	12	
711/1-2#	de Adamich	20	rtd	fuel injection
711/2	Beuttler	22	rtd	disqualified for entering pits via loop
711/3	Pescarolo	10	rtd	suspension

Austrian GP, Osterreichring, 15.8.71

711/3-2	Pescarolo	13	6	new monocoque
711/6	Peterson	11	8	
711/4#	Galli	15	12	
711/2	Beuttler	19		running but unclassified
711/1-2	Lauda	21	rtd	handling problems, GP début

Oulton Park Gold Cup, 21.8.71 (run in two heats)* ++

701/9	Jarier	22	10	Goodwin Racing Services, F1 début
701/6	Trimmer	14	rtd	crash (Frank Williams)
711/2	Beuttler	5	rtd	fuel injection
711/3-2	Pescarolo	2	rtd	crash, winner of heat one

Italian GP, Monza, 5.9.71

711/6	Peterson	6	2	0.06s behind Gethin (BRM)
701/9	Jarier	23	12	
711/4	Galli	19	rtd	electrics
711/1-2#	de Adamich	18	rtd	engine
711/3-2	Pescarolo	10	rtd	gearbox housing, fastest lap
711/2	Beuttler	16	rtd	engine

Canadian GP, Mosport Park, 19.9.71

711/6	Peterson	6	2	
711/4	Galli	20	16	
711/2	Beuttler	22	running but unclassified	
711/5	Barber	24	rtd	oil pressure
711/3-2	Pescarolo	DNS	accident in practice	

United States GP, Watkins Glen, 3.10.71

711/6	Peterson	11	3	
711/1-2#	de Adamich	25	11	
711/5	Barber	24	18	
711/3-2	Pescarolo	20	rtd	engine
711/4	Galli	23	rtd	broken front wheel and resulting suspension problems

WC Victory Race, Brands Hatch, 24.10.71*

711/6	Peterson	4	16	
711/3-2	Pescarolo	15	rtd	crash

(race stopped at 14 laps after Jo Siffert's fatal accident)

A seventh 711 (711/7) was made as a show car and sent to Sweden.

711/1 was virtually destroyed during the International Trophy at Silverstone, but was rebuilt around an undamaged chassis plate. By any reckoning the post-Silverstone car should have been 711/6 but has to be referred to above as 711/1-2.

711/3 received a new monocoque for the Austrian GP, but since Frank Williams had blanched at the factory price, he had had it made up by Maurice Gomm.

Mike Beuttler's 701/11 was converted by the works to F5000 spec before the end of the season.

Frank Williams's 701/6 received new tub (Tyrrell spare) after Oulton Park crash.

Drivers' Championship:

1,	Stewart (Tyrrell)	62
2,	*Peterson*	*33*
3,	Cevert (Tyrrell)	26
17,	*Pescarolo*	*4*

Constructors' Championship:

1,	Tyrrell	73
2,	BRM	36
3=	*March and Ferrari*	*33*

European Formula Two Championship (European Trophy)

Rouen	Ronnie Peterson
Mantorp Park	Ronnie Peterson
Tülln-Langenlebarn	Ronnie Peterson
Vallelunga (Rome GP)	Ronnie Peterson
Vallelunga (Madunina GP)	Mike Beuttler

1, Ronnie Peterson	March-Cosworth	54
2, Carlos Reutemann	Brabham-Cosworth	40
3, Dieter Quester	March-BMW	27
4, Tim Schenken	Brabham-Cosworth	27
5, François Cevert	Tecno-Cosworth	22
6, Wilson Fittipaldi	March-Cosworth	16

Non-Championship F2 races

Mallory Park	Henri Pescarolo
Monza Lottery	Dieter Quester
Imola	Carlos Pace
Swedish Gold Cup	Ronnie Peterson
Brands Hatch	Ronnie Peterson

Shell Super Oil (British) F3 Championship

1, David Walker	Lotus-Ford	86
2, Roger Williamson	March-Ford	56
3, Bev Bond	Ensign and March-Ford	48
4, Colin Vandervell	Brabham-Ford	21
5, Barrie Maskell	Chevron-Ford	16
6, Jochen Mass	Brabham-Ford	16

Lombard North Central (British) F3 Championship

1, Roger Williamson	March-Ford	90
2, Colin Vandervell	Brabham-Ford	63
3, Jody Scheckter	EMC and Merlyn-Ford	28
4, Alan Jones	Brabham-Jones	21
5, David Purley	Ensign-Ford	20
6, Bernard McInerney	Brabham-Ford	13

Other Categories

Six times South African National Champion John Love ran 701/11 in the South African F1 championship before buying a Surtees TS9, but was usually beaten by Dave Charlton (Lotus 72) and Jackie Pretorius (Brabham BT 26).

Helmut Kelleners used a 8.3-litre March 717-Chevrolet in the Interserie Championship (it was actually his 707 modified by the works), but only achieved one points score, third at Helsinki. Part of the problem came from the overstretched engine, part from experiments with the car's bodywork. Before the end of the season he switched to a Porsche 917.

March Production 1972

Type	Description	Number Made	Running Total
721	Formula 1	4	22
721X	Formula 1	2	24
721G	Formula 1	6	30
722	Formula 2	20	46
722	Formula Atlantic	4	22
72B	Formula B (USA)	20	42
723	Formula 3	20	57
72A	Formula 5000	1	1
728	FF1600 (USA)	6	23
	Total	83	202

721. Revised 711 with more than 50 detail modifications but the same overall layout. Full-width nose replaced 711-style 'Spitfire' wing after first race. Eifelland car (721/4) had special body by Luigi Colani.

721X. 711-style monocoque and front suspension but rear suspension by inboard high-mounted coil springs operating through cranks and levers. Chief difference to the 721 was the gearbox, which used Alfa Romeo internals in a March casing and was mounted ahead of the rear axle line in order to reduce the polar moment of inertia.

721G and 722A. 722 chassis to rear bulkhead with 721 rear end and extra tankage. 60in front and rear track, 94in wheelbase.

Junior Formulae monocoque cars. Broadly the same as 1971, but new bodywork with chisel nose and side radiators; in rear suspension parallel lower arms replaced the former lower wishbone.

Two-litre engines replaced 1600cc units in Formula Two.

March Formula One Racing Record

*Non-Championship F1 race #Combined F1 and F5000 race

Argentine GP, Buenos Aires, 23.1.72

		Q	race	
721/1	Peterson	10	6	driver ill during meeting
721/3	Pescarolo	15	8	(Frank Williams)
721/2	Lauda	22	11	

South African GP, Kyalami, 4.3.72

721/1	Peterson	9	5	new bodywork
721/2	Lauda	21	7	last race for this chassis
721/3	Pescarolo	22	11	
721/4	Stommelen	24	13	Eifelland
711/3-2	Pace	25	17	Frank Williams

Race of Champions, Brands Hatch, 19.3.72*

721/4	Stommelen	12	10	
721X/1	Peterson	8	11	first appearance of 721X, delayed by loose wheel

Brazilian GP, Interlagos, 30.3.72*

721/1	Peterson	3	2	no clutch, slow puncture
711/2	Bueno	10	6	last classified runner
721/3	Pescarolo	8	rtd	jammed throttle, lap 1
711/3-2	Pace	7	rtd	jammed throttle, lap 1

Only 12 starters

International Trophy, Silverstone, 23.4.72#

721/3	Pescarolo	7	rtd	overheating

Spanish GP, Jarama, 1.5.72

711/3-2	Pace	16	6	
721/3	Pescarolo	19	11	
721/4	Stommelen	17	rtd	crashed
721X/1	Lauda	25	rtd	sticking throttle
721X/2	Peterson	9	rtd	differential
721G/1	Beuttler	DNQ		first appearance of 721G

Monaco GP, 14.5.72

721/4	Stommelen	25	10	
721X/2	Peterson	15	11	ZF differential replaced Weismann
721G/1	Beuttler	23	13	
721X/1	Lauda	22	16	
711/3-2	Pace	24	17	
721/3	Pescarolo	9	rtd	crash

Oulton Park Gold Cup, 29.5.72*

721X/2	Peterson	9	rtd	crash, 721 rear suspension and Hewland FG400 gearbox internals

Belgian GP, Nivelles, 4.6.72

711/3-2	Pace	11	5	
721X/2	Peterson	14	9	last race for 721X
721/4	Stommelen	20	11	
721X/1	Lauda	25	12	
721/3	Pescarolo	19	16	throttle problems
721G/1	Beuttler	22	rtd	drive-shaft

GP Republica Italiana, Vallelunga, 18.6.72*

721G/1	Beuttler	6	5	
721/1	Lauda	4		crashed in practice
721/3	Pescarolo		rtd	broken front wishbone when second

Only seven starters

French GP, Clermont-Ferrand, 2.7.72

721G/3	Peterson	9	5	works switched to 721G
721/4	Stommelen	15	16	
711/3-2	Pace	11	rtd	engine
721G/1	Beuttler	24	rtd	ran out of fuel
721G/2	Lauda	23	rtd	drive-shaft, car became team spare
721/3	Pescarolo			crashed in practice, driver blinded by dust.

British GP, Brands Hatch, 15.7.72

721G/3	Peterson	8	7	spun from fourth place two laps from home when engine cut due to fuel problems
721G/4	Lauda	19	9	
721/4	Stommelen	25	10	
721G/1	Beuttler	23	13	
711/3-2	Pace	13	rtd	broken differential

German GP, Nürburgring, 30.7.72

721G/3	Peterson	4	3	highest WC finish of 1972
721G/1	Beuttler	27	8	
711/3-2	Pace	11		running but unclassified
721G/4	Lauda	24	rtd	leaking fuel tank
721/3-2	Pescarolo	9	rtd	crashed, new monocoque
721/4	Stommelen	14	rtd	electrics

Austrian GP, Österreichring, 13.8.72

721G/4	Lauda	22	10	
721G/3	Peterson	11	12	low fuel pressure
721/4	Stommelen	17	15	
711/3-2	Pace	18		running but unclassified
721G/1	Beuttler	24	rtd	fuel metering unit
721/3-2	Pescarolo			crashed in practice

Italian GP, Monza, 10.9.72

721G/3	Peterson	24	9	
721G/1	Beuttler	25	10	
721G/4	Lauda	20	13	
711/3-2	Pace	18	rtd	crash
721/3-2	Pescarolo	DNQ		

Canadian GP, Mosport Park, 24.9.72

711/3-1	Pace	18	9	not running at end
721/3-2	Pescarolo	21	13	
721G/1	Beuttler	24	15	
711/6	Barber	22	running but unclassified	
721G/3	Peterson	3	rtd	crashed in second place
721G/4	Lauda	19	disqualified for receiving outside assistance to restart after throttle jammed.	

United States GP, Watkins Glen, 8.10.72

721G/3	Peterson	26	4	
721G/1	Beuttler	21	13	
721/3-2	Pescarolo	22	14	
711/6	Barber	20	16	
721G/4	Lauda	25	19	fuel injection problems
711/3-2	Pace	15	rtd	throttle linkage

John Player Challenge Trophy Race, Brands Hatch, 22.10.72*

721/4	Watson	10	6	(Hexagon) rebodied, Watson's F1 début
721G/3	Peterson	2	8	led early stages
721G/1	Beuttler	16	11	
721/3-2	Pescarolo	13	rtd	accident damage
721G/5	Migault	crashed in practice, first and only race for car		

721G/5 was used by Daniel Rouveyran as a hill-climb car in 1973.
761G/6 was built as a show car and sent to Sweden.

Drivers' Championship:

1,	Fittipaldi (Lotus)	61
2,	Stewart (Tyrrell)	45
3,	Hulme (McLaren)	39
9,	*Peterson*	*12*
18,	*Pace*	*3*

Constructors' Championship:

1,	Lotus	61
2,	Tyrrell	51
3,	McLaren	47
6,	*March*	*15*

Rothmans 50,000 (Brands Hatch, Formula Libre)

711/3-2	Pescarolo	5	3	
721G/2	Purley	13	rtd	engine fire

European Formula Two Championship

Outright Wins

Thruxton Peterson

Maximum Points Finishes (non-graded drivers)

Thruxton Lauda
Enna Depailler

1, Mike Hailwood	Surtees-Cosworth	55
2, Jean-Pierre Jaussaud	Brabham-Cosworth	37
3, Patrick Depailler	March-Cosworth and Elf-Cosworth	27
4, Carlos Reutemann	Brabham-Cosworth	26
5, Niki Lauda	March-Cosworth	24
6, David Morgan	Brabham-Cosworth and Tui-Cosworth	23

Niki Lauda won the (British) John Player Championship from Ronnie Peterson, both in March-Cosworths. This combined results from the three British rounds of the European F2 Championship plus two races at Oulton Park, the second one receiving double points. Lauda won the poorly supported first Oulton Park race, came second at Mallory Park and in the second Oulton Park race, and third at Thruxton. Peterson won both Thruxton and the second Oulton Park event.

Jochen Mass won the non-Championship Eifelrennen (Nürburgring) in a March-Cosworth.

Shell Super Oil (British) F3 Championship

1, Roger Williamson	March and GRD-Ford	78
2, Colin Vandervell	Ensign-Ford	44
3, Jacques Coloun	Martini-Ford	26
4, Mike Walker	Ensign-Ford	23
5, Rikki von Opel	Ensign-Ford	21
6, Tony Brise	Brabham and GRD-Ford	18

Lombard North Central (British) F3 Championship

1, Rikki von Opel	Ensign-Ford	61
2, Tony Brise	Brabham and GRD-Ford	55
3, Andy Sutcliffe	GRD-Ford	53
4, Roger Williamson	March and GRD-Ford	30
5, Damian Magee	Palliser and Brabham-Ford	24
6, Bob Evans	March-Ford	21

Forward Trust (British) F3 Championship

1, Roger Williamson	GRD-Ford	50
2, Rikki von Opel	Ensign-Ford	48
3, Mike Walker	Ensign-Ford	46
4, Tony Brise	Brabham and GRD-Ford	18
5, Barrie Maskell	Lotus-Ford	13
6, Andy Sutcliffe	GRD-Ford	10

Yellow Pages Formula Atlantic Championship

1, Bill Gubelman	March-Ford	105
2, Cyd Williams	March-Ford	102
3, John Nicholson	Lyncar-Ford	52
4, Bob Sailsbury	Brabham-Ford	46
5, Vern Schuppen	March-Ford	44
6, Chris Meek	March 712 and Brabham-Ford	40

SCCA Formula B Championship

1, Chuck Sarich	March-Ford	80
2, Tom Outcault	March-Ford	60
3, Bob Lazier	March-Ford	59
4, Dave McConnell	GRD-Ford	50
5, Gordon Smiley	Merlyn-Ford	35
6, Jim Sarich	March-Ford	33

Other Categories

John Cannon ran a 722A-Oldsmobile (the engine was sometimes called a 'Rover' for politic reasons) in FA/5000 and put the car on pole at its first race, at Nivelles. Thereafter the engine appeared not to be on a par with the Chevrolet units which were otherwise standard wear and the car did not keep up with the opposition (mainly Lola) in terms of development. Despite that, Cannon was still a regular points finisher and in a very wet race at Silverstone in August came home a close second.

Xavier Perrot in a 722-Cosworth won six of the eight rounds of the European Hill Climb Championship and secured the title by a country mile.

Nick Williamson (March 712-Hart) won the RAC British Hill Climb Championship.

March Production 1973

Type	Description	Number Made	Running Total
731	Formula 1	0	30*
732	Formula 2	14	60
733	Formula 3	36	83
73A	Formula 5000	6	7
73B	Formula Atlantic/B	22	64
73S	Group 5 2 litre	19	19
	Total	97	299

* March' s own records maintain that five F1 cars were built in 1973, but in fact none were made and the four surviving 721Gs were up-rated.

All 1973 single seater Marches had front-mounted radiators set in a full-width nose cone and the junior formulae cars were further revisions of the 1971 series. F3 and FF cars used new Hewland Mk 9 gearbox.

731. Up-rated 721G with narrower (56in) front and rear (58in) track and longer (97in) wheelbase. New deformable side structures from Spanish GP onward.

73A. As 731 but 60in front track, 61in rear, and a 98in wheelbase.

73S. Built to use up the BMW engines March had to take to get an exclusive deal. Suspension and running gear same as F2 car.

March Formula One Racing Record

Argentine GP, Buenos Aires, 28.1.73

721G/1	Beuttler	18	10	
721G/4	Jarier	17	rtd	gear linkage

Brazilian GP, Interlagos, 11.2.73

721G/4	Jarier	15	rtd	gearbox
721G/1	Beuttler	21	rtd	overheating

South African GP, Kyalami, 3.3.73

721G/4	Jarier	18	13	gearbox problems
721G/1	Beuttler	23	15	crashed

Spanish GP, Montjuich Park, 29.4.73

721G/2	Beuttler	19	7	ex-team spare, updated to 731 spec
721G/4	Pescarolo	18	8	updated to 731 spec

Belgian GP, Zolder, 20.5.73

721G/2	Beuttler	20	11	not running at the end, crash
721G/4	Jarier	16	rtd	crash

Monaco GP, 3.6.73

721G/3	Hunt	18	9	not running at the end, was sixth when engine blew, Hesketh car, up-dated to '73 spec, GP début
721G/1	Purley	23	rtd	fuel leak, updated car, GP début
721G/2	Beuttler	20	rtd	engine
721G/4	Jarier	14	rtd	gearbox

Swedish GP, Anderstorp, 17.6.73

721G/2	Beuttler	21	8	
721G/4	Jarier	20	rtd	throttle
721G/1	Wisell	14	retired on warming-up lap	

French GP, Paul Ricard, 1.7.73

721G/3	Hunt	14	6	
721G/2	Wisell	22	rtd	fuel leak, overheating
721G/4	Jarier	7	rtd	drive shaft

British GP, Silverstone, 14.7.73

721G/3	Hunt	11	4	fastest lap
721G/2	Beuttler	23	11	
721G/4	Williamson	21	rtd	involved in multiple crash
721G/1	Purley	15	crashed in practice	

Dutch GP, Zandvoort, 29.7.73

721G/3	Hunt	7	3	revised bodywork
721G/1	Purley	21	rtd	stopped to help Roger Williamson
721G/2	Beuttler	23	rtd	electrics
721G/4	Williamson	18	fatal accident caused by a tyre	

German GP, Nürburgring, 5.8.73

721G/1	Purley	23	15
721G/2	Beuttler	20	16

Austrian GP, Österreichring, 19.8.73

721G/1	Jarier	10	rtd	engine
721G/2	Beuttler	11	rtd	crashed, hit from behind
721G/3	Hunt	9	rtd	fuel system

Italian GP, Monza, 9.10.73

721G/1	Purley	24	9	
721G/2	Beuttler	12	rtd	gear lever
721G/3	Hunt	crashed in practice		

Canadian GP, Mosport Park, 23.9.73

721G/3	Hunt	15	7	
721G/1	Jarier	22	19	
721G/2	Beuttler	20	rtd	engine

United States GP, Watkins Glen, 7.10.73

721G/3	Hunt	4	2	0.668s behind, fastest lap
721G/2	Beuttler	26	10	
721G/1	Jarier	17	11	not running at the finish, crashed two laps from home when lying seventh

Drivers' Championship:

1,	Stewart (Tyrrell)	71
2,	Fittipaldi (Lotus)	55
3,	Peterson (Lotus)	52
8,	*Hunt*	*14*

Constructors' Championship:

1,	Lotus	92
2,	Tyrrell	82
3,	McLaren	58
5,	*March*	*14*

European Formula Two Championship

Mallory Park	Jean-Pierre Jarier
Hockenheim	Jean-Pierre Jarier
Nivelles	Jean-Pierre Jarier
Rouen	Jean-Pierre Jarier
Monza	Roger Williamson
Mantorp Park	Jean-Pierre Jarier
Karlskoga	Jean-Pierre Jarier
Enna	Jean-Pierre Jarier
Salzburgring	Vittorio Brambilla
Albi	Vittorio Brambilla
Vallelunga	Jacques Coulon

Maximum Points Score (ungraded driver)

Pau	Jean-Pierre Jarier

1, Jean-Pierre Jarier	March-BMW	78
2, Vittorio Brambilla	March-BMW	44
3, Jochen Mass	Surtees-Cosworth	42
4, Patrick Depailler	Elf-Cosworth	38
5, Jacques Coulon	March-BMW	32
6, Bob Wolleck	Motul-Cosworth	23

Japanese F2 Champion: Motahuru Kursawa

John Player (British and European) F3 Championship

1, Tony Brise	GRD and March-Ford	123
2, Alan Jones	GRD-Ford	121
3, Russell Wood	March-Ford	119
4, Jacques Lafitte	Martini-Ford	112
5, Ian Taylor	March-Ford	78
6. Musami Kuwashima	GRD-Ford	76

Lombard North Central (British) F3 Championship

1, Tony Brise	GRD and March-Ford	52*
2, Richard Robarts	GRD and March-Ford	52
3, Mike Wilds	Ensign and March	33
4, Russell Wood	March-Ford	29
5, Alan Jones	GRD-Ford	25

* Brise took the title with the greater number of wins.

Forward Trust (British) F3 Championship

1, Ian Taylor	March-Ford	64
2, Tony Brise	GRD and March-Ford	42
3, Richard Robarts	GRD and March-Ford	32
4, Mo Harness	Ensign and March-Ford	24
5, Leonel Friedrich	March-Ford	23

Italian F3 Champion: Carlo Giorgio, Ensign and March-Ford

Swedish F3 Champion: Conny Andersson, Brabham and March-Ford

Yellow Pages (British) Formula Atlantic Championship

1, Colin Vandervell	March-Ford	92
2, John Nicholson	Lyncar-Ford	88
3, Geoff Friswell	March-Ford	52
4, David Purley	March 722-Ford	50
5, Ken Bailey	March 722-Ford	30
6, Tom Price	Royale and Motul	29

BP (British) Formula Atlantic Championship

1, John Nicholson	Lyncar-Ford	92
2, Colin Vandervell	March-Ford	79
3, David Purley	March 722-Ford	71
4, Ken Bailey	March 722-Ford	36
5, Tom Pryce	Royale and Motul	32
6, Geoff Friswell	March-Ford	30

Other Categories

March sold six 73A (FA/5000) cars, all of which went to America. The L & M Continental Championship that year was dominated by Brian Redman's Lola T330 and Jody Scheckter's Trojan and the only top six finish a March achieved was Hutchinson's fourth place in the second round of the series, at Laguna Seca.

The European 2 litre Sports Car Championship was a three-way battle between Lola, Chevron and Abarth, who finished in that order in the Manufacturers' Championship. March 73S-BMWs took one second (Hezemans, Enna), two fourths (Serblin, Paul Ricard; Nesti, Misano), a fifth (Turizio, Imola) and two sixth places (Peltier, Clermont-Ferrand; Hezemans, Österreichring). The 73S showed some promise during the winter Springbok Series in South Africa, but with the factory concentrating on F2, the model did not receive the development work which might have kept it competitive. The whole series was dominated by the Ford-Cosworth FVA engine while almost all Marches had the BMW unit, so it remains a debatable point whether or not the main weakness was the car or the engine, or a combination of both.

Jimmy Mieusset (732-BMW) won the European Hill Climb Championship.

March Production 1974

Type	Description	Number Made	Running Total
741	Formula 1	2	32
742	Formula 2	30	90
743	Formula 3	29	112
74A	Formula 5000	2	9
74B	Formula Atlantic/B	13	77
74S	Group 5 2 litre sports	11	30
	Total	87	386

741. New monocoque but built on previous lines, new full-width nose cone, side-radiators, large rear wing mounted further back, wider front track (58in) making it the same as the rear track, and 98in wheelbase. Hewland DG300 gearbox.

All customer cars were up-dates of 1973 models, but the works F2 cars had F1 style nose cones, side radiators, revised suspension geometry and F1 style brakes.

In F3 two litre engines, with 24mm restrictor, replaced 1600cc units.

March Formula One Racing Record

Argentine GP, Buenos Aires, 13.1.74

741/2	Ganley	19	8	first race for March
741/1	Stuck	23	rtd	transmission
721G/3	Hunt	5	rtd	overheating, briefly led race

Brazilian GP, Interlagos, 21.1.74

721G/3	Hunt	16	9	
741/2	Ganley	18	rtd	ignition switch
741/1	Stuck	13	rtd	drive-shaft

Grand Prêmio Presidenta Medici, Brasilia, 3.2.74*

742/2	Ganley	10	6	
741/1	Stuck	11	rtd	gear linkage
721G/3	Hunt	12	rtd	broken wing mounting

NB only 12 starters

South African GP, Kyalami, 30.3.74

741/1	Stuck	7	5	
741/2	Brambilla	19	10	GP début

International Trophy, Silverstone, 7.4.74

741/2	Takahara	13	11

Spanish GP, Jarama, 28.4.74

741/1	Stuck	13	4
741/2	Brambilla	crashed in practice	

Belgian GP, Nivelles, 12.5.74

741/2-2	Brambilla	31	9	
741/1	Stuck	10	rtd	clutch

Monaco GP, 26.5.74

741/2-2	Brambilla	15	rtd	crash
741/1	Stuck	9	rtd	crash

Swedish GP, Anderstorp, 9.6.74

741/2-2	Brambilla	17	9	not running at finish
741/1-2	Wisell	16	rtd	suspension

Dutch GP, Zandvoort, 22.6.74

741/2-2	Brambilla	15	11	
741/1-2	Stuck	20	rtd	crash

French GP, Dijon-Prenois, 7.7.74

741/1-2	Brambilla	16	11	
741/1-2	Stuck	DNQ	see notes for explanation	

British GP, Brands Hatch, 20.7.74

741/2-3	Brambilla	18	rtd	fuel pressure
741/1-2	Stuck	9	rtd	crash
721G/3	Wilds	DNQ		Hesketh entry

German GP, Nürburgring, 4.8.74

741/1-3	Stuck	20	7
741/2-3	Brambilla	23	13

Austrian GP, Österreichring, 18.8.74

741/2-3	Brambilla	20	6	
741/1-3	Stuck	15	rtd	rear suspension

Italian GP, Monza, 8.9.74

741/1-3	Stuck	16	rtd	engine mounting bolts
741/2-3	Brambilla	13	rtd	crash

Canadian GP, Mosport Park, 22.9.74

741/1-3	Stuck	23	rtd	fuel pressure
741/2-3	Brambilla	DNQ		

United States GP, Watkins Glen, 6.10.74

741/2-4	Brambilla	25	rtd	metering unit
741/1-3	Stuck	DNQ		

Drivers' Championship:

1,	Fittipaldi (McLaren)	55
2,	Regazzoni (Ferrari)	52
3,	Scheckter (Tyrrell)	45
16,	*Stuck*	*5*
18=	*Brambilla*	*1 pt*

Constructors' Championship:

1,	McLaren	73
2,	Ferrari	65
3,	Tyrrell	52
9,	*March*	*6*

March 741/1-3 later cannibalized to make 751/4.

French GP – Brambilla qualified in 741/2-2 but crashed it. Stuck, unhappy with the handling of 741/1-2, was unable to qualify in it and Brambilla crashed his usual car before Stuck could attempt to qualify in it, thus Brambilla, the only driver to qualify, raced the only raceworthy car.

European Formula Two Championship

Montjuich Park	Stuck
Hockenheim	Stuck
Pau	Depailler
Salzburgring	Lafitte
Mugello	Depailler
Karlskoga	Peterson (Depailler 2nd, max points)
Enna	Stuck
Hockenheim	Depailler
Vallelunga	Depailler

NB Only non-March-BMW win was taken by Jean-Pierre Jabouille, Alpine-BMW (aka Elf 2) at mid-season Hockenheim race.

1, Patrick Depailler	March-BMW	54
2, Hans-Joachim Stuck	March-BMW	43
3, Jacques Lafitte	March-BMW	31
4, Jean-Pierre Jabouille	Alpine-BMW	20
5, David Purley	March and Chevron-BMW	13
6, Michel Leclère	Alpine-BMW	11

Japanese F2 Champion: Masahiro Hasemi, 724-BMW

Japanese Grand Champion: Masahiro Hasemi: 742-BMW

Forward Trust (British) F3 Championship

1, Brian Henton	March-Ford and Toyota	73
2, Tony Rouff	GRD-Ford	51
3, José Santo	March-Ford	36
4, Alex Ribeiro	GRD-Ford	36
5, José Chateaubriand	March-Ford and Toyota	33
6, Danny Sullivan	March and Modus-Ford	27

Lombard North Central (British) F3 Championship

1, Brian Henton	March-Ford and Toyota	78
2, Alex Ribeiro	GRD-Ford	60
3, Tony Rouff	GRD-Ford	54
4, Josa Chateaubriand	March-Ford and Toyota	32
5, Nicholas Von Preussen	March-Ford	29
6, Derek Lawrence	Ehrlich-Ford	17

Italian F3 Champion: Alberto Colombo, March-Toyota

Prolifac F3 Champion: Giorgio Francia, March-Toyota

John Player (British) F Atlantic Championship

1, John Nicholson	Lyncar-Ford	132
2, Jim Crawford	March-Ford	127
3, Tony Brise	Modus-Ford	101
4, Alan Jones	March-Ford	97
5, Dave Morgan	Chevron-Ford	85
6, Ray Mallock	Brabham-Ford	66

Other Categories

Alpine Renault enjoyed a clean sweep of the European 2-litre Sports Car Championship with its drivers taking the first three places in the final table. Fourth in the series was Jean Ragnotti, whose best result with his March 74S was second in the opening round using a BMW engine, but then, in common with most other BMW users, he switched to Ford for reasons of economy but still managed two-thirds in the seven-race series.

March 742-BMWs won six of the seven rounds of the European Hill Climb Championship with Freddy Amweg and Roland Salomon each scoring a win and Jimmy Mieusset taking four wins and the title.

Mike Wilds (March 74A-Chevrolet) took two seconds in the European F5000 series.

March Production 1975

Type	Description	Number Made	Running Total
751	Formula 1	5	37
752	Formula 2	25	115
753	Formula 3	22	134
75A	Formula 5000	1	10
75B	Formula Atlantic/B	12	89
75R	Formula Renault	8	8
75S	Group 5 2-litre sports	5	35
	Total	78	464

New lower, wider and stiffer monocoque with built-in deformable structures used by F1, F5000 and F2 cars while other single-seaters used the 1971-series narrow tub and all had 741-style nose cone and side radiators, but the body from the nose cone to the front of the cockpit was much smoother. Junior formulae cars had full rear bodywork characterized by a series of notches.

751. Track varied but as narrow as 50in front, 55in rear, longer (100in) wheelbase.

75S. Radical new body which made the, by then, well-handing 1973-series of sports cars perhaps the class of the field, but the 2-litre class had collapsed by the time it was introduced.

Junior formulae cars strengthened at the back with a cast cross-beam in place of previous fabricated beams.

March Formula One Racing Record

In mid-season Roger Penske Racing abandoned its own Penske PC1 and switched to a March (751/5).

Argentine GP, Buenos Aires, 12.1.75

741/2	Brambilla	12	9	only one car entered

Brazilian GP, Interlagos, 26.1.75

741/2	Brambilla	17	rtd	engine

South African GP, Kyalami, 1.3.75

751/1	Brambilla	7	rtd	broken oil cooler, first race for 751
741/2	Lombardi	26	rtd	fuel pressure, GP début, 741' s last race

Race of Champions, Brands Hatch, 16.3.75*

751/1	Lombardi	11	rtd	handling, later rebuilt with new tub

International Trophy, Silverstone, 12.4.75*

751/1	Lombardi	14	12	

Spanish GP, Montjuich Park, 27.4.75

751/3	Brambilla	5	5	half-points, race stopped prematurely
751/2	Lombardi	24	6	first WC (half) point scored by female driver

Monaco GP, 11.5.75

751/3	Brambilla	5	rtd	steering, damaged in incident with Pryce
751/2	Lombardi DNQ			

Belgian GP, Zolder, 25.5.75

751/2	Lombardi	23	rtd	engine
751/3	Brambilla	3	rtd	brakes, led race

Swedish GP, Anderstorp, 8.6.75

751/2	Lombardi	24	rtd	metering unit
751/3	Brambilla	1	rtd	drive-shaft, led race and pole position.but see main text for explanation

Dutch GP, Zandvoort, 22.6.75

751/2	Lombardi	23	14	
751/3	Brambilla	11	rtd	crash

French GP, Paul Ricard, 6.7.75

751/2	Lombardi	26	18	
751/3	Brambilla	8	rtd	rear damper

British GP, Silverstone, 19.7.75

751/5	Donahue	15	5	entered as 'Penske'
751/3	Brambilla	5	6	first race with narrow front track
751/2	Stuck	14	rtd	crash
751/1-2	Lombardi	22	rtd	engine

German GP, Nürburgring, 3.8.75

751/1-2	Lombardi	25	7	
751/5	Donahue	19	rtd	puncture
751/3	Brambilla	11	rtd	puncture & suspension
751/2	Stuck	7	rtd	water leak

Austrian GP, Österreichring, 17.8.75

751/3	Brambilla	8	1	1st WC win for works car, race stopped, half WC points
751/2	Lombardi	20	17	
751/1-2	Stuck	4	rtd	crash
751/5	Donahue	fatal accident in practice		

Swiss GP, Dijon (France), 24.8.75*

751/3	Brambilla	12	11	

Italian GP, Monza, 7.9.75

751/3	Brambilla	9	rtd	clutch
751/6	Stuck	16	rtd	suspension, after incident
751/1-2	Lombardi	24	rtd	crash, brake failure

United States GP, Watkins Glen, 7.10.75

751/3	Brambilla	6	7
751/6	Stuck	13	8

Drivers' Championship:

1,	Lauda (Ferrari)	64½
2,	Fittipaldi (McLaren)	45
3,	Reutemann (Brabham)	37
11,	*Brambilla*	*6½*
15,	*Donahue*	*2**
21,	*Lombardi*	*½ pt*

Constructors' Championship:

1,	Ferrari	72½
2,	Brabham	54
3,	McLaren	53
8,	*March*	*7½**

* Donahue in the Penske March scored 2 points, but these were awarded to the Penske team. Had March been allowed to count these, it would have finished 6= (with Shadow) in the Constructors' Championship.

March 751/1-2 given chassis number 761/3 at end of season.

March 751/3 severely damaged in practice for the US GP (Brambilla) and later cannibalized for 1976 cars.

March 751/4 (originally 741/1) used as spare race car for Lombardi (taken to meetings crated up), formed basis of 1976 test car, 761/5. In 1977 this car was bought and raced by Brian Henton.

March 751/5 written off in practice for Austrian GP, Penske Racing reverted to Penske PC1 for United States GP (John Watson). In practice for the US GP Watson also drove the new Penske PC3, which was based on the March 751.

European F2 Championship

Mugello	Flammini
Silverstone	Leclère
Zolder	Leclère
Nogaro	Tambay
Rome	Brambilla

1, Jacques Lafitte Martini-BMW 60
2, Michel Leclère March-BMW 36
3, Patrick Tambay March-BMW 36

4, Gérard Larrousse	Alpine-BMW	26
5, Jean-Pierre Jabouille	Alpine-BMW	24
6, Maurizio Flammini	March-BMW	22

Non-Championship F2 races

Magny Cours	Leclère
Santamonica	Flammini

Japanese F2 Champion: Kazuyoshi Hoshino, 725-BMW

Japanese Grand Champion: Noritake Takahara

BP Visco-Static (British) F3 Championship

1, Gunnar Nilsson	March-Toyota	74
2, Alex Ribeiro	March-Toyota	59
3, Danny Sullivan	Modus-Toyota	59
4, Patrick Neve	Safir-Ford	50
5, Larry Perkins	Ralt-Toyota	40
6, Ingo Hoffman	March-Toyota	34

Italian Championship: 1, Luigi Pavesi, March-Toyota

Swedish Championship: 1, Conny Ljunfeldt, March 743-Toyota

Canadian Formula Atlantic Championship

1, Bill Brack	Chevron-Ford	112
2, Bertil Roos	March-Ford	94
3, Tom Klauser	Lola-Ford	92
4, Elliott Forbes-Robinson	Lola-Ford	75
5, Gilles Villenueve	March-Ford	69
6, Howdy Holmes	Lola-Ford	59

Other Categories

Despite the fact that March had dominated the previous two years of Formula Atlantic in Britain, only three drivers bought 75Bs and none figured strongly.

In the Shellsport European 5000 Championship, RAM Racing began the season with a Chevron and a number of different drivers. Then it switched to a March 75A powered by a Cosworth-Ford GAA 3.4-litre V6 engine and, driven by Alan Jones, comfortably led at Thruxton until encountering problems which saw it finally finish third. It then won the next two rounds, at Brands Hatch and Silverstone, but in the final races of the year while it was the class of the field while it ran, it usually suffered engine problems. Jones eventually finished seventh equal in a championship dominated by Lola drivers.

Michel Pignard (March 75S-BMW), Markus Hotz (752-BMW), and Jimmy Mieusset (742-BMW) all won rounds of the European Hill Climb Championship, Mieusset scoring two wins.

March Production 1976

Type	Description	Number Made	Running Total
761	Formula 1	6	43*
762	Formula 2	19	134
763	Formula 3	16	150
76A	Formula 5000	2	12
76B	Formula Atlantic/B	20	109
76S	Group 5 2-litre sports	2	37
76S	Group 5 3-litre sports	1	38
	Total	66	530

NB This is the official works figure, but includes up-rated 751s. 751/1-2 became 761/3, 751/4 became 761/5 and 751/6 became 761/2. On the other hand- 761/1 had four tubs during the season and 761/3 had two tubs yet kept their original identities.

761. Stiffer monocoque, some weight saving, wider track front (56in) and rear (58in) wheelbase variable depending on circuit, 100in standard (swb) or 109in using spacer between engine and gearbox. Choice of nose cones depending on circuit.

All other cars up-rated 1975 models with revised rear suspension in which the bottom parallel arms were replaced by a wishbone.

March Formula One Racing Record

Brazilian GP, Interlagos, 25.1.76

761/2	Stuck	14	4	
761/3	Lombardi	22	14	
761/1	Brambilla	7	rtd	oil leak

South African GP, Kyalami, 6.3.76

761/1	Brambilla	6	8	flatted tyres
761/2	Stuck	18	12	
761/3	Peterson	9	rtd	crash

Cars used new, more rounded, nose cones with extended lip; Brambilla ran with larger radiators

United States GP West, Long Beach, 28.3.76

761/3	Peterson	6	10	
761/2	Stuck	18	rtd	crash
761/1	Brambilla	8	rtd	crash
761/4	Merzario	DNQ		

Race of Champions, Brands Hatch, 14.3.76*

761/1	Brambilla	16	4

16 starters

International Trophy, Silverstone, 11.4.76*

761/2	Brambilla	2	2

Spanish GP, Jarama, 2.5.76

761/1+	Brambilla	6	rtd	accident damage to rear suspension
761/2	Stuck	17	rtd	gear selection problem
761/3+	Peterson	16	rtd	transmission
761/4	Merzario	16	rtd	gear linkage

+revised front suspension with shorter wishbones, new air boxes

Belgian GP, Zolder, 16.5.76

761/2	Stuck	15	rtd	suspension
761/4	Merzario	21	rtd	engine
761/3	Peterson	10	rtd	accident, taking avoiding action
761/1	Brambilla	5	rtd	drive shaft

All four cars had new front suspension, air-boxes, and revised rear wing mounting

Monaco GP, 30.5.76

761/2	Stuck	6	4	
761/3-2+	Peterson	3	rtd	crash, spun on oil, new monococque
761/1	Brambilla	9	rtd	suspension
761/4	Merzario	DNQ		crashed in practice

+original front suspension for this race only; all cars ran in swb form

Swedish GP, Anderstorp, 13.6.76

761/3-2	Peterson	9	7	
761/1-2	Brambilla	15	10	new tub, see notes
761/4-2	Merzario	19	14	
761/2	Stuck	20	rtd	engine

French GP, Paul Ricard, 4.7.76

761/2	Stuck	15	7	
761/4-2	Merzario	18	9	
761/3-2	Peterson	6	19	fuel metering unit when in 3rd
761/1-2	Brambilla	9	rtd	oil pressure

British GP, Brands Hatch, 18.7.76

761/3-2	Peterson	7	rtd	fuel pressure
761/4-2	Merzario	9	rtd	drive shaft when in fourth place, set third fastest lap of race,then joined Wolf-Williams
761/1-2	Brambilla	10	rtd	broken front suspension pick-up point after colliding with Peterson
761/2	Stuck	17	rtd	crash

German GP, Nürburgring, 1.8.76

761/4-2	Brambilla	13	rtd	crash, 3rd accident of weekend*
761/3-2	Peterson	11	rtd	crash,
761/2	Stuck	4	rtd	clutch

*Brambilla crashed 761/1-3 (re-tubbed after Brands Hatch) in practice and detroyed the tub

Austrian GP, Österreichring, 15.8.76

761/6	Peterson	3	6	new car, led race, brake problem
761/1-3	Brambilla	7	rtd	crash
761/2	Stuck	11	rtd	fuel pressure

All cars in swb form. Karl Oppitzhauser entered 761/4-3 (re-tubbed after Brambilla's crash), but was not allowed to run

Dutch GP, Zandvoort, 29.8.76

761/1-5	Brambilla	7	6	
761/6	Peterson	1	rtd	led race, oil pressure
761/2	Stuck	18	rtd	engine

Italian GP, Monza, 12.9.76

761/6	Peterson	8	1	lap record
761/1-5	Brambilla	15	7	
761/2	Stuck	6	rtd	crash

Canadian GP, Mosport Park, 3.10.76

761/6	Peterson	2	9	led, handling problem, worn dampers
761/1-5	Brambilla	3	14	
761/2	Stuck	8	rtd	handling problem

United States GP, Watkins Glen, 10.10.76

761/2	Stuck	6	5	
761/1-5	Brambilla	4	rtd	burst tyre
761/6	Peterson	3	rtd	front suspension bulkhead

Japanese GP, Fuji, 24.10.76

761/1-5	Brambilla	7	rtd	engine
761/2	Stuck	17	rtd	electrics
761/6	Peterson	10	rtd	engine cut out

Drivers' Championship:

1,	Hunt (McLaren)	69
2,	Lauda (Ferrari)	68
3,	Scheckter (Tyrrell)	49
10,	*Peterson*	*10*
13,	*Stuck*	*8*
19=	*Brambilla*	*1*

Constructors' Championship:

1,	Ferrari	83
2,	McLaren	74
3,	Tyrrell	71
7,	*March*	*19*

March 761/1 received the tub from 761/3 for the Swedish GP. After a crash at the Nürburgring it was rebuilt with monocoque number 761/10. It crashed again at the Österreichring and was rebuilt with an unnumbered tub. By strict reckoning, 761/1 had ceased to exist on anything but a carnet and its chassis plate. It was then rebuilt as a six-wheeler (non-drivable) for March's press release of its new concept and was then dismantled and used as the basis for March 761B/2.

March 761/2 was converted to a six-wheeler for the concept's first two test sessions. In early 1977 it was sold to Space Racing as a four-wheeler for Brett Lunger.

March 761/3 had a new monocoque, 761/6, for the Swedish GP while tub 761/3 (originally 751/1-2) was used in Brambilla's car, 761/1. It crashed during the German GP and was rebuilt with a new tub, 761/8, for the Austrian GP, where it became the team spare. Sold to John Macdonald in 1977 and modified by Howden Ganley (wheelbase and track increased) for Boy Hayje to drive.

March 761/4 was extensively damaged during practice for the Monaco GP and rebuilt around a new monocoque, 761/9. As 741/4-2 it was crashed by Brambilla during the German GP and rebuilt with an unnumbered tub (making it 761/4-3) and sold to Karl Oppitzhauser.

March 761/5 (née 741/1, 751/4) was converted into a six-wheeler for the Rothmans' Press Day at Silverstone in February 1977 and then re-converted to four wheels and sold to Brian Henton.

March 761/6 (which had monocoque 761/7) was the team spare from early in July until the Austrian GP, when it became Ronnie Peterson's race car. At the end of the season it was used as the basis for 761B/1. In August 1977 it was re-converted to 761/6 for Ronnie Peterson, who shipped it home.

March 761/7 did not race in 1976 but was built using an updated, unnumbered, previously used March 751 monocoque for Frank Williams in 1977.

European Formula Two Championship

Hockenheim	Hans-Joachim Stuck*
Thruxton	Maurizio Flammini
Hockenheim	Hans-Joachim Stuck*
Rouen	Maurizio Flammini
Santamonica	Hans-Joachim Stuck*

**Graded driver, results did not count towards Championship.*

1, Jean-Pierre Jabouille	Elf-Renault	53
2, René Arnoux	Martini-Renault	52
3, Patrick Tambay	Martini-Renault	39
4, Michel Leclère	Elf-Renault	33
5, Alex Ribeiro	March-BMW	31
6, Maurizio Flammini	March-BMW	26

Japanese F2 Champion: Noritake Katahara, 762-BMW

Japanese Grand Champion: Noritake Katahara, 762-BMW

European F3 Championship

1, Riccardo Patrese	Chevron-Toyota	52 (56)
2, Conny Andersson	March-Toyota	52 (54)
3, Bruno Giacomelli	March-Toyota	36
4, Marc Surer	March and Chevron-BMW	13
5, Bertrand Shäfer	Ralt-BMW	12
6, Piercarlo Ghinzani	March-Toyota	11

BP (British) F3 Championship

1, Rupert Keegan	March 743-Toyota and Chevron-Toyota	74*
2, Bruno Giacomelli	March-Toyota	71
3, Geoff Lees	Chevron-Toyota	31
4, Stephen South	March-Toyota	27
5, Mike Young	Modus-Toyota	21
6, Tiff Needell	Safir-Toyota	11

**Although Keegan switched to a Chevron B34 in July, four of his seven F3 wins (both British Championships) were achieved with his March 743.*

Shellsport (British) F3 Championship

1, Bruno Giacomelli	March-Toyota	79
2, Rupert Keegan	March 743-Toyota and Chevron-Toyota	62
3, Geoff Lees	Chevron-Toyota	42
4, Mike Young	Modus-Toyota	36
5, Ian Flux	Ralt-Toyota	29
6, Stephen South	March-Toyota	21

IMSA (USA) Formula Atlantic Championship

1, Gilles Villenueve	March-Ford	80
2, Price Cobb	March-Ford	45
3, Elliott Forbes-Robinson	Tui-Ford	45
4, Bobby Brown	Chevron-Ford	41
5, Tom Klausler	Lola-Ford	38
6, Johnny Gerber	Chevron-Ford	22

Canadian Formula Atlantic Championship

1, Gilles Villeneuve	March-Ford	120
2, Bertil Roos	Ralt-Ford	72
3, Bill Brack	Chevron-Ford	67
4, Price Cobb	March-Ford	66
5, Tom Klausler	Lola-Ford	58
6, Bobby Rahal	March-Ford	57

Other Categories

In the Shellsport 5000 Championship Damien Magee (March 75A-Cosworth GAA) won two rounds and finished runner-up in the series to David Purley (Chevron B30-Cosworth GAA) and Ray Mallock won a round at Snetterton in a 75B-BDX.

Ian Scheckter won the South African F Atlantic Championship in his 76B-Ford.

Stanislave Sterzel ran a 75S-BMW entered by Walter Wolf in the World Championship for Sports Cars, pairing with 'Gimax' in the longer events. Sterzel came sixth in the Nürburgring 300 Km and, with 'Gimax', third in the Coppa Florio. Other Marches appeared intermittently without distinguishing themselves and it was largely thanks to Sterzel that March finished sixth of 12 marques in the overall Championship and fourth of eight marques in the 2-litre category.

Pierre Maublanc, Michel Pignard, Markus Hotz and Jimmy Mieusset all won rounds of the European Hill Climb Championship in 762-BMWs.

March Production 1977

Type	Description	Number Made	Running Total
771	Formula 1	2	45
761B	Formula 1	2	47*
240	Formula 1	0	**
772	Formula 2	8	142
772P	Formula 2	21	44
773	Formula 3	18	138
77B	Formula Atlantic/B	29	138
	Total	61	591

*Three 761Bs were raced in 1977, but 761B/1 was built from 761/6 and was reconverted to 761/6 for Ronnie Peterson to keep after the 1977 Austrian GP. 761B/2 was made from 761/1-5 which ended 1976 with tub 761/10.

**Six-wheeler, 2 extra rear wheels added to existing 761(s), therefore car made but does not appear in production figures. For full details of chassis used, see notes in the 1976 appendix.

761B. Up-rated 761 with improved twin-caliper brakes, revised uprights, and a shorter wheelbase (98.4in).

771. New, wider, monocoque, fuel carried more to the centre of the car, front-mounted radiator, 104.3in wheelbase.

2.4.0. Front track 56in, rear track 69.8in, wheelbase 97.4in to first rear axle line, 121in to second rear axle line.

72P. F2 car run by the works using the narrow (pre-1975) Formula Atlantic tub.

782. Does not appear in March production figures for 1977 as a separate entity but prototype car (one of the two 77Ps) was used by Bruno Giacomelli to win the final round of the European Championship at Donington.

All other cars uprated 1976 models.

March Formula One Racing Record

Argentine GP, Buenos Aires, 9.1.77

761B/2	Ribeiro	20	rtd	gearbox
761B/1I.	Scheckter	17	rtd	battery lead disconnected

Only 21 starters

Brazilian GP, Interlagos, 23.1.77

761B/1I.	Scheckter	17	rtd	final drive, oil line fracture
761B/2	Ribeiro	21	rtd	engine, dropped valve

South African GP, Kyalami, 5.3.77

761/2	Lunger	23	14	Space Racing
761/3-3	Hayje	21	rtd	gearbox, RAM Racing
761B/1	Stuck	18	rtd	engine, substituting for Ian Scheckter (injured in F. Atlantic race)
761B/2	Ribeiro	17	rtd	engine

United States GP West, Long Beach, 3.4.77

761B/1	Henton	18	10	substituting for Ian Scheckter
761/2	Lunger	21	rtd	crash
J761B/2	Ribeiro	22	rtd	loss of gearbox oil

Race of Champions, Brands Hatch, 19.3.77*

761/5	Henton	10	4	British F1 Racing Team
761/3-3	Hayje	12	7	
761B/3	Ribeiro	15	rtd	electrics

16 starters

Spanish GP, Jarama, 8.5.77

761/2	Lunger	25	10	
761B/1	I. Scheckter	17	11	
761/7	Neve	22	12	Frank Williams car
761B/2	Merzario	21	rtd	damaged nose section (private entry)
761B/3	Ribeiro	DNQ		
761/3-3	Hayje	DNQ		
761/5	Henton	DNQ		

After this race Brett Lunger switched to a McLaren M23

Monaco GP, 22.5.77

761B/3	Ribeiro	DNQ	accident
761B/1	I. Scheckter	DNQ	earlier accident injury exacerbated by minor shunt, driver withdrew, also drove 771/1 in practice
761B/2	Merzario	DNQ	
761/3-3	Hayje	DNQ	

Belgian GP, Zolder, 5.6.77

761/7-2	Neve	24	10	
761B/2	Merzario	14	14	
761/3-3	Hayje	27		running but unclassified
761B/1	I.Scheckter	21	rtd	crash
761B/3	Ribeiro	DNQ		
761/5	de Dryver	DNQ		Brian Henton' s car

Swedish GP, Anderstorp, 19.6.77

761/7-2	Neve	20	15	
761B/1	I. Scheckter	21	rtd	broken CV joint
761B/3-2	Ribeiro	DNQ		
761/3-3	Hayje	DNQ		
761/8	Kozarowitsky	DNQ		RAM Racing

French GP, Dijon-Prenois, 3.7.77

761B/1	I. Scheckter	20	running but unclassified	
761B/2	Merzario	18	rtd	gearbox
761/7-2	Neve	DNQ		
761B/3-2	Ribeiro	DNQ		

British GP, Silverstone, 16.7.77

761/7-2	Neve	26	10	
761B/1	I. Scheckter	24	rtd	crash
761B/2	Merzario	17	rtd	drive shaft
761B/3-2	Ribeiro	DNQ		
761/5	Henton	DNQ		
761/3-3	Sutcliffe	DNQ	did not pre-qualify	
761/8	Kozarowitsky	DNQ	did not pre-qualify	

German GP, Hockenheimring, 31.7.77

761B/3-2	Ribeiro	20	8	last finisher still running
761B/1	I. Scheckter	18	rtd	suspension and handling
761/7-2	Neve	DNQ		
761B/2	Merzario	DNQ		

Austrian GP, Österreichring, 14.8.77

761/7-2	Neve	22	9	
761B/1	I. Scheckter	24	rtd	crash
761B/3-2	Ribeiro	DNQ		
761/5	Henton	DNQ		

Dutch GP, Zandvoort, 28.8.77

771/2	I. Scheckter	25	10	first race for 771
761B/3-2	Ribeiro	24	11	
761/7-2	Neve	DNQ		
761B/2	Merzario	DNQ		
761/3-3	Hayje	DNQ		
761/6	Bleekemolen	DNQ		

Italian GP, Monza, 11.9.77

761/7-2	Neve	24	7	
771/2	I. Scheckter	17	rtd	transmission
761B/3-2	Ribeiro	DNQ		

United States GP East, Watkins Glen, 2.10.77

761B/3-2	Ribeiro	23	15	
761/7-2	Neve	24	18	
771/1	I. Scheckter	21	rtd	crash

Canadian GP, Mosport Park, 9.10.77

761B/3-2	Ribeiro	23	8	last finisher still running
771/1-2	I. Scheckter	18	rtd	engine
761/7-2	Neve	21	rtd	oil pressure

Japanese GP, Fuji, 23.10.77

761B/3-2	Ribeiro	23	12
771/1-2	I. Scheckter	visa problems, not permitted to enter Japan	

Drivers' Championship:

1,	Niki Lauda (Ferrari)	72
2,	Jody Scheckter (Wolf)	55
3,	Mario Andretti (Lotus)	47

Constructors' Championship:

1,	Ferrari	95
2,	Lotus	62
3,	McLaren	60

No March driver scored a World Championship point.

March 761B/1 (Ian Scheckter's car) was withdrawn from team after Austrian GP to be converted back to 761/6 for Ronnie Peterson's personal use.

March 761B/2 (née 761/1-4) used by Ribeiro until Long Beach and then sold to Arturo Merzario.

March 761B/3-2 sprayed in ATS colours at the end of the season for use as a show car. In May 1978 was cannibalized to refettle 781/2 and very little remained.

March 761B/4 did not race but was built as six-wheeled show car, autumn.

March 771/1 severely damaged in United States GP East and rebuilt for Canadian GP using the monocoque from 771/2.

March 771/2 used as test car and then monocoque flown out to North America to repair 771/1. The remaining components were used to make 781/1.

March Engineering withdrew from F1 at the end of 1977 and its FOCA membership was sold to ATS along with various effects.

European F2 Championship

Hockenheimring	Jochen Mass (772P)*
Nürburgring	Jochen Mass (772P)*
Vallelungha	Bruno Giacomelli (772P)
Mugello	Bruno Giacomelli (772P)
Donington Park	Bruno Giacomelli (782 prototype)

**Graded driver, so did not score points*

1,	René Arnoux	Martini-Renault	52
2,	Eddie Cheever	Ralt-BMW	40
3,	Didier Pironi	Martini-Renault	38
4=	Bruno Giacomelli	March-BMW	32
4=	Riccardo Patrese	Chevron-BMW	32
6,	Keijo Rosberg	Chevron-Hart	25

March won five races, Martini won four, Chevron two and Ralt and Boxer took one apiece

BP (British) F3 Championship

1,	Derek Daly	Chevron-Toyota	69
2=	Stephen South	March-Toyota	56
2=	Eje Elgh	Chevron-Toyota	56
4,	Geoff Lees	Chevron-Toyota	41
5,	Derek Warwick	Ralt-Toyota	40
6,	James King	March-Toyota	22

Vandervell (British) F3 Championship

1,	Stephen South	March-Toyota	75
2,	Brett Riley	March-Toyota	58
3,	Derek Warwick	Ralt-Toyota	41
4,	Geoff Brabham	Ralt-Toyota	36
5=	Eje Elgh	Chevron-Toyota	34
5=	Derek Daly	Chevron-Toyota	34

European F3 Championship

1, Piercarlo Ghinzani	March-Toyota	58 (61)
2, Anders Olofsson	Ralt-Toyota	46
3, Nelson Piquet	March and Ralt-Toyota	33
4, Beppe Gabbiani	Chevron-Toyota	26
5, Oscar Pedersoli	Ralt-Toyota	24
6, Piero Necchi	Ralt-Toyota	22

Italian F3 Champion: Piercarlo Ghinzani

Shellsport International Group 8 Championship

1, Tony Trimmer	Surtees TS19-DFV 3.0	181
2, Guy Edwards	March 75A-DFV 3.0	129
3, Val Musetti	March 752-GAA 3.4	85
4, Tony Rouff	Ralt-BDG 2.0	80
5, Emilio da Villota	McLaren M23-DFV 3.0	76
6, Divina Galica	Surtees TS19-DFV 3.0	74

Guy Edwards won three rounds of the championship, Musetti won one.

Canadian Formula Atlantic Championship

1, Gilles Villeneuve	March-Ford	114
2, Bobby Rahal	March 76B-Ford	92
3, Binl Brack	March-Ford	87
4, Keijo Rosberg	Chevron-Ford	82
5, Price Cobb	March-Ford	82
6, Tom Gloy	March-Ford	82

Other Categories

Pierre Maublanc (772-BMW) and Markus Hotz (762-BMW) each won rounds of the European Hill Climb Championship, but long-time March exponent, Jimmy Mieusset, defected to Ralt.

Ian Scheckter won the South African (Formula Atlantic) Championship breaking the six-year reign of Dave Charlton.

March Production 1978

Type	Description	Number Made	Running Total
781	Formula 1	2	49
782	Formula 2	29	173
772	Hill climb car	11	74
783	Formula 3/SuperVee3	11	99
78B	Formula Atlantic/B	19	157
77B	Formula Atlantic/B	11	58
	Total	83	674

No March appeared in an international F1 race in 1978. Two cars, however, were built for John MacDonald's RAM team to run in the Aurora British F1 Championship. 781/1 was built with limited tankage, but 781/2 was prepared for Patrick Neve to run in the Belgian GP, although, in the event, financial problems precluded this. Both were basically 771s and parts from 771/2 were used to build 781/1.

New monocoques for all cars with more angular sides as a result of new machinery to simplify production, but the principles on which they were built remained the same as the 1971 series. All 1978 single-seaters had front-mounted radiators.

782. New slim monocoque with driver moved forward, cars ran half-length sliding skirts during the latter part of the season.

Other cars light up-dates of previous models.

European Formula Two Championship

Thruxton	Bruno Giacomelli
Hockenheim	Bruno Giacomelli
Nürburgring	Alex Ribeiro*
Pau	Bruno Giacomelli
Rouen	Bruno Giacomelli
Nogaro	Bruno Giacomelli
Enna	Bruno Giacomelli
Misano	Bruno Giacomelli
Hockenheim	Bruno Giacomelli

*March 782-Hart

1, Bruno Giacomelli	March-BMW	78
2, Marc Surer	March-BMW	48
3, Derek Daly	Chevron-Hart	27
4, Eddie Cheever	March-BMW	23
5, Keke Rosberg	Chevron-Hart	16
6= Piero Necchi	March-BMW	13
Ingo Hoffman	March-BMW	13

European F3 Championship

1, Jan Lammers	Ralt-Toyota	71 (72)
2, Anders Olofsson	Ralt-Toyota	71
3, Patrick Gaillard	Chevron-Toyota	49
4, Teo Fabi	March-Toyota	45
5, Michael Bleekemolen	Chevron-Toyota	30
6= David Kennedy	Argo-Toyota	24
Derek Warwick	Ralt-Toyota	13

BP (British) F3 Championship

1, Nelson Piquet	Ralt-Toyota	101
2, Derek Warwick	Ralt-Toyota	72
3, Chico Serra	March-Toyota	72
3, Philip Bullman	Chevron-Toyota	22
5, Tiff Needell	March-Triumph	22
6, Rob Wilson	Ralt-Toyota	20

Vandervell (British) F3 Championship

1, Derek Warwick	Ralt-Toyota	162 (164)
2, Nelson Piquet	Ralt-Toyota	124
3, Chico Serra	March-Toyota	78
4, Rob Wilson	Ralt-Toyota	49
5, Brett Riley	March-Triumph	30
6= John Bright	March-Toyota	24
Tiff Needell	March-Triumph	24

North American Labatt Formula Atlantic Championship

1, Howdy Holmes	March-Ford	131
2, Keke Rosberg	Chevron-Ford	114
3, Price Cobb	March-Ford	103
4, Jeff Wood	March-Ford	88
5, Bobby Rahal	Ralt-Ford	68
6, Tom Gloy	March-Ford	60

Other Categories

Ian Scheckter took his hat-trick of South African Championships, which was run to Formula Atlantic, and Teo Fabi won the New Zealand Formula Atlantic Championship.

Helmut Henzler (March 783-VW) won the European Formula SuperVee seriew.

David Franklin (March 722) won the RAC British Hill Climb Championship.

Kazuyoshi Hoshino (782-BMW) was Japanese Grand Champion.

March Production 1979

Type	Description	Number Made	Running Total
792	Formula 2	32	206
793	Formula 3	25	224
79A	Formula B	3	161
79B	Formula Atlantic/B	23	184
79C	Formula 3	1	225
79V	Formula SuperVee	21	21
	Total	105	779

792. Ground effect car with sliding skirts, new narrow tub with honeycomb inserts and engine as a stressed member with steel side-frames. Inboard front suspension by lower wishbones and top rocker arms, rear suspension by lower wishbones, top and bottom links, single radius arms and inboard springs. Wheelbase 100in, front and rear track 60in. Front-mounted radiator with side wings.

Toleman's 782s raced with full-length sliding skirts.

79A. Formula B/Atlantic/Pacific car based on 792.

79C. F3 car based on 792 built by the works as a prototype and tested by Chico Serra, but in view of the fact that skirts were permitted only for 1979 in Formula Three it was not raced.

Junior formulae cars broadly the same as 1978, with front radiators and full-width nose cones. The March 793 had sliding skirts which were permitted in F3 only in 1979, but this was not a serious 'ground effect' design since little work was done on the venturi and the outboard suspension was likewise not ideal. Skirts were not permitted in Formula Atlantic, where the Ralt RT1 continued to prove it was superior to the non-ground effect Marches.

March Engines Ltd of Cowley built a special version of the BMW M1 coupé which was entered at Le Mans as a Group 5 car, but homologation problems saw it put into Group 6. Driven by Guy Edwards, Dieter Quester and Ian Grob it qualified in midfield but was not permitted to start under the race's 'class by class' qualifying regulations. Neither this car, nor its sister, appears in March Engineering's records.

Formula Two European Championship

Hockenheim	Keke Rosberg
Thruxton	Rad Dougall
Nürburgring	Marc Surer
Vallelunga	Marc Surer
Hockenheim	Stephen South
Enna	Eje Elgh
Donington Park	Derek Daly

1,	Marc Surer	March-BMW	38
2,	Brian Henton	Ralt-Hart	36
3,	Derek Daly	March-BMW	33
4,	Eddie Cheever	Osella-BMW	32
5=	Stephen South	March-BMW	19
	Rad Dougall	March-Hart and Ralt-Hart	19
	Beppe Gabbiani	March-BMW	19

Japanese F2 Champion: Keiji Matsumoto, March 792-BMW

European F3 Championship

1, Alain Prost	Martini-Renault	67
2, Michael Bleekemolen	March-Toyota	28
3, Slim Borguud	Ralt-Toyota	23
4, Mauro Baldi	March-Toyota	22
5, Richard Dallest	Martini-Toyota	21
6, Michele Alboreto	March-Toyota	21

Vandervell (British) F3 Championship

1, Chico Serra	March-Toyota	103
2, Andrea de Cesaris	March-Toyota	90
3, Mike Thackwell	March-Toyota	71
4, Stefan Johansson	March-Toyota	54
5, Brett Riley	March-Triumph	40
6, Kenny Acheson	March-Toyota	35

North American Labatt Formula Atlantic Championship

1, Tom Gloy	Ralt-Ford	199 (208)
2, Kevin Cogan	Ralt-Ford	163
3, Jeff Wood	March-Ford	143
4, Howdy Holmes	March-Ford	136
5, Bob Earl	Ralt-Ford	127
6, Rick Koehler	Excalibur-Ford	60

Other Categories

Ian Scheckter won his fourth consecutive South African Championship with a March (Formula Atlantic). March also won the Constructors' Championship in the European SuperVee series, but this was an honorary title if ever there was one.

Norman Dickson (792-BMW) won the F2 class of the British 'Aurora' F1 Championship.

March Production 1980

Type	Description	Number Made	Running Total
802	Formula 2	25	206
803	Formula 3	27	252
80A	Formula Atlantic/B	25	209
80V	Formula SuperVee	16	37
	Total	93	872

802. Same monocoque and layout as 792 but without sliding skirts. Chisel nose, front aerofoils, and side radiators, venturi side pods.

803. Front-mounted radiator in chisel nose with side wings, improved venturi side pods, rocker arm front suspension with inboard springs, began the season with outboard rear suspension but rocker arm rear adopted mid-season.

Formula Atlantic, as 803 but with full-width nose cone with front radiator

March Engines of Cowley also built three 'Orbiter' Indycars based on special honeycomb 79A used in Tasman series.

European Formula Two Championship

Hockenheim	Teo Fabi
Misano	Andrea de Cesaris
Hockenheim	Teo Fabi

1, Brian Henton	Toleman-Hart	61
2, Derek Warwick	Toleman-Hart	42
3, Teo Fabi	March-BMW	38
4, Siegfried Stohr	Toleman-Hart	29
5, Andrea de Cesaris	March-BMW	28
6, Richard Dallest	AGS-BMW	23

Japanese F2 Champion: Mashahiro Hasemi, 802-BMW

Japanese Grand Champion: Mashahiro Hasemi

European F3 Championship

1, Michele Alboreto	March-Toyota	60
2, Thierry Boutsen	Martini-Toyota	54
3, Corrado Fabi	March-Alfa Romeo	50
4, Mauro Baldi	Martini-Toyota	45
5, Philippe Alliot	Martini-Toyota	39
6, Philippe Streiff	Martini-Toyota	18

Vandervell (British) F3 Championship

1, Stefan Johansson	March and Ralt-Toyota	97
2, Kenny Acheson	March-Toyota	95
3, Roberto Guerrero	Argo-Toyota	95
4, Thierry Tassin	Argo-Toyota	40
5, Rob Wilson	Ralt-Toyota	40
6, Mike White	March-Toyota	37

Italian F3 Champion: Michele Alboreto, March 803-Alfa Romeo

North American Mamiya Formula Atlantic Championship

1, Jacques Villeneuve	March-Ford	178
2, Tom Gloy	Ralt-Ford	168
3, Steve Saleen	Ralt-Ford	140 (147)
4, Price Cobb	March-Ford	121
5, Jeff Wood	Ralt-Ford	114
6, Rogello Rodriguez	Ralt-Ford	110 (111)

Other Categories

March was the most successful constructor in the European SuperVee Championship, but it was a series that nobody outside of it took very seriously.

March Production 1981

Type	Description	Number Made	Running Total
811	Formula 1	6	55
812	Formula 2	11	242
813	Formula 3	12	264
81A	Formula B (USA)	9	218
81A	Formula Atlantic/Pacific	5	223
81C	Indianapolis	9	9
81H	Hill climb	1	1
81P	G.T.P.	1	1
81S	Sports 2000	5	5
817	Can-Am	3	6
	Total	62	934

811. Aluminium alloy monocoque with cast magnesium bulkheads, front and rear suspension by inboard coil springs, top rocker arms and lower wishbones; front track 68in; rear track 63.25in; wheelbase 106in; Cosworth DFV engine; Hewland FGA gearbox; AP brakes; weight 632.6kg.

81C. Based on 811, strengthened monocoque, Cosworth DFX engine, Weismann transverse gearbox.

81P. Built for BMW by March Engines, entered as BMW M1C and used both straight-six engine, 3.5-litre engine and 2-litre 4-cylinder turbo unit. Became basis of March IMSA/Group C series of cars.

817. Based on 811 with full-width body and 5-litre Ghevrolet engine.

812. New monocoque and body but rocker arm suspension all round similar to 802, wheelbase 101.4in, front track 59.04in, rear track 58.12in.

813. Broadly similar to 812 but with smaller critical dimensions and front-mounted radiator in slim nose cone with side wings.

81A. New body retaining full-width nose cone and front radiator, new rocker arm rear suspension.

81S. Monocoque with semi-stressed engine, double wishbone front suspension, top links, lower wishbones and radius arms at rear, coil springs outboard all round. 2 litre Ford engine with Hewland Mk 9 gearbox.

March Formula One Racing Record

South African GP (FOCA only race, non-Championship), Kyalami, 7.2.81

881/2	Daly	17	11	
881/3	Salazar	19	rtd	gearbox

19 starters

United States GP West, Long Beach, 15.3.81

881/2	Daly	DNQ
881/3	Salazar	DNQ

Brazilian GP, Rio de Janeiro, 29.3.81

881/2	Daly	DNQ	crashed in practice when wishbone pulled out of monocoque
881/3	Salazar	DNQ	

Argentine GP, Buenos Aires, 12.4.81

881/1	Daly	DNQ	original (heavy) tub
881/3	Salazar	DNQ	

San Marino GP, Imola, 3.5.81

881/3	Salazar	23	rtd	oil pressure
881/1	Daly	DNQ		collapsed rear damper found after practice

Lotus absent, else Salazar would not have qualified, both cars strengthened at front of monocoque

Belgian GP, Zolder, 17.5.81

881/5	Daly	DNQ	misunderstanding with scrutineers
881/4	Salazar	DNQ	

New cars with honeycomb inserts in chassis

Monaco GP, 31.5.81

881/5	Daly	DNQ	drive shaft broke in pre-qualifying
881/4	Salazar	DNQ	spun during pre-qualifying

Hydro-pneumatic suspension, after Monaco Salazar joined Ensign

Spanish GP, Jarama, 21.6.81

881/4	Daly	22	16	new profile side pods

French GP, Dijon-Prenois, 5.7.81

881/4	Daly	20	rtd	engine

Avon crossply tyres used for first time

British GP, Silverstone, 18.7.81

881/6	Daly	17	7	in effect an 811B, 8th fastest race lap

German GP, Hockenheim, 2.8.81

881/6	Daly	21	rtd	steering tie rod

Austrian GP, 16.8.81

881/6	Daly	19	11

Dutch GP, Zandvoortl 30.8.81

881/6	Daly	19	rtd	broken suspension

Italian GP, Monza, 13.9.81

881/6	Daly	19	rtd	gearbox

Canadian GP, Montreal, 27.9.81

881/6	Daly	20	8

Caesar's Palace GP, a car park in Las Vegas, 17.10.81

881/6	Daly	DNQ

Drivers' Championship:

1,	Nelson Piquet (Brabham)	50
2,	Carlos Reutemann (Williams)	49
3,	Alan Jones (Williams)	46

Constructors' Cup:

1,	Williams	95
2,	Brabham	61
3,	Renault	54

No March driver scored a Championship point

European Formula Two Championship

Nürburgring	Thierry Boutsen
Mugello	Corrado Fabi
Enna	Thierry Boutsen

1, Geoff Lees	Ralt-Honda	51
2, Thierry Boutsen	March-BMW	37
3, Eje Elgh	Maurer-BMW	35
4, Stefan Johansson	Toleman-Hart	30
5, Corrado	March-BMW	29

6, Mike Thackwell	Ralt-Honda	22

Japanese F2 Champion: Satoru Nakajima, March 812-Honda
Japanese Grand Champion: Naohiko Fujita

USAC Gold Crown National Championship

Pocono 500 — A.J. Foyt

CART PPG Indy Car World Series

Milwaukee 200 — Tom Sneva
Phoenix 150 — Tom Sneva

1, Rick Mears	Penske-Cosworth	304
2, Bill Alsup	Penske-Cosworth	177
3, Pancho Carter	Penske-Cosworth	168
4, Gordon Johncock	Wildcat-Cosworth	142
5, Johnny Rutherford	Chapparral-Cosworth	120
6, Tony Bettenhausen	Phoenix-Cosworth	107
8, Tom Sneva	*March 81C-Cosworth*	*96*

European F3 Championship

1, Mauro Baldi	March-Alfa Romeo	94
2, Alain Ferté	Martini-Alfa Romeo	63
3, Philippe Alliot	Martini-Alfa Romeo	41
4, Philippe Streiff	Martini-Alfa Romeo	36
5, Oscar Larrauri	March-Toyota	32
6, Emanuele Pirro	Martini-Toyota	19

Marlboro (British) F3 Championship

1, Jonathan Palmer	Ralt-Toyota	105
2, Thierry Tassin	Ralt-Toyota	92
3, Raul Boesel	Ralt-Toyota	81
4, Mike White	March-Alfa Romeo	38
5, David Leslie	Ralt-Toyota	29
6, Dave Scott	Ralt-Toyota	29

North American Formula Atlantic Championship

1, Jacques Villeneuve	March-Ford	166
2, Rogelio Rodriguez	Ralt-Ford	130
3, Whitney Ganz	Ralt-Ford	124
4, Norm Hunter	Ralt-Ford	105
5, Allen Berg	Ralt-Ford	84
6, Tommy Grunnah	March-Ford	82

Other Categories

Ralt completely dominated the Robert Bosch/VW SuperVee Championship with the best March driver being Arie Luyendyk with three thirds and fourth in the series. By the end of the season, the SuperVee Championship became recognized as the premier junior single-seater category in North America.

Teo Fabi (March 817-Chevrolet) took four wins and a second in the Can-Am Championship and finished a close runner-up in the series to Geoff Brabham' s VDS-Chevrolet.

In the American IMSA GT Championship David Hobbs drove the March-developed BMW M1C which, despite a disadvantage in engine size (it ran with either a 3.5-litre normally aspirated unit or a 2-litre turbo) proved very fast if fragile. Hobbs' best results were a fourth (Portland), a fifth (Mid-Ohio) and two sixths (Riverside and Laguna Seca).

March Production 1982

Type	Description	Number Made	Running Total
822	Formula 2	13	255
827	Can-Am	0	6
82A	Formula Atlantic/B	5	228
82C	Indianapolis	20	20
82G	Group C and G.T.P.	4	5
82S	Sports 2000	5	10
	Total	48	981

821. Aluminium alloy monocoque with cast magnesium bulkheads, front suspension by inboard coil springs, top rocker arms and lower wishbones; rear suspension by inboard coil springs, top rocker arms and lower wishbones; front track 68in; rear track 66in; wheelbase 106in; Cosworth DFV engine; Hewland FGA gearbox; Lockheed brakes; weight 580kg.

82C. Up-dated 81C with longitudinal gearbox. March transverse box appeared during the season and supplied to some teams.

822. Up-date of the 812 but with a slightly narrower tub, improved aerodynamics, and new rear suspension geometry.

82G. Honeycomb monocoque, coil spring and wishbone front and rear suspension. Made in both Group C and IMSA GTP versions, engines various.

827. Re-bodied 817 with aerodynamics by Dr Max Sardou.

82S. Lightly updated 81S.

82A. Virtually the same as 81A.

NB For the first time in March's history, no F3 cars were made.

March Formula One Racing Record

Chassis numbers continue from 1981 but do not appear in March production figures because March Grand Prix was in effect a separate entity.

South African GP, Kyalami, 23.1.82

821/8	Mass	22	13	
821/7	Boesel	21	15	

Pirelli radial tyres

Brazilian GP, Rio de Janeiro, 21.3.82

821/8	Mass	22	10	
821/9	Boesel	17	rtd	puncture, spun off

United States GP West, Long Beach, 4.4.82

821/8	Mass	21	8	
821/9	Boesel	23	9	

San Marino GP, Imola, 25.4.82

No March GP entries – FISA/FOCA dispute

Belgian GP, Zolder, 9.5.82

821/9	Boesel	24	8	
821/8	Mass	25	rtd	engine
821/7	de Villota	DNQ		entered by Onyx Race Engineering

Monaco GP, 23.5.82

821/8	Mass	DNQ	
821/9	Boesel	DNQ	
821/7	de Villota	DNQ	crashed in pre-qualifying

Switch to Avon crossply tyres

United States GP, Detroit, 6.6.82

821/8	Mass	18	7	
821/9	Boesel	21	rtd	crash
821/7	de Villota	DNQ		

Carbon fibre side pods

Canadian GP, Montreal, 13.6.82

821/8	Mass	22	11	
821/10	Boesel	21	rtd	engine+
821/7	de Villota	DNQ		

Dutch GP, Zandvoort, 3.7.82

821/11	Mass	24	rtd	engine; stiffer tub, wider front track
821/10	Boesel	22	rtd	engine
821/7	de Villota	DNQ		

British GP, Brands Hatch, 18.7.82

821/11	Mass	25	10	wider track front and rear
821/10	Boesel	DNQ		

French GP, Paul Ricard, 25.7.82

821/10	Mass	26	rtd	crash
821/10	Boesel	DNQ		no mistake over chassis number, see note++

German GP, Hockenheim, 8.8.82

821/7	Boesel	24	rtd	puncture
821/11	Keegan	DNQ		Jochen Mass withdrew after first practice due to cracked ribs sustained in the French GP

Austrian GP, Österreichring, 15.8.82

821/11	Keegan	24	rtd	bent steering arm
821/7	Boesel	DNQ		

Swiss GP, Dijon-Prenois, 29.8.82

821/7	Boesel	24	rtd	gearbox
821/11	Keegan	22	rtd	spun

Italian GP, Monza, 12.9.82

821/11	Keegan	DNQ
821/7	Boesel	DNQ

Michelin radial tyres, pull-rod front suspension

Caesar' s Palace GP, a car park in Las Vegas, 25.9.82

821/7	Keegan	25	12
821/11	Boesel	24	13

+Boesel started Canadian GP in 821/9 which was destroyed in start-line crash, he made the re-start in 821/10.

++In the French GP, Boesel practised in 821/10 and Mass practised in 821/11. Mass elected to use 821/10 for the race and it was written off.

Drivers' Championship:

1,	Keke Rosberg (Williams)	44
2=	Didier Pironi (Ferrari)	39
2=	John Watson (McLaren)	39

Constructors' Cup:

1,	Ferrari	74
2,	McLaren	69
3,	Renault	62

No March driver scored a Championship point

European Formula Two Championship

Thruxton	Johnny Cecotto
Mugello	Corrado Fabi
Vallelunga	Corrado Fabi
Pau	Johnny Cecotto
Hockenheim	Corrado Fabi
Donington Park	Corrado Fabi
Mantorp Park	Johnny Cecotto
Misano	Corrado Fabi

1, Corrado Fabi	March-BMW	57
2, Johnny Cecotto	March-BMW	56 (57)
3, Thierry Boutsen	Spirit-Honda	50 (51)
4, Stefan Bellof	Maurer-BMW	33
5, Beppe Gabbiani	Maurer-BMW	26
6, Phillipe Streiff	AGS-BMW	22

Japanese F2 Champion: Sartoru Nakajimi, 822-BMW

European F3 Championship

1, Oscar Larrauri	Euroracing 101-Alfa Romeo*	91
2, Emanuele Pirro	Euroracing 101-Alfa Romeo*	62
3, Alain Ferté	Martini-Alfa Romeo	42
4, James Weaver	Ralt-Toyota	33
5, Didier Theys	Martini-Alfa Romeo	30
6, Philippe Alliot	Martini-Alfa Romeo	25

Italian F3 Champion: Enzo Coloni March 813-Alfa Romeo

**March Engineering ceased production of F3 cars during 1981 and no serious competitor used a March chassis thereafter for they were clearly no longer competitive. An exception was Euroracing, whose '101' cars were based on the team's March 813s. These obsolete cars won nine of the 15 rounds of the European Championship but clearly should not have done. In fact they were greatly helped by Michelin, but James Weaver in a Ralt running on Yokohamas took three wins and a second from the four races he contested.*

CART PPG Indy Car World Series

Cleveland 500	Bobby Rahal
Milwaukee 200	Tom Sneva
Elkhart Lake 200	Hector Rebaque
Michigan 150	Bobby Rahal
Pheonix 150	Tom Sneva

1, Rick Mears	Penske-Cosworth	294
2, Bobby Rahal	March-Cosworth	242
3, Mario Andretti	Wildcat-Cosworth	188
4, Gordon Johncock	Wildcat-Cosworth	186
5, Tom Sneva	March-Cosworth	144
6, Kevin Cogan	Penske-Cosworth	136

Other Categories

A 'works' Group C March 82G-Chevrolet 5.7 appeared in practice for the Silverstone Six Hours (Jeff Wood and Eje Elgh) and at Le Mans (Wood, Elgh and Patrick Neve, retired electrics) and was then converted to IMSA spec and sold to the States, where it finished at Mosport and Mid-Ohio and sixth at Road America (drivers: Randy Lanier and Marty Hinze).

82Gs were a little more comfortable in IMSA and Bob Garretson's car, fitted with a 5.7-litre Chevrolet engine, finished second in the Sebring 12 Hours (drivers; Bobby Rahal, Mauricio De Narvaez, and Jim Trueman). This car also ran at Le Mans (Rahal, Trueman and Skeeter McKitterick), where it was slower than the 'works' car and retired with a split fuel tank. The 3.5-litre BMW-powered car of David Cowart and Kenper Miller took third at Road Atlanta, fifth at Road America, and sixth at Riverside. Most races were won by Porsche 935s or, to a lesser degree, Lola T600-Chevrolets.

Three considerably modified March 75S-BMWs appeared in the Fuji Six Hours and qualified 6th, 8th and 18th in a field of 36. Masakuza Nakamura and Kiyashi Misaki brought theirs home third, while Haruhiti Yanagida and Shinji Uchida finished tenth, which was not bad going for a seven-year-old car.

Danny Sullivan's Newman Racing March 827-Chevrolet took a win and three seconds in the Can-Am Championship, and Sullivan finished third overall behind Al Unser Jnr's (Lola-based) Frissbee-Chevrolet and Al Holbert's VDS-Chevrolet.

Apart from the Euroracing 101s, March 813s continued to appear in national F3 Championships and Kurt Thiim took third place in the Knutsrop round of the European Championship and since it was behind the Euroracing pair, it might be said to count as a March

1–2–3. In Britain only rarely did a March appear (best result, Phil Dowsett, seventh at Snetterton in September) but among 813 users in Italy was Ivan Capelli.

Graham Duxbury (822-Mazda) won the South African 'Sigma' National Championship.

Ralt dominated the North American Formula Atlantic Championship, with the best March results being a pair of fourths by Allen Berg. Ralt' s domination was even more complete in the SuperVee series with the best March finish being a fifth by Brad Hulings in a two-year-old car.

The British F1 Championship was in a sorry state with only five rounds and a handful of starters in each, so Val Musetti's second at Thruxton in a March 811 (four finishers) didn't amount to much.

March Production 1983

Type	Description	Number Made	Running Total
822	Formula 2	1	256
832	Formula 2	25	281
83C	Indianapolis	21	50
83G	Group C and G.T.P.	5	10
83S	Sports 2000	8	18
	Total	60	1041

832. New monocoque and aerodynamic package; composite stiffeners added mid-season.

83C. Robin Herd's last design. Last of the 81C series with March-designed transverse gearbox and pull-rod front and rear suspension as base car, but during the season a 'road circuit' kit was offered with longitudinal Hewland DGB gearbox and rocker-arm rear suspension.

All other cars up-dates of previous designs.

In Formula One, RAM Racing entered its cars as March-RAMs, but they were Marches only in the paperwork and so have been excluded from this appendix.

European Formula Two Championship

Silverstone	Beppe Gabbiani
Hockenheim	Beppe Gabbiani
Thruxton	Beppe Gabbiani
Nürburgring	Beppe Gabbiani
Vallelunga	Beppe Gabbiani

1, Jonathan Palmer	Ralt-Honda	68 (75)
2, Mike Thackwell	Ralt-Honda	51
3, Beppe Gabbiani	March-BMW	39
4, Phillipe Streiff	AGS-BMW	25
5, Christian Danner	March-BMW	21
6, Jo Gartner	Spirit-BMW	14

Japanese F2 Champion: Geoff Lees, March-Honda, the first occasion a driver had won both the European and Japanese F2 Championships

Japanese Grand Champion: Kazuyoshi Hoshino, March-BMW

CART PPG Indy Car World Series

Milwaukee 150	Tom Sneva
Indianapolis 500	Tom Sneva
Pocono 500	Teo Fabi
Riverside 500	Bobby Rahal
Lexington 210	Teo Fabi
Laguna Seca 300 Km	Teo Fabi
Pheonix 150	Teo Fabi

1, Al Unser	Penske-Cosworth	151
2, Teo Fabi	March-Cosworth	146
3, Mario Andretti	Lola-Cosworth	133
4, Tom Sneva	March-Cosworth	96
5, Bobby Rahal	March-Cosworth	94
6, Rick Mears	Penske-Cosworth	92

IMSA GTP Championship (USA)

1, Al Holbert	March-Chevrolet and March-Porsche	204
2, Bob Tullius	Jaguar XJR-5	121
3, Jim Trueman	March-Chevrolet and March-Porsche	113
4, Bob Akin	Porsche 935	113
5, John O'Steen	Porsche 935	95
6, Bill Adam	Jaguar XJR-5	78

Other Categories

A March 83G-Nissan 2.1-litre turbo ('Nissan Silvia') ran in Japan and was seventh, and first non-Porsche, in the WCM Fuji 1000 Km (Kazuyoshi Misaki and Akira Hagiwara), while a March 75S-Toyota was eighth (Kiyoshi Misaki and Masakuza Nakamura) on an equal number of laps.

The March-developed BMW M1C appeared in some IMSA rounds fitted with a Chevy engine. It did not set the world alight.

Ian Scheckter returned to serious racing with a March 832 and won his fifth South African National title, the Sigma Championship, which specified Mazda rotary engines. Ian's domination was such that he won the last 13 races of the season and continued his run the following year.

March Production 1984

Type	Description	Number Made	Running Total
842	Formula 2	20	301
84C	Indianapolis	47	97
84G	Group C and GTP	7	17
84S	Sports 2000	3	21
	Total	77	1118

84C. Entirely new aluminium honeycomb monocoque with composite top section, tub five inches shorter than 83C achieved by shorter but higher fuel cell, much larger (by 7 inches) front crushable structure. Pull-rod front suspension, rocker arm rear, wheelbase 111.87in, front track 66in, rear track 63in. Engine tilted at three degrees to the horizontal to improve under-car aerodynamics. New 4/5-speed longitudinal March gearbox.

842. New honeycomb monococque with composite top section, honeycomb and machined aluminium bulkheads, 'flat-bottomed' to comply with new regulations, engine tilted at four degrees to the horizontal. New pull-rod front suspension.

Sports cars all up-dates of previous models.

Formula Two European Championship

Hockenheim	Pascal Fabre

1, Mike Thackwell	Ralt-Honda	72
2, Roberto Moreno	Ralt-Honda	44
3, Michel Ferte	Martini-BMW	29
4, Phillipe Streiff	AGS-BMW	27
5, Christian Danner	March-BMW	23
6, Thierry Tassin	March-BMW	18
Emanuele Pirro	March-BMW	18

At the end of 1984 Formula Two was dropped in favour of Formula 3000 save in Japan, where it continued until the end of 1986.

Japanese F2 Champion: Satoru Nakajima, March-Honda

Japanese Grand Champion: Kazayoshi Hoshino, March-BMW

CART PPG Indy Car World Series

Phoenix 150	Tom Sneva
Indianapolis 500	Rick Mears
Milwaukee 200	Tom Sneva
Portland 200	Al Unser Jnr
Phoenix 150	Bobby Rahal

Laguna Seca 300 Km	Bobby Rahal
Las Vegas 200	Tom Sneva

1, Mario Andretti	Lola-Cosworth	176
2, Tom Sneva	March-Cosworth	163
3, Bobby Rahal	March-Cosworth	137
4= Rick Mears	March-Cosworth	110
4= Danny Sullivan	Sheirson-Cosworth and Lola-Cosworth	110
6, Al Unser Jnr	March-Cosworth	103

IMSA Camel GT Championship (USA)

1, Randy Lanier	March-Chevrolet	189
2, Bill Whittington	March-Chevrolet	168
3, Derek Bell	Porsche 962	164
4, Al Holbert	Porsche 962	136
5, Sarel van der Merwe	March-Porsche	105
6, Brian Redman	Jaguar XJR-5	97

Other Categories

Thg Pegasus Racing 84G-Buick turbo (a Buick-backed entry) appeared at Le Mans (drivers: Ken Madren, M.L. Speer and Wayne Pickering), qualified 35th and retired after 95 laps with engine trouble.

Mazda bought an 84G and fitted it with a twin-rotor turbo-charged Wankel engine. It raced only once, in the Fuji 1000 Km (drivers: Yoshimi Katayama and Takashi Yorino), where it qualified 16th and finished eighth and second Group C2 car home. Thus March-Mazda (the nominal priority had changed) finished ninth in the Group C2 Championship.

Ian Scheckter won his sixth South African National Championship in his 832-Mazda and continued his '83 run of 13 straight wins with a further five at the start of the year before his first defeat. Eighteen successive wins in a national championship is surely a record while Scheckter's sixth title equalled the scores of John Love and Dave Charlton.

March Production 1985

Type	Description	Number Made	Running Total
85B	Formula 3000	16	16
85C	Indianapolis	44	141
85G	Group C and GTP	11	38
85J	Formula 2 (Japan)	11	312
85O	Oldsmobile record car	2	2
	Total	84	1202

85B. The 842 with a two-inch longer monocoque with flatter sides.

85C. New honeycomb monocoque incorporating extra bulkhead to protect brake master cylinders, lower fuel cell, increased use of composites, pull-rod front suspension, rocker arm rear, front track, 66in, rear track 63in, wheelbase 110.2in.

85G. Further update of 82G series but with revised aerodynamics. Narrower gearbox helped improve under-car air flow.

85J. Virtually the same as the 842.

European Formula 3000 Championship

Thruxton	Emanuele Pirro
Vallelunga	Emanuele Pirro
Pau	Christian Danner
Österreichring	Ivan Capelli
Zandvoort	Christian Danner
Donington Park	Christian Danner

1, Christian Danner	March-Cosworth	51 (52)
2, Mike Thackell	Ralt-Cosworth	45
3, Emanuele Pirro	March-Cosworth	38
4, John Nielsen	Ralt-Cosworth	34
5, Michel Ferté	March-Cosworth	17
6, Gabriele Tarquini	March-Cosworth	14

Japanese F2 Champion: Satoru Nakajima, March-Honda

Japanese Grand Champion: Kazuyoshi Hoshino

CART PPG Indy Car World Series

Indianapolis 500	Danny Sullivan
Michigan 500	Emerson Fittipaldi
Elkhart Lake 200	Jacques Villeneuve
Pocono 500	Rick Mears
Lexington 200	Bobby Rahal
Montreal	Johnny Rutherford
Michigan 200	Bobby Rahal
Laguna Seca 300 Km	Bobby Rahal
Phoenix 150	Al Unser Snr
Miami	Danny Sullivan

1, Al Unser Snr, March-Cosworth	151
2, Al Unser Jnr, Lola-Cosworth	150
3, Bobby Rahal, March-Cosworth	134
4, Danny Sullivan, March-Cosworth	125
5, Mario Andretti, Lola-Cosworth	114
6, Emerson Fittipaldi, March-Cosworth	104

NB March's first Indycar Championship.

Other Categories

Although a large number of Marches raced in IMSA, the series was dominated by various Porsche 962s with the only serious challenge coming from the Bob Tullius (unofficial works) Jaguar team. The only March performance worth recording was at Miami, where David Hobbs and Darin Brassfield brought their 85G-Chevy home second followed by a similar car driven by Emerson Fittipaldi and Tony Garcia.

In the last race of the season, at Daytona, David Hobbs drove a modified 85G fitted with a BMW 2-litre turbocharged engine which he put on the front row of the grid, and although the engine failed in the race, BMW (North America) was sufficiently encouraged to commission a full programme for 1986, buying no fewer than six 86Gs.

Marches quite often appeared in Group C and the highlight of the season was Kazuyoshi Hoshino' s win in the foreshortened Fuji 1000 Km in an 85G-Nissan with Masahiro Hasami fifth in a similar car. Unfortunately the win was undermined by the withdrawal of most of the European entries in protest at starting the race in impossible conditions but, given his practice performance, Hoshino would probably have won anyway.

An 85G-Porsche came 22nd at Le Mans (Christian Danner, Graham Duxbury and Almo Copelli) and 84G-Porsches came seventh at Spa (Danner, Costas Los, Pascal Witmeur) and Brands Hatch (Anders Olofsson, Los, Divina Galica), but in 1985 the Championship was for teams, not makes.

March Production 1986

Type	Description	Number Made	Running Total
86A	ARS	20	20
86B	Formula 3000	19	35
86C	Indianapolis	38	179
86G	Group C and GTP	11	38
88J	Formula 2 (Japan)	15	327
	Total	103	1305

86A. March 85B chassis, 3½-litre normally aspirated Buick V6 engine, control tyres and control engine rebuilds. In America called 'Wildcats' after Pat Patrick's former Indycar marque.

86C. New monocoque, still honeycomb aluminium with composite top section (all composite tubs banned under CART rules); engine 2) degrees from horizontal; new body; pull rod front suspension, rocker arm rear but springs horizontal and parallel to gearbox.

86B. Same mechanicals and tub as 85B but changed in detail to fit complete revision of aerodynamics, notably re-profiled side pods moved eight inches forward and high engine cover. One-inch spacer between oil tank and Hewland FBG gearbox.

86G. Two distinct cars, one for BMW which derived from 85G with body by McLaren, North America, with the radiators mounted on each side of the cockpit and suspension layout superficially the same as 82G. Buick-engined car was to this spec and like the BMW cars was supplied as a rolling chassis with underbody.

Nissan cars had the same monocoque but with titanium front roll hoop, fabricated aluminium rear hoop, entirely new body, traditional coil spring and double wishbone, but different geometry to IMSA cars.

All other cars up-dates of 1985 models.

FIA Formula 3000 International Championship

Vallelunga	Ivan Capelli
Spa	Philippe Alliot
Österreichring	Ivan Capelli
Le Mans	Emanuele Pirro
Jarama	Emanuele Pirro

1, Ivan Capelli	March-Cosworth	39
2, Emanuele Pirro	March-Cosworth	32
3, Pierluigi Martini	Ralt-Cosworth	27
4, Michel Ferté	March-Cosworth	26
5, Luis Perez Sala	Ralt-Cosworth	24½
6, John Nielsen	Ralt-Honda	18

Japanese F2 Champion: Satoru Nakajima, March-Honda

CART PPG Indy Car World Series

Phoenix 200	Kevin Cogan
Long Beach	Mike Andretti
Indianapolis 500	Bobby Rahal
Milwaukee 200	Mike Andretti
Meadowlands	Danny Sullivan
Cleveland	Danny Sullivan
Toronto	Bobby Rahal
Michigan 500	Johnny Rutherford
Lexington	Bobby Rahal
Montreal	Bobby Rahal
Michigan 250	Bobby Rahal
Elkhart lake	Emerson Fittipaldi
Laguna Seca	Bobby Rahal
Phoenix 200	Mike Andretti

1, Bobby Rahal, March-Cosworth	179
2, Mike Andretti, March-Cosworth	171
3, Danny Sullivan, March-Cosworth	147
4, Al Unser Jnr, Lola-Cosworth	137
5, Mario Andretti, Lola-Cosworth	136
6, Kevin Cogan, March-Cosworth	115

Other Categories

Nissan entered two V6-engined cars at Le Mans, one an 85G (James Weaver, Masahiro Hasemi and Takao Wada), one an 86G (Kazuyoshi Hoshino, Keiji Matsumoto and Aguri Suzuki). The 86G retired after six hours with a broken crankshaft while the 85G came home 16th, 83 laps behind the winner.

A private 84G-Porsche (Costas Los, Neil Crang and Raymond Touroul) also ran at Le Mans but retired after 169 laps with an electrical fault.

In the Fuji 1000 Km, the Nissan cars were generally slow and the best finish was Hoshino/Hasemi, who came tenth.

In IMSA BMW (North America) ran a team of 2-litre turbocharged March 86Gs which were entered as BMW GTPs. The programme had an unsettled start due to a late decision to do the season but after reorganization the cars were extremely quick and the team was unlucky not to have won at least four races, but in the event took only one, when Davy Jones and John Andretti won the second Watkins Glen race.

Privateers in IMSA rarely figured in the results apart from an 85G-Buick driven by Whitney Ganz, who finished second at Atlanta (with John Paul Jnr) and third at Charlotte and Lime Rock with, respectively, Bob Lobenberg and Jim Crawford.

1986 saw the first year of the American Racing Series, an F3000 equivalent, devised by Pat Patrick and Robin Herd. It did not, however attract a great deal of interest among drivers and most of the time there were only about a dozen starters, but every single race was won by a March called a 'Wildcat'.

March Production 1987

Type	Description		Number Made	Running Total
871	Formula 1		3	58
87B	Formula 3000		37	72
87C	Indianapolis		33	212
87G	Group C and GTP		3	41
87P	Formula 1	1	59	
	Total		77	1382

87P. Formula One car based on 87B which was entered for the Brazilian GP to fulfil March Racing's obligation to FISA rules. F3000 fuel cell meant it could not have finished the race even had it started.

871. Carbon fibre monocoque, front suspension: inboard coil springs, pull-rods and double wishbones; rear suspension: inboard coil springs, pull-rods and double wishbones; front track 71in; rear track 65in; wheelbase 108in; Cosworth DFV engine; March 6-speed gearbox; AP brakes; weight 520kg.

87B. New, slim, honeycomb monocoque with composite top section but mechanically similar to 842-86B series.

87C. Basic 86C tub and layout retained but new rear structure, new profiles in side pods.

87G. Updated 86G. All three cars bought by Nissan, which ran them as 'Nissan R87Es'. Later rebodied and developed these ran as 'Nissan R88Cs'.

March Formula One Racing Record

Brazilian GP, Rio, 12.4.87

87P/1	Capelli	23	DNS	ran out of engines, modified F3000 car

San Marino GP, Imola, 3.5.87

871/1	Capelli	22	rtd	ignition

Belgian GP, Spa, 17.5.87

871/1	Capelli	21	rtd	oil pressure

Monaco GP, 31.5.87

871/1	Capelli	22	6	2nd 'atmo' car

United States GP, Detroit, 21.6.87

871/1	Capelli	22	rtd	battery broken by Nakajima's Lotus

French GP, Paul Ricard, 5.7.87

871/1	Capelli	22	rtd	engine, new wiring loom, new rear wing

British GP, Silverstone, 12.7.87

871/1	Capelli	24	rtd	gearbox

German GP, Hockenheim, 26.7.87

871/3	Capelli	24	rtd	broken rotor arm

Hungarian GP, Hungaroring, 9.8.87

871/1	Capelli	18	10	3rd 'atmo' car

Austrian GP, Österreichring, 16.8.87

871/3	Capelli	23	11	1st 'atmo', new bodywork and rear wing

Italian GP, Monza, 6.9.87

871/1	Capelli	25	13	2nd 'atmo' car, Hart prepared engine

Portuguese GP, Estoril, 21.9.87

871/1	Capelli	22	9	1st 'atmo' car

Spanish GP, Jerez, 27.9.87

871/1	Capelli	19	13	3rd 'atmo' car

Mexican GP, Autodromo Hermanos Rodrigue, 18.10.87

871/1	Capelli	20	rtd	engine, wider front track

Japanese GP, Suzuka, 1.11.87

871/1	Capelli	22	crashed	collided with Arnoux

Australian GP, Adelaide, 15.11.87

871/1	Capelli	23	rtd	spin

871/2 was used as the spare car at Monaco and Detroit, but in the pits at Paul Ricard the jack which was supporting it collapsed and the tub was ruined.

Drivers' Championship:

1,	Piquet, Williams	73
2,	Mansell, Williams	61
3,	Senna, Lotus	57
19=	*Capelli*	*1*

Constructors' Cup:

1,	Williams	137
2,	McLaren	76
3,	Lotus	53
11=	*March*	*1*

Jim Clark Trophy (3.5-litre normally aspirated engines):

1,	Palmer, Tyrrell	95
2,	Streiff, Tyrrell	74
3,	Alliot, Lola	43
4,	*Capelli*	*38*

Colin Chapman Trophy (3.5-litre normally aspirated engines):

1,	Tyrrell	169
2,	Lola	50
3,	AGS	41
4,	*March*	*38*

FIA Formula 3000 International Championship

Vallelunga	Stefano Modena
Pau	Yannick Dalmas
Birmingham	Stefano Modena
Imola	Stefano Modena
Jarama	Yannick Dalmas

1, Stefano Modena	March-Cosworth	40 (41)
2, Luis Perez Sala	Lola-Cosworth	33
3, Robert Moreno	Ralt-Honda	30
4, Mauricio Gugelmin	Ralt-Honda	29
5, Yannick Dalmas	March-Cosworth	20
6, Michel Trollé	Lola-Cosworth	16½

CART PPG Indy Car World Series

Phoenix 200	Roberto Guerrero
Indianapolis 500	Al Unser Snr
Milwaukee 200	Mike Andretti
Cleveland	Emerson Fittipaldi
Toronto	Emerson Fittipaldi
Michigan 500	Mike Andretti
Pocono 500	Rick Mears
Lexington 200	Roberto Guerrero
Pennsylvania	Mike Andretti
Miami 200	Mike Andretti

1, Bobby Rahal, Lola-Cosworth	188
2, Mike Andretti, March-Cosworth	158
3, Al Unser Jnr, March-Cosworth	107
4, Roberto Guerrero, March-Cosworth	106
5, Rick Meass, Penske PC16 and March 86C-Cosworth	102
6, Mario Andretti, Lola-Ilmor	100

Other Categories

Nissan bought three 87Gs which were slightly updated 86Gs modified to take the new 3-litre VEJ30 V8 engine (which was ineligible for IMSA) and two were run at Le Mans (Hoshino/Takahashi/Matsumoto and Hasemi/Suzuki/Wada) under the name 'Nissan R87E', but neither finished. The Le Mans Company ran an 86G (aka 'Nissan R86V') with one of the V6 engines (Anders Olofsson, Alain Ferté and Patrick Gonin) and this proved extremely impressive during qualifying but during the race Gonin crashed.

As usual, the only other major race NISMO entered was the Fuji 1000 Km and while the V8 cars were slow, Takao Wada put the Le Mans Company's V6 car on pole, but a tyre blow-out ruined its chances and it could finish no higher than 13th. Of the two 87Gs, one lasted three laps before a tyre blow-out and the other was simply slow and finished a lacklustre 16th.

March was a dead issue in IMSA and the best result was at Sears Point, when Gianpiero Moretti and Whitney Ganz brought a 85G-Buick home sixth.

March Production 1988

Type	Description	Number Made	Running Total
881	Formula 1	4	63
88B	Formula 3000	2	294
88C	Indianapolis	20	232
88GC	Grand Champion	8	8
88G	Group C and GTP	1	42
86A	RS	4	24
	Total	59	1441

881. Carbon-fibre monocoque, front suspension: inboard coil springs, pull-rods and double wishbones; rear suspension: inboard coil springs pull-rods and double wishbones; front track 70in; rear track 66in; wheelbase 112.4in; Judd CV engine; March 6-speed gearbox; AP carbon brakes; weight 520kg.

88B. Updated 87B.

88C. 'Scaled-down' Indycar, overall dimensions and layout as 87C.

88G. Monocoque lower in cockpit area. Single car made for the Le Mans Company which fitted a Nissan V6 engine.

88GC. Grand Champion car for Japan, Can-Am style single-seater sports body made in Japan and fitted to modified 88B chassis.

March Formula One Racing Record

Brazilian GP, Rio, 3.4.88

881/3	Capelli	9	rtd	overheating, started from pit lane after 811/1 overheated on warm-up lap when water rail detached
881/2	Gugelmin	13	rtd	transmission

San Marino GP, Imola, 1.5.88

881/2	Gugelmin	9	15	both cars had larger front wings
881/3	Capelli	20	rtd	gearbox

Monaco GP, 15.5.88

881/3	Capelli	22	10	
881/2	Gugelmin	14	rtd	electrics

Cut-away body around gearbox plus small oil radiator for the transmission, new front wings, slightly shorter wheelbase (881/4) tried by Capelli in practice.

Mexican GP, Autodromo Hermanos Rodriguez, 29.5.88

881/3	Capelli	10	16	lost four laps with gearbox problems
881/2	Gugelmin	16	rtd	electrics

New airbox and rear wing, modified fuel system.

Canadian GP, Montreal, 12.6.88

881/3	Capelli	14	5	
881/2	Gugelmin	18	rtd	gearbox

Larger front wings.

US GP, Detroit, 19.6.88

881/2	Gugelmin	13	rtd	overheating, split radiator, when 5th
881/3	Capelli	DNS		injured in practice accident

French GP, Paul Ricard, 3.7.88

881/2	Gugelmin	16	8	
881/3	Capelli	10	9	new front suspension pick-up points

British GP, Silverstone, 10.5.88

881/2	Gugelmin	5	4	fastest non-turbo qualifier
881/3	Capelli	6	rtd	electrics

Both cars had new front suspension pick-up points and new c/w pinions. Capelli used high-compression engine

German GP, Hockenheim, 24.7.88

881/3	Capelli	7	5	first non-turbo finisher
881/2	Gugelmin	10	8	

Hungarian GP, Hungaroring,7.8.88

881/2	Gugelmin	8	5	
881/3	Capelli	4	rtd	misfire

New front wing with longer nose and revised side plates

Belgian GP, Spa, 28.8.88

881/5	Capelli	14	5	
881/2	Gugelmin	13	rtd	spun-off, clutch

Both cars used short nose

Italian GP, Monza, 11.9.88

881/5	Capelli	11	5
881/2	Gugelmin	13	8

Both cars used short nose

Portuguese GP, Estoril, 25.9.88

881/5	Capelli	3	2nd	fastest non-turbo qualifier
881/2	Gugelmin	5	rtd	engine, 2nd fastest non-turbo qualifier

Both cars had new pick-up points for rear shockers, long nose with two-piece front wing, additional cooling duct on right-hand pod

Spanish GP, Jerez, 2.10.88

881/2	Gugelmin	11	7	
881/5	Capelli	6	rtd	engine, when 3rd

Long nose with large front wing

Japanese GP, Suzuka, 30.10.88

881/2	Gugelmin	13	10	
881/5	Capelli	4	rtd	reason for retirement a mystery, fastest non-turbo qualifier, first non-turbo car to lead a GP since 1984

Australian GP, Adelaide, 13.11.88

881/5	Capelli	9	6	
881/2	Gugelmin	19	rtd	accident, hit by Nakajima

Drivers' Championship

1,	Senna, McLaren-Honda	90 (94)
2,	Prost, McLaren-Honda	87 (105)
3,	Berger, Ferrari	41
7=	*Capelli, March*	*15*
12=	*Gugelmin, March*	*5*

Constructors' Cup

1,	McLaren	199
2,	Ferrari	65
3,	Benetton	46
5=	*March*	*20*

881/1 used as spare, not raced.
881/4 used as spare, written off in practice for US GP.
881/6 new car for Gugelmin in Japan but damaged in practice.

FIA International F3000 Championship

Enna Pierluigi Martini

1, Roberto Moreno	Reynard-Cosworth	43
2, Olivier Grouillard	Lola-Cosworth	34
3, Martin Donnelly	Reynard-Cosworth	30
4, Pierluigi Martini	March-Cosworth	23
5, Bertran Gachot	Reynard-Cosworth	21
6, Mark Blundell	Lola-Cosworth	18

CART PPG Indy Car World Series

Long Beach	Al Unser Jnr
Toronto	Al Unser Jnr
Meadowlands	Al Unser Jnr
Miami	Al Unser Jnr

1, Danny Sullivan	Penske-Ilmor	182
2, Al Unser Jnr	March-Ilmor	149
3, Bobby Rahal	Lola-Judd	136
4, Rick Mears	Penske-Ilmor	129
5, Mario Andretti	Lola-Ilmor	126
6, Mike Andretti	March-Cosworth and Lola-Cosworth	119

Other Categories

Nissan modified its 87Gs and these were run as Nissan R88Cs and after its redesign the V8 engine was given the designation VHR 30.

At Le Mans an R88C (Win Percy, Allan Grice and Mike Wilds) finished 14th, 50 laps down on the winning Jaguar, while a second car (Kazuyoshi Hoshino, Takao Wadi and Aguri Suzuki) retired with engine trouble. The two V6 cars, an 87G and an 88G (which was entered as an 88S) were driven by, respectively, Akio Morimoto, Lamberto Leoni and Anders Olofsson, and Toshio Suzuki, Michel Trollé and Danny Ongais. Both retired on lap 74 because the electronic engine management system had not been correctly mapped for commercial grade petrol.

At Fuji all the cars were outclassed and the best result was Hoshino, Kenji Takahasi and Grice, who finished ninth in a Nissan R88C.

Seven of the top ten finishers in the Japanese F3000 Championship used March cars, but unfortunately all but one switched to Lola or Reynard chassis soon into the season. The exception was Ross Cheever, who switched from a March 88B to an 87B.

March Production 1989

Type	Description	Number Made	Running Total
CG891	Formula 1	4+1	67+1*
89B	Formula 3000	7	301
89P	Indianapolis (Porsche)	4	
89C	Indianapolis (Alfa Romeo)	2	238
89GC	Grand Champion	2	10
86A	ARS	10	34
	Total	29 +1	1470+1**

* This represents March production to June 1989, by which point the F1 and F3000 projects had been sold to Leyton House. A fifth CG891 was built for Leyton House and raced by Capelli in the Australian GP.

** The 86As and 89Cs were made in the Ralt factory at Weybridge. Though Ralt junior formulae cars from October 1988 on might be included in the March production figures, they have been excluded from the running total. For the record, 37 examples of the Ralt RT33 Formula 3 car were made. In effect, the Weybridge arm became the main production base for March.

CG891. Designated 'CG' in memory of Cesare Gariboldi. Completely new car with slimmer and slightly less rigid monocoque and larger cockpit but using the same overall mechanical layout of the 881 except that the transverse gearbox was ahead of the rear axle line (as on the 721X) and the rear coil springs and dampers had been moved from alongside the gearbox to on top of it to prevent overheating and create better air-flow at the rear of the car. Narrow-angle (76-degree) Judd EV engine exclusive to March and aerodynamics revised to fit – there was also a 'fast circuit' body with a short nose. After early failures a new gearbox/oil reservoir casing was provided.

89B. Entirely new F3000 car designed by Ralph Bellamy, all-composite monocoque (the first customer car in March's history to be so made), and pull-rod suspension front and rear. Wheelbase 102.5in, front track 67.25in, rear track 62in.

89CE. Superficially similar to 88C but with push-rod suspension all round. It was a completely re-engineered car. Main work done by the late Maurice Phillippe with development continuing under Nick Wirth. Alfa Romeo V8 engine exclusive to 1989 cars but the mechanical technology was intended to be used in 1990 production cars, which did not materialise. Wheelbase 112.2in (road circuits), 115.2in (ovals), front track 67.5in, rear track 63.5in, two-shaft gearbox.

89GC. Grand Champion car based on 89B but with bodywork designed and built by Leyton March, the first time March made a complete Grand Champion car.

89P. Entirely new Indycar designed by Gordon Coppuck for Porsche, push-rod suspension all round, honeycomb and composite tub, front track 66.6in, rear track 63.5in, wheelbase 116.2in (ovals), 112.2in (road circuits), March '2½'-shaft gearbox used as part of the aerodynamic package with the gear linkage running inside the casing.

March Formula One Racing Record

Please note that Ivan Capelli and Mauricio Gugelmin are set down in alphabetical order, there was not a number-one driver, though Capelli had been with the team from the start.

Brazilian GP, Interlagos, 26.3.89

881/5	Capelli	7	rtd	cracked rear upright
881/6	Gugelmin	12	3	

San Marino GP, Imola, 23.4.89

881/5	Capelli	13	rtd	accident
881/6	Gugelmin	19	rtd	gearbox

Monaco GP, 7.5.89

CG891/2	Capelli	22	11	classified but not running (electrics)
CG891/1	Gugelmin	14	rtd	seized engine

Mexican GP, Autodromo Hermanos Rodriguez, 28.5.89

CG891/2	Capelli	4	rtd	lap one, cv joint
CG891/3	Gugelmin	DNQ		problems in practice then rain came when ready to try for a quick lap

United States GP, Phoenix, 4.6.89

CG891/2	Capelli	11	rtd	transmission
CG891/3	Gugelmin	16		black-flagged for adding brake fluid during pit stop

Canadian GP, Montreal, 18.6.89

CG891/3	Capelli	21	rtd	accident
CG891/2	Gugelmin	17	rtd	electrics

French GP, Paul Ricard, 9.7.89

CG891/4	Capelli	12	rtd	electrics when in second place
CG891/2	Gugelmin	10		running but unclassified, clutch problems, crashed on first lap in CG891/3, fastest lap in race

British GP, Silverstone, 16.7.89

CG891/4	Capelli	8	rtd	gearbox
CG891/1	Gugelmin	6	rtd	gearbox, intended to use CG891/2 but water leak on the starting grid meant Gugelmin started from pit lane in spare car

Both cars ran in long wheelbase form, two extra inches achieved by angling the front suspension forward.

German GP, Hockenheim, 30.7.89

CG891/4	Capelli	22	rtd	electronics
CG891/3	Gugelmin	12	rtd	gearbox

Hungarian GP, Hungaroring, 13.8.89

CG891/4	Capelli	14	rtd	drive pegs
CG891/3	Gugelmin	13	rtd	electrics

Belgian GP, Spa, 27.8.89

CG891/2	Capelli	11	12
CG891/3	Gugelmin	9	7

Italian GP, Monza, 10.9.89

CG891/4 Capelli 18 rtd engine
CG891/3 Gugelmin 25 rtd throttle linkage

Portuguese GP, Estoril, 24.9.89

CG891/4 Capelli 24 rtd engine
CG891/3 Gugelmin 14 10

Spanish GP, Jerez, 1.10.89

CG891/4 Capelli 19 rtd transmission
CG891/3 Gugelmin 26 rtd accident

Japanese GP, Suzuka, 22.10.89

CG891/5 Capelli 18 rtd front suspension
CG891/3 Gugelmin 20 7

Australian GP, Adelaide, 5.11.89

CG891/5 Capelli 16 rtd radiator
CG891/3 Gugelmin 25 7

Drivers' Championship

1, Prost 76 (81)
2, Senna 60
3, Patrese 40
16= Gugelmin 4

Constructors' Cup

1, McLaren-Honda 141
2, Williams-Renault 77
3, Ferrari 39
12, March-Judd 4

CART PPG Indy Car World Series

Teo Fabi (March 89P-Porsche) took sixth in the Phoenix 200, third in the Milwaukee 200, and fourth at Detroit, Portland, Toronto, Pocono and Elkhart Lake. Fabi was second in the Michigan 500 and won at Mid-Ohio. He finished fourth in the Championship. The win at Mid-Ohio on 3rd September was the last to be achieved by a works March. The highest finish by a March 89CE-Alfa Romeo was eighth (Roberto Guerrero) at Detroit.

Other Categories

The best result by a Leyton March 89B in a European F3000 race was second place at Vallelunga (Fabrizio Giovanardi). This became a 'win' after the disqualification of Martin Donnelly's Reynard for a technical infringement. When the result was finally established, it marked the last win by a March in a Formula 3000 race. Almost immediately, Giovanardi switched to a Reynard and scored no more points. The only other points finish was Gary Brabham's fifth place at Brands Hatch.

Masanori Sekiya took pole and won the July Grand Champion race at Suzuka in his Leyton House-entered 89GC.

NISMO entered two 3-litre V8 'Nissans' (March 87Gs) and the 3.2-litre V6 88G at Suzuka in the opening round of the FIA World Sports-Prototype Championship. They were not on the leading edge of the pace except in a wet practice session where Takao Wada (V6 88G) set third fastest time. In the race, Kazuyoshi Hoshino and Toshio Suzuki had a troubled run to finish fourth behind two Sauber-Mercedes and a Porsche, but ahead of the leading Jaguar.

The 88G, further detuned to try to make it reliable, was entered at Le Mans under the umbrella of the French Cougar team and ran as the Cougar-Nissan C22. Driven by Takao Wada, Akio Morimoto and Anders Olofsson, it had transmission problems and couldn't top 190mph on the Mulsanne Straight (a Sauber-Mercedes topped 250mph) so could qualify no higher than 14th. It was running in 19th place after 17 hours when an oil leak ruined the engine.

1990

For reasons already given the position at March had become so confused that there is no longer any point in detailing production figures. For the record, six examples of the CG901 were built, but only five were seen in public. CG901/4 was written off following an accident in testing at Imola prior to the first race of the European season.

The Ralt side of the business continued to look after the mass market and no fewer than 81 Ralt RT33 Formula Three cars were made. They dominated the F3 Championship in Britain, but in most other national series the Reynard 903 tended to have the upper hand. A straw in the wind was that Dallara was becoming ever stronger.

CG901. Designed by Adrian Newey and developed by Gustav Brunner. It used the Judd EV V8 engine and LH March's own six-speed transverse gearbox. The CG901 followed the general lines of the CG891, but in response to new regulations the driver's feet were behind the (imaginary) front axle line. Before the end of the year a CG901 had been tested using a new V10 engine from Ilmor (which now makes engines for McLaren-Mercedes), an engine which had been commissioned by LH March and was officially called Leyton House.

LH March Formula One Racing Record

United States GP, Phoenix, 11.3.90

CG901/1 Capelli 26 rtd electrics
CG901/2 Gugelmin 25 14

Brazilian GP, Interlagos, 25.3.90

CG901/1 Capell DNQ
CG901/2 Gugelmin DNQ

San Marino GP, Imola, 13.5.90

CG901/1 Capelli 18 rtd accident
CG901/3 Gugelmin 12 rtd electrics

Monaco GP, 27.5.90

CG901/1 Capelli 23 rtd brakes
CG901/3 Gugelmin DNQ

Canadian GP, Montreal, 10.6.90

CG901/2 Capelli 24 10
CG901/3 Gugelmin DNQ

Mexican GP, Mexico City, 24.6.90

CG901/2 Capelli	DNQ		
CG901/3 Gugelmin	DNQ		

French GP, Paul Ricard, 8.7.90

CG901/3 Capelli	8	2	led race on laps 33 to 77 of 80 laps, but lost victory due to fuel pick-up problem
CG901/5 Gugelmin	9	rtd	engine

British GP, Silverstone, 15.7.90

CG901/3 Capelli	10	rtd	fuel pipe
CG901/5 Gugelmin	DNQ		fuel pump

German GP, Hockenheim, 29.7.90

CG901/6 Capelli	10	7	
CG901/5 Gugelmin	14	rtd	stone in engine

Hungarian GP, Hungaroring, 12.8.90

CG901/6 Capelli	16	rtd	transmission
CG901/5 Gugelmin	17	8	

Belgian GP, Spa, 25.8.90

CG901/6 Capelli	12	7	
CG901/5 Gugelmin	14	6	

Italian GP, Monza, 9.9.90

CG901/3 Capelli	16	rtd	engine cut out
CG901/5 Gugelmin	10	rtd	engine

Portuguese GP, Estoril, 23.9.90

CG901/6 Capelli	12	rtd	engine
CG901/5 Gugelmin	14	12	

Spanish GP, Jerez, 30.9.90

CG901/6 Capelli	19	rtd	leg cramp
CG901/5 Gugelmin	12	8	

Japanese GP, Suzuka, 21.10.90

CG901/6 Capelli	13	rtd	misfire
CG901/5 Gugelmin	16	rtd	engine cut out

Australian GP, Adelaide, 4.11.90

CG901/6 Capelli	14	rtd	sticking throttle
CG901/5 Gugelmin	16	rtd	rear brakes

Drivers' Championship

1, Senna	78
2, Prost	71 (73)
3, Piquet	43 (44)
10= Capelli	*6*
18, Gugelmin	*1*

Constructors' Cup

1, McLaren-Honda	121
2, Ferrari	110
3, Benetton-Ford	71
7, LH March-Judd	*7*

CART PPG Indy Car World Series

The March-Porsche team fielded two cars, one for Teo Fabi and one for John Andretti, nephew of Mario and son of Mario's twin brother Aldo, whose career in motor racing was terminated at an early stage by a serious accident. Though nominally number-two, Andretti scored two fifth places and was 10th in the Championship while Fabi was 14th overall, thanks to third place at Meadowlands. Fabi did, however, put his car on pole at Detroit.

Before the end of the season Porsche announced that it was to terminate its involvement in CART.

The March-Alfa Romeo project came to nothing. After a struggle to qualify at Indianapolis, Patrick Racing ordered a Lola T90/00 and finished the season with Lola.

Other Categories

There was no other category in which a March built in 1990 competed.

1991

Not a single car using the March name was made in 1991. There were, however, 68 cars made under the Ralt name. The figure broke down to 56 RT35 Formula Three cars and 12 RT23 Formula 3000 cars.

Karl Wendlinger replaced Ivan Capelli for the last two Grands Prix of the year. Wendlinger had Daimler-Benz behind him.

LH March Formula One Racing Record

United States GP, Phoenix, 10.3.91

CG911/1 Capelli	18	rtd	gearbox
CG911/2 Gugelmin	23	rtd	gearbox

Brazilian GP, Interlagos, 24.3.91

CG911/1 Capelli	15	rtd	engine
CG911/2 Gugelmin	8	rtd	driver unwell

San Marino GP, Imola, 26.4.91

CG911/4 Capelli	22	rtd	spin
CG911/2 Gugelmin	15	12	

Monaco GP, 12.5.91

CG911/4 Capelli	18	rtd	brake fluid
CG911/2 Gugelmin	15	rtd	throttle cable

Canadian GP, Montreal, 2.6.91

CG911/4 Capelli	13	rtd	engine
CG911/2 Gugelmin	23	rtd	engine

Mexican GP, Mexico City, 16.6.91

CG911/4 Capelli	22	rtd	engine over-revved
CG911/2 Gugelmin	21	rtd	engine

French GP, Magny-Cours, 7.7.91

CG911/4 Capelli	15	rtd	spin, avoiding accident
CG911/2 Gugelmin	9	7	

British GP, Silverstone, 14.7.91

CG911/4 Capelli	16	rtd	spin
CG911/2 Gugelmin	9	rtd	chassis vibration

German GP, Hockenheim, 29.7.91

CG911/4 Capelli	12	rtd	engine misfire
CG911/2 Gugelmin	16	rtd	gearbox

Hungarian GP, Hungaroring, 11.8.91

CG911/4 Capelli	9	6
CG911/1 Gugelmin	13	11

Belgian GP, Spa, 25.9.91

CG911/4 Capelli	12	rtd	engine
CG911/1 Gugelmin	15	rtd	engine

Italian GP, Monza, 8.9.91

CG911/4 Capelli	12	8
CG911/1 Gugelmin	18	15

Portuguese GP, Estoril, 22.9.91

CG911/4 Capelli	9	17	broken nose cone
CG911/5 Gugelmin	7	7	

Spanish GP, Barcelona, 29.9.91

CG911/4 Capelli	8	rtd	collision
CG911/5 Gugelmin	13	7	

Japanese GP, Suzuka, 20.10.91

CG911/5 Gugelmin	18	8	
CG911/4 Wendlinger	22	rtd	collision

Australian GP, Adelaide, 3.11.91

CG911/5 Gugelmin	14	14
CG911/4 Wendlinger	26	20

Drivers' Championship

1, Senna	96
2, Mansell	72
3, Patrese	53
18= Capelli	*1*

Constructors' Cup

1, McLaren-Honda	139
2, Williams-Renault	125
3, Ferrari	55.5
12, Leyton House-Ilmor	*1*

Other Categories

Jean-Marc Gounon won the Formula 3000 race at Pau driving a Ralt RT23 and finished sixth in the European Formula 3000 Championship.

Rubens Barrichello won the British Formula Three Championship in a Ralt RT35 (from David Coulthard, also in a Ralt). Christophe Bouchet took the French F3 series in a Ralt RT33 (from Olivier Panis in a Ralt RT35). Tom Kristensen (Ralt RT35) won the German Formula Three Championship. Domenico Schiattarella (RT35) was runner-up in the Italian Formula Three series, which was dominated by Dallara. The only other Ralt driver in the top six – and he was sixth – was Jacques Villeneuve. Also using Ralts were Alfonso Giaffone Neto, who won the Sud-Am Formula Three Championship, and Marco Gueiros, who took the Brazilian F3 title.

1992

As before, Ralt looked after the customer cars, but production was down to 35 units – 30 Formula 3 cars, two Formula 3000 cars and three for Toyota Atlantic in North America.

With Leyton House out of the picture, the Formula One team was renamed March F1. Because of financial constraints the team ran their 1991 cars so no new March cars were made. 1992 marked the end of the March story.

March Formula One Racing Record

South African GP, Kyalami, 1.3.92

CG911/5 Wendlinger	7	rtd	overheating
CG911/3 Belmondo	DNQ		

Mexican GP, Mexico City, 22.3.92

CG911/5 Wendlinger	19	rtd	accident
CG911/3 Belmondo	DNQ		

Brazilian GP, Interlagos, 5.4.92

CG911/5 Wendlinger	9	rtd	clutch
CG911/3 Belmondo	DNQ		

Spanish GP, Barcelona, 3.5.92

CG911/5 Wendlinger	9	8
CG911/3 Belmondo	DNQ	

San Marino GP, Imola, 17.5.92

CG911/5 Wendlinger	12	12
CG911/3 Belmondo	24	13

Monaco GP, 31.5.92

CG911/5 Wendlinger	16	rtd	gearbox
CG911/3 Belmondo	DNQ		

Canadian GP, Montreal, 14.6.92

CG911/5 Wendlinger	12	4	
CG911/3 Belmondo	20	14	

French GP, Magny-Cours, 5.7.92

CG911/5 Wendlinger	21	rtd	gearbox
CG911/3 Belmondo	DNQ		

British GP, Silverstone, 12.7.92

CG911/2 Wendlinger	21	rtd	gearbox
CG911/3 Belmondo	DNQ		

German GP, Hockenheim, 26.7.92

CG911/2 Wendlinger	10	16	
CG911/3 Belmondo	22	13	

Hungarian GP, Hungaroring, 16.8.92

CG911/2 Wendlinger	23	rtd	accident
CG911/3 Belmondo	17	9	

Belgian GP, Spa, 30.8.92

CG911/2 Wendlinger	18	11	
CG911/3 Naspetti	21	12	

Italian GP, Monza, 13.9.92

CG911/2 Wendlinger	17	10	
CG911/3 Naspetti	24	rtd	collision with Wendlinger

Portuguese GP, Estoril, 27.9.92

CG911/2 Wendlinger	22	rtd	gearbox
CG911/3 Naspetti	23	11	

Japanese GP, Suzuka, 25.10.92

CG911/4 Lammers	23	rtd	clutch
CG911/3 Naspetti	26	13	

Australian GP, Adelaide, 8.11.92

CG911/4 Lammers	25	12	
CG911/3 Naspetti	23	rtd	gearbox

Drivers' Championship

1, Mansell	108
2, Patrese	56
3, Schumacher	53
12= Wendlinger	*3*

Constructors' Cup

1, Williams-Renault	164
2, McLaren-Honda	99
3, Benetton-Ford	91
9, March-Ilmor	*3*

For the record: Under new management, March made four RT37 Formula Three cars in 1993, along with 17 RT40 Toyota Atlantic cars. Two Ralt RT94C Formula Three cars were made 1993/4 and it is likely that some RT41 Toyota Atlantic cars were made under the umbrella of March, but it is impossible say how many were actually completed before the Ralt brand became independent.